Cross-examinations of
law and literature

Cambridge Studies in American Literature and Culture

Editor

Albert Gelpi, Stanford University

Advisory Board

Nina Baym, University of Illinois, Champaign-Urbana
Sacvan Bercovitch, Harvard University
Richard Bridgman, University of California, Berkeley
David Levin, University of Virginia
Joel Porte, Harvard University
Mike Weaver, Oxford University

Other books in the series

Robert Zaller, *The Cliffs of Solitude*
Peter Conn, *The Divided Mind*
Patricia Caldwell, *The Puritan Conversion Narrative*
Stephen Fredman, *Poet's Prose*
Charles Altieri, *Self and Sensibility in Contemporary American Poetry*
John McWilliams, *Hawthorne, Melville, and the American Character*
Mitchell Breitwieser, *Cotton Mather and Benjamin Franklin*
Barton St. Armand, *Emily Dickinson and Her Culture*
Elizabeth McKinsey, *Niagara Falls*
Albert J. Von Frank, *The Sacred Game*
Marjorie Perloff, *The Dance of the Intellect*
Albert Gelpi, Editor, *Wallace Stevens*
Ann Kibbey, *The Interpretation of Material Shapes in Puritanism*
Sacvan Bercovitch and Myra Jehlen, *Ideology and Classic American Literature*
Karen Rowe, *Saint and Singer*
Lawrence Buell, *New England Literary Culture*
David Wyatt, *The Fall into Eden*
Steven Axelrod and Helen Deese, Editors, *Robert Lowell*
Jerome Loving, *Emily Dickinson*
Brenda Murphy, *American Realism and American Drama, 1880–1940*
Paul Giles, *Hart Crane*
Richard Gray, *Writing the South*

Cross-examinations of law and literature

Cooper, Hawthorne, Stowe, and Melville

BROOK THOMAS

University of Massachusetts at Amherst

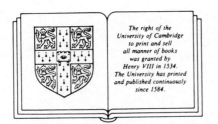

The right of the
University of Cambridge
to print and sell
all manner of books
was granted by
Henry VIII in 1534.
The University has printed
and published continuously
since 1584.

CAMBRIDGE UNIVERSITY PRESS

CAMBRIDGE

LONDON   NEW YORK   NEW ROCHELLE

MELBOURNE   SYDNEY

Published by the Press Syndicate of the University of Cambridge
The Pitt Building, Trumpington Street, Cambridge CB2 1RP
32 East 57th Street, New York, NY 10022, USA
10 Stamford Road, Oakleigh, Melbourne 3166, Australia

© Cambridge University Press 1987

First published 1987

Printed in the United States of America

Library of Congress Cataloging-in-Publication Data
Thomas, Brook.
Cross-examinations of law and literature.
(Cambridge studies in American literature and culture)
1. American fiction – 19th century – History and
criticism.   2. Law in literature.   3. Law and literature.
4. Law – United States – History and criticism.
I. Title. II. Series.
PS374.L34T56   1987   813'.3'09355   86–20756
ISBN 0 521 33081 5

British Library Cataloguing-in-Publication applied for

To Ramsay and Nancy and their families

Contents

Acknowledgments

David Levin and Robert A. Ferguson read the entire manuscript with critical and knowledgeable eyes. They are model professional colleagues. Jonathan Arac, Sacvan Bercovitch, Maxwell Bloomfield, Everett Emerson, Winfried Fluck, Bruce Franklin, Michael Gilmore, Myra Jehlen, and Michael Rogin read parts at various stages. My thoughts were shaped through conversations with many. I especially thank Lee Edwards and Michael Wolff in Amherst and Craig Howes, John Rieder, and Rob Wilson in Honolulu. Nancy Castle did a splendid job of typing (and then wrote an essay for me on "Bartleby"). Mary Coty and Doris Newton typed revisions. The University of Hawaii, Manoa, provided a travel grant to get the project started. Once again the literature department at the University of Constance in the Federal Republic of Germany gave me a chance to try out my ideas on its students.

I have reworked material previously published:

> "*The House of the Seven Gables:* Reading the Romance of America," *PMLA* 97 (1982):195–211.
>
> "*The Pioneers,* Or the Sources of American Legal History: A Critical Tale," *American Quarterly* 36 (1984):86–111.
>
> "The Legal Fictions of Herman Melville and Lemuel Shaw," *Critical Inquiry* 11 (1984):24–51.
>
> "*The House of the Seven Gables:* Hawthorne's Legal Story," *The University of Mississippi Studies in English* 5 (1985–7).

I also want to acknowledge you, reader, for having an interest in this topic. *Caveat emptor!*

Abbreviations

The following abbreviations are used for important works cited in the text:

B   Herman Melville. "Bartleby, the Scrivener: A Story of Wall-Street." In *Great Short Works of Herman Melville,* ed. Warner Berthoff. New York: Harper and Row, 1969.

BB   Herman Melville. *Billy Budd, Sailor (An Inside Narrative),* ed. Milton R. Stern. Indianapolis: Bobbs-Merrill, 1975.

BC   Herman Melville. "Benito Cereno." In *Great Short Works of Herman Melville,* ed. Warner Berthoff. New York: Harper and Row, 1969.

BR   Nathaniel Hawthorne. *The Blithedale Romance.* Vol. 3 in *The Centenary Edition of the Works of Nathaniel Hawthorne,* ed. William Charvat, Roy Harvey Pearce, and Claude M. Simpson. Columbus: Ohio State University Press, 1965.

CM   Herman Melville. *The Confidence-Man: His Masquerade,* ed. H. Bruce Franklin. Indianapolis: Bobbs-Merrill, 1967.

Dred   Harriet Beecher Stowe. *Dred; A Tale of the Great Dismal Swamp.* 2 vols. Boston: Phillips, Sampson, 1856.

E   Herman Melville. "The Encantadas or Enchanted Isles." In *Great Short Works of Herman Melville,* ed. Warner Berthoff. New York: Harper and Row, 1969.

HSG   Nathaniel Hawthorne. *The House of the Seven Gables.* Vol. 2 in *The Centenary Edition of the Works of Nathaniel Hawthorne,* ed. William Charvat, Roy Harvey Pearce, and Claude M. Simpson. Columbus: Ohio State University Press, 1965.

Key   Harriet Beecher Stowe. *A Key to Uncle Tom's Cabin.* Boston: John P. Jewett, 1853.

MD   Herman Melville. *Moby-Dick; or The Whale,* ed. Charles Feidelson, Jr. Indianapolis: Bobbs-Merrill, 1964.

MF Nathaniel Hawthorne. *The Marble Faun*. Vol. 4 in *The Centenary Edition of the Works of Nathaniel Hawthorne,* ed. William Charvat, Roy Harvey Pearce, and Claude M. Simpson. Columbus: Ohio State University Press, 1965.

MM Nathaniel Hawthorne. *Mosses from an Old Manse*. Vol. 10 in *The Centenary Edition of the Works of Nathaniel Hawthorne,* ed. William Charvat, Roy Harvey Pearce, and Claude M. Simpson. Columbus: Ohio State University Press, 1965.

PB/TM Herman Melville. "The Paradise of Bachelors and the Tartarus of Maids." In *Great Short Works of Herman Melville,* ed. Warner Berthoff. New York: Harper and Row, 1969.

Pierre Herman Melville. *Pierre; or, The Ambiguities*. Vol. 7 in *The Writings of Herman Melville,* The Northwestern-Newberry Edition, ed. Harrison Hayford, Hershel Parker, and G. Thomas Tanselle. Evanston and Chicago: Northwestern University Press and Newberry Library, 1971.

Pioneers James Fenimore Cooper. *The Pioneers; or the Sources of the Susquehanna: A Descriptive Tale,* ed. James Franklin Beard. Albany: State University of New York Press, 1980.

R Herman Melville. *Redburn, His First Voyage, Being the Sailor-boy Confessions and Reminiscences of the Son-of-a-Gentleman, in the Merchant Service*. Vol. 4 in *The Writings of Herman Melville,* The Northwestern-Newberry Edition, ed. Harrison Hayford, Hershel Parker, and G. Thomas Tanselle. Evanston and Chicago: Northwestern University Press and Newberry Library, 1969.

SL Nathaniel Hawthorne. *The Scarlet Letter*. Vol. 1 in *The Centenary Edition of the Works of Nathaniel Hawthorne,* ed. William Charvat, Roy Harvey Pearce, and Claude M. Simpson. Columbus: Ohio State University Press, 1965.

TT Nathaniel Hawthorne. *Twice-Told Tales*. Vol. 9 in *The Centenary Edition of the Works of Nathaniel Hawthorne,* ed. William Charvat, Roy Harvey Pearce, and Claude M. Simpson. Columbus: Ohio State University Press, 1965.

UTC Harriet Beecher Stowe. *Uncle Tom's Cabin,* ed. Alfred Kazin. New York: Bantam Books, 1981.

WJ Herman Melville. *White-Jacket: or The World in a Man-of-War*. Vol. 5 in *The Writings of Herman Melville,* The Northwestern-Newberry Edition, ed. Harrison Hayford, Hershel Parker, and G. Thomas Tanselle. Evanston and Chicago: Northwestern University Press and Newberry Library, 1970.

An Opening Statement

Accepting a new chair of law established at Harvard College in 1829, Supreme Court justice Joseph Story welcomed the foundation of a "temple, sacred to the majesty of the law."[1] Often, in antebellum America, law was described in sacred terms. As Abraham Lincoln put it, "Let reverence for the laws . . . become the *political religion* of the nation."[2] But if reverence for the law was the political religion of the nation, some recognized that it would take more than law to guarantee that reverence. In 1833, a devout believer in the sacredness of law, Rufus Choate, argued that whereas law appeals to the rational faculties in man, it is literature that speaks "directly to the heart and affections and imaginations of the whole people." Since man is both rational and emotional, the diverse people of America would truly be united only when the nation's laws were complemented by a unifying literature. "The influence of a rich literature of passion and fancy upon society must not be denied merely because you cannot measure it by the yard or detect it by the barometer." Read "in every parlor, . . . in every lawyer's office," poems and romances "must do something, along with more palpable, if not more powerful agents, towards moulding and fixing that final, grand, complex result, – the national character. A keen, well-instructed judge of such things said, if he might write the ballads of a people, he cared little who made its laws." As envisioned by Choate, this national literature would make the country forget its "recent and overrated diversities of interest" and "reassemble, as it were, the people of America in one vast congregation." It would do so by returning us to the country's past. "Reminded of our fathers," he argues, "we should remember that we are brethren." Differences would be "merged in an expanded, comprehensive, constitutional sentiment of old, family, fraternal regard."[3]

Choate expounded these ideas in a talk entitled "The Importance of Illustrating New-England History by a Series of Romances Like the Waverly Novels." Late in his life Herman Melville remembers Choate's

1

eloquence, which grew out of careful study of Cicero and other classical orators. "Rufus Choate, the Boston advocate, when inspired to his best before an audience, how he exhilarated and elevated and transported his hearers. But he is gone; and all those fireworks of elfish passion and wit, where are they?"[4] Lawyers like Choate no longer dominated the legal profession in postbellum America. Their disappearance marked the breakup of a configuration of law and letters recently described by Robert A. Ferguson.

Choate's emphasis on the role of literature in shaping the consciousness of the American people is characteristic of the thinking that resulted from this configuration. According to Ferguson, in the first years of the American republic the "lawyer's assertiveness as ideological guardian . . . encouraged him to dominate republican culture and to create strong affinities between law and literature." An understanding of literature was considered essential to proper training in law. But as Ferguson also tells us, "The lawyer's deliberate combination of intellectual breadth, artistic insight, and political commitment" did not last. Even as Choate delivered his talk, that synthesis was giving way to a narrow professionalism that concentrated on training lawyers in the technicalities of the law. In part the legal man of letters was a victim of social transformations in Jacksonian America that redefined the role of the lawyer in the republic, transformations that he often resisted. But he was also a victim of his own legalistic vision. As Ferguson admits, the configuration of law and letters was "inherently conservative." Choate's program for writers of historical romances perfectly illustrates this conservatism.[5]

According to Choate, historical romances should not be "substitutes *for* history, but supplements to it," supplying the vivid and positive details of the past that are lacking in standard histories. The effect would be to make literature "cooperate with history" so as to engrain in the public imagination the truly sacred nature of America's political institutions. To do so a fiction writer would have to be more selective than a historian. The writer of America's Waverly novels should never forget that the story he tells must accommodate the "show of things to the desires and the needs of the immortal nature. . . . He remembers that it is an heroic age to whose contemplation he would turn us back; and as no man is a hero to his servant, so no age is heroic of which the whole truth is recorded. He tells the truth, to be sure, but he does not tell the whole truth, for that would be sometimes misplaced and discordant."[6]

The aesthetic advocated by legal men of letters like Choate clearly subordinated literature to law. One result was the sacrifice of originality to order, individuality to social duty. According to Ferguson, the writers of the American Renaissance reacted against the constraints of this aesthetic by stressing individual originality. But Choate's call for the selective use of history in works of fiction shows that more is at stake than a "contest between order and originality."[7] For Choate, the popular imagination would reveal respect for law only if it had proper respect for the history of our republican institutions. Therefore, preservation of the present order depended upon the public's perception of the past. Choate hoped that through a proper narration of the past a national literature would shape the public's respect for the laws of the present. The writers of the American Renaissance challenged the neoclassical aesthetic of the republican man-of-letters tradition not only by stressing individual originality but also by constructing alternative narratives of the past. We can see the extent of this challenge if we imagine Nathaniel Hawthorne in the audience as Choate delivered his speech in Salem.

Arguing that "much of what history relates . . . chills, shames and disgusts us," producing "discordant and contradictory emotions," Choate recommends leaving out accounts of the "persecution of the Quakers, the controversies with Roger Williams and Mrs. Hutchinson."[8] This recommendation almost seems a direct rebuke to Salem's Hawthorne. In 1832 "The Gentle Boy" had appeared in the *Token*. It dealt explicitly with the persecution of the Quakers. In 1830 Hawthorne had published a sketch of Anne Hutchinson in the *Salem Gazette*. He followed it ten years later with one of both Roger Williams and Anne Hutchinson, in *Grandfather's Chair*.[9] *The Scarlet Letter* explicitly evokes the memory of Hutchinson. Furthermore, when in "Roger Malvin's Burial" (1832) Hawthorne did write about one of the topics Choate suggested for fictional treatment – King Phillip's War – he certainly did not impart to his reader a reverence for our fathers. Indeed, the literature of the American Renaissance does not complement the law in the way Choate hoped that it would. Whereas Choate wanted to use the emotional appeal of literature to supplement history and elicit public support for the country's legal system, the history that literature relates often risks raising the discordant and contradictory emotions Choate wanted to suppress. Offering a less selective and less heroic narration of the country's past, it allows us to see what was excluded and marginalized by the country's submission to rule by law.

A major purpose of my study is to use selected literary texts from the American Renaissance to help define the legal ideology of the period. Part I examines the transformation of American property law and the image of the judiciary in James Fenimore Cooper's *Pioneers* and Hawthorne's *House of the Seven Gables*. Cooper provides a transition between the neoclassical aesthetic of the law-and-letters tradition and the romantic one of later writers such as Hawthorne. The rest of the book is concerned primarily with readings of Melville's fiction, which more than any other lends itself to analysis of the legal ideology of the time. Part II treats the legal questions arising from two different forms of labor in antebellum America: chattel slavery in the South, and so-called wage slavery in the North. I start with chapters comparing Melville's treatment of chattel slavery in "Benito Cereno" with Harriet Beecher Stowe's in *Uncle Tom's Cabin*. I then turn to Melville's images of exploitation at home and at sea in *White-Jacket* and *Pierre*, read in the context of the legal debate over chattel slavery. This chapter leads to a consideration of "Bartleby, the Scrivener" in terms of the free-labor ideology of the North. Part II ends with a short chapter relating *The Confidence-Man* to the laws of contract that provided a foundation for the free-labor system. Part III consists of two chapters on *Billy Budd*, the only text that I examine written after the Civil War. Composed in the late nineteenth century but set in the late eighteenth century, *Billy Budd* frames the period, thus allowing me to examine continuities as well as changes in legal history. In Captain Vere's "forms, measured forms," it raises questions about the role of formalism within the Anglo-American legal tradition, as well as about the triumph of formalism after the Civil War. It also offers an occasion to reconsider the typical nineteenth-century narrative that poses questions of justice in terms of a conflict between the individual and society. Finally, by drawing attention to the ideological implications of how histories are constructed, it lets me reflect upon my own attempt to write a historical narrative.

My use of literary texts to help define the legal ideology of antebellum America draws from and tries to expand upon work by members of the critical legal-studies movement. Interested in the social implications of the law, many members of the critical legal-studies movement recognize the limitations of a reflection theory, which explains the law as a mirror of society's existing power structure. In the liberal version, for instance, law reflects the competing demands of society's interest groups, whereas in orthodox Marxism law reflects capitalist control of political power and therefore serves the ruling class. This model does not adequately explain how law operates in Western democracies, because in addition to reflecting existing power structures, a legal system becomes an arena of conflict wherein power is sought. But if law is not merely a reflection of social conditions, it remains a social text that responds to its historical situation by finding ways to resolve social conflicts. Although the law's ability to maintain order by peacefully resolving conflict is often seen as its most positive function, the critical legal-studies movement reminds us of the extent to which the rhetoric of the law helps to maintain order at the price of disguising or denying the conflicts produced by the existing order, thereby helping to legitimate that order. Such a view of the law raises new questions, for the law can no longer be explained merely by analysis of the social conditions to which it responds. As Robert Gordon puts it, "If what is important about law is that it functions to 'legitimate' the existing order, one starts to ask *how* it does that."[10]

One of the most important ways in which the law fulfills its legitimizing function is through its rhetoric. As G. Edward White argues, "It was [John] Marshall's supreme mastery of the existing rhetorical conditions of his time that gave his admittedly partisan results their unassailable quality."[11] The persuasive effect of Marshall's highly praised logic was indebted to his masterly use of what Peter Gabel and Jay M. Feinman have called the "ideological imagery" of the law, its use of images and metaphors that help to convince the public of its impartiality.[12] To give a flavor of lawyers' use of such imagery, I will occasionally quote fairly lengthy passages. It is important to add, however, that it was not only their use of the rhetoric of the time that made their language persuasive. As Alexis de Tocqueville observed, respect for the law pervaded the very language Americans spoke. According to Chancellor James Kent,

> We live in the midst of the common law; we inhale it at every breath, imbibe it at every pore; we meet with it when we wake and when we lie down to sleep, when we travel and when we stay at home; and it is interwoven with the very idiom that we speak and we cannot learn another system of laws, without at the same time, another language.[13]

Constituted by a language full of the rhetoric of their republican system of government, individual subjects in America were more easily made subject to the country's laws.

As important as the language and imagery of law are in legitimating an existing political structure, they are both part of a larger, if less obvious, aspect of legal rhetoric. According to the late Chancellor Kent Professor of Law and Legal Studies at Yale University, Robert Cover, "No set of legal institutions or prescriptions exists apart from the narratives that locate it and give it meaning." Whereas we normally consider a judicial opinion to be the product of legal reasoning, Cover's insight into the inseparability of law and narrative reminds us that the persuasiveness of a decision depends upon an implied narrative that makes its reasoning seem logical. To try, as Cover proposes, to understand law "in the context of the narratives that give it meaning" is to try to reconstruct the cultural narratives that grant the law its authority.[14] One way to accomplish this task is to compare a culture's law with its literature, since literature, in a much more obvious way than law, reveals the stories that a culture tells about itself. Of course, as the difference between the narratives Choate proposed and the ones Hawthorne produced reveals, the literary narratives of the American Renaissance often demystify the narratives that serve to legitimate the legal order. It is precisely literature's ability to produce alternative narratives to the dominant ones of a culture that makes it so valuable in exposing the ideology of the legal system.

It would be a mistake, however, to assume that literature's capacity to generate narratives contesting a period's legal ideology makes literature an inherently subversive cultural institution. As Choate knew, literature can serve the dominant ideology, as well as challenge it. Even narratives that seem subversive can turn out indirectly to support the ideology they seem to subvert. Furthermore, a narrative that challenges one aspect of the law can support another, just as a narrative that subverts the legal ideology in one period can support the legal ideology of another. Thus, a second purpose of this study is to examine the ideological implications of major texts of the American Renaissance, especially those representing some aspect of the law.

An ideological analysis assumes that literature is a social text, one intricately connected to the social and historical conditions of its production and reception. Yet to assume that literature is a social text is not necessarily to assume the reflection theory that dominates most traditional ideological studies of literature. Indeed, a distinctive quality of the novels that I will examine is their fictionality. Recognition of the fictional aspect of much of literature has led critics interested in ideological analysis to consider a work as an imaginative response to its historical situation, rather than a reflection of the situation.[15] Thus, just as recent ideological analysis of the law has rejected a reflection theory, so has recent ideological analysis of literature.

If law, like literature, is related to the narratives a culture tells about itself, so literature, like law, responds to its historical situation by seeking ways to resolve social contradictions. Whereas legal discourse is conscious of its effort to resolve social contradictions but often unconscious of its narrative basis, literature is conscious of its narrativity while often unconscious of how its narratives are generated as a response to social contradiction. The similarities between legal and literary discourse show how close their social functions are to myth as described by Claude Lévi-Strauss.[16] Nonetheless, legal discourse much more explicitly promotes social cohesion, whereas literature more often offers utopian projections and possibilities. Literature's potentially utopian aspect does not, however, move it into a realm beyond ideology. Its resolutions of social contradictions may be different from those offered by a culture's legal system, but, as Fredric Jameson has argued, a literary narrative often amounts to a "strategy of containment" that disguises or diffuses the social contradictions that helped to generate it in the first place.[17] Easier to recognize in works offering explicitly utopian – often nostalgic – solutions, such strategies of containment are also present in seemingly pessimistic works, which, as Theodor Adorno has argued, can express their utopian impulse through a negative dialectic.[18] Even open-ended texts that refuse to resolve conflicts, such as many of Hawthorne's and Melville's, reveal an ideology, since such a strategy can lead to a world view in which social contradictions can be explained by a metaphysics of ambiguity.

Reading my literary texts in the context of legal history can enhance an analysis of their ideology in a variety of ways. As should be clear from the preceding discussion, a critic intent on ideological analysis cannot be content with recovering the surface meaning of a text but must reconstruct its historical horizon, in order to re-pose the questions to which its narrative is an imaginary solution. A knowledge of legal history can greatly facilitate this act of reconstruction.

Furthermore, legal history can help us measure how accurately literary works portray legal issues. My dissatisfaction with a reflection theory of literature does not mean that I regard the accuracy of literary representation as unimportant for an understanding of its ideology. If literature does not directly reflect a historical reality, it does offer narratives that are representative of how a culture reacts to the social contradictions of its time. Moreover, literature is never merely a reflection of existing cultural narratives. Because literature can come alive only through the minds of readers who live in the historical world, it helps to produce narrative responses, as well as to reproduce them. As fiction from *Don Quixote* to *Madame Bovary* to *Huckleberry Finn* has shown, readers of fiction often confuse the world they read about with the world they inhabit. It was Choate's awareness of the power of literature to shape a culture's image of itself that made him want to control the production of literary texts. Thus, even though literature defies a simple reflection model, any ideological analysis must still consider the accuracy of its representation.

I can make this point clearer by briefly referring to a story told time and again in American literature: the story about the conflict between the individual's need for freedom and society's need for order provided through rule by law. Of course, this conflict is not confined to American literature; it is as old as literature itself. But it takes on a special significance in a culture that prides itself on the legal protection of individual rights. Central to the narrative of most of the works I will analyze, this narrative remains one of the most common ones that Americans invoke when trying to explain their occasional or frequent dissatisfaction with the law. Sometimes a writer chooses individual freedom over rule by law – other times, rule by law over individual freedom. Yet the terms of the conflict remain the same. Rule by law stands for social order, but it risks constraining individual freedom, which in turn risks disrupting social order. Relying on Morton Horwitz's work in legal history, however, we get a very different story about the conflict between the individual and the law in American history. According to Horwitz, during the antebellum period American law was transformed in the economic realm to release individual freedom rather than constrain it.[19] If historically the law did not control possessive individualism the way we are told it should, we need to reexamine the role that law played in America's development.

As this example shows, the very terms of the conflict between the individual and society, so eloquently expressed by antebellum writers, risk ideological distortion. I can say this even though I will argue that we should not see their works as a reflection of their time but as a response to social, economic, and legal transformations. It is, indeed, the persuasive power of this imagined narrative to explain contradictions within the American legal system that grants it such ideological force; hence the importance that I place on using legal history to reconsider this narrative and related ones opposing public to private and head to heart. That reconsideration will not make the obviously false claim that people did not feel a conflict between head and heart or that individuals did not come into conflict with the law, but it will question whether such narratives can offer an adequate explanation of the inequities produced and perpetuated by the American legal system.

Not all writers narrate the conflict between the individual and society in the same way. Cooper's version in *The Pioneers* is different from Melville's in *Billy Budd*. Such differences should remind us that, although I have stressed the status of literary texts as cultural narratives, not all narratives having to do with the law are the same. *The Pioneers* and *The House of the Seven Gables* offer very different resolutions to the conflict over the ownership of a piece of property. "Benito Cereno" and *Uncle Tom's Cabin* are very different responses to slavery.

These individual differences bring me to a third aspect of my study. I want to help account for the differences by suggesting the type of contact that the writers had with the legal profession. For instance, I interweave my discussion of *The Pioneers* with an examination of the Federalist philosophy of Chancellor James Kent, a friend of Cooper's father and a member of Cooper's own Bread and Cheese Club in New York City, paying careful attention to Kent's response to the New York State constitutional convention of 1821, which occurred one year before Cooper began his book.[20] My discussion of *The House of the Seven Gables* draws on the legal philosophy of U.S. Supreme Court justice Joseph Story, Salem's most famous judge and a figure connected with Salem's notorious White murder case of 1830, which was a source for Hawthorne's romance. My analysis of *Uncle Tom's Cabin* begins with an analysis of *State v. Mann,* a North Carolina slave case that Stowe wrote about at length in *A Key to Uncle Tom's Cabin*. Finally, the economic and fugitive slave law decisions of Massachusetts's Chief Justice Lemuel Shaw inform my discussion of the legal issues presented in the fictions of his son-in-law, Herman Melville.

I pair legal and literary figures both to organize my material and to make a historical point. The writers of this period mark a break in the connection between law and letters, yet they remain direct heirs to that tradition. Cooper was not trained as a lawyer and thus is not one of the figures that Ferguson treats at length in *Law and Letters*. Nonetheless, Cooper's contact with the Jay family, as well as with Kent and the Bread and Cheese Club, placed him in the same social milieu. With its explicit political themes, his fiction adheres to the lawyer-writer's desire to use literature to shape the country's sense of self-definition. He is a transitional figure, however, because the major concern of his fiction is how to respond to the destruction of the republican ideal fostered by the lawyer-writers.

More than Cooper, Hawthorne and Melville adhere to the aesthetic arising during the American Renaissance, an aesthetic that Ferguson claims "excludes the legal mind from the literary enterprise."[21] By drawing on legal history in my readings of Hawthorne and Melville, I hope to show that this exclusion was not as rigorous as Ferguson claims. Writers of the American Renaissance did not so much exclude the legal mind as search for alternatives to it, especially as it moved increasingly toward a rigid formalism. If that search means that the legal mind is not as apparent as in the works produced by the configuration of law and letters, it also means that the legal mind continues to influence the shape and even content of works in the American Renaissance. We have a better understanding of how and why that is so when we remember that the aesthetic of the American Renaissance was forged by writers with close social and familial ties to members of the legal profession. The Melville family, for instance, was close to the same circle frequented by Cooper. In 1826 Herman's mother wrote to her own mother, proudly reporting that Herman's ten-year-old brother Gansevoort had sat next to Chancellor Kent during a staged school performance.[22] Through Shaw's connection with the Melville family, a connection that started before Herman was born, Melville throughout his life had social access to some of the most important lawyers of the time.

Ironically, the very closeness of literary and legal figures that a generation earlier produced the configuration of law and letters might have contributed to the aesthetic that appears to exclude the legal mind. Struggling for public recognition, Melville and Hawthorne must have been acutely aware of having much less power and influence than their lawyer friends and relatives. Hawthorne, about to lose his job at the Custom House, appealed to those powerful friends, most notably George Hillard, for help. Hillard – one of Joseph Story's prize pupils, a law partner of Charles Sumner, and a true man of letters who had edited an edition of Spenser – did try to help his friend. But in arguing that he should not be fired from his job, Hawthorne rested his case on the contention that he

was an artist and that art was by definition apolitical.[23] This split between politics and aesthetics is familiar to students of literature in the
twentieth century. Analyzing some of the major texts of the American
Renaissance in the context of legal history will help us understand the
historical situation that helped to create it.

Of course, the claim that art is above politics is not new with the
American Renaissance. Even the neoclassical aesthetic of the lawyer-
writers described by Ferguson considered art above "politics" in the
narrow sense. Similarly, American writers a generation before Hawthorne also recognized that to choose a career as an artist rather than as a
lawyer potentially meant to lose practical power and influence. Despite
these similarities, the new aesthetic differed from the old aesthetic because it moved toward a split from politics in even the larger sense.

To understand how the difference between the old and new aesthetic
arose, we can look at the writers' responses to the practical bent of
American society. As different as the romantic aesthetic was from the
earlier neoclassical one, the two were alike in that both had to confront a
public that considered art impractical. Indeed, people like Choate and
Story bucked a powerful segment of American society when they advocated the arts. Choate campaigned unsuccessfully to have the Smithso-
nian Institute support the arts rather than science and technology. Story,
in a lecture entitled "Developments of Science and Mechanic Art," also
made a pitch for the fine arts, although he was fully aware of the practical
bias of his audience. Declaring that fine arts are not only the "grace and
ornament of society" but also "intimately connected with its solid com-
forts," Story claimed that "far more than gratifying our taste, increasing
our circle of innocent enjoyment, and refining our feelings," the arts
create jobs. "They not only create a demand for labor; but make that
very labor a means of subsistence to many, who must otherwise be idle
and indolent."[24] In creating jobs for marble cutters, printers, and other
craftsmen, the arts become useful; otherwise they are a mere frill.

Story and Choate defended the arts, but clearly their defense would
cause trouble for someone embracing a romantic aesthetic. Although
Story and Choate advocated the arts, they continued to subordinate them
to social needs, especially the need of American society to be ruled by
laws instead of men. As long as their aesthetic reigned, the choice between a legal and literary career was clear. A lawyer-writer like Charles
Brockden Brown might have temporarily chosen the "barren laurel"
over the "useful olive," but his training made it clear that to do so was to
place individual needs above those of the nation.[25] In contrast, when
Emerson addressed the question of vocation, he justified in nationalistic
terms the individualism associated with a career as the American Scholar.
If for lawyers a literary career ultimately lacked practicality, spokesmen

for the aesthetic of the American Renaissance rejected the law precisely because of its practicality. Understanding why Shelley called poets the "unacknowledged legislators of the world," they embraced a new religion of art in competition with America's religion of the law.

Nonetheless, the questioning of the legal mind during the American Renaissance was not merely the result of changes within the artistic mind. In part this questioning was a response to changes within the legal profession itself. Even an unreserved defender of the law such as Story decried the trend in his profession toward narrow specialization. For him, lawyers should be well-read in classical literature because it trained lawyers to respond to universal truths and thus to rise above narrow concerns, whether of partisan politics or purely technical aspects of the law. The prospect of a profession made up entirely of technical practitioners of the law depressed him, and it caused people like Emerson and Thoreau to reject the legal mentality.

The story is more complex, however, because, paradoxically, Story and his allies were in part responsible for the change in the profession they so lamented. According to Ferguson, "Technical competence triumphed over general learning and philosophical discourse as case law accumulated."[26] The accumulation of case law was a logical consequence of a philosophy shared by Story that both demanded the supremacy of law and resisted legal codification. The growth of the market economy supported by Story led to more and more situations that required legal intervention. Even his effort in *Swift v. Tyson* (1842) to establish a universal commercial law resulted in more rather than fewer cases. With so many cases to master, a practicing lawyer no longer had the time to study classical literature.

Story's belief in the existence of a universal commercial law points to one of the major reasons why his legal philosophy laid the foundation for its own undoing. Despite his claim that his philosophy was classical, his economic beliefs were based on those of eighteenth-century Britain. In linking his belief in universals with a support of the market economy, he and his allies developed a legal philosophy that gave a concentration on commerce universal moral justification. Thus, when Thoreau and Emerson attacked the legal profession for its undue emphasis on practicality, they did not confine their attack to petty practitioners but singled out Story's friend Daniel Webster, who was identified with commercial interests. For them the problem with the legal profession was not merely that it was comprised of too many technical specialists but that even its mightiest minds adhered to a logic that misled the public about universal values. In trying to marry universals and commerce, the great legal thinkers in antebellum America made way for the triumph of a narrow technical expertise within their profession, forcing writers of the American Renaissance to turn to a different conception of art to find the universal values that Story had sought in the law. The belief that art, not law, was the seat of universal values became so powerful in intellectual circles that after Story's death his own son rejected the law to pursue a career as an artist.

Story's son, William Wetmore Story, did not pursue his career as an artist in America. Instead, as so many artists after him were to do, he left for Europe. The United States was no more supportive of the arts during the American Renaissance than earlier. This lack of support was especially difficult for serious writers of fiction, like Hawthorne and Melville, and contributed to a theory of fiction that split art and politics even farther apart. On the one hand, Hawthorne and Melville lived in a society that considered the arts impractical, an ornament to provide entertainment or comfort for the female population. On the other, they confronted a society that inherited suspicion, felt by Puritans and by adherents of the Scottish Common Sense School, of fictional works as subversive of reality.[27] As we have seen, Rufus Choate eloquently argued for writers of fiction by challenging both of these beliefs. Choate's defense of fiction, however, was based on the narrow neoclassical aesthetic against which the writers of the American Renaissance reacted. Finding that their fictions did indeed contain the subversive elements feared by some segments of the American public, writers adopted strategies to protect themselves. Hawthorne, for instance, announced that his works had nothing to do with politics, and at times not even with the historical world. The price that the writers paid for this protection, however, was an increasingly marginalized role in society. In dissociating their work from political reality, they confirmed the public's belief that literature was no more than an ornament.

Of course, not all of the fiction writers of the time self-consciously pronounced their works to be divorced from politics. Harriet Beecher Stowe's *Uncle Tom's Cabin* addressed an explicit political question, and exerted immediate influence, precisely by asserting its connection with the historical world. But her novel connected politics and art by challenging the legal mind, instead of appealing to it. Based on evangelical religion, not a religion of art or law, it adhered to an aesthetic of sentiment, rather than that of either the American Renaissance or the configuration of law and letters.[28] Emphasizing the split between law and morality more than the split between politics and art, the aesthetic underlying *Uncle Tom's Cabin* has correctly been associated with the Beecher family's involvement with religious revivalism. Nonetheless, even Stowe had important legal connections that stretched from her birth in Litchfield, Connecticut, the location of one of the country's first law schools, to her reliance on antislavery lawyers to defend her portrayal of slavery laws.

Her legal connections remind us, as do those of Hawthorne and Melville, that the writer's aesthetic was shaped in part by the breakup of an aesthetic that tried to link morality, law, and letters. In turn, Stowe's aesthetic, which tried to unite sentiment and art, influenced the shape of the aesthetic of the American Renaissance adopted by Hawthorne and Melville.

In bringing together the law and literature of the period, I hope to offer a better understanding of the conditions that led to the split between morality and law and between politics and art. At the same time, an understanding of those conditions makes it clear why a study such as mine is necessary in the first place. Mine is only one of many recent attempts to link law and literature. Such studies are part of a general attempt to bring literature and law together with other disciplines, an attempt necessitated by the movement toward the specialization and professionalization of knowledge into increasingly isolated disciplines in the nineteenth century. As more and more people try to relate law and literature, we should recognize that in bringing together two disciplines that have been historically severed, we risk violating the criteria that both have evolved to define legitimate knowledge. For instance, my method might cause legal scholars to complain that I lack the professional training to understand the complexities of law. Similarly, literary scholars might complain that my account of literary history is not really "literary" because I use historical evidence improperly and subordinate literary history to another history.[29] Such objections are important and should be addressed.

On the one hand, my justification for venturing into the field of legal analysis is similar to that of John Dewey, who noted that "discussions and theories which have influenced legal practice . . . introduced and depended upon a mass of non-legal considerations: considerations popular, historical, political, moral, philosophical, metaphysical and, in connection with the latter, theological."[30] That Dewey leaves out literary considerations only serves to emphasize the need to draw on literature for legal analysis. On the other hand, I hope that my use of certain legal texts in conjunction with literary texts will remind us of the extent to which the category of literature is itself historically defined. In the 1918 *Cambridge History of American Literature,* for example, an entire chapter is devoted to Daniel Webster and another to "Publicists and Orators, 1800–1850." Texts discussed in the latter chapter include John Marshall's great opinions and Story's and Kent's legal treatises. In contrast, Melville is listed as a poet of the Civil War.[31]

By now it should be clear that in bringing law and literature together I am trying to go beyond the boundaries of what has been defined as literary analysis. The major purpose of my study is to tell a story about

American culture – not always to recover the author's conscious intention. When Melville wrote "Bartleby," he did not set out to question the legal decisions supporting the northern system of free labor. For him, "Bartleby" was much more a metaphysical than a social text. Nonetheless, when we compare Melville's narrative with those decisions, we have a better understanding of their ideological assumptions. In addition, legal history helps us to reconstruct the historical situation in which this bizarre narrative could be imagined. Thus, although I rarely claim that the law is a primary cause in the production of the fiction I discuss, I do claim that reading the fiction in the context of legal history can help us understand its cultural significance.

Having made this claim, I need to say a word about my use of biographical evidence to tell a cultural story. Because biographical evidence has often been used to recover an author's intention, my use of it might cause confusion, especially since the economy of my narrative dictates that I use legal figures for two sorts of evidence. On the one hand, I use them to emphasize the connections that writers of literature had with the legal profession. On the other, I use them to reconstruct aspects of legal history relevant to my discussion of a particular text. In the first case the biographical connection is essential; in the second it is not. In either case, my major concern is not to produce a positivistic influence study. With occasional exceptions, when I draw on the legal opinions of Kent, Story, and Shaw I am not arguing that these opinions are "sources" in the traditional sense of the word. Instead, I use their opinions to illustrate the legal philosophies of people close to the authors. For the purposes of my study it is not so important to establish that writers had firsthand knowledge of a specific opinion as to establish that they knew the opinions behind the opinions.

Nonetheless, there remain times when a legal case, incident, or figure does serve as a source in the traditional sense, as does the White murder case for *The House of the Seven Gables,* the Fugitive Slave Act of 1850 for *Uncle Tom's Cabin,* or the *Somers* affair for *Billy Budd.* In drawing on cases like these, as well as those that are not traditional sources, I can be accused of mixing my evidence. I would be on safer ground, it would seem, not to bring these two types of evidence together. Not to do so, however, would be to risk distorting the complex process by which the legal issues of a culture get inscribed in the work of an individual author. My use of biographical evidence is not intended to reduce a cultural study to biography but to suggest the process by which some issues directly affect a writer, others are mediated through family and social connections, and some are generally accessible through the culture at large. For instance, few educated people in the United States at the time would have been unaware of the *Somers* affair, the Webster murder case,

and the Fugitive Slave Act cases. That Melville also had personal connections with each one only serves to make their relevance to his works
more complex.

I cite these three examples intentionally, because I have one more point
to make about my use of evidence. So far I have distinguished between
traditional sources and other evidence. But, as these three examples
show, the criteria used to establish historical sources may not be as
objective as they seem. If we were to rely on normal criteria, only the
Somers affair would qualify as a source for one of the literary works I
discuss, and even its status as a source has been questioned, despite its
mention in *Billy Budd*.[32] The status of the Webster murder case and the
Fugitive Slave Act cases as sources would certainly be questioned, since
we can find no empirical evidence indicating that Melville had them in
mind as he wrote. But clearly there is something arbitrary about the
standards that determine legitimate source evidence in literary studies
when they so often depend upon a scholar's ability, years later, to recover mention of an incident on a piece of paper, as if only what is
written down could have been important. This objection is especially
applicable in the case of Melville, who, in *Billy Budd,* questions the
objectivity of such documentary evidence.

To say this is not to deny the importance of trying to discover whether
an author actually knew about a case or had access to knowing about it
while writing. Such knowledge does make a difference, and when appropriate I will note whether we can establish either, but I will not exclude a
case merely because it cannot be established beyond a reasonable doubt as
a "source." On the one hand, these cases serve, as I have noted, as
cultural evidence giving us a sense of the legal thought to which individual writers would have been exposed. On the other, I hope to show
that the inclusion of some evidence is so appropriate to particular texts
that we might be led to wonder whether its previous exclusion has
something to do with the criteria that professional literary critics have
used to lay down the law as to what constitutes legitimate evidence in
textual analysis. If so, what appears to be the exclusion of the legal mind
from the aesthetic of the American Renaissance may in part be due to
modern criticial procedures, procedures shaped, in turn, by that very
aesthetic.

Indeed, one result of the specialization and professionalization of
knowledge that contributed to the breakup of the law-and-letters configuration was the establishment of disciplines each with its own criteria for
legitimate knowledge. Although professional specialization led to
important advances in knowledge, it also led to the production of catego-
ries that excluded certain types of questions.[33] The separation of law and
literature is a case in point. In rejoining the two, in order to study the

period in American history in which they were severed, I am not claiming that law is the key that will provide a full understanding of the period's literature, nor that literature is the key that will provide a full understanding of the period's law. I am not even claiming to offer complete readings of the literary texts I analyze, since my concentration on the law clearly emphasizes some aspects at the expense of others. The law and literature of the time were shaped by many more factors than one another. In order to compare these two disciplines, I will often have to refer to aspects of social and economic history. In fact, precisely because both law and literature responded – in different ways – to social transformations, I can claim that in weaving together a narrative from law and literature we can explore aspects of America's cultural history that our tendency to concentrate on only one field of study has consigned to a realm of silence. Specifically, a cross-examination of law and literature can help us reconstruct the narratives that different segments of American society imagined in response to the social and economic transformations that they experienced, as well as the narratives that helped to legitimize and structure those transformations.

As I have made clear, a variety of literary narratives were generated at this time. Nonetheless, I will repeatedly refer to the "dominant legal ideology of the time" or "orthodox legal thought." Such labels perhaps seem to imply that the period spawned only one variety of legal thought. Clearly, this is not the case. Jeffersonian lawyers differed from Federalist lawyers, and Jacksonian from Whig. When I refer to the dominant legal ideology of the period, I do not do so to refer to the way all lawyers thought. Instead, I refer to the thought associated most often with prominent Whig lawyers, such as Story, Kent, Webster, Choate, and Shaw. In lumping their thought together I do not want to imply that no individual differences existed. Although Story and Kent are often linked, they did not agree on everything. If Story and Webster were allies, Story occasionally ruled against his friend in Supreme Court cases. Shaw had a long and distinguished career and shared many views with Kent and Story, but he was by no means a legal scholar with the same breadth of knowledge. Despite their individual differences, however, these Whig lawyers had identifiable similarities. They strongly advocated judicial supremacy, arguing that a disinterested judiciary was necessary to check the partisan designs of legislatures. They also supported a strong federal government and urged that law encourage national growth through the support of commerce. Their program did not achieve immediate dominance. In fact, as Ferguson argues, to many the breakup of the configuration of law and letters signaled the defeat of their ideal vision for the American republic. But even though at the end of their lives a number of these figures felt that they had failed in their efforts to make reverence for the law the political religion of the land, their formative influence on the shape of American law is universally recognized. The dominance of their ideology has to do with the manner in which it was institutionalized in America's legal system, so that its influence continues to be felt today. The fact that the writers I treat had close connections with Whig lawyers makes the inclusion of their works even more appropriate in an analysis of the ideological assumptions that underlie the American legal system.

My emphasis on ideological analysis, especially that of the law, also needs an important qualification. To argue that the period's legal thinking is ideological is not to argue that the law was solely an instrument serving the interests of dominant groups. To a large extent it was, and yet it was also more. The faith in rule by law that Americans inherited from the British grew out of a struggle in the sixteenth and seventeenth centuries between the aristocracy and the agrarian and mercantile bourgeoisie. The rising middle class appealed to rule by law to limit the arbitrary power of the aristocracy. The laws established by the bourgeoisie often reflected its interests, and continued to do so as this class consolidated its power. Since submission to rule by law meant submission to bourgeois rule, the powerful rhetoric praising the fairness of the law was inevitably ideological.

Nonetheless, as E. P. Thompson argues, "The law may be rhetoric, but it need not be empty rhetoric." If the bourgeoisie used rule by law as an instrument of class power, "It was inherent in the very nature of the medium which they had selected for their own self-defense that it could not be reserved for the exclusive use only of their own class. The law, in its forms and traditions, entailed principles of equity and universality which, perforce, had to be extended to all sorts and degrees of man." Thus, law has remained a central arena of conflict for groups challenging the rule of the bourgeoisie itself, because, for the law to function effectively as ideology, it has to seem just. It cannot seem just without at times upholding its own logic and criteria of equity – without at times actually being just. In other words, the ideal of the law contains within it a standard of equity that allows us to measure the failure of individual laws to correspond to that standard. This ideal aspect of rule by law has caused Thompson himself to proclaim, "The notion of the regulation and reconciliation of conflicts through rule by law – and the elaboration of rules and procedures which, on occasion, made some approximate approach towards the ideal – seems to me. . . a cultural achievement of universal significance."[34] My own study draws on this ideal in an essential way, since my ideological analysis is enabled by it.

To believe in some ideal notion of justice is not necessarily to believe in a transcendental, ahistorical standard for judgment. As Thompson emphasizes, the ideal that he and I speak of is a cultural achievement, understood only in its proper historical development and context. A historical understanding of an ideal notion of justice can help counter a recent ahistorical trend in legal and literary scholarship. A critic like Stanley Fish, believing as I do that there is no knowledge outside of situations, goes on militantly to legislate against the use of notions such as impartiality, objectivity, disinterestedness, and neutrality.[35] But Fish's banishment of these notions makes sense only if we think of them ahistorically. Certainly there is no disinterested stance outside of history, and yet a historical situation itself can generate a notion of disinterestedness. A pure state of disinterestedness might be counterfactual, but it is imagined within particular historical contexts.

For instance, throughout my study I will argue that the social inequities existing within antebellum America made the judiciary's claim to disinterestedness invalid, and thus a political act. Nonetheless, my criticism depends upon the very notion of disinterestedness that the judiciary helped define. It might be "logical," but certainly not historical, to discount this notion of disinterestedness that people believed in and that continues to shape our notion of the law. Indeed, this example makes clear how much my study depends upon the tradition that it criticizes. My analysis owes much to the work of the very people whose legal thought comes in for some of my most comprehensive criticism. Judges like Kent, Story, and Shaw were not terrible men; they were sincere proponents of justice. This is not to say that their legal philosophies always led to justice. As I will try to show, they often served to legitimize the ascendance of a particular class by making the laws that benefited its rule seem just, but their defense of justice still provides a standpoint from which to criticize their practices.

Having remarked upon the way in which the tradition I study has helped to shape my presuppositions about both law and literature, I will end this introduction by acknowledging that my interest in that tradition is also shaped by present concerns. This can be seen most clearly in my selection of literary texts. I have self-consciously chosen canonized texts. Widely read today, expecially by college and university students, these texts continue to influence the public's attitude toward the law. Thus the critical debate over how they are read is inevitably a political debate. Drawing on legal history, the readings to follow are my contribution to that present debate.

Part I

Individuals, Judges, Property

1

The Pioneers; or the Sources of American Legal History: A Critical Tale

Few would argue with the statement that *The Pioneers* is a novel about the transformation of America from wilderness to civilization. That transformation, as Henry Nash Smith put it, was "conceived in terms of the antithesis between nature and civilization, between freedom and the law, that has governed most American interpretations of the westward movement." For Smith, "The narrative turns constantly about the central issue of the old forest freedom versus the new needs of a community which must establish the sovereignty of law over the individual."[1] George Dekker has refined Smith's definition of the conflict by pointing out that the issue is not simply law versus freedom. Natty's "freedom" results from his obedience to a strict code of law, internalized from his direct experience of nature. In many ways Natty's code is more rigorous than Temple's.[2] Yet Dekker does not really change the terms of the conflict. It remains what Perry Miller called "the great issue of the nineteenth century, the never-ending case of Heart versus Head." Should Natty's natural sense of justice, personal and from the heart, be sacrificed to a socially imposed rule of law, impersonal and guided by disinterested rationality? "Yes," Cooper seems to say, even though *his* heart seems to sympathize with Natty, so much so that he gives America, in Perry Miller's words, "its first universally accepted folk symbol."[3]

It is not my purpose in this chapter to question the received critical opinion about Cooper's portrayal of the conflict between Natty and the law. Instead my purpose is to examine that portrayal historically and critically.

As both Smith and Miller argued, *The Pioneers* reveals that many Americans have come to accept the necessity of the legal order, despite their nagging sense that it infringes on their freedom. This is not to say that all who think about law in terms similar to Cooper's have read Cooper, but it is to say that more Americans get their sense of the role that law played in civilizing America from literary works and works of popular culture than from reading legal history. If *The Pioneers* does not directly reflect a historical reality, it does offer a persuasive way to narrate the conflict between the individual and the law that so many Americans have felt. Variations of that narrative are inscribed in our cultural attitude toward law. Studying *The Pioneers* historically and critically allows us to examine the assumptions that narrative generates. As Cooper tells it, Natty's sacrifice, though lamentable, is inevitable, because Judge Temple's laws are necessary for the orderly civilizing of America. We get a very different sense of the conflict when we juxtapose Cooper's fictional narrative with an interpretation of antebellum law relying on the evidence of actual court cases and statutes. Judge Temple's legal order may not have been the only possible order available.

The first step toward understanding the historical context of Cooper's work is to recognize that *The Pioneers* represents not just one historical transformation but two. *The Pioneers* is set in 1793–4, but it also provides us with a glimpse of what the land surrounding Templeton was like in its wilderness state before 1793 and what it was like at the time Cooper wrote the book in 1821–2. The glimpse of the past comes through the eyes of Judge Temple and is strategically located in the twenty-first of forty-one chapters; that is, in the very center of the book. It occurs just before the scenes in which the pioneers wastefully slaughter countless pigeons and bass, thereby contrasting an image of undisturbed wilderness with an image of nature abused by the settlers' extravagance. The glimpse of the land at the time of writing comes in the first few pages of the book. What this initial description reveals is that even though Natty's wilderness has been transformed in the thirty years since the action of the book, it has not been laid waste. A just system of laws seems to have successfully checked the destruction of nature.

> Beautiful and thriving villages are found interspersed along the margins of the small lakes or situated at those points of the streams which are favourable to manufacturing; and neat and comfortable farms, with every indication of wealth about them, are scattered profusely through the vales, and even to the mountaintops. . . . Academies, and minor edifices of learning, meet the eye of the stranger, at every few miles, as he winds his way through this uneven territory; and places for the worship of God, abound with that frequency which characterizes a moral and reflecting people, and with that variety of exterior and canonical government which flows from unfettered liberty of conscience.[4]

This idyllic scene is not, as similar ones will be in later Cooper works, set in the past. It is in the present and includes a suggestion of what the model of proper government should be.[5]

> In short, the whole district is hourly exhibiting how much can be done, in even a rugged country, and with severe climate, under the dominion of mild laws, and where every man feels a direct interest in the prosperity of a commonwealth, of which he knows himself to form a part. (*Pioneers* 15–16)

This description might have owed some of its optimism to the Era of Good Feeling that reigned in America at this time. Yet as Cooper wrote these words, this ideal of a republican commonwealth had already been severely threatened. Cooper's opening description implies that the legal system that had come down intact from 1793 had allowed the wilderness to be transformed into a romantic, picturesque, and productive landscape. In 1821, however, the state of New York held a convention to revise its constitution. Responding to social transformations occurring in the last thirty years, the convention marked the "passage from republican aristocracy to prudent democracy in the politics of New York."[6] A look at the debate at the 1821 convention over the character of the law will help us to understand Cooper's portrayal of the law.

By 1821, Federalist political power had noticeably shrunk. Federalists, adopting the new name of Independent Republicans, were even overshadowed by their anti-Democratic allies, who followed De Witt Clinton. In opposition, the Democrats insisted that they represented the people, against those with property. However, rallying behind the moderate leadership of Martin Van Buren rather than a more radical, egalitarian faction, they were not quite the threat to property that their own rhetoric and that of their opponents would suggest. Though responsive to popular sentiment, the Van Buren Bucktails strongly believed in social order and the maintenance of private rights under the rule of law. When Van Buren spoke against New York's "aristocracy," he was not making a claim for popular rule. The governing elite (to which Cooper belonged) was sustained by social position and family connection. Van Buren wanted to replace it with a new leadership of the rising powerful – the Albany Regency. The constitution that had ruled New York State from the Revolution until 1821 was an object of Van Buren's attack because it, along with residual elements of the old Dutch patroon system, protected the interests of what the Federalists called the "guardian class."

The old constitution of New York reflected the elitist beliefs of its most famous architect, John Jay, a Federalist friend of William Cooper and a man whom James Cooper admired. Built into the constitution were provisions designed to control the extravagance of the masses. Suffrage was limited to well-to-do property holders. A Council of Appointments was established, which made certain that those in control of the state government were responsible for local appointments. Finally, there was the Council of Revision, which had veto power over any act that the legislature might pass. Made up of seven men, including all five members of the state supreme court, the governor, and the chancellor of the court of equity, the Council of Revision guaranteed the guardian class control of the state's laws through the judiciary.

Given the makeup of the convention, it was clear that the principles of the old constitution were doomed to defeat. The two councils were abolished and the voting requirements changed. Nonetheless, a few powerful individuals made a spirited effort to "save for posterity those principles and practices which had been tried and sanctified by time."[7] Their major spokesman, Yale-educated Chancellor James Kent, the former chief justice of the New York Supreme Court, is an important figure for our purposes. A Federalist of the "old school," Kent had been a friend of Cooper's father, William. When James Fenimore Cooper moved to New York City in 1822, Kent became his friend and joined his Bread and Cheese Club. Kent's *Commentaries on the American Law* (1826–30) won him a reputation as the "American Blackstone." Its four volumes had a profound influence on the training of American lawyers, going through twelve editions by 1873 and selling well enough to earn Kent five thousand dollars a year. In the *Commentaries* and Kent's comments at the 1821 convention, we can see in detail a historical counterpart of a political philosophy similar to Cooper's fictional Judge Temple. This is not to argue that we should consider Kent the model for Temple, rather than the much more obvious model of William Cooper. Nonetheless, in imagining his fictional character, Cooper could have drawn on a legal philosophy similar to that of New York's most famous judge.[8]

Kent's speeches at the 1821 convention were described even by his opponents as an "elegant epitaph" for the old constitution. An important part of his argument denied American exceptionalism. "Dare we flatter ourselves . . . that we are a peculiar people, who can run the career of history exempted from the passions which have disturbed and corrupted the rest of mankind?" For him the threat of rule by the passions was associated with the threat of rule by a specific group of people – those without property. The threat could be controlled so long as government remained in the hands of those with property. When it was proposed that the property holding requirement for voters in senatorial elections should be lowered, the chancellor responded,

> The apprehended danger from the experiment of universal suffrage applied to the whole legislative department, is no dream of the imagination. It is too mighty an excitement for the moral condition of men to endure. The tendency of universal suffrage is to jeopardize the rights of property, and the principles of liberty. There is a constant tendency in

> human society, and the history of every age proves it; there is a constant tendency in the poor to covet and to share the plunder of the rich; in the debtor to relax or avoid the obligations of contract; in the majority to tyrannize over the minority, and trample down their rights; in the indolent and profligate to caste the whole burthen of society upon the industrious and virtuous; and there is a tendency in ambitious and wicked men to inflame those combustible materials.[9]

For Kent, ownership of property was a sign of an individual's good character and ability to govern. Riding the circuit in 1810, he had contrasted the squatters and insolvent emigrants in Delaware and Tioga counties, who supported "democratic" ideas, with the settlers whose attachment to the rights of property kept them from confusing license with liberty. He was proud that the Federalist system had apparently controlled the passions of the "indolent and profligate" and allowed the "industrious and virtuous" to construct improvements such as canals and turnpikes, thus opening the wilderness to cultivation and making possible the rise of commerce. His account of these developments is almost identical with Cooper's description of how the rude, fierce, and licentious pioneers yielded to a population of self-restrained and responsible yeomen who cultivated the wilderness.

> The expedients of the pioneers who first broke ground in the settlement of this country, are succeeded by the permanent improvements of the yeoman, who intends to leave his remains to moulder under the sod which he tills, or, perhaps, of the son, who, born in the land, piously wishes to linger around the grave of his father. – Only forty years have passed since this territory was a wilderness. (*Pioneers* 16)

An understanding of the issues debated in 1821 lets us see that Cooper's opening description could well carry with it the message that James Kent delivered on the convention floor: In changing the old constitution, the people of New York State risked abandoning the very system that had given them prosperity. Indeed, although Cooper's point of view is not identical with Kent's, he did sympathize with Kent and his allies at the convention.[10]

Cooper sympathized with the old school because he shared their paternalistic concept of government. As John P. McWilliams, Jr., has put it, "Cooper's conception of law and government is entirely protective and preventive." In *The American Democrat,* Cooper argued that

> man is known to exist in no part of the world, without certain rules for the regulation of his intercourse with those around him. It is a first necessity of his weakness, that laws, founded on the immutable principles of natural justice, should be framed, in order to protect the feeble against the violence of the strong; the honest from the schemes of the dishonest; the temperate and industrious, from the waste and indolence of the dissolute and the idle.[11]

Judge Temple's role in the early history of Templeton illustrates Cooper's notion of how a disinterested member of the guardian class could fulfill his patriarchal function. During the first year of settlement, famine threatened the pioneers. "It was a season of scarcity; the necessities of life commanded a high price in Europe, and were greedily sought after by speculators. The emigrants, from the east to the west, invariably passed along the valley of the Mohawk, and swept away the means of subsistence, like a swarm of locusts" (*Pioneers* 234). As Temple tells his daughter, "I had hundreds, at that dredful time, daily looking up to me for bread" (234). To save people, the judge had food delivered from Pennsylvania. In his social vision the poor need enlightened rulers, like himself, to guard over them. "The poor," the judge believes, "are always prodigal . . . where there is plenty, and seldom think of a provision against the morrow" (260). For the judge, therefore, "The first object of my solicitude . . . is to protect the sources of this great mine of comfort and wealth, from the extravagance of the people themselves" (221). Judge Temple's laws provide that protection.

Despite Cooper's sympathy with Kent's social vision, his own social vision differed from Kent's in important ways. When the Federalist party dissolved, Kent became a Whig and Cooper a Democrat. The most important difference between their political philosophies concerned the role of commerce in the republic. Kent, in trying to save doomed republican institutions, had at times adopted an almost Jeffersonian rhetoric to advocate rule by "free and independent lords of the soil." Nonetheless, Kent's major concern was the growth of commerce. For him, prosperity depended on encouraging commerce. In the 1821 convention, he looked ahead to the future: "We are no longer to remain plain and simple republics of farmers, like the New England colonists, or the Dutch settlements on the Hudson. We are fast becoming a great nation, with great commerce, manufactures, population, wealth, luxuries, and with the vices and miseries that they engender."[12] Although Kent feared the power that the rise of industry might give to the growing population of propertyless laborers in New York City, he was too good a Hamiltonian not to recognize the value of manufacturing to commerce. Kent's answer was for commerce and agriculture to ally themselves against the potentially disruptive political power of manufacturers who, with skillful management, might control the vote of laborers. His appeal to this alliance at the convention was an astute political move, for in emphasizing the threat of New York City's poor, he played on the fears of Van Buren's Bucktails, who were afraid of losing political power to the city. With the support of the Bucktails, Kent was able to counter the radical calls for universal suffrage and maintain a reduced property requirement for senatorial elections. Kent could tolerate, even encourage, the rise of manufacturing centers, so long as an independent propertied class remained in political ascendancy.

By contrast, Cooper's vision of the ideal republic remained agrarian. Although he included manufacturing in his opening description in *The Pioneers,* he placed it in a pastoral setting. Cooper, unlike Kent, distrusted the commercial class. "No government that is essentially influenced by commerce has ever been otherwise than exclusive, or aristocratic."[13] Nor did the creator of Natty Bumppo share Kent's disdain for all of those without property. Although he believed in the necessity of a guardian class, Cooper did not believe in a property restriction for suffrage. But his portrayal of Natty shows that when he wrote *The Pioneers* Cooper may not have been as aware as Kent of the threat that the urban poor could pose to his ideal agrarian republic. Cooper's representative man without property is a woodsman, not an urban laborer – a man who refuses to possess the land, not one who covets it. Nonetheless, the part of Cooper's social vision that eventually led him to support the Jacksonians accounts for much of the power of his narrative.

The Pioneers does not merely represent Temple's point of view. It also suggests potential contradictions in his logic, contradictions more apparent as the old constitution of New York State was dismantled and various inheritors of the Federalists' republican vision tried to relocate within the American political scene, some eventually supporting the Whigs, some the Democrats. By pointing out these potential contradictions, Cooper raised doubts about the right of the guardian class and its judiciary to rule. Whereas Judge Temple claims that his laws are impartial, Cooper showed that they could be manipulated to help some more than others. Whereas the guardian class based its right to rule on its ownership of the land, Judge Temple may have gained his title by dispossessing the rightful owners of the soil.

Finally, although the judge claims to base his legal system on eternal, natural laws, he comes into conflict with the man in closest contact with those laws – Natty Bumppo. For Cooper, Natty is the most serious threat to Temple's authority, for if Temple's laws come into conflict with Natty, what right do they have to rule? Rule by law, not men, was defended in America because it kept might from making right. But Natty's conflict with the law raises the ironic possibility that "might makes right here, as well as in the old country" (*Pioneers* 21). Furthermore, the law itself may be the means by which might is made right. As Natty laments, "Might makes right, and the law is stronger than an old man" (135). It is Cooper's obvious sympathy for common people like Natty, who struggle against an obfuscating, legalistic elite, that distinguishes his politics from those of a James Kent.[14]

In the convention, Elisha Williams, Kent's ally, had criticized landless men like Natty, who, on the spur of the moment, might swing their packs on their shoulders and disappear, leaving the stable yeoman and his son with the burden of defending and developing society. In championing Natty, Cooper defended the "democratic" man who eventually became a folk hero for challenging the propertied class's distrust of the common man. In the final section of this chapter, we will see that the democratic vision associated with Natty has as many contradictions as the social vision associated with Judge Temple. Before looking at Natty's conflict with Temple, we need to consider the first two threats to Temple's authority and how Cooper manages to resolve them. We can start to place those threats in historical context by examining some complaints made at the 1821 convention that the judiciary drawn from the guardian class was not as impartial as it claimed to be.

Americans today almost universally agree that an independent judiciary is essential to ensure that government is not manipulated to favor powerful and partisan factions. James Kent's defense of the Council of Revision at the 1821 convention shows, however, that support of an independent judiciary can grow out of a fear of popular rule. For Kent, a major threat to proper rule by law was the legislature, that potentially dangerous voice of the people. In his *Commentaries on the American Law*, Kent argued that legislative bodies are "presumed to partake with a quicker sensibility of the prevailing temper and irritable disposition of the times and to be much more in danger of adopting measures with precipitation and of changing them with levity. A mutable legislation is attended with a formidable train of mischiefs to the community." In the old constitution, the Council of Revision was designed to control the whims of the legislature. Made up of six judges and the governor, the council had veto power over legislation. The theory was that judges, more attentive to eternal principles of justice than to the "irritable disposition of the times," could safeguard the community from any "mischiefs" the legislature might commit. To eliminate the Council of Revision would be to lessen the power of what Kent in his *Commentaries* called an "independent judiciary, venerable by its gravity, its dignity, and its wisdom."[15]

The Bucktails at the convention did not necessarily agree with Kent's notion of the judiciary and its role on the council. They did not disagree with the need for impartial judges, but they claimed that the council was a voice of conservatism and thus a partisan body. The Federalists, losing political power in the legislature, continued to exert it through the council. Van Buren turned Kent's defense of the judiciary on its head and argued, "I object to the Council because . . . it tends to make our judges politicans." As members of the council, judges were no longer merely interpreters of the law; judges helped to make the law. To these charges

Kent responded that he himself, as a member of the council, had endeavored to "discharge his trust without regard to party influence and with a single reference to the intrinsic merits of the bills that have been submitted."[16] Yet the delegates at the convention, aware of the chancellor's record, were not convinced. The chancellor himself became the object of attacks. Erastus Root urged the convention to abolish the court of chancery over which Kent presided. Although the effort failed, a similar one was successful in the 1846 convention. What Kent's enemies did accomplish, however, was to set a retirement age for the court, forcing Kent to step down as chancellor in 1823.

One of Kent's actions, which turned many Democrats against him, was his support of Judge William Cooper's questionable election practices in 1792, the year before the action in *The Pioneers* is supposed to take place. Cooper's father was not the impartial figure we see in the fictional Judge Temple. In the 1792 election for governor of New York, William Cooper's friend John Jay narrowly lost to George Clinton. The Federalists blamed his loss on the Board of Canvassers' decision to ignore votes cast in Otsego, because of irregularities. Kent, outraged at what seemed to be a partisan move to block Jay's election, visited Cooperstown in the fall of 1792 and lent his support to his friend William Cooper. The anti-Federalist legislature, however, was equally outraged. It uncovered enough election irregularities in Cooperstown to pass a resolution calling for Cooper's impeachment. Although the investigation did not lead to Cooper's removal from office, it did reveal why Dixon Ryan Fox could call William Cooper the "mirror of partisan perfection as a Federalist squire." In order to deliver up to seven hundred votes for the Federalists, Cooper had threatened tenants with reprisals. One testified that the judge "had been round to the people and told them that they owed him, and that unless they voted for Mr. Jay, he would ruin them." Another told how "Judge Cooper then said to me, 'What, then, young man, you will not vote as I would have you – you are a fool, young man, for you cannot know how to vote as well as I can direct you, for I am in public office.' "[17] If Kent, the most prestigious member of the independent judiciary, supported such practices by the "owners of the soil," it was little wonder that his opponents were not convinced when he argued at the 1821 convention that to lower the voting requirements would be to let unscrupulous men control the votes of the poor. Scrupulous men – including a judge – were already doing so.

Of course, to point out William Cooper's and James Kent's partisan politics is not necessarily to discredit James Fenimore Cooper's belief in an independent judiciary. Judge Temple is neither Cooper nor Kent. He is a fictional character who, as McWilliams has argued, exactly fits Cooper's "idealized sketch of the American County Judge."[18] What is at stake in Cooper's fiction is the general principle, not the historical actuality.

To be sure, in Cooper's fictional world, partisan use of the law in the name of the law does occur. Even though the laws in Templeton are sanctioned by Temple, they are too often executed by unscrupulous, self-interested or unreflecting men such as Richard Jones or Hiram Doolittle. Cooper even hints that the old system was flawed in its method of appointing those who would administer the law. Richard Jones, thanking Temple for his position as sheriff, refers to the practice of the Council of Appointments. "First, duke, let me thank you for your friendly interest with the Council and the Governor, without which, I am confident that the greatest merit would avail but little" (*Pioneers* 200). Appointments attained through connection and influence rather than merit are not impartial, and abuses will follow. The worst abuser is Doolittle, the representative of the rising, acquisitive middle class. Greed, not impartial considerations of justice, lies behind Doolittle's obtaining a warrant to search Natty's hut. Thinking that Natty has silver hidden, Doolittle wants a look. Like Aristabulus Bragg and 'Squire Timms, in Cooper's later works, Doolittle knows how to use the law to further his self-interest, because he is trained as a lawyer. Cooper's unsympathetic treatment of lawyers like Doolittle shows the extent to which he sympathized with the widespread antilawyer sentiment of his day. By no means did he give undivided support to the legal profession.[19]

Yet although Cooper acknowledged that individuals trained in the law could manipulate the system for personal gain, he reinforced the lawyers' most powerful claim, that only an independent judiciary could prevent abuse of the law. By the end of the book, it is Judge Temple who has restored order. He can do so because he maintains a clear social vision that keeps him above the petty squabbles that govern the almost laughable final outbreak of hostilities in Templeton.

Cooper's portrayal of Temple's power is even more compelling because earlier the judge has had to wrestle with a case that would seem the supreme test of his judicial character. He has to uphold the law by passing judgment on the man who has saved his daughter's life. The feelings of the father come into conflict with the duty of the judge. Yet Temple knows his duty well. It is to let the law speak, no matter what the private man interpreting the law feels. Answering Edwards's plea that he be lenient in judging Natty, Temple responds that his judgment will be "whatever the law demands, notwithstanding any momentary weakness I may have exhibited, because the luckless man has been of such eminent service to my daughter" (*Pioneers* 344). As Cooper portrays it, judicial impartiality is defined in terms of the conflict between head and heart. Much as we might regret it, the head must triumph, because to have the heart rule would be to risk having rule by men. It would be to risk having one man above the law, and to have one man above the law is to risk having a legal system in which might makes right. The only way to ensure rule by law, not men, is to make certain that the men who rule are strong enough to be ruled by the law rather than their personal feelings.

Cooper's portrayal of Judge Temple was so compelling that it helped to diffuse complaints such as those made by Van Buren and others at the 1821 convention that the judiciary as it stood helped to maintain a legal system with an inbuilt bias in favor of the rich. In Cooper's work, the legal system protects the weak, not the powerful. Partisanship in the name of the law results from individual acts, not the nature of the legal system itself. Finally, it is precisely because the system is overseen by judges drawn from an independent guardian class that greedy, acquisitive individuals can be controlled.

We get a very different view of the role of the judiciary and the legal system in this period if we rely on recent research done by legal historians. In the early years of the republic, American law underwent a major transformation from an eighteenth-century concept of substantive justice to an instrumental concept of the law, which saw the law as an instrument for social change and allowed a "release" of economic energy that reshaped the vast American continent. As Morton Horwitz has carefully demonstrated, the transformed legal system, far from controlling abuses of power by acquisitive individuals like Hiram Doolittle, "enabled emergent entrepreneurial and commercial groups to win a disproportionate share of wealth and power in America."[20]

In other words, abuses of justice may have been more systemic than individual. Horwitz has also demonstrated that judges' interpretations played a major role in transforming the law to aid commerce. The judges responsible included the historical counterparts of a judge like Temple, who claimed to represent the conservative tradition. A closer look at the career of James Kent will let us see how historically, if not fictionally, the conservative legal tradition in America, although claiming to maintain the old social order, may have laid the foundation for its collapse.

The American conservative tradition that Kent and Temple represent has its roots in beliefs much closer to the political philosophy of the British Whigs than that of the Tories. Kent's biographer has called his life a "Study in Conservatism." What a close look at that life reveals is that American conservatism has, from the start, encouraged commerce. Whereas Kent claimed to base his legal philosophy on eternal truths, his economic beliefs were based on the fairly recent works of Adam Smith.

To be sure, Smith did claim an ahistorical universality for his laws of economics. Yet if the economic principles that Smith defended were eternal, it took a certain amount of innovation to found a political system on them. According to Kent, the strength of the U.S. Constitution was that for the first time the governmental functions specified in *The Wealth of Nations* were "almost in so many words recognized and declared to be the end of the government of the union." Although Kent's personal "constitution" was conservative – he called himself a "disciple of the old school" with "an aversion to innovation, except by cautious steps"[21] – he supported a political constitution that British conservatives found radical.

Kent's conservatism was a conservatism that lent support to the rights of first developers, enterprising men who risked all to improve the conditions of the country. Defending the temporary monopoly granted to Robert Fulton and Robert R. Livingston for the use of the steamboat in New York State waters, Kent argued that they had engaged in a hazardous adventure with "patient industry, at great expense, under repeated disappointments, and while constantly exposed to be held up, as dreaming projectors, to the *whips and scorns of time*. . . . The prize has been dearly earned and fairly won."[22] Kent would, no doubt, have felt the same way about William Cooper or the fictional Judge Temple, who, even if they did not invent a steamboat, constructed a social system designed to improve the land. Not surprisingly, Kent himself was a pioneering entrepreneur who invested in a variety of enterprises aimed at improving the country's internal commerce. Kent was also one of the most important of the judges who worked to transform an old system of law to meet new economic conditions.

To aid commerce, Kent expanded the doctrine of *caveat emptor* – "Buyer beware" – in equity cases. He also sought to expand the variety and volume of credit by developing rules for bank checks. In *Mann v. Executors of Mann* (1814), he ruled that money was not only "gold and silver, or the lawful circulating medium of the country. It may be extended to bank notes, when they are known and approved of, and used in the market as cash."[23] Perhaps most important, he aided the development of the new market economy by promoting types of business organization, such as the corporation, more appropriate for expanding the economy than the individual proprietorship and simple partnership.[24]

From our twentieth-century standpoint the contradiction within Kent's conservative philosophy is not hard to see. Like Temple, he saw himself as a check on the abuse of power. His position as the chancellor of the court of chancery points to his role as a defender of the old system of substantive justice against those who would manipulate the law to use it merely as an instrument of social change. The purpose of his legal system, like Temple's, was not only to encourage a release of economic energy but to control that energy. If Kent and Temple clearly favored economic development, it was controlled development that they approved. Nonetheless, in transforming the law to encourage commerce Kent helped to undercut controls built into the older system. For instance, although he promoted corporations, as a member of the Council of Revision Kent had tried to limit the use of the corporate form for "extraordinary businesses" performing a public service, such as canals and turnpikes. Yet once the corporate form was established, it was difficult to limit its use. Similarly, like Judge Temple, Kent supported laws for the regulation of fisheries and the preservation and growth of migratory game, yet once first developers had profited from using the land's resources, it was difficult to stop the next generation of developers from wanting to profit as well. Since, in New York State, game laws were based on the premise that ownership of all game was vested in the state, it seemed logical that all citizens should benefit from the use of the game – yet Temple disagreed. At the tavern he argues for a return to the European concept of game as a class possession. "I hope to live to see the day, when a man's rights in his game shall be as much respected as his title to his farm" (*Pioneers* 160).[25] Indeed, many of the issues of the 1821 convention came down to a conflict between people like Kent, who were intent on maintaining the property and profits of those who benefited from an initial release of economic energy, and a rising middle class asking for the same opportunity and rights to develop the land and to expand commerce as the generation before it had done. The part of Kent's philosophy that supported the pioneering entrepreneur made way for the overthrow of his conservative principles. We can see this contradiction best in his defense of the owners of the soil.

Basing his decisions on the eternal principles embodied in the common law, Kent hoped to guarantee the preservation of life, liberty, and property – especially property. At the 1821 convention, Kent argued that life and liberty were seldom jeopardized; it was property that must be protected from assault. Fearful of calls for economic leveling, he argued that to base a social system on an ideal of economic equality would be to base it on a false foundation. It would contradict the traditional wisdom and laws of nature that judges were sworn to obey. "A state of equality as to property is impossible to be maintained, for it is against the laws of our nature, and if it could be reduced to practice, it would place the human race in a state of tasteless enjoyment and stupid activity which would degrade the mind and destroy the happiness of social life."[26]

To protect property was to protect all that Kent held valuable about society. At the convention Kent made an argument that revealed his rationale for this view. "The great body of people are now owners . . .

of the soil. . . . Their habits inspire them with a correct spirit of freedom
and justice; they are the safest guardians of property and the law."[27]
Laws protected property, and the propertied protected the laws. Together they guaranteed prosperity. For Kent, Dorfman writes, "The
substantial and independent landlords were the backbone and foundation
of national economic prosperity and power."[28]

Yet Kent undercut what seemed to be his own agrarian vision by
recognizing approvingly changes in U.S. law that altered common-law
tradition and increasingly regarded the land as a commodity whose value
was determined by the market. "In no other part of the civilized world
[as in the United States] is land made such an article of commerce and of
such incessant circulation."[29] Kent's legal opinions, although seemingly
aimed at providing a stable foundation for the growth of the American
economy, actually provided a foundation for a legal system that based
itself on something very unstable and whimsical: the necessities of the
marketplace.

Well aware of how commerce influenced American attitudes toward
the land, Alexis de Tocqueville remarked that for most Americans agriculture itself was a trade and that they developed the land or built improvements "on the speculation" that "a good price may be obtained for
it."[30]

A nineteenth-century Englishman recorded a similar impression.

> There is as yet in New England and New York scarcely any such thing
> as local attachments – the love of a place because it is a man's own –
> because he has hewed it out of the wilderness, and made it what it is; or
> because his father did so, and he and his family have been born and
> brought up, and spent their happy youthful days upon it. Speaking
> generally, every farm from Eastport in Maine to Buffalo on Lake Erie,
> is for sale.[31]

In light of such accounts, we can see to what extent Cooper's opening
description in *The Pioneers* is an imaginative construct. New York State
in the 1820s does not seem to have been an agrarian community based on
the "permanent improvements of the yeoman, who intends to leave his
remains to moulder under the sod he tills" (*Pioneers* 16). Yet without
imagining such a community, Cooper would have had no foundation for
his ideal political system. And if he was to imagine that community as a
present possibility, he needed to imagine that the rightful owner of the
land was someone who resisted the tendency to turn it into a commodity. The support that the American legal system gave to the commercialization of the land made such an owner difficult to find.

Once the land became recognized as a commodity, speculation was
inevitable. William Priest wrote, "Were I to characterize the United
States, it would be by the appellation of the land of speculation."[32] Yet

for Cooper, speculators threatened to undermine the foundation of an agrarian republic in which individual landowners earned their property through labor rooted in the soil. For Cooper the real value of land increases only through intrinsic improvements accomplished through labor. Because the farmer intends to stay on his land, his improvements are motivated by love of the land, not desire to reap a profit when it is sold. All of the profit that the self-sufficient farmer makes is returned to the land to improve its productivity. With each farmer increasing the intrinsic value of his farm through labor and self-improvement, the republic is bound to thrive. In contrast, speculation discourages farmers from laboring to increase the intrinsic value of the land. Rather than provide stability by cultivating the land, speculators relied on market fluctuations to gain "unearned" wealth. Increased value, determined by something outside of the land itself brought about by speculation, is unnatural, fictional, and suspect. In *The Chainbearer,* set shortly after the American Revolution, the narrator describes how landlords increased the productivity of their land by reinvesting any profit they might have made in improvements to the land. "Not a dollar" of rent, he argues, "ever left the settlement." In contrast, he evokes the specter of current practices of speculation. "Legal speculations were then nearly unknown; and he who got rich was expected to do so by manly exertions, openly exercised, and not by the dark machinations of a sinister practice of the law."[33]

In *The Pioneers,* Cooper personifies the speculator in Jotham Riddel, described by Judge Temple as "that dissatisfied, shiftless, lazy, speculating fellow! he who changes his country every three years, his farm every six months, and his occupation every season! an agriculturalist yesterday, a shoemaker to-day, and a schoolmaster tomorrow! that epitome of all the unsteady and profitless propensities of the settlers, without one of their good qualities to counterbalance the evil!" (*Pioneers* 317). Yet Temple himself, having bought his land cheaply during the Revolutionary War, could be accused of speculation. Indeed historically, those who held legal title to large tracts of American land, including Chancellor Kent and Kent's friend William Cooper, were often speculators.

Speculators' claims did not go unchallenged. Title disputes were common. Some of the most important reached the U.S. Supreme Court, which had to weigh the claims of speculators against those of Indians, individual squatters, and state legislatures operating in the name of the people. In one of the most important of these cases, the Supreme Court upheld the claim of a Loyalist relative to land confiscated by the State of Virginia during the Revolutionary War, just as in *The Pioneers* Cooper returns Temple's land to the Effingham family.[34]

Although it would be an exaggeration to claim that Cooper alluded specifically to this or any other well-known dispute, it does seem safe to say that when he cast doubt on Judge Temple's right to his property, he recalled the widespread disputes over land titles in the early years of the republic. He also emphasized how much was at stake in these disputes. If "impartial" judges appealed to the rhetoric of the eternal rights of property upon which the country's legal system was founded to support claims to property only recently, and sometimes fraudulently acquired, the entire legal system would be based on a false foundation. Judges would be using the law to favor a few, rather than to guarantee justice for all.

Challenged by Edwards, Temple defends his claim to his land by pointing to the authority of the law. "I hold under the patents of the Royal Governors, confirmed by an act of our own State Legislature, and no court in the country can affect my title" (*Pioneers* 237). Yet while even Edwards admits the legality of Temple's claim – "Doubtless, sir, your title is both legal and equitable" – Cooper reminds us that Temple's right may be based on his power to use the law as an instrument of his will, rather than on a natural right to the land. If it were not for the "money of Marmaduke Temple, and the twisty ways of the law," Natty tells us, the land would still be a "comfortable hunting-ground" (291). Judge Temple's legal system stands for the eternal principles of justice, and yet his own claim to the land seems to lack the authority of first possession. His laws, like Chancellor Kent's, seem weighted to favor first developers. A first developer, Judge Temple is one of those Christians who "dispossessed the original owners of the soil" (83) and who now use the law to protect their claims to the soil.

Faced with this irreconcilable difference between what the law purports to do and what it does, Cooper imagines a fictional solution that contains the threat of the potential contradiction that his narrative has exposed in Temple's legal ideology. The land is not the Indians' after all. They had given it as a gift to Edwards's grandfather, who had passed it on to Edwards's father, a friend of Temple. During the Revolutionary War, Edwards's father, remaining loyal to the Crown and fearing the loss of his fortune in America, entrusted his wealth to Temple. "We differed in politics. If the cause of this country was successful, the trust was sacred with me, for none knew of the father's interest. If the crown still held its sway, it would be easy to restore the property of so loyal a subject as Col. Effingham" (439). When the British lost, Colonel Effingham's real estate was sold, and Temple became the "lawful purchaser." "It was not unnatural to wish that he might have no bar to its just recovery" (440). Because all this time Temple is loyal to his friend and holds Effingham's estate in trust for the family, Temple's claim to the land gains solid authority. Temple is not what he seemed to be – a first developer using the law to purchase dispossessed property cheaply for his own profit. Instead, he uses the law to restore the property to its rightful owners, and, in addition, through his industry has multiplied the value of the estates "a hundredfold." When Oliver Effingham marries Elizabeth Temple at the end of the story, the conflict over the land reaches its harmonious resolution – harmonious except that Natty and Indian John are dispossessed of the land. Before concluding by looking closely and critically at the implications of Natty's dispossession, I want to emphasize the conservatism of Cooper's conclusion.

The marriage between the Effingham and Temple families unites two different theories about the basis of authority for the American legal system. After the Revolutionary War, advocates of British common law debated those advocating the construction of a new legal code for America.[35] The common law was described in organic metaphors. It was a body that had grown over time so that it closely corresponded with eternal laws of nature. The other system was described in architectural terms. It would be constructed to fit the unique requirements of the American situation. The problem with the common law was that it grew out of British, not American, soil. The problem with the architectural metaphor was that the system constructed was too obviously man-made and thus lacked the natural authority of tradition possessed by the common law with its organic metaphor. America needed a legal system that would embody the timeless truths of the common law but was adapted to the American environment.

One solution, with which Cooper seems to sympathize, was to adopt English common law but to have wise judges interpret it so as to adapt it to American needs. So long as farsighted judges were in control, there was no need for the legislature to enact entirely new legal codes. For instance, novelist and Pennsylvania supreme court justice Hugh Henry Brackenridge argued that great judges were the architects of the legal system. For Brackenridge, the majority of judges were content to inherit the existing system, but the great judge, "*a skillful architect* . . . who can have the whole edifice in his mind . . . can remove at once, or alter, what was originally faulty or has become disproportioned in the building."[36]

Cooper makes Temple an obvious representative of this view of the law. His very name is architectural.[37] His mansion, or the "castle," as the townspeople call it, was constructed from the native materials of the land, fashioned by the architectural pair of Richard Jones and Hiram Doolittle, the same two who will administer his legal system. Though "far from uncomfortable," the house, a mixture of a variety of styles, lacked proportion, because the roof was "by far the most conspicuous part of the whole edifice" (*Pioneers* 44). The roof was so large because the practical American, Jones, had decided to break with tradition. "A roof, Richard contended, was a part of the edifice that the ancients always endeavoured to conceal, it being an excrescence in architecture that was only to be tolerated on account of its usefulness" (43–4). At first Jones tried to conceal the size of the roof by painting it in such a way so that it would seem part of the natural sky. Unsuccessful, he "ended the affair by boldly covering the whole beneath a color that he christened 'sunshine,' a cheap way, as he assured his cousin, the Judge, of always keeping fair weather over his head" (44).

The architectural oddities of Temple's mansion expose the problem with the architectural metaphor for a system of laws. Man-made, the system of laws is not part of nature but tries instead to offer a substitute for nature. Rather than deriving its authority from nature, it might support a social system that threatens nature. In a field near the mansion lay the "ruin of a pine or a hemlock that had been stripped of its bark, and which waved in melancholy grandeur its naked limbs to the blast, a skeleton of its former glory" (45). Temple's legal system allows for rapid change, but despite Temple's claim that his laws will check man's extravagance, it is not until the end of the book that Cooper assures us that his laws will lead to the "permanent improvements of the yeoman" in evidence in 1821–2. "Five years had wrought greater changes, than a century would produce in countries, where time and labor have given permanency to the works of man" (46). Temple's laws gain the sanctity that his name implies they should have only when it becomes clear that his laws coincide with the "natural rights" of the Effinghams.[38] Appropriately, when old Effingham is finally allowed to appear, his condition is described as reflecting the "decay of nature" (437).

Cooper's social vision turned out to be even more conservative than that of the conservative New York Federalists, whose thinking he came so close to sharing. As we have seen, despite widespread complaints that the old paternalistic notion of republican government had an inbuilt bias in favor of the guardian class, Cooper imagined a narrative in which abuses of the law, under the rule of this regime, were individual, not systemic. In this way, Cooper's romance supported the Federalist theory of government. Nonetheless, the Federalist ideal of a republic that encouraged commerce posed a threat to Cooper's agrarian ideal. His imaginary solution to this threat was a narrative that made certain that the authority of the guardian class was rooted in the soil. In transferring ownership of the land from his representative founding Federalist to the son of a Loyalist, Cooper betrayed a nostalgia that idealized a pre-Revolutionary past.

Despite his talk, Judge Temple is not a man of the land in the same way that Edwards is. Edwards, who can live comfortably in both Temple's mansion and Natty's hut, represents the British agrarian tradition, which distrusted the commercialization of the land as much as Cooper did. That for Cooper the ideal representative of agrarian values was the son of a man who fought against the Revolution shows how much his social vision was rooted in the past. That he saw fit to restore authority over the land to the son of a Loyalist shows how for him maintaining rights of property was more important than taking advantage of the Revolution to realign society. That the historical figure who corresponds most closely to Edwards, because he served William Cooper as secretary, was Moss Kent, the brother of James Kent, might also indicate how much Cooper had wished for Kent's legal system actually to embody the marriage of British and American systems he posited as his ideal. Cooper, we are told, "had a boyish admiration for Moss Kent and for a time called himself James Kent Cooper."[39] In legal circles it was, after all, James Kent who was praised for incorporating the eternal truths of British law into American law.

For Cooper, nature, like society, underwent perpetual change. His use of the seasons as an organizing principle emphasized this natural flux. Yet underlying that change were eternal truths. As Daniel Peck has argued, Cooper's major aesthetic achievement was the creation of timeless natural images.[40] These images reflect the stability that eternal natural laws provide. They were the foundation of Cooper's politics as well as his aesthetics. When man-made laws are based on the eternal truths found in nature, they stabilize the unpredictable fluctuations of society. Oliver Effingham's marriage to Elizabeth Temple helps to guarantee that stability for Templeton.

Yet surely a better representative than Edwards of the eternal truths found in nature is Natty. To call Cooper's political vision more conservative than that of the conservative New York Federalists seems to ignore his great sympathy for his democratic hero. To concentrate, as I have so far, on the role of Temple and Effingham would seem to emphasize Cooper's conservative vision at the expense of his democratic vision. Yet by now it should be clear that to align conservatism with the Federalists and progressivism with the Democrats is to fall prey to a simplification often duplicated in both Federalist and Democratic rhetoric. The agrarianism at the heart of Cooper's vision, which I have claimed makes it more conservative than the Federalists', is clearly Jeffersonian and was inherited by the Jacksonians. That Cooper found it necessary to associate this agrarianism with either the heir of a British Loyalist or a man dispossessed of his land shows how difficult it was to retain the vision without lapsing into nostalgia. To examine Natty's conflict with Temple is to see, as Marvin Meyers has shown, that Jacksonian democracy is not as progressive as it portrayed itself.

Indeed, Cooper has often been called a democratic writer because he champions Natty, the self-sufficient man of nature, the uncivilized, rugged individual with a pure heart that is capable of telling right from wrong. The tragedy, as Cooper sees it, is that Natty's powerful, individual code of democratic conduct, developed from his close contact with nature, inevitably comes into conflict with Judge Temple's code of civil law that is necessary for the orderly development of the new republic. If Cooper was able fictionally to contain the threats to the authority of man-made law posed by the disparity between the execution of the law and the principle of the law, and by the possibility that the legal system has dispossessed the rightful owners of the soil, he did not resolve the conflict between Natty and the law. Each seems to have powerful claims to authority.

To keep from regressing into a situation in which might makes right, society needs laws to check the possessive individualism of people like Hiram Doolittle. Yet those laws, designed to be fair by making no man above them, seem unable to distinguish between Doolittle's possessive individualism and Natty's self-sufficient individualism. Natty can find a space where he can enjoy freedom only outside of society, in the wilderness or on the frontier. Even so, Natty can exist outside of society only because he is self-contained and strong. Natty is not the only one to leave Templeton for the West at the end of the book. Hiram Doolittle heads west as well.[41] On the western frontier Natty will have to cope with unscrupulous men like Doolittle and lawless men like Ishmael Bush. The value of Judge Temple's system is that it controls or banishes such men. By the time of *The Prairie,* even Natty recognizes that the law is needed to maintain social order: "The law – 'tis bad to have it, but I sometimes think it is worse to be entirely without it. Age and weakness has brought me to feel such weakness at times. Yes – yes, the law is needed when such as have not the gifts of strength and wisdom are to be taken care of."[42]

What my analysis of legal history would seem to indicate, however, is that Natty is thrust from society on false premises. Whereas in Cooper's fiction the law is necessary to control possessive individualism, in history, as Horwitz's work demonstrates, the law helped encourage it. If so, Cooper's narrative would seem to be weighted in favor of the law, against Natty's self-sufficient individualism – yet it is not. To see why, we will have to look at the assumptions underlying Cooper's view of the law.

Cooper's legal system is a Lockean vision in which each distinct, self-governing person provides for himself from the abundance of nature. In order to improve economic well-being, individuals enter into commerce. The danger of entering into commerce is that the individual's natural rights will be violated. Thus, men form a social contract and devise laws to guarantee each individual the birthrights of life, liberty, and property against intrusions from the state or others. Freedom, therefore, is defined as independence from the wills of others – self-sufficiency – and no individual embodies freedom more than Natty. Thus, when the judge's game laws restrict Natty's freedom by threatening his natural means of subsistence, Temple's legal system would seem to be caught in a contradiction. Far from guaranteeing Natty's freedom, it denies it. Indeed, because Temple's laws are man-made, they are not perfect. Natty's conflict with them points to the inevitable distance between man-made laws and the natural laws that Natty's individualism embodies. When Natty removes himself from society, he exists as a continual reminder of the inability of man's written laws to coincide with the higher laws of nature. Natty is, as it were, too pure to exist in the fallen world of civilization. Our hearts are with Natty, our minds with Temple and his problem of having to deal with people who lack Natty's self-restraint and intuitive judgment.

We get a very different view of Natty's conflict with Temple's laws, however, if, rather than deriving an economic system and legal system from Locke's state of nature, we follow C. B. Macpherson's analysis and perceive that the Lockean state of nature might owe its formulation to the capitalist economic system gaining ascendancy in Locke's day.[43] The capitalist mode of production replaced the interdependent social bonds of feudalism with the new set of individualistic social relations that we find reflected in Locke's vision of the state of nature. Although belief in freedom as independence from the wills of others served the interests of capitalism, capitalist society, by subordinating human beings' wills to a system of market relations, did not necessarily deliver the freedom that its ideology promised. Looked at from this point of view, Natty's forest freedom serves an entirely different function than commonly supposed. So long as we believe with Cooper in natural law, Natty's forest freedom will challenge the authority of Temple's man-made law, yet if we see natural law as a man-made construct, we can start to see how Natty's forest freedom grows out of the same assumptions that justify Temple's legal system. Perhaps the reason Natty cannot find freedom in society is that the definition of freedom as independence from the wills of others is a fiction. Instead of recognizing this possibility, Cooper champions Natty's forest freedom, thereby asserting the existence of the very self-sufficient man of nature needed to construct Judge Temple's legal system. Natty and figures like him – Robinson Crusoe, for instance – become the necessary fictional products of people sharing Cooper's assumptions about the law.

Natty's individualism has been read for years as the "democratic" alternative to Federalist and Whig conservatism, but it is really no alternative. Natty is at least as cónservative a figure as Edwards. As David Noble has shown, Natty's role in the book is to serve "Major Effingham, the last direct symbol of English culture. . . . His final constructive achievement is to keep his commander alive until his rightful claim to be a part of the American frontier is recognized."[44] Later in his career Cooper saw the possibility of an ideal reconciliation between British and American culture diminish. As a result, he wrote works that locate the idyllic moment of American society farther and farther back in the past, as he traces Natty's life from old age to youth.[45] It is quite appropriate that in all of these works, Natty, the symbol of forest freedom, serves conservative British interests.

Insofar as Natty became a representative hero for Jacksonian democrats, we can start to see how the nostalgic agrarian strain that Marvin Meyers has uncovered in their political vision could coexist with policies advancing market capitalism. For instance, the Jacksonian Indian policy was supposed to turn the West into an arcadia populated by countless self-sufficient, landowning farmers. Accumulation of Indian land was also a major factor, however, in bringing about a market revolution that rendered the small, self-sufficient farmer obsolete. Andrew Jackson, believed by his admirers to have been "educated in Nature's school," gained political support by claiming – and believing – that freehold agriculture would restore republican virtue. Nonetheless, as Michael Rogin argues, "He helped impose a system of materialism, dependence, and impersonal authority on others."[46]

Confronted with a system in which economic self-sufficiency was impossible, Jackson's "common man" was to find a "free" figure like Natty more and more appealing. As a result, whereas conservatives in England feared the radical potential of a literate working class, Americans adopted as a folk hero a man who could not even read the laws that imprisoned him. Natty, of course, is not unintelligent. Except perhaps for Indian John, no one can match his ability to "read" the signs of nature. In his forest freedom Natty has no need to master book learning or carry society's paper money, since he has immediate access to nature's laws inscribed in his heart. Yet this nostalgic vision that rejects all products of civilization as unnatural does nothing to alter the direction that civilization will take. When Natty heads west, the laws he finds so oppressive remain in force.

Too often, lovers of democracy, who are convinced by works like

Cooper's that the loss of freedom is the cost of civilization, have a tendency to neglect the possibility of increasing human freedom within civilization. For instance, within *The Pioneers* it is Cooper's failure to resolve the conflict between Natty and society that makes it easier for him to contain the historical conflicts discussed earlier. If Cooper admits a disparity between what the law stands for and its execution, that disparity is more tolerable once we believe that pure freedom can exist only outside of society. If Cooper shows that Temple's legal system might have dispossessed the rightful owners of the soil, that act of dispossession is easier to take once we believe that more "natural" souls like Natty and Indian John would prefer dispossessing themselves to compromising with the fallen ways of society. Throughout Cooper's works, historical conflicts are displaced by the "eternal," personal ones of the individual versus society and the heart versus the head.

If we look once again at Cooper's portrayal of the "never ending case of Heart versus Head," we can see this displacement at work. Cooper affirms the fairness of Judge Temple's legal system by demonstrating Temple's impartiality. That impartiality is proved when Temple refuses to allow his feelings as father to get in the way of his duty as judge. By basing his decision against Natty on the rule of reason rather than the rule of the heart, he avoids the risk of having one man above the law. Yet to define judicial impartiality in terms of the conflict of heart versus head is to succumb to another risk. It is to risk limiting our examination of the guarantees for justice in a political system to an examination of the "character" of the judge. It is to risk emphasizing a personal conflict taking place *within* the judge at the expense of social and historical conflicts. This is not to argue that a judge's character lacks importance, but it is to argue that there cannot be political justice without a fair set of laws in the first place, since an impartial interpretation (and even administration) of partial laws does not produce impartial justice.

Judge Temple's laws are often called impartial because each individual – including Natty – is treated equally under them. However, to guarantee individuals equal treatment under the law does not necessarily guarantee justice, as Anatole France indicated when he remarked on the majestic equality of the French law that forbids rich and poor alike to sleep under the bridges of the Seine.[47] Considerations of political justice cannot be separated from social and historical considerations of class, race, and gender.[48] As Karl Marx put it, a legal system that stops at guaranteeing individuals equal treatment under the law never goes beyond treatment of egotistical man – that is, man as an individual separated from the community. Political emancipation should not be separated from human emancipation. Yet it is the effect of Cooper's fiction ultimately to pose the question of justice in terms of a conflict between an individual and society. It has been the purpose of this chapter to show that the very terms of this conflict, as Cooper depicts it and as much of our culture perceives it, are deceptive, since Natty's forest freedom and Temple's legal system are based on the same individualistic ideology.

On May 29, 1826, the Bread and Cheese Club met in New York City to honor Cooper before his departure for Europe. His friend James Kent offered a toast that nicely sums up the effect of Cooper's fiction. Cooper, Kent declared, was the "genius which has rendered our native soil classic ground, and given to our early history the enchantment of fiction."[49] Indeed, it was only through fictionalizing history that Cooper could give classic ground to American soil, for the American legal system that Cooper depicts is not founded on "eternal truths" but on the fiction of self-sufficient individualism.

2

The House of the Seven Gables:
Hawthorne's Legal Story

Written a generation after *The Pioneers,* Nathaniel Hawthorne's *House of the Seven Gables* deals with similar conflicts. Both novels imagine a dispute over the legitimate ownership of a piece of property, a dispute involving a member of the judiciary. Both construct an architectural metaphor to comment on the structure of the American political system. But although Hawthorne and Cooper both aligned themselves politically with the Democratic party, Hawthorne's narrative appears more democratic than Cooper's. In *The House of the Seven Gables* the land is returned to a plebean, not a Loyalist family, and Judge Pyncheon presents an image of the judiciary in total contrast to Cooper's impartial Judge Temple. Moreover, whereas Cooper offers a narrative of the past that ultimately grants the American legal system the monumental quality needed to give the republic a solid foundation in natural law, Hawthorne's sketch of the history of the House of the Seven Gables suggests that the present system has a faulty foundation.

Such a narrative would seem to turn Hawthorne into a radical. But ironically, the very aspect of Hawthorne's vision that gives him a radical potential also leads to his conservatism. For Hawthorne does not stop with exposing the false foundation of the present system of government. He goes on to question the possibility that any human product can intentionally be made to coincide with natural law. Thus Hawthorne suggests that the democratic alternative is subject to the same criticism it levels against the conservative system represented by Judge Pyncheon. To make matters even more complicated, Hawthorne's narrative succumbs to its own undermining. A product of Hawthorne's imagination, it is, as Hawthorne self-consciously reminds us, founded on human subjectivity, not natural truth.

In the next two chapters I want to explore Hawthorne's complex vision by interweaving my discussion of his fictional narrative with an account of the period's legal history, paying careful attention to events within his hometown of Salem. In this chapter I will concentrate on the subversive potential of the story Hawthorne tells. In the next I will examine how Hawthorne's romantic narrative ultimately evades the historical and political conflicts that helped to generate it in the first place.

In part, Hawthorne's subversive vision can be traced to his Puritan heritage, which refuses to grant to any human constructs the divine authority accorded to nature. Frequently, in Hawthorne's works, humans try unsuccessfully to construct permanent monuments in a temporal world. In "The Ambitious Guest," a youth sheltered by a New England family in a winter storm declares, "It is our nature to desire a monument."[1] Afraid of being forgotten in the grave, he proudly boasts, "I cannot die till I have achieved my destiny. Then, let Death come! I shall have built my monument!" (*TT* 328). The story ends in his burial under an avalanche, "His name and person utterly unknown; his history, his way of life, his plans, a mystery never to be solved, his death and his existence equally a doubt" (333). Similarly, in *The House of the Seven Gables,* Colonel Pyncheon constructs his solid house as a monument to himself, hoping to combat the flow of time. But the house, which the colonel had hoped would provide a foundation for the reign of a long line of heirs who would keep his name alive, serves the opposite purpose. As soon as Colonel Pyncheon possesses Maule's land, the well that provides the stream of life dries up, and as soon as the house is completed the colonel dies, turning his proposed monument into his tomb. Finally, as time goes on, the family he tried to plant and endow gradually dies out. Nature, often in the form of death, shows the folly of human attempts to build monuments in a temporal world.

But if Hawthorne's Puritan heritage taught him the universal lesson that death is the "only guest who is certain, at one time or another, to find his way into every human dwelling" (*HSG* 16), the social conditions at the time he wrote would have reinforced his skepticism about humankind's ability to erect lasting monuments. The fear of economic speculation and social instability that Cooper felt while writing *The Pioneers* was stronger than ever a generation later. The rapid social transformations in Jacksonian America made it harder to imagine a solution in which the country's legal system had the permanent authority of natural law and tradition. As one lawyer put it, "The powerful hand of progress has been prying under the pedestal of the most time-honored institutions of law. Edifices, built with the granite of Littleton, the cement of Coke, the trowel of Blackstone, the masonic genius of a hundred justiciaries, have been set swaying as if they were fresh and flexible, instead of being covered with the moss of many generations."[2]

The hand of progress had a peculiar effect on Hawthorne's Salem. In

"The Custom-House" Hawthorne notes a fall in Salem's commerce as he describes what "half a century ago, in the days of old King Derby, was a bustling wharf, – but which is now burdened with decayed wooden warehouses, and exhibits few or no symptoms of commercial life" (*SL* 2–3). Once a major port, Salem steadily lost trade to its rival, Boston. As a result, many important families moved from Salem. Those that stayed risked losing power or being replaced by other families, which in turn risked losing power. The fall of houses like the Derbys certainly would have affected Hawthorne's imagination as he contemplated the sins involved in the desire to accumulate wealth in order to "plant and endow a family" (*HSG* 185).

In "The Sister Years" Hawthorne writes that the "game of politics" can be understood as well in Salem as in the nation's capital. "Human weakness and strength, passion and policy, Man's tendencies, his aims and modes of pursuing them, his individual character, and his character in the mass, may be studied almost as well here as on the theatre of nations" (*TT* 338). In *The House of the Seven Gables* Hawthorne uses the history of Salem to present an allegory about national politics. The dispute over the rightful ownership of the House of the Seven Gables becomes a dispute over who has the right to rule the American system of government. Hawthorne's choice of a piece of property as the central symbol in his allegory is appropriate not only because the architectural metaphor suggests the American attempt to construct a political system but also because one of the major political debates of the time was between those with established property and those without. We can better understand the political implications of Hawthorne's narrative by looking at the transformation of American property law.

Morton Horwitz identifies three stages in the development of American property law in antebellum America. If they are not as pure as implied, they are useful for my analysis. Appropriate to a static, feudal economy, the property rights that the colonies inherited from common law favored the maintenance of the status quo. Landowners were limited to "natural" – that is, "agrarian" – use of the land. If two owners' natural use came into conflict, another rule – "First in time is first in right" – could be invoked. This rule opposed development by granting the first developer of the land prior rights. If a landowner complained that a dam that had existed for years on a neighbor's land flooded property scheduled for development as pasture, the owner would have no case. But, if the neighbor built a new dam that flooded pasture already in use, the injured party would prevail.

So long as the economy remained static and little development took place, the two theories of property rights – natural use and priority – complemented one another, but as the economy developed, they came into conflict. As Horwitz argues, "If priority is measured not from a common denominator of natural use but from the time that a new technology appears, the theory of natural use continues to enforce its anti-developmental premises, but a rule of priority now confers an exclusive property right on the first developer."[3] If traditionally the rule of priority had been used to keep someone from developing land in a way that would disturb a neighbor's "natural" enjoyment of the land, now the rule was used to justify an owners' right to develop the land as desired.

This reinterpretation of property rights by early nineteenth-century judges ensured a victory for developers at the expense of those who wanted to maintain an agrarian economy. As claims based on the rule of natural use lost power, a new rule replaced it. This rule balanced the claims of individual owners that a development harmed their land against the social benefits resulting from the new development. Since it was felt that private investors needed some inducement to risk capital in projects beneficial to the entire public, the "balancing test" was often used to allow developers privileges unheard of a generation before.

Those who favored the rise of commerce in the republic felt that these privileges were necessary because development was essential for the country's well-being. The desire to encourage development also led to the legal support of corporations. Only corporations seemed able to pool enough capital to finance large-scale improvements, such as the turnpikes, bridges, and (later) railroads necessary to expand commerce. Without guarantees concerning the legal status of their investments in corporations, investors would not risk necessary capital. In the famous *Dartmouth College* case, the U.S. Supreme Court provided the hoped-for guarantees.

The *Dartmouth College* case arose over a dispute between the college and the state legislature of New Hampshire. The legislature had amended the school's charter to make it more responsive to state needs, in a manner similar to Jefferson's proposed University of Virginia, but powerful members of the college wanted to preserve its elitist, private nature. A battle developed between the college and the newly declared university. The suit that developed went to the New Hampshire Supreme Court, where the legislature's amendment was upheld. The college then enlisted the aid of Daniel Webster and took the case to the U.S. Supreme Court. After one of Webster's most memorable oratorical displays, the court held the Dartmouth Act invalid, under the impairment-of-contracts clause of the Constitution.

Even though a case involving a small college would seem to have little economic impact, the court's decision was welcomed by the rising commercial class because it established the principle of the vested rights of corporations. According to Edward S. Corwin, the doctrine of vested rights sets out "with the assumption that the property right is fundamental" and "treats any law impairing *vested rights*, whatever its intention, as a bill of pains and penalties, and so void."[4] The doctrine alleviated fears of the wealthy that their property would be threatened by the leveling tendencies of legislatures. First formulated by the courts in *Fletcher v. Peck* (1810), the doctrine of vested interests asserted judicial over legislative authority on matters of property. It did so by broadly interpreting the contract clause of the Constitution to forbid states from passing laws "impairing the obligation of contracts." Although the Constitution is silent on whether legislative grants as well as agreements between private parties were to be regarded as contracts, the court declared that they were. This interpretation, claims Leonard Levy, created a vital "link between capitalism and constitutionalism."[5] By extending the principle of vested rights to corporations, the *Dartmouth College* case created a link between constitutionalism and *corporate* capitalism. New corporations of all kinds could appeal to their original charters as sacred contracts under the law, not to be altered by legislative attempts to control them.

The *Dartmouth College* case clearly marked the movement to the second stage in the development of the American law of property. The agrarian bias of the common law had been transformed to favor first developers whose interests were now protected by new laws. But not all of the American people were pleased with the exclusive rights granted the newly entrenched commercial elite, especially those granted to corporations. In terms of future development, the problem with the exclusive rights granted first developers was that too many privileges might be granted. For instance, under traditional common law, private corporations with a public function were bound by so many charter obligations as to make them as much instruments of common welfare as vehicles for private enterprise, but under the new laws many public-service organizations turned into private, profit-making organizations, making the theory justifying their special favors outdated. Under the new conditions, such corporations enjoyed the benefits of a public corporation without its obligations. Thus, just as the old agrarian laws had favored those already possessing wealth, so, after an initial redistribution of wealth, did the new laws. As a result, the law was once again reinterpreted and transformed, this time to encourage competition, by undermining the privileges granted a generation earlier. The case pointed to as marking the transformation from the second stage of law to the third is *Charles River Bridge v. Warren Bridge* (1837).[6]

In 1785 the state of Massachusetts had granted a corporation an almost exclusive franchise to build a toll bridge across the Charles River. By 1827 the corporation was collecting tolls of thirty thousand dollars a year. In an effort to spark competition, the legislature chartered the new

Warren Bridge Corporation, which promised that its bridge would be toll-free in six years. The Charles River Bridge Corporation, loosely connected with Harvard College, claimed that the new bridge violated its charter, and the company hired Daniel Webster and Lemuel Shaw to present its case in the Massachusetts courts. The company failed to gain relief, but, still employing Webster, appealed to the U.S. Supreme Court, where its case was finally heard in 1837. In this appearance before the highest court in the land Webster lost.

In his opinion, the new Jacksonian chief justice, Roger B. Taney, agreed that the law must accommodate itself to new economic conditions, but he offered a different theory on how best to do so. For Whigs, the essential elements for economic progress were certainty of expectation and predictability of legal consequences. For instance, in his dissenting opinion, Justice Joseph Story argued that in allowing the new bridge to be constructed the state legislature had made the legal consequences of Charles River Bridge Corporation investments unpredictable. He could "conceive of no surer plan to arrest all public improvements, founded on private capital and enterprise, than to make the outlay of that capital uncertain, and questionable both as to security, and as to productiveness."[7] But Taney argued that granting exclusive rights eventually impedes the march of public improvement by disrupting the system of fair competition upon which the country was founded. The chartering of the Warren Bridge Corporation had not discouraged but encouraged economic development.

Whigs took this defeat hard. That the highest court in the land had agreed to give up its regulatory control to state legislatures seemed to them a threat to the republic. Their gloom was confirmed even before the Court adjourned for the year when the panic of 1837 swept the country. In the public sphere, Jacksonian policies seemed to have triumphed, and the United States seemed to have given itself over to irrational control.

Democrats, of course, did not agree. Three essays in the *Democratic Review* outlined the Democrats' version of recent legal history. Two of the essays appear in issues that also contain stories by Hawthorne. The essays make a number of the same points about the judiciary that are implied by Hawthorne in *The House of the Seven Gables*.[8] Writing on the Supreme Court, one author decries the "blind veneration which has heretofore sealed the eyes of a very large portion of the public, whenever their looks have been directed towards that sacro-sanct tribunal, in prostrate submission to its presumed infallibility." In another essay we hear that "courts are composed of men, liable to the same impulses as the rest of their countrymen. And whenever it shall please Providence to let us

alone because we be joined to our idols, and vice and corruption shall be
the characteristics of the nation, judges will not have escaped the con-
tagion." The only way to guarantee a responsible judiciary, therefore, is
to "let the people keep the watch." Until the courts are made accountable to the people, the nation's judicial system will be "based on a false
principle."[9]

Unresponsive to the people, the Supreme Court, one of the essayists
says, had pursued under Marshall a "career of high-handed judicial legislation" resulting in many injustices. Similar to Hawthorne's moral in
The House of the Seven Gables, the general aim of the essays in the *Democratic Review* was to establish "in the public mind . . . distinct ideas of the
errors of the past" in order to "effectually guard against their possible
recurrence in the future."[10] The essays therefore concentrate on exposing
the bias of the Marshall court, especially in *Fletcher v. Peck* and *Dartmouth
College.* According to Whig lawyers, the *Charles River Bridge* decision
had overturned the immutable principles of law on which these earlier
cases were based. The *Democratic Review* essays argue, however, that
these principles had only recently been constructed. Based on the ingenious "speculation" of individual judges, these decisions of the Marshall
court are not binding, and it is the duty of a new court to "make and act
upon their own interpretation of the Constitution."[11] To do so would be
to restore to the people power that the courts had invested in themselves
and in corporations.

This was certainly the lesson of a short story entitled "Martha Gardner, or Moral Re-action" that appeared in *American Monthly Magazine*
shortly after the *Charles River Bridge* case. The author was the Democratic lawyer William Austin, a classmate of Joseph Story at Harvard, where
he declined election to Phi Beta Kappa because he disliked secret societies. Austin achieved literary fame for his *Letters from London,* written
during his stay in London as a young lawyer in 1802–3. Rufus Choate
claimed that no book in the Dartmouth College library was more read.
Students were fascinated by Austin's description of statesmen and advocates. An amateur writer of stories, Austin is best remembered today as
the author of "Peter Rugg, the Missing Man," a story Hawthorne loved.
Peter Rugg even makes an appearance in "A Virtuoso's Collection."
Col. Thomas Wentworth Higginson noted the Hawthornesque quality
of "Peter Rugg" and called Austin a "Precursor of Hawthorne."[12] No
one, however, has remarked upon the similarities between "Martha
Gardner" and *The House of the Seven Gables.*

Martha Gardner inherited a small house from Sir Francis Willoughby,
who founded the first settlement in Charlestown, Massachusetts, adjoin-
ing the old ferry dock. For years she kept a small shop where she sold
sweetmeats, nuts, and apples, until her house was burned by the British

during the battle of Bunker Hill. Rebuilding the house after the war, she lived in it until she died in 1809 – but not without difficulty. In 1785 the Charles River Bridge was erected near the door of her house. Just as Colonel Pyncheon desired Maule's land, so the wealthy Charles River Bridge Corporation desired Martha's land. Haunted in her dreams by the corporation, Martha is sure she will lose her house, especially because she thought all the deeds and documents had been burnt in the war. Providentially, she dreams of the location of the long-lost deed and saves her house. But this is not enough. Two more times she must go to court to save her house from the powerful corporation. According to the author, the tale illustrates "Moral Reaction," because the recent defeat of the Charles River Bridge Corporation in the Supreme Court can be attributed to Martha Gardner's willingness to stand up to the threat posed to individuals by corporations.

Written over a decade later, *The House of the Seven Gables,* with its tale of a cent shop, a lost deed, and a final miraculous triumph of the common people over the rich, seems to offer the same political message as "Martha Gardner" and the essays on the Supreme Court in the *Democratic Review*. If Hawthorne's romance makes no explicit mention of a corporation, his Judge Pyncheon embodies all of the characteristics that the Democrats attributed to corporations. In "Martha Gardner" the author claims that of the three parts of man – the animal, the intellectual, and the moral – the moral is neglected by corporations. "The Corporation of Charles River Bridge was composed of many men, in that day, well remembered now for their public and private worth. Less than five of them would have redeemed Nineveh. But, unhappily, the animal and intellectual part of Corporations generally govern the body, and conscience is a non-corporate word."[13] Such a description anticipates Hawthorne's description of his judge. In addition, Hawthorne provides a remarkably accurate account of the three stages of American property law, told from a Jacksonian perspective.

In the first chapter Hawthorne sketches the history of the House of the Seven Gables. According to his fictional narrative, when New England was settled the agrarian principles of natural use and the rule that "First in time makes first in right" clearly coincided. Matthew Maule made natural use of his land by clearing it with his own hands for agrarian development. That pastoral, agrarian economy is violated, however, when Colonel Pyncheon asserts his power in the legislature to come up with a grant allowing him to take over Maule's land. The way in which the Pyncheons first bend the law to accumulate property and then appeal to it to protect their property recalls the way in which a rising commercial class benefited first from a reinterpretation of property laws and then from a rhetoric about the eternal sanctity of property rights that was used to protect property only recently acquired.

In questioning the legitimate authority of laws of property, Hawthorne questions one of the foundations of the legal system of the United States. Although the United States claimed to have broken with its British past, it had inherited one of eighteenth-century Britain's strongest beliefs – the belief in the natural right to property. As we saw in the last chapter, legal figures like Chancellor James Kent strongly agreed with John Locke, who said, "Governments have no other end but the preservation of property."[14] In *Fletcher v. Peck,* Justice Johnson went so far as to claim that property becomes an intimate part of an owner's existence, "as essentially so as the blood that circulates through his system."[15] In general, Americans would have agreed with Edward Christian, the editor of Blackstone's *Commentaries on the Laws of England,* when he refers to "that law of property, which nature herself has written upon the heart of all mankind."[16]

Hawthorne's tale shows that the law of property is indeed written but implies that nature may not be its author. The status given to a deed of property confirms the idea that an owner's authority to possess land is embodied in a text. A deed allows the person whose name is affixed to it to claim ownership of a piece of land. In a sense the document and the piece of property merge. The owner of the deed is the owner of the land. The owner's name coincides with the land. The House of the Seven Gables is located on Pyncheon Street, and the tree beside the house is called the Pyncheon-elm.

Hawthorne, however, questions the natural connection between the deed to the property and the property itself. Masquerading as a document written by nature, the Pyncheon deed was actually written by a biased state legislature. And although "no written record of this dispute [between Pyncheon and Maule] is known to be in existence" (*HSG* 7), the Pyncheons maintain their right to the property on the basis of another document – a will. They then protect this right of inheritance as a natural right by still other documents – laws passed by a legislature whose point of view reflects the will of the powerful, not the will of the people. Although the specific authorship of these documents is never acknowledged, Hawthorne's tale makes us see that all documents extend someone's will onto a printed text and that many attempt to shape a world to conform to that will.

Hawthorne's reminder that all documents – including legal ones – have human, not natural authors questions more than the law of property. One of the first examples of what Max Weber calls a legal, rational system of government, the United States, more than most governments

at the time, placed authority in written documents. Britain had its unwritten common law and constitution, whereas the United States had
declared its independence in one document and constituted itself in another. Expressing the will of the people, both the Declaration of Independence and the Constitution were originally granted authority because
they supposedly embodied natural law. But what if they, like the deed to
the Pyncheon land, expressed the will of a few, not the natural rights of
all? If the legal documents essential to the maintenance of America's rule
by law do not embody the authority they claim, the entire structure of
government may rest on a false foundation.

For instance, the system imposed on present-day Salem has no foundation in natural law; it is accepted, just as the Pyncheons' claim to their
land is accepted, because of years of usage. The Pyncheons' continued
possession of their house shows how we come to accept as a fact of
nature anything that has existed for a long time. Although built by
human hands, the House of the Seven Gables is considered as natural as
the elm that grows next to it. The Pyncheon-elm, "now fourscore years
of age, or perhaps nearer a hundred . . . gave beauty to the old edifice,
and seemed to make it a part of nature" (*HSG* 27). Just as the house is
considered a part of nature, so too is the patriarchal system of inheritance
that renews the Pyncheons' right to the land, existing "in the line marked
out by custom, so immemorial, that it looks like nature" (23). The
narrator, however, lets us know that the Pyncheons' status and rank are
the result not of a natural right but of a counterfeit right. "There is
something so massive, stable, and almost irresistably imposing, in the
exterior presentment of established rank and great possessions, that their
very existence seems to give them a right to exist; at least, so excellent a
counterfeit of right, that few poor and humble men have moral force
enough to question it, even in their secret minds" (25). Hawthorne's
narrative of the Pyncheons' history forces us to question the right of such
exterior shows to exert influence. What we learn is that the normative
rules, ranks, and institutions of society are not norms of nature; they
only appear so because they have acquired stability over the years.

The political allegory that Hawthorne presents in his first chapter is a
gloomy one, for it indicates that far from breaking with the corruption of
the past, the United States has repeated its evils, using a new set of
characters. Indeed, in questioning the Pyncheons' claim to the House of
the Seven Gables, Hawthorne also questions the impersonal claim to
authority made by all three branches of the U.S. government. The legislature's conduct in the Pyncheon–Maule dispute indicates how easily that
popularly elected body can be influenced by wealth. Admittedly, as the
narrator tries to assure us, this case of the legislature's buckling under the
influence of the powerful occurred at a time "when personal influence

had far more weight than now" (*HSG* 7). Unfortunately, we lose confidence in this assurance later in the chapter, when he describes how young Clifford escaped execution for murder: "The young man was tried and convicted of the crime; but either the circumstantial nature of the evidence, and possibly some lurking doubt in the breast of the Executive, or, lastly – an argument of greater weight in a republic, than it could have been under a monarchy – the high respectability and political influence of the criminal's connections, had availed to mitigate his doom from death to perpetual imprisonment" (22). Here the executive branch exerts the authority, but the effect is the same: The Pyncheons' rank and status, rather than impersonal considerations of justice, continue to rule. That not even the judicial branch of the government is immune to personal influence is shown by the way in which, urged on by the colonel's loud cries, "Clergymen, judges, statesmen, – the wisest, calmest, holiest persons of their day" – convicted Matthew Maule of witchcraft (8). Disguised as rationality purging irrationality, irrational forces of greed and egotism gain power and deprive Maule of his land.

The lesson Hawthorne draws from the most notorious event in Salem's legal history totally undermines the distinction that the conservatives of the period made between republican and democratic rule, which, as we saw in the last chapter, was essential to their justification of rule by an enlightened elite. As a president of Harvard College wrote, summarizing the thought of Fisher Ames,

> A republick is that structure of an elective government, in which the administration necessarily prescribe to themselves the general good as the object of all their measures; a democracy is that, in which the present popular passions, independent of the publick good, become a guide to the rulers. In the first, the reason and interests of the society govern; in the second, their prejudices and passions. . . . True republican rulers are bound to act, not simply as those who appoint them *would,* but, as they *ought;* democratick leaders will act in subordination to those very passions which it is the object of government to control. . . . Then it is, that men, not laws, govern.[17]

Given the Salem witch trials, "which should teach us, among its other morals, that the influential classes, and those who take upon themselves to be leaders of the people, are fully liable to all the passionate error that has ever characterized the maddest mob" (*HSG* 8), Hawthorne is not so confident that republican principles will prevail. And there is more. Through Judge Pyncheon he suggests that the irrationality displayed by the judges in the witch trials persists in present-day America. The U.S. system of government has not eliminated irrational control of power; instead, it allows those who can master its forms to pursue their personal dreams under the mask of disinterestedness.

Significantly, the most famous judge to come from Hawthorne's Salem, Joseph Story, offered an interpretation of the Salem witch trials in opposition to Hawthorne's. In 1828 Story delivered a speech in Salem entitled "History and Influence of the Puritans." Directing himself to his ancestors' darkest hour, Story offers an explanation of their actions. "We may lament, then, the errors of the times, which led to these persecutions. But surely our ancestors had no special reasons for shame in a belief, which had the universal sanction of their own and all former ages; which counted in its train philosophers, as well as enthusiasts; which was graced by the learning of prelates, as well as the countenance of kings; which the law supported by its mandates, and the purest judges felt no compunctions in enforcing."[18] Although lamentable, the Puritans' errors were not irrational, since they were supported by the established laws of the society. In the remainder of this chapter I want to look closely at the legal career of this man who defended the witch-trial judges, especially his connection with one of Salem's most famous murder trials. To do so will let us better understand how Hawthorne could so confidently declare Salem a laboratory for studying national politics.

Born in nearby Marblehead, Joseph Story came to prominence as a lawyer in Salem, where he lived until he moved to Cambridge in 1829 to accept a chair as professor of law at Harvard. He was appointed the youngest member of the U.S. Supreme Court by President Madison in 1811, a position he held along with his chair at Harvard until his death in 1846. This remarkably talented man is often linked with James Kent in accounts of the formative era of American law, but Story supplanted the New Yorker as the foremost legal scholar of his day by publishing numerous books, including the monumental three-volume *Commentaries on the Constitution*. Story and Kent were close professional friends and often praised one another's work. In 1823, Kent, after his forced retirement as chancellor, traveled to Boston and Cambridge. The climax of his journey was Harvard's Phi Beta Kappa banquet, presided over by Justice Joseph Story, who toasted "our distinguished guest, who so administered the law of the land, as to make New York the land of the law." Kent responded by proposing, "Massachusetts, the land of Story as well as song."[19]

Their mutual respect grew out of their shared conservative views. Like Kent, Story clearly favored the expansion of commerce and judicial control of popularly elected legislatures. "That government can scarcely be deemed free," Story warned, "where the rights of property are left solely dependent upon the will of a legislative body, without restraint."[20] During his service on the bench of the Supreme Court, Story played a major role in bringing about transformations in American property law. In

Dartmouth College, for instance, it was Story's concurring opinion, not Marshall's opinion of court, that explicitly extended corporate privilege to private business enterprises. In a preliminary ruling on the case, Story was very concerned to make a clear distinction between public and private corporations, since a better case could be made for legislative control over public corporations than private ones. "A bank, whose stock is owned by private persons, is a private corporation, although . . . its objects and operations partake of a public nature. The same doctrine may be affirmed of insurance, canal, bridge, and turnpike companies. In all these cases, the uses may, in a certain sense, be called public, but the corporations are private."[21] Writing to Chancellor Kent, Story celebrated the outcome of the case: "Unless I am very much mistaken, these principles will be found to apply with an extensive reach to all the great concerns of the people, and will check any undue encroachments upon civil rights, which the passions or the popular doctrines of the day may stimulate our State Legislatures to adopt."[22]

Given Story's fear of encroachments caused by the passions of the people, it is interesting to find that he was involved in the second most famous event in Salem's legal history, an event that caused people to recall the witch trials two hundred years earlier: the Joseph White murder case. Given Hawthorne's portrayal of the judiciary in his romance, it is even more interesting to find that the White murder is a likely source for *The House of the Seven Gables.* According to George Parsons Lathrop, Hawthorne's son-in-law, "In all probability Hawthorne connected with [the Pyncheon murder], in his mind, the murder of Mr. White."[23] Leading to the most sensational murder trial in America up to that time, the White murder could have easily tantalized the imagination of a writer of romances. Providing a particularly telling insight into the fluctuating fortunes of some of Salem's most prominent families in a time of social change, it gives us a sense of the power structure in Hawthorne's Salem. Involving legal figures of national fame, it lets us see how Hawthorne's story of squabbles among Salem families takes on national significance. My account of its events will necessarily take us both forward and backward in Salem history, and sometimes into the arena of national politics.

In April 1830 Captain Joseph White, a rich Salem merchant (on whose ships Hawthorne's father had served), was found murdered in his bed. The town was in an uproar, fearing that the lives and property of respectable citizens were no longer safe. A committee of vigilance was formed, made up of twenty-seven leading citizens. Its vigorous pursuit of the murderers added to the climate of crisis, as critics recalled the witch hunts two hundred years earlier. Some suspected White's servants, who had reported the murder. Some thought that White, eighty-two, had been involved in a love affair and was the victim of a jealous rival. Others speculated that a black had committed the crime, in revenge for the large profits that White had made from the African slave trade. Suspicion was also directed at White's lawyers and his nephew. Soon, however, two sets of brothers, the black sheep of two prominent Salem families – Frank and Joseph Knapp, and Richard and George Crowninshield – were accused of the murder.

Three years earlier, Joseph Knapp, a captain on one of White's ships, had married Mary Beckford, the beautiful daughter of White's niece and longtime housekeeper. Accusing Knapp of fortune hunting, White had removed him from command and cut his favorite Mary out of his will. Joseph Knapp mistakenly believed that if the will could be destroyed, his mother-in-law would inherit half the fortune, so he hired Richard Crowninshield to murder White, while Knapp, still having the run of the house, was to steal the will. Crowninshield murdered White, and Knapp stole a document, but the wrong one. White's real will was safe in the keeping of his lawyers. In the real will, the major inheritor of a great fortune was the once-suspect nephew Stephen White, a Massachusetts state senator and the brother-in-law of Joseph Story. Story wrote his good friend Daniel Webster that his brother-in-law "will get 150 to 200 thousand dollars. Three of my nieces will receive about 25,000 each."[24]

Although Story had a personal stake in the trial, he stayed in the background as controversy about the case made news throughout the country. Privately, however, he arranged for Webster to aid the prosecution. Webster, having recently debated the Constitution with Robert Young Hayne on the Senate floor, was at the height of his career. He was also tired. But he owed his friend a favor. Many give Story credit for providing the "Defender of the Constitution" with the constitutional theory that he used against Hayne. As Theodore Parker noted, "Mr. Webster was in the habit of drawing from that deep and copious well of [Story's] legal knowledge, whenever his own bucket was dry."[25] Webster accepted his friend's request and traveled to Salem.

Because of numerous complications – including Joseph Knapp's confession in exchange for immunity, the sudden death of presiding Chief Justice Parker from apoplexy, and Joseph's subsequent loss of immunity when he refused to testify at his brother's trial – the prosecution's task was not easy. In addition to these complications there was the obstacle of a Massachusetts law at that time stating that no accessory to a crime could be convicted without the conviction of a principal. A principal had to be present at the commission of the crime. To be regarded as present the accused need not be directly at the scene of the murder. It was sufficient, if the individual had cooperated in the act by watching to give an alarm or by assisting in escape. The obvious principal in this case was Richard Crowninshield. Told of this legal technicality, Richard promptly hanged himself in his cell, making the conviction of his brother and the two Knapps problematic.

Webster's task became the difficult one of proving that Frank Knapp, the only one of the remaining three who had even been in Salem the night of the crime, was a principal, even though he had not been directly at the scene. In devising his strategy Webster drew on the legal expertise of Story. Their combined efforts were successful in bringing about Frank's conviction, paving the way for Joseph's trial and conviction. Later George Crowninshield was acquitted. Some attributed his acquittal to the absence of Webster at his trial. Webster, after all, had been given personal credit for Frank's conviction. His summary statement at that trial has been called the "greatest ever delivered to an American jury."[26] In his "Eulogy on Daniel Webster," Rufus Choate called it a "more difficult and higher effort of mind than that more famous 'Oration for the Crown.' "[27] But not all of those impressed by the power of Webster's speech were impressed by its fairness. One critic went so far as to call Frank's conviction an "example of judicial murder."[28] Enough Salem residents were outraged at Webster for helping hang two members of a prominent Salem family so that he was never again warmly welcomed by them in their town. Others were understandably upset at the irregularity of having Webster brought in from outside to serve the prosecution, especially since, contrary to his official denial, he was paid one thousand dollars by Story's brother-in-law, the same fee paid to Crowninshield to commit the murder.

The resentment grew when Webster, who had stayed at Stephen White's house during the trial, later received a gift of a yacht from White. Salem residents would also have known that in 1831 William Paige, younger half-brother of Webster's first wife, had married Harriette White, one of White's daughters and also a niece of Story's, and that in 1836 Webster's son Fletcher had married another such daughter and niece, Caroline White. Part of Joseph White's fortune trickled into the hands of the Webster family.

Another reason why Webster's being allowed to argue the case for the prosecution drew criticism was that Robert Rantoul, a young Jacksonian Democrat from nearby Beverly, who would later battle Story over the codification of Massachusetts law, was not allowed to argue the defendants' case because he was not a member of the court. Rantoul remained as an assistant for the defense, and his tireless efforts alienated White's friends in Salem so much that he, like Webster, found himself unwelcome in Salem after the trial. The Webster – Rantoul opposition points to a political aspect of the trial that historical distance too often lets us forget but that was certainly remembered by Hawthorne, who started *The House of the Seven Gables* in the midst of an election pitting his Whig enemy, Upham, against Democrat Rantoul and an antislavery candidate who was campaigning against Webster's Fugitive Slave Act.

In addition, Hawthorne had personal reasons for being sensitive to the political implications of the White affair. His replacement at the Custom House, Allen Putnam, had been a witness at the trial, discrediting the testimony of another witness who swore that Frank Knapp had been in his company just before his departure home. The discredited witness was Zachariah Burchmore, a good friend of Hawthorne's and a correspondent who was one of the first to hear about Hawthorne's plans to write *The House of the Seven Gables*. Finally, the Crowninshields were Hawthorne's distant cousins. As any Salem resident would have known, the Crowninshield family had come into conflict with Story before.[29]

The ascent of the Crowninshield family is an important part of Salem history in itself. The Crowninshields rose by opposing "King Derby," who dominated commercial life in Salem at the turn of the century. Staunch Federalists, the Derbys were aligned with the Essex Junto, a group that exerted powerful influence on Bay State politics. Opposing them, the Crowninshields became Jeffersonian Republicans, a political allegiance dictated more by local than national issues. At first the Derbys were able to contain the Crowninshield threat. For instance, in 1802 they maneuvered to eject the Republicans, including the Crowninshields and the Hathornes, from Salem's Court Ball. In 1806, however, the Crowninshields increased their power when Salem was scandalized by a divorce trial involving the daughter of Elias Hasket Derby and her husband Nathaniel West. The two had been separated since 1803, after a quarrel between West and his brothers-in-law over the division of the Derby estate. During the trial, testimony unearthed a record of loose morality that permanently damaged the Derby name, a damage aggravated by charges that the Derbys had used their influence to corrupt the judges. By the end of 1806 the Derby hegemony had crumbled, and the Crowninshields gained increased influence in Salem. One of their allies was a young Republican lawyer from nearby Marblehead who, along with Samuel Dexter, had helped to defend Nathaniel West in the divorce trial. His name was Joseph Story.

Story's rise to prominence soon outstripped that of the Crowninshields and was achieved partially at their expense. In 1811, Story, Stephen White, and Benjamin W. Crowninshield served on the first board of directors of the Salem Merchants Bank, with Crowninshield as president. In 1815 Story replaced Crowninshield as president, a position he was to hold for twenty years. If the local Salem diarist Dr. William Bentley can be trusted, Story rose in the Massachusetts legislature by depriving the same Crowninshield of the speakership. In 1808 he maneuvered him out of a seat in Congress. This election launched Story on a national career, for it sent him to Washington with the support of the New England "Yazoos."

The Yazoos were a group of New England speculators who had been involved in an infamous land scandal in Georgia. In 1795 the Georgia legislature, enticed by bribes, sold thirty-five million acres of its western territory to four land companies for half a million dollars, even though the title to much of the land was in dispute – some claimed by the Spanish government, some by the federal government, and some by Indian tribes. Learning of the circumstances of the sale, the Georgia public expressed its anger by electing a new legislature, which repealed the sale. On the very day that the sale was repealed, the New England Mississippi Land Company, made up of a number of important New England politicians and businessmen, bought eleven million acres of land from one of the companies. For over a decade the title to the land was in dispute. Gambling that a profit was still to be made, the New England company held onto its claim and refused offers of a refund by the state of Georgia. In the meantime, the land greatly increased in value as it was transformed from wilderness into cotton plantations made more and more productive after the invention of the cotton gin.

With North and South involved, the dispute became national as the New England company sought compensation from the federal legislature. When Joseph Story first went to Congress, he went as a paid lobbyist for the Yazoos. He also went as a newly married man, having recently married for the second time. His new bride was the daughter of Judge William Wetmore, one of the original investors in the New England Company.

The New England Yazoo strategy depended on the outcome of a suit brought by Robert Fletcher of New Hampshire against John Peck of Massachusetts over the sale of a deed to Yazoo land – the famous *Fletcher v. Peck* case we have already looked at regarding the doctrine of vested rights. Some historians consider it a collusive suit, arranged between friendly adversaries in order to have the issues decided by the courts.[30] When John Quincy Adams left Washington to become ambassador to Russia, Story succeeded him as Peck's counsel before the Supreme Court. John Marshall, whose long friendship with Story started at this time, decided in Story's favor, declaring that the 1796 Georgia legislature had no right to repeal the 1795 grant, for to do so would be to violate a contract. The court's decision no more led to the Yazoos taking possession of the land than Hawthorne's fictional Pyncheons could use the long-lost Indian deed to take possession of their Maine land. Nonetheless, the decision did prompt Congress to enact a generous compensation law that gave a number of influential New Englanders a large profit – and a personal debt to Story.

Story's role in the Yazoo affair clearly marked his arrival as a man of affairs. A year after *Fletcher v. Peck* (1810) and only five years after he helped to reveal scandal in the Derby family, he found himself a member of the U.S. Supreme Court. On the bench, Story's politics seemed to change. Although he had started his career as a Jeffersonian Republican, allied with the Crowninshields against the Federalist establishment in Salem, he became a spokesman for conservative interests and a friend of Chancellor Kent. Story claimed that it was the country's ideas on the law that changed – not his. Nonetheless, there were those in Salem who remembered his switch in party loyalty and questioned his motivation.

Salem residents would also have known that even as a judge Story continued to be involved in Crowninshield family affairs. In 1817 he sat on the Supreme Court as it decided the bankruptcy case of *Sturgis v. Crowninshield,* disallowing a Crowninshield's attempt to discharge past debts. Other ways in which Story might have antagonized the Crowninshields are suggested in a letter from Mrs. Crowninshield to her husband Benjamin, the secretary of the Navy, in Washington.

> Yesterday afternoon I had the pleasure of seeing Judge Story. . . . He told me you may be home in May. . . . He likewise says you have fine times with the girls in the house. . . . [I also understand there are] so many ladies that almost every evening you send for music and dance. Now you have never told me this and I have many times asked you how you pass your evenings but not a word in reply. I hope in the course of your evenings you sometimes recollect you have a wife at home peering over her knitting and two daughters studying their lessons by her side.[31]

Finally, as the White murder trials proceeded in 1830, another Crowninshield lost his race for Congress, probably in part as a result of negative publicity from the trials.

Whether or not Hawthorne was offended by Story's involvement in the White murder case and by his dealings with Hawthorne's distant cousins is not clear. In a letter to his relative John Dike that refers to the trials, Hawthorne does not seem very concerned. He does not mention the Crowninshields at all, and of the Knapps he writes, "For my part, I wish Joe to be punished, but I should not be very sorry if Frank were to escape."[32]

What does seem certain is that Hawthorne drew extensively on the circumstances surrounding the White murder in *The House of the Seven Gables,* as he had in his 1834 story "Mr. Higginbotham's Catastrophe."[33] In both the historical event and Hawthorne's romance, wills and lost documents are confused. A niece has the possibility of inheriting a large fortune. A judge dies of apoplexy. Someone may avoid a stiffer penalty because of the "high respectability and political influence of the criminal's connection" (*HSG* 22). Furthermore, both involve plots within in a rich man's family over inheritance. That both involve scandal among the well-to-do leads us to one of the most important similarities. Hawthorne draws his lesson about the influential classes' liability to passionate error from the Salem witch trials. He could just as easily have drawn it from events in Salem in 1830. Involving some of Salem's most prominent families, the White murder led to trials that gave Hawthorne a close view of how four of the most important shapers of American law – Story, Webster, Choate, and Rantoul – wielded power. Of these four, Story especially invites comparison with Hawthorne's fictional representative of the legal profession.

Like Judge Pyncheon, Story combined a legal career with a commercial one. He too presided over meetings of bank directors and had considerable financial investments, investments aided by his ruling in *Dartmouth College* that a bank is a private corporation. In addition, Story's rise to power, allegedly at the expense of the Crowninshields, along with his participation in the Yazoo affair, recalls the rise of the Pyncheons, accomplished at the expense of the Maules through influencing the legislature and the courts to get favorable decisions with respect to property. Such actions caused some to claim that Story, like Hawthorne's fictional judge, concealed a shifty nature behind his stately public pose. In *The Prose Writers of America* (1847), which includes selections by both Hawthorne and Story, the editor compares Story to Kent and Marshall and concludes that his friends will have a "more solid and permanent" fame because the Massachusetts judge was "perhaps too sedulous a student of the tone and tendencies of the day, and his want of decidedness and precision often leaves it extremely doubtful what were his own opinions."[34] The page opposite the frontispiece of this book, which Hawthorne must have seen, prominently displays a vignette of Salem's most famous judge adopting a stately smile.

It may seem scandalous to compare Judge Pyncheon to one of the most honored American judges of the nineteenth century, yet it is not surprising to find that one of Hawthorne's contemporaries thought of Justice Story as he read *The House of the Seven Gables*. On the flyleaf of a copy of the first edition of *The House of the Seven Gables* discovered by Norman Holmes Pearson, a former owner wrote,

> There seems no doubt that Hawthorne, from some pique or other, has to a sufficient extent to have annoyed Judge Story not a little, had he lived to read these pages, though not enough to ground an action of libel on, introduced very unpleasant allusions to the late Mr. Justice Story in this volume. We know that in preceding work, Mr. H. treated some very respectable old people in Salem, who had incurred his dis-

pleasure, in a similar way; & there is therefore nothing strange in this attack. Probably, Mr. H. having been a Revenue officer in the district of which Judge Story had jurisdiction, some ill-feeling arose out of their official intercourse. These instances, of a vague, indefined resemblance, are numerous, though unconnected as a whole. There was never in N. England that I can learn of, but one *Pyncheon* family and almost the last (female) descendant of it, Judge Story married. Judge Story & a Mr. Crowninshield were nephews of the late Mr. White, a wealthy gentleman of Salem whom the latter murdered by night, destroying his will &c. (see p. 335) Crowninshield was hung, however. The sketches in Ch. VIII.[35]

Although the contemporary is a bit confused – Story was not a nephew of Captain Joseph White – he does correctly suggest Story's involvement in the White murder affair. He also correctly identifies Story's first wife, who died shortly after her marriage, as a descendant of the Pynchon family that felt so unfairly attacked by Hawthorne's use of its name in his fiction. Further, although there is no record that any ill feeling arose out of Hawthorne's official dealings with Story, there is a possibility that Hawthorne might have harbored some secret, if ill-founded and minor, resentment against this famous man from Salem. In 1850 Hawthorne took some pride in his own fame. He wrote his friend Horatio Bridge that he was Salem's "most distinguished citizen; for [it has] no other that was ever heard of beyond the limits of the Congressional district." Such a man might well have remembered that as he himself struggled to gain fame, Joseph Story was already better known not only as a judge but also, by some, as an author. In *Prose Writers of America,* Hawthorne is represented by four selections, Story by six.[36]

But there is no need to search for personal disputes or secret jealousies. Given Hawthorne's fascination with the possibility that the lives of even the greatest public figures concealed some private sin, Salem's Justice Story would have raised intriguing possibilities for Hawthorne's imagination. Story's solid reputation would have made him more, rather than less, interesting for Hawthorne. Hawthorne's sister wrote him that having expected Judge Pyncheon to resemble Hawthorne's enemy in the Custom House affair, the Reverend Charles W. Upham, she was surprised to find the fictional judge so "weighty."[37]

Of course to argue that Hawthorne drew on Story's reputation for his portrait of Judge Pyncheon is not to suggest that Story is the definitive model. The similarity between Judge Pyncheon and Story does not, for instance, rule out similarities that other critics have found between Pyncheon and Upham. Judge Pyncheon cannot be reduced to one historical figure. The safest hypothesis is that Hawthorne drew on a number of sources (including Story's friend Webster), none of whom will ever be identified with certainty as a model because Hawthorne was so reluctant to admit that he had one.[38] He told members of the Pynchon family that he had used its name in complete innocence; he never admitted that his character resembled Upham; and, in the anonymous commentator's view, his "unpleasant allusions" to Justice Story were "not enough to ground an action of libel on."

Furthermore, to compare Story with Judge Pyncheon is not to argue that Story was a hypocrite. If Story was not as saintly as political allies made him out to be – he had a number of political enemies; if his rise to prominence suggested strong ambition to some (Dr. Bentley of Salem referred to him as an "Ambitious wretch")[39] and if his personal judgment was not always above reproach, for the most part he deserves his reputation as a well-intentioned lover of justice. In drawing on Story's involvement in the bizarre events of the White murder case, I am fully aware of Lathrop's warning that "such resemblances as these between sundry elements in the work of Hawthorne's fancy and details of reality are only fragmentary, and are rearranged to suit the author's purposes."[40] To be sure, it is precisely Hawthorne's imaginative rearrangement of events that interests me. To study that rearrangement is to understand better the political implications of Hawthorne's portrayal of a judge and legal issues. If I am not trying to question Story's personal integrity, I do want to call attention to the ideology that he shared with many other well-intentioned members of the legal profession in the antebellum years. Precisely because Story's personal reputation is so respectable, to bring Story's legal career to bear on our discussion of Judge Pyncheon is to turn our attention away from reading Hawthorne's romance in terms of petty squabbles between minor personalities and to move toward reading it in terms of the contending ideologies of the period. Because Story eloquently represents the orthodox legal ideology, he would be an ideal figure to draw on even if there were no biographical connection with Hawthorne. That there is only adds to the story.

To compare Story to Judge Pyncheon is to see the political implications of both the rhetoric that Story's friends used to praise him and that which Hawthorne uses to describe his judge. The monumental reputation that Story enjoyed – and in some circles continues to enjoy – resulted partially from rhetoric typical of his time, rhetoric used to offer reassurance that the judiciary could combat the instability caused by the country's rapid social transformations, rhetoric that elevated members of the judiciary to a higher moral status than mere politicians. To muster confidence in judicial authority, this rhetoric relied heavily on metaphors of brightness and monumentality. Using this rhetoric to frame Hawthorne's portrait of his judge will in turn allow us to use the lens of Hawthorne's fiction to see how politically loaded such rhetoric was.

In a letter to Story in 1833, Chancellor James Kent wrote, "I consider your work to be an incomparable monument of sound and healthy and incontestable constitutional principles." Three years later Kent wrote,

> We live in a very perilous time, in which our fair and splendid fabrics of Governments, and our wide and deep jurisprudence, are threatened to be weakened and disturbed to the very foundations. May you have health, and then I know you will not lack perseverance, to accomplish all your plans, and along the stream of time to gather all your fame, and prove a stable and impregnable bulwark against all dangerous innovation, and all ferocious assault, of the splendid structures created by the wisdom and patriotism of our fathers.[41]

Charles Sumner, delivering the annual Phi Beta Kappa address at Harvard the year after Story died, praised Story in similar terms. Sumner begins by calling Story a jurist and then goes on to compare a jurist to a "mere lawyer or judge." An ordinary member of the legal profession can be likened to a "well-graced actor, of whom only uncertain traces remain, when his voice has ceased to charm." He is an "artisan" of the law. He might be surrounded by all the tokens of worldly success, but "his labors are on the things of to-day. His name is written on the sandy margin of the sounding sea, soon to be washed away by the embossed foam of the tyrannous wave. Not so the name of the jurist. This is inscribed high on the immortal tablets of the law. The ceaseless flow of ages does not wear away their indestructible front; the hour-glass of time refuses to measure the period of their duration." A jurist, like Story, "does not live for the present merely, whether in time or place. He lifts himself above its petty temptations, and, yielding neither to the love of gain nor to the seductions of a loud and short-lived praise, perseveres in those serene labors which help to build the mighty dome of justice, beneath which all men are to seek shelter and peace." Sumner illustrates Story's commitment to the timeless principles of jurisprudence by citing his response to a conversation a few days before the illness that caused his death. Told that a "wish had been expressed by many to see him a candidate for the highest political office of the country," Story "replied at once, spontaneously, and without hesitation, 'That the station of President of the United States would not tempt him from his professor's chair, and the calm pursuit of jurisprudence.' "[42]

In refusing the possibility of pursuing worldly ambition by accepting a political office at the end of his life, Story acts in direct contrast to Hawthorne's fictional Judge Pyncheon, who dies while a small group of powerful men wait at a private dinner to offer him their party's nomination for governor. Nonetheless, the rhetoric that the narrator mockingly employs to describe why the elite regard the judge as an ideal candidate is rhetoric that recalls the praise heaped upon Story. For these "practiced politicians," with the skill to "steal from the people without its knowledge, the power of choosing its rulers," there is no worthier candidate than the judge, no one "more wise and learned, more noted for philanthropic liberality, truer to safe principles, tried oftener by public trusts, more spotless in private character, with a larger stake in the common welfare, and deeper grounded by hereditary descent, in the faith and practice of Puritans" (*HSG* 274). That there was also no historical judge who was a better candidate to fit this description than Justice Story is shown by Henry James's description of the distinguished judge: "All the light, surely, that the Puritan tradition undefiled had to give, it gave with free hands, in Judge Story – culture, courtesy, liberality, humanity, at their best, the last finish of the type and its full flower."[43]

Written years after Hawthorne died, James's description of Story could not possibly have influenced Hawthorne. Nonetheless, it illustrates something Hawthorne was very sensitve to: how official reputations are constructed. James praises Story in a biography of Story's son commissioned by the Story family, *William Wetmore Story and His Friends*. Hawthorne knew William Wetmore Story, first in Salem, then through their mutual friend George Hillard, and finally in Rome. William Wetmore had studied law and even written legal treatises. Sharing a practice with Hillard and Charles Sumner, his father's two most prized pupils, he had a promising career ahead of him, but after his father's death he abandoned the law to become a writer and a sculptor. He moved to Rome and became an important member of a circle of expatriate artists that at one time or another included Margaret Fuller, the Brownings, Henry James, and Hawthorne. Hawthorne made his friend famous when, in *The Marble Faun,* his romance about a secret homicide, he alludes to William Wetmore's statue of Cleopatra. But it is another statue that concerns us. Although William Wetmore abandoned his father's profession, he continued to honor him. His first important sculpture was a commissioned portrait of his dead father. Story completed it in 1849, and it was placed in the chapel in Mount Auburn Cemetery near Boston. Describing the portrait in his biography, James marvels at its ability to capture the judge's character: "It expressed the character that made one exclaim 'What a *lovable* great man!' "[44]

Through his art, Story's son is able to materialize the monumental rhetoric used to enhance Justice Story's reputation. The statue, existing years later as a lasting monument to his father's greatness, evokes even more rhetoric of praise when it receives the sanction of one of America's most famous writers. One need not deny the love a son felt for his father or Story's truly admirable accomplishments when one notices that Hawthorne was very skeptical of this process by which unblemished reputations are made. For instance, "The Great Stone Face" is often read

as questioning the monumental reputation of Daniel Webster, who, according to *Prose Writers in America,* had "written his name in our history," had "graven it indelibly on the rocks of our hills."[45] This story was
published only one year after the statue of Webster's friend was displayed
to the public. Within another year Hawthorne started *The House of the
Seven Gables.* If the most famous judge in Salem's history represented all
the light that the Puritan tradition had to give, its most famous fictional
judge represents its darkness.

In his two-volume *Life and Letters of Joseph Story* (1851), William Wetmore Story describes his father's physical appearance.

> The muscular action of his face was very great, and its flexibility and
> variety of expression remarkable. Its outward form and feature seemed
> like a visible text, into which every thought and emotion translated
> themselves, – a luminous veil, which moved with every vibration of
> the inward life. His face was a benediction. Through it shone a benign
> light, whose flame was fed by happy thoughts and gentle desires. . . .
> while he spoke, his face was haunted by a changeful smile, which
> played around it, and flashed across it with auroral light.[46]

Judge Pyncheon also has a variety of expression and a face that can be
read as a visible text, but when the veil is lifted on Judge Pyncheon's face
it reveals not the "genuine benignity of soul, whereof it purported to be
the outward reflection" but something "cold, hard, immitigable, like a
day-long brooding cloud" (*HSG* 119). Outwardly expressing a shining
brightness, Judge Pyncheon embodies darknesss.

Hawthorne's relentless undercutting of any attempts to turn human
beings or human institutions into bright, eternal monuments to perfection clearly gives his narratives a radical edge. It would seem to align him
with the politics of his reformer-artist Holgrave, who in radical Jacksonian style advocates the destruction of all monuments to the past. In the
law, the Jacksonians' target was precisely the type of rhetoric that
granted legal decisions the authority of eternity. For instance, in one of
the *Democratic Review* essays on recent legal history that appeared side by
side with Hawthorne's fiction, Charles J. Ingersoll demystifies the doctrine of vested interests established by the Marshall court. Arguing that
the doctrine is a construct of Whig lawyers, Ingersoll points to Story's
role in giving it the appearance of a timeless sacred principle. As Ingersoll
points out, the notion that a legislative act was a contract was first
suggested by Story as he argued the Yazoo case before the Supreme
Court. Accepted by his friend Marshall, it was extended by Marshall
nine years later to include charter trusts. "Judge Story then threw in bank
charters to boot . . . ; of course in his commentaries he repeats his own
arguments and those of the judge who was prevailed on to adopt them,
and they pass as law." Ingersoll clearly singles out the commentaries of

Story and Kent for confusing judicial legislation with time-honored principles of law. In them "one may trace the humble parentage, monstrous
birth, and inordinate growth of judicial constructive prepotency."[47] Ingersoll's answer was that the new Supreme Court justices needed to
reinterpret the Constitution to restore power to the people.

Indeed, this is exactly what Jacksonians felt they were doing. If so far
my analysis of *The House of the Seven Gables* has concentrated on its
power to unmask the rhetoric so vital to Whig ideology, we should not
forget that by the time Hawthorne wrote his book the Jacksonians had
had their "revolution." The political allegory that Hawthorne offers in
his first chapter takes us only as far as the first two stages of the transformation of American property law. As gloomy as that account is, the rest
of his narrative records a third stage, in which the land is returned to a
descendant of its original owner. That rectification of past wrongs is
accomplished through the seeming triumph of Holgrave's Jacksonian
principles. Indeed, Holgrave's opinions on reform have similarities with
Taney's decision in the *Charles River Bridge* case. Just as Holgrave proposes that each generation should be able to restructure society to serve
its present interests, so Taney ruled that considerations of public interests
at the present time were more important than maintaining the conditions
under which a corporation was originally chartered. In contrast, the
Pyncheons' desire to have the present generation bound by the wills of
the past recalls Story's defense of the sanctity of contract. Whereas Story
saw the triumph of Jacksonian principles as a threat to the nation's stability, Hawthorne portrays it as an attempt to return property to its
rightful owners.

As we saw in the last chapter, however, the Jacksonian version of
American history has its own problems. In Cooper's hands it risks falling
prey to a nostalgia for a nonexistent, innocent agrarian past. To be sure,
Hawthorne's Jacksonian vision is different from Cooper's. Nonetheless,
Hawthorne seems to assent to a nostalgic view of American history in
which there was a time of innocence when one could gain possession of the
land and carve out one's destiny without encountering restrictions from
the past and without violating another's rights. It is this belief in a
continent existing in "unscribbled serenity"[48] outside human history that
establishes Matthew Maule's right to the land that Colonel Pyncheon
deceitfully wrested from him. As the narrator says, describing the ground
for Maule's defense of his land against Colonel Pyncheon's claims, "For
several years, he succeeded in protecting the acre or two of earth which,
with his own toil, he had hewn out of the primeval forest, to be his garden-
ground and homestead" (*HSG* 7). It is this same myth that seems to give
the settlers in Maine a firmer right to the land than the Pyncheons have.
After all, the Pyncheons base their claim on a written deed; the pioneer

settlers base theirs on "real" deeds. The tragedy of American history appears to be that the rhetorical authority of written deeds has replaced the natural authority of real deeds.

But Hawthorne does not assent to this version of the past uncritically. His narrative provides moments that invite its demystification. One, the mention of the Indian deed, is never fully developed. Another, Holgrave's conversion to conservatism, is a vital part of Hawthorne's imaginative resolution of the conflicts he has exposed at the core of the American legal system. Serving to emphasize the latent conservatism within the Jacksonian vision, the conversion of Hawthorne's radical-artist also suggests the conservatism at the heart of Hawthorne's aesthetic vision. As William Wetmore Story's switch of careers suggests, the legal and the artistic mind may have more in common than first meets the eye. Having concentrated on the radical aspects of Hawthorne's legal story in this chapter, I will examine the conservative aspects of his romance in the next. We can start by looking at his incomplete but suggestive reminder that the Indians, not the Maules, were the original owners of the soil.

3

The House of the Seven Gables: Hawthorne's Romance of Art

The Jacksonian version of American history questioned the disproportionate share of property held by the rich. According to Jacksonians, this wealth was rarely earned by labor. Furthermore, very often the rich had displaced the original owners of the soil and then used their power and influence to make that displacement legal. In contrast, the Whig version of history legitimized the division of wealth by constructing a continuous line of inheritance and acquisition from the original, rightful owners of the soil to the present-day owners. These contrasting versions of the past led to different narratives about the Indians' claim to the land.

In his speech entitled "History and Influence of the Puritans," Joseph Story tried to explain how the Indians had lost their land. Story expresses great sympathy for them. He admits that they have been dealt with unjustly. He denies European claims to either possession or discovery. "If, abstractly considered, mere discovery could confer any title, the natives already possessed it by such prior discovery. If this were put aside, and mere possession could confer sovereignty, they had that possession, and were entitled to sovereignty."[1] In the landmark *Cherokee Nation v. Georgia* case a few years later, Story stuck to his beliefs and recorded one of his rare dissents with Marshall when the chief justice denied the Cherokees the status of a foreign nation.

But in his Salem speech Story goes on to argue that the Puritans, unlike other European settlers, had not dealt with the Indians unjustly. "Let our consolation be, that our forefathers did not precipitate the evil days. Their aim was peace; their object was the propagation of Christianity." The Puritans, Story argues, "constantly respected the Indians in their settlements and claims to the soil." This respect grew out of the feature that distinguished the Puritans from all other settlers: their republican institutions. "The basis of their institutions was, from the first settlement, republican. The people were the admitted source of all power." In New England the dispossession of the Indians could not be attributed to a violation of their rights. It was a melancholy inevitability of history. "By a law of their nature, they seemed destined to a slow, but sure extinction. . . . By their very nature and character, they can neither unite themselves with civil institutions, nor with safety be allowed to remain as distinct communities." Faced with the possibility that it was the introduction of civil institutions, not the inevitability of history, that caused the Indians to disappear, Story concludes, with a slight hesitation, that civil institutions are part of civilization and that the advance of civilization is inevitable. "It may be so; perhaps in the wisdom of Providence, it must be so."[2]

What is important to note in this account is how Story constructs a continuity from the Puritans' claim to the land and the claims of the propertied class of his day. The claim is legitimized in the name of the republican institutions that have existed uninterrupted in America from the time of the Puritans onward, institutions that the propertied class guaranteed against threats posed by Jacksonians, especially the Jacksonian tendency not to honor the sanctity of contracts established in the past.

In *The Pioneers* Cooper comes up with a similar narrative in order to resolve the problem of the Indians' claim to the land. Also expressing great sympathy for the Indians' plight and believing in the necessity to honor the sanctity of contracts and to establish continuity between the past and present, Cooper has the Indians give the land to Edwards's grandfather as a gift. Cooper's narrative, however, has a major difference from Story's. Suspicious of the commercial class and sharing the agrarian values inherited by the Jacksonians, Cooper gives the land to a representative of the agrarian past, not the commercial present. Furthermore, the land is given by word of mouth and personal trust. The claim to it need not be incarnated in a paper document.

Hawthorne's narrative is different from both Cooper's and Story's, although it shares aspects of both. Regarding the Pyncheon land in Maine, Hawthorne seems to come up with a solution similar to Story's. The Indian deed establishes a seemingly legitimate line of ownership from the Indians to the present-day ruling class, but Hawthorne grants no sanctity to the line of inheritance established by written documents. Sharing Cooper's distrust of the rising commercial elite, Hawthorne imagines a more radical Jacksonian narrative by implying that the Indian deed would not be honored by white settlers of the land, who "would have laughed at the idea of any man's asserting a right – on the strength of mouldy parchments, signed with the faded autographs of governors and legislators, long dead and forgotten – to the lands which they or their fathers had wrested from the wild hand of Nature, by their own sturdy toil."[3] Such a statement combines two aspects of Jacksonian ideology. First, it expresses the doctrine of the sovereignty of the living generation, a doctrine partially underlying the *Charles River Bridge* decision and one questioned by Cooper. Each generation should be able to escape the bondage of past generations by maintaining the right to reinterpret a legal document according to present conditions. Second, the statement implies that the virgin condition of America allowed a reenactment of the Lockean state of nature in which ownership was established by labor. The emphasis on labor allowed Jacksonians to make their claim that the original white settlers were the rightful owners of the soil because their labor had first developed the land, whereas the Indians had allowed it to remain in its "natural," uncivilized state.

Although this radical Jacksonian narrative counters both Story's and Cooper's narratives by exposing a break in the legitimate line of inheritance from the original owners of the soil to the present-day owners, it is in turn undercut by the existence of the Indians, whose presence exposes the false foundation of any claim by white settlers to own land according to the right of first possession. When Matthew Maule thought he was innocently marking out the boundaries of his garden spot on a virgin continent, he was in effect anticipating the crime of Colonel Pyncheon: establishing a claim to land by ignoring prior claims to it. To be sure, Hawthorne never explicitly accuses the Maules of stealing the land from the Indians, nor would he want to, but he does implicitly link the Edenic moment that allows the Maules to claim first possession with the romance. Holgrave, alone with Phoebe in the garden, exlaims, "Could I keep the feeling that now possesses me, the garden would every day be virgin soil, with the earth's first freshness in the flavor of its beans and squashes; and the house! – it would be like a bower in Eden, blossoming with the earliest roses that God ever made" (*HSG* 214). If the freshness of the Edenic moment is possible only in a romance, the Maules' claim to the land is based on a fictional foundation, an imagined moment outside of history.

Hawthorne's questioning of the Maules' innocence is made more explicit when he emphasizes their similarities to the corrupt Pyncheons. For instance, the Pyncheons try to establish control over a piece of land; the Maules repeat the crime, metaphorically, by trying to acquire "empire over the human spirit" (*HSG* 212). The similarities between the two families are most obvious when we compare the reformer Holgrave with his enemy, the conservative Judge Pyncheon. To stress similarities between Hawthorne's artist and judge is to invite a comparison between Hawthorne's artistic mind and the period's legal mind, especially in the way both respond to the rise of commerce in America.

Holgrave, who champions change and flux, would seem to be the total opposite of Judge Pyncheon, who shares the lawyer's love of order and stability. Holgrave's friends – "reformers, temperance-lecturers, and all manner of cross-looking philanthropists" – according to Hepzibah, "acknowledged no law and ate no solid food, but lived on the scent of other people's cookery" (*HSG* 84). Nonetheless, Holgrave's profession as an artist betrays his affinity with the judge. In his portraits he is able to fix flux – even the varying expression of the judge – to capture the essence of a personality. Holgrave can live in flux and embrace it because he believes in the artistic individual's access to fixed, permanent laws. Although Holgrave makes Phoebe uneasy because he "seemed to unsettle everything around her, by his lack of reverence for what was fixed," Hawthorne immediately adds "unless, at a moment's warning, it could establish its right to hold its ground" (177). As Hepzibah says, "I suppose he has a law of his own!" (85). Whereas Holgrave's dislike of the judge shows that his artistic version of the truth conflicts with the official, legal version, his conversion to conservatism at the end of the book shows how the artist's desire to find eternal truths can lead to political conservatism. Thus, Holgrave's conversion is not, as Rudolph Abele claims, Hawthorne's "complicating of the theme of egalitarianism with that of art, and so producing the kind of muddle in the book that Hawthorne's mind was always in about his respective loyalties to art and politics," but one of the most important ways in which he links the two.[4]

According to Marvin Meyers, changing social and economic conditions in antebellum America "made instability the natural condition of American life."[5] As we have seen through the example of Joseph Story, the legal profession had a double response to those changes. On the one hand, the profession encouraged the rise of the new economy by transforming the law to suit its needs. On the other, it sought security from the increasing sense of instability in the monumental, formal qualities of the law. Constructed according to the solid eighteenth-century values of perspicuity, elegance, and logic, the law was to provide a firm foundation to order an economy that seemed to defy all laws because its only control was the formless passions of the masses. Most important in a time of flux, the edifice of the law housed eternal truths. Jurists were of the guardian class because, specially trained in the law, which Story granted the status of a science, they had privileged access to those eternal truths. Sumner, for instance, said that Story's legal reasoning had the certainty of geometry.[6]

Judges of the period were not the only ones to react to the new economic conditions by seeking eternal truths. If public law, as Hawthorne suggests, did not house stable truths, they must be sought elsewhere. "Commercial times," Emerson had argued in "The Transcendentalists," give rise to idealism. "The materialist," Emerson wrote, "believes his life is solid." But he is deluded.

> The sturdy capitalist, no matter how deep and square on blocks of
> Quincy granite he lays the foundation of his banking-house or Ex-

> change, must set it, at last, not on a cube corresponding to the angles of
> his structure, but on a mass of unknown materials and solidity . . .
> which . . . lies floating in soft air, and goes spinning away, dragging
> bank and banker with it at a rate of a thousand miles the hour, he knows
> not whither, – a bit of bullet, now glimmering, now darkling through a
> small cubic space on the edge of an unimaginable pit of emptiness.[7]

Caught in a market system that rendered the value of things subjective,
turned nature itself into a commodity, and seemed beyond human control, men needed to seek stable truths in transcendental laws. For Emerson it was the imaginative artist's special role to see those transcendental
truths, just as for Story it was the trained jurist's to discover eternal
truths in the law.

By making this comparison I do not want to minimize the difference
between the transcendentalists and the lawyers. Although Story started
his career as a poet and continued to write poetry all of his life, and
although he strongly urged his law students to study literature as a source
of eternal truths, he was uncomfortable with nineteenth-century poets.
His models were the eighteenth-century figures of Pope and Johnson,
whose balance and reason expressed "truth," not the modern poets'
"ideal sketches of the imagination."[8] Story's eternal truths were "public"; the transcendentalists' "private." But despite their differences both
Story's and Emerson's social visions depended on keeping the public
sphere separate from the private. Story wrote a poem called "The Power
of Solitude" and then embarked on a public career. Emerson, finally
bringing himself to speak on the Fugitive Slave Law, starts his address,
"I do not often speak to public questions; – they are odious and hurtful,
and it seems like meddling or leaving your work."[9] Despite the important conflict between Emerson's private law and society's public law on
the slavery issue, Emerson maintains the same split between the public
and the private that was at the heart of the antebellum legal system. That
split had important consequences.

The separation of public and private spheres allowed people like Story
to defend the impartiality of the judiciary. Story was not so naive as to
believe that judges were without private beliefs or interests, but he did
believe that when a man delivered his public opinions as a judge he
could, to a large extent, suppress his private opinions. Similarly, private
business matters could be kept separate from matters of public policy, so
long as a public figure did not reap direct financial gain from one of his
own public decisions. Thus Story saw no conflict of interest in his role in
the *Dartmouth College* case when he, a bank president, went out of his
way to protect banks by calling their charters private contracts. In retrospect, however, we can see that in this case Story wrote into American
corporate law the very distinction between public and private that justified his judicial impartiality. The result was not at all impartial.

The split between private and public was so pronounced that public and private law could be dominated by different theories. Private law was dominated by an instrumental theory, public law by a formal theory. The same judge could adhere to both theories simultaneously. According to Horwitz, for instance, "more than any other jurist of the nineteenth century, Joseph Story brought each of these two contradictory tendencies to their highest fulfillment. His private law opinions are, by and large, highly utilitarian and self-consciously attuned to the goals of promoting pro-commercial and developmental legal doctrines. By contrast his public opinions are usually starkly formalistic."[10] This is not as paradoxical as it seems. As we have seen, the instrumental theory allowed for a transformation of commercial law so as to encourage low-cost development and economic expansion. The formal theory forged constitutional doctrines under the contract clause granting constitutional status to "vested rights" and thus limiting political interference into the "private realm" by public legislatures. In other words, public-law decisions that claimed to be apolitical by refusing to interfere with the private realm were actually extremely political, since the split between public and private itself became a foundation for public policy. Whereas someone like Story argued that the public good demanded that private business matters be protected from the political designs of legislatures, because to do so ensured the most productive economy and thereby helped to promote the commonwealth, he did not acknowledge that the major beneficiaries of such a policy were members of a new commercial elite.

By the time Hawthorne wrote *The House of the Seven Gables,* that now established elite benefited even further when the formalism dominating public law gained more power in private law. According to Horwitz, this intrusion of formalism into the realm of private law disguised "both the recent origins and foundations in policy and group self-interest of all newly established legal doctrines." The laws protecting the wealthy now had the "appearance of being self-contained, apolitical, and inexorable."[11]

In his portrait of Judge Pyncheon, Hawthorne offers a splendid image of the double character of antebellum law by showing whose interests are served by an outward show of form. Judge Pyncheon's formal, public self veils a shifty private self. Far from disinterested and rational, the formal public self is a tool used both to promote the judge's private interests in the present and to hide deeds that promoted his interests in the past. As Hawthorne makes clear, merely keeping one's beliefs private does not mean that they do not affect one's public role. To know the public person, one must know the private person.

> As regards the Judge Pyncheon of to-day, neither clergyman, nor legal
> critic, nor inscriber of tombstones, nor historian of general or local

politics, would venture a word against this eminent person's sincerity as a christian, or respectability as a man, or integrity as a judge, or courage and faithfulness as the oft-tried representative of his political party. But, besides these cold, formal, and empty words of the chisel that inscribes, the voice that speaks, and the pen that writes for the public eye and for a distant time – and which inevitably lose much of their truth and freedom by the fatal consciousness of so doing – there were traditions about the ancestor, and private diurnal gossip about the Judge, remarkably accordant in their testimony. It is often instructive to take the woman's, the private and domestic view, of a public man. (*HSG* 122)

But if Hawthorne's Judge Pyncheon illustrates the inevitable distortion in the cold, formal style written for the public eye, he also demonstrates how deeply Hawthorne shares an assumption found in most literary artists of the period. Truth is to be found in the private realm. So two years later, when Hawthorne took up the "pen that writes for the public eye and for a distant time" to compose the campaign biography of Franklin Pierce, he emphasized his intimate knowledge of his college friend's private character. For Hawthorne, politics was basically not a question of issues but of character.[12]

In *The House of the Seven Gables*, for instance, the corruption that Hawthorne exposes in Salem can be explained by the corrupt heart of Judge Pyncheon or by the private greed of the small group of politicians who want to nominate him as governor. When the judge suddenly dies, Maule's curse is magically lifted, and the book can come to what seems to be a happy ending. Thus, although Hawthorne condemns his Puritan ancestors who participated in the witch trials, he seems to retain their world view that explains social contradiction in terms of a conspiracy theory, an explanation readily seized upon by many Jacksonians who referred to the "Monster Bank" and who called Justice Story's friend Webster "Black Dan." If we turn once again to my comparison between Story and Judge Pyncheon, we can see how inadequate this conspiracy theory is as an explanation. Although Story served the same commercial interests as Judge Pyncheon, he was not evil. In fact, his sincere concern for the welfare of his country, his family, and his students is moving. If he had enemies, he did not have a heart that, like Judge Pyncheon's, threw a "great black shadow over everything" (*HSG* 306). The way in which judges, even honorable ones, can help perpetuate social injustice needs a more complex explanation than Hawthorne's fiction provides, for ultimately Hawthorne diverts our attention from the historical perspective that his romance offers to an exploration of the universal character of the human heart, including his own.

No matter how telling Hawthorne's criticism of the ideology of the legal profession might be, it loses some of its power, because Hawthorne, the judger of judges, in his heightened self-consciousness hints that he is not exempt from his own criticisms. If judges like Story relied on a distinction between the public and private self, so did Hawthorne, who referred to his fiction as a veil covering his private self. It was, he pleaded, the public self that readers should judge. Hawthorne's image of the self he tried to sell to the public shares an important similarity with the public image that judges tried to project. In antebellum America, judges were not the only professionals claiming to be above the squabbles of local politics; artists made the same claim. Hawthorne, in fact, made precisely this claim in protesting his dismissal from the Custom House. Appointed an artist, he should not, he felt, be the victim of petty politics.[13] Yet, as readers of "The Custom-House" and *The House of the Seven Gables* knew and should know, Hawthorne's works can be very political on a local and even, I have argued, a national level. Like Judge Pyncheon, Hawthorne conceals his politics behind a public role. And (again like Judge Pyncheon) Hawthorne covers up a gloomy disposition by putting forth a sunny face to the public in *The House of the Seven Gables*. That forced sunshine, like the judge's sunny smile, is in part motivated by commercial interests, as Hawthorne, hopeful of increased sales, tried to open up "commerce," in both senses of the word, with his consuming public.[14]

Eleven years to the day before Ralph Waldo Emerson delivered his famous lecture "The American Scholar," Joseph Story addressed the Phi Beta Kappa Society of Harvard and linked the spirit of free trade with the spirit of free inquiry characteristic of a liberal republic. At times sounding very much like Emerson, Story praised the prevailing "spirit of free inquiry" that questioned the sometimes arbitrary authority of the past:

> Nothing is more common, in the history of mankind, than a servile adoption of received opinions, and a timid acquiescence in whatever is established. It matters not, whether a doctrine or institution owes its existence to accident or design, to wisdom or ignorance, or folly, there is a natural tendency to give it an undue value in proportion to its antiquity.

Enthusiastically declaring that one of the most important characteristics of the age was the "bold and fearless spirit of its speculations," he went on to describe what this meant in the field of law:

> In jurisprudence, which reluctantly admits any new adjunct, and counts in its trains a thousand champions ready to rise in defense of its formularies and technical rules, the victory has been brilliant and decisive. The civil and the common law have yielded to the pressure of the times, and have adopted much, which philosophy and experience have recommended, although it stood upon no text of the Pandects, and claimed no support from the feudal policy.

The result was the creation of commercial law, "started into life with the genius of Lord Mansfield" and developed by others like him.[15]

For Story, the spirit of speculation that made way for the creation of commercial law also brought about a "literary revolution" that profited from the "establishment of a new and mighty empire, the empire of public opinion." This new empire had turned the age into the "age of reading" and had drastically altered the condition of authors. Previously, authors had depended upon the "smiles of a favored few." Now they had the public as their patrons. "No longer the humble companions or dependents of the nobility," authors "constitute the chosen ornaments of society, and are welcomed to the gay circles of fashion and the palaces of princes." With the rewards of authorship "almost as sure and regular as those of any other profession," authors can address themselves "not to the present generation alone, but aspire to instruct posterity."[16]

Less than twenty years later Justice Story had completely reversed his optimistic view about the empire of public opinion established by America's political revolution. Writing to Justice John McLean, he despaired: "My heart sickens at the profligacy of public men, the low state of public morals – & the utter indifference of the people to all elevated virtue & even self-respect – They are not only the willing Victims but the Devotees of Demagogues – I had a letter a few days ago from Chancellor Kent, in which he utters language of entire despondency. Is not the *Theory* of our govt. a total failure?"[17]

As we saw in the last chapter, Hawthorne would have distrusted the elitist political implications of Story's lament. He reminds us that those who consider themselves most elevated are capable of the basest acts. Further, he could have argued that the support of commerce by people like Story and Kent had helped contribute to the sad state of affairs that they now regretted, since it had allowed considerations of money, not morality, to rule in the development of American law. Indeed, the White murder case gave Hawthorne a close view of how money influenced our system of justice. According to Webster, the White murder was a "cool, calculating, money-making murder. It was all 'hire and salary, not revenge.' It was the weighing of money against human life; the counting out of so many pieces of silver against so many ounces of blood."[18] Webster's assessment takes on a certain irony, since Webster himself was known as the lawyer who sold his services to the highest bidder on Wall Street and who, in the White trial, was accused of manipulating the law to bring about a "judicial murder," after having accepted the same fee as the alleged murderer. Webster's emphasis on the role of money reminds us that Joseph White himself was a murder victim, because, as a captain of commerce in a center of trade, he had been able to accumulate a large amount of capital. His accumulated wealth is itself a sign of the rise of commerce in the American economy, a rise that affected all areas of America, including Hawthorne's Salem. Raised in the same Salem as Captain White, Joseph Story, whose early expertise was in admiralty and maritime law, played a major role in transforming American law to accommodate commercial interests. In contrast, Salem's most famous writer had serious reservations about the increasing influence that commercial life had on American life.

Although Hawthorne differed with Story on the role of commerce in America, he also shared some of Story's ideas. To argue that Hawthorne saw the potential for evil in those of "elevated" morals as well as of low is not to argue that Hawthorne trusted the masses. Indeed, he had good reason to share Story's despair at the public's indifference to eternal moral truths: For years the public had proved its lack of taste by refusing to buy his books. With the public his patron, Hawthorne found himself not welcomed to the gay circles of fashion but only – when he was lucky – granted a boring job in a custom house. A democratic writer, not a powerful, conservative judge, Hawthorne had even more reason to despair than Story.

In 1844 Story could blame the failure of public opinion on the misguided policies of the Jacksonian revolution, which had moved the country away from its republican ideals. Writing in 1850, Hawthorne would have to admit that what triumphed in the wake of the Jacksonian revolution were not the basic values Jacksonians had promised to restore but values increasingly dictated by the marketplace. If the *Charles River Bridge* decision did not, as Story had predicted, prove disastrous for commerce, neither did it combat the instability in social and economic life that Jacksonians blamed on Whig support of the Bank and corporations. Historically, the conservative values of the Pyncheons were not replaced by the nostalgic and idealized agrarian values of Phoebe and Holgrave but by values even more acquisitive and selfish than those of the Whig elite, values represented by the young consumer of cookies, Ned Higgins.[19] Just as the radical reformer-artist Holgrave turns out to share traits with his conservative enemy the judge, so the democratic writer Hawthorne had more in common with someone like Story than with the consuming public that increasingly dictated the shape of American politics and art. Democratic as it seems, the resolution in which he restores the land to the Maules is Hawthorne's own strategy of containment. Hawthorne recognizes this resolution for what it is: simultaneously a nostalgic and utopian vision, a product of the form of the romance as conceived by Hawthorne, a form that depends upon the split between public and private yet also exposes the limitations resulting from maintaining that split. The same social transformations that influenced American law also influenced the aesthetic laws to which Hawthorne submitted himself in writing his own version of a legal story. We need to examine the political implications of those aesthetic laws.[20]

In the preface to *The House of the Seven Gables* Hawthorne makes a seemingly clear distinction between the novel and the romance: The novel "is presumed to aim at a very minute fidelity, not merely to the possible, but to the probable and ordinary course of man's experience"; the romance, in contrast, concerns the possible, not the probable. "While, as a work of art, it must rigidly subject itself to laws, and while it sins unpardonably, so far as it may swerve aside from the truth of the human heart – [the romance] has fairly a right to present that truth under circumstances, to a great extent, of the writer's own choosing or creation" (*HSG* 1).

Part of Hawthorne's purpose in submitting to the laws of the romance is to be certain that he avoids Colonel Pyncheon's sin of manipulating man-made laws in order to make an illegitimate claim to authority over a piece of land. The last sentence of the preface pleads that the "book may be read strictly as a Romance, having a great deal more to do with the clouds overhead, than with any portion of the actual soil of the County of Essex" (3). By "laying out a street that infringes on nobody's private rights, and appropriating a lot of land which had no visible owner, and building a house, of materials long in use for constructing castles in the air" (3), Hawthorne clearly aligns himself with Matthew Maule, who, like a writer of romance, seems to have maintained his innocence by claiming his land without violating anyone's private rights. With their imaginary powers, the Maules are Hawthorne's representatives of the romance, and the Pyncheons, with their command of the forms and usages of the everyday world, are his representatives of the novel.

The Jacksonian aspect of Hawthorne's narrative tells how the worldly representatives of the novel usurp power from the innocent representatives of the romance. Its ironic aspect suggests that representatives of the romance are not as innocent as they seem. Warning us against the sins of Colonel Pyncheon, Hawthorne repeats them. The entire description of Colonel Pyncheon's motives in building his house can be read allegorically as Hawthorne's self-conscious comment on his motives in constructing his own *House of the Seven Gables*. Like the colonel's house, Hawthorne's romance becomes a monument to its founder, an attempt to resist the flow of time. If the colonel writes a will stipulating that his portrait remain affixed to the wall of the room in which he dies, thus allowing the "ghost of a dead progenitor" to haunt the interior of the house, Hawthorne, though hiding behind a veil, scatters haunting traces of his presence in his work. As the narrator remarks about the human desire to build stately edifices, "With what fairer and nobler emblem could any man desire to shadow forth his character?" (229).

Thus Hawthorne's writing of his romance, like the colonel's construction of his house, becomes a way to escape the constraints of a temporal world. Nonetheless, Hawthorne faces one constraint that the wealthy Colonel Pyncheon did not have to face: the constraint of the marketplace. How can an author write for eternity while pleasing the tastes of a time-bound public? In this sense, Hawthorne comes much closer to Colonel Pyncheon's heir Hepzibah, who has to set up her cent shop to establish commerce with the world of the street. Ironically, the worldly wares Hawthorne tries to sell are the very romances through which he tries to escape the world of time. At one point in his life Hawthorne had even hoped that his career as a professional constructor of fictional castles in the air would provide him with enough capital to build a house and thus, like Colonel Pyncheon, to be able to plant and endow a family.

Increasingly in Hawthorne's works, to inhabit the world of romance meant to escape the constraints imposed by the everyday world of commerce. At the end of *The House of the Seven Gables,* two men of the street watch the barouche carry Clifford, Hepzibah, Holgrave, and Phoebe to the country home of Judge Pyncheon.

> "Well, Dixey," said one of them, "what do you think of this? My wife kept a cent-shop, three months, and lost five dollars on her outlay. Old Maid Pyncheon has been in trade just about as long, and rides off in her carriage with a couple of hundred thousand – reckoning her share, and Clifford's and Phoebe's – and some say twice as much! If you choose to call it luck, it is all very well; but if we are to take it as the will of Providence, why, I can't exactly fathom it!" "Pretty good business!" quoth the sagacious Dixey. "Pretty good business!" (318–19)

Hepzibah, who at the beginning of the book was forced to open commerce between the enclosed world of the House of the Seven Gables and the everyday world of Salem, is magically relieved of that demand.

Working in the midst of commerce in the Custom House, Hawthorne complained, that he could not write a romance "with the materiality of this daily life pressing so intrusively upon me" (*SL* 38). The romancer, he writes, needs the atmosphere of moonlight, which makes all details it shines upon "seem to lose their actual substance, and become things of the intellect" (36). Hawthorne admits, however, that he could have used those everyday details to have written a better book than *The Scarlet Letter.* "The wiser effort would have been, to diffuse thought and imagination through the opaque substance of to-day, and thus to make it a bright transparency; to spiritualize the burden that began to weigh so heavily; to seek, resolutely, the true and indestructible value that lay hidden in the petty and wearisome incidents, and ordinary characters, with which I was now conversant" (38).

In some ways *The House of the Seven Gables,* which draws so heavily on the everyday reality of Salem, is Hawthorne's attempt to write that unwritten book. Although proclaiming itself a romance, it combines aspects of both the novel and the romance, as defined by the preface. An imaginary construct, it has, as Henry James noted, "more literal actuality" than Hawthorne's other romances, and, as we have noted, it offers a close approximation of transformations occurring within the legal world.[21] Just as the Pyncheons and Maules come to share more and more qualities, so the barriers between romance and novel collapse. Hawthorne's characters are supposed to be pure products of his imagination, and yet readers cannot help associating them with actual figures from Salem history. The House of the Seven Gables is supposed to be a "castle in the air," but people travel to Salem to see the real house. Finally, midway through his tale Hawthorne admits, "A romance on the plan of Gil Blas, adapted to American society and manners, would cease to be a romance" (*HSG* 176). The implication: In America, romances are ordinary experiences, and the ordinary is akin to romance. To write a romance with an American setting is to write a novel.

This merger of the romance with the novel presents a problem for Hawthorne. In the preface to *The Blithedale Romance* he complains that American writers of romances are not allowed a "certain conventional privilege" granted to European writers. In Europe the romancer's work is not "put exactly side by side with nature; and he is allowed a license with regard to every-day Probability" (*BR* 2). Thus, when he writes *The Marble Faun,* Hawthorne chooses Italy as the site of his tale, because it afforded a "sort of poetic or fairy precinct, where actualities would not be so terribly insisted upon as they are, and must needs be, in America" (*MF* 3). Whereas Hawthorne wants to find the indestructible value hidden in the ordinary, America's insistence on actuality does not give his imagination the freedom he needs to find it. Furthermore, American life is in such flux that it threatens any attempt to construct something indestructible. Ironically, then, Hawthorne embraces the private, imaginative world of the romance and tries to establish a strict separation between it and the world of the novel, precisely because American life makes the merger of romance and novel inevitable.

In *The House of the Seven Gables* the intrusion of historical reality so threatens to break the "impalpable beauty of [Hawthorne's] soap-bubble . . . by the rude contact of some actual circumstance" (*SL* 38) that Hawthorne has to retreat from it. Evoking the atmosphere of romance at the end of the book, Hawthorne tries to defuse the disruptive intrusion of history. Daniel Webster, in his famous address to the jury in Frank

Knapp's trial, vividly describes the beams of the moon that lit up innocent Captain White's face at the moment when he was ruthlessly murdered. In Hawthorne's romance, flickering moonbeams light up the figure of the dead Judge Pyncheon, immobile in his oaken chair. Hawthorne's moon-beams transform a sudden tragic death into a happy ending. Under moonlight the class struggle that Hawthorne has portrayed throughout his work, the need to reform a world of inequities, even death itself, prove to be illusory, merely part of the imaginative vision of the "writer's own choosing or creation" (*HSG* 1).

Having described the Edenic feeling evoked while he is alone with Phoebe in the garden, Holgrave adds, "Moonlight, and the sentiment in man's heart, responsive to it, is the greatest of renovators and reformers. And all other reform and renovation I suppose, will prove to be no better than moonshine!" (214). Later, when Holgrave and Phoebe acknowledge their love, they

> transfigured earth and made it Eden again, and themselves the first two dwellers in it. The dead man, so close beside them, was forgotten. At such a crisis, there is no Death; for Immortality is revealed anew, and embraces everything in its hallowed atmosphere.
> But soon the heavy earth-dream settled down again! (307)

Historical reality is but an earth-dream; the Edenic moment of romance reality.

What our examination of the period's legal history should let us see is that paradoxically an important aspect of the historical reality from which Hawthorne retreats is a market system that made value "fiction-al." In explaining why Joseph Story's position as a bank president ex-emplified a transformation in economic orders, Story's biographer offers a valuable description of the new market conditions.

> The rise of banking cut the fabric of tradition with an especial sharp-ness. Though the significance of the change was barely grasped and rarely articulated, the growing importance of banking amounted to a revolution in the traditional system of credit, which forced profound changes in outlook and values. Sharply challenged were the old agrarian views under which gold and silver, like fields and flocks, were the true essence of wealth. Rather, wealth was changing in form to the intangi-ble – to paper bank notes, deposit entries on bank ledgers, shares in banks, in turnpikes, in canals, and in insurance companies. More important, perhaps, debt was no longer necessarily the badge of im-providence and misfortune. And from the creditor's point of view debt, in the form of bank notes or bank deposits, became an instrument of power.[22]

In the new economy, the old theory that value was determined by the inherent properties of an object gave way to a theory that the value of an object was determined by the laws of supply and demand. Increasingly, the laws of the market, with all of its whimsical fluctuations and disregard for eternal moral truths, dictated what was valuable in American society. Even someone like Justice Story, who claimed to uphold solid values by basing his legal decisions on eternal principles, adjusted the country's laws to coincide with the laws of the marketplace. If the most solid men of the time turned out to be Judge Pyncheon-like as they swayed to the demands of the market, it is no wonder that Hawthorne turned to imaginative romances to find a world in which "true" value would be more secure.

At Vanity Fair, in "The Celestial Rail-road," Hawthorne offers a description of the new market economy and how it undermines moral values.

> There was a sort of stock or scrip, called Conscience, which seemed to be in great demand, and would purchase almost anything. Indeed, few rich commodities were to be obtained without paying a heavy sum in this particular stock, and a man's business was seldom very lucrative unless he knew precisely when and how to throw his hoard of conscience into the market. Yet as this stock was the only thing of permanent value, whoever parted with it was sure to find himself a loser in the long run. (*MM* 200)

The new economy made value so easy to fictionalize that true value was impossible to find in the everyday world and had to be sought in imaginative fictions.

The problem is that imaginative fictions have no securer foundation than the market in Vanity Fair. Both are based on speculations. In "Peter Goldthwaite's Treasure" Hawthorne explicitly links the imaginative speculations of romancers with the economic speculations of investors. Led on by his dreams of wealth, Peter the romancer quits the business that he shares with a solid, businesslike partner and searches for a buried treasure in the house that he inherited from his father. He finally discovers the treasure, only to find that it consists of worthless paper money. In the meantime, during the quest he has torn apart and destroyed his house, the only thing of real value that he owned.

Hawthorne's imaginative sketches would seem to share a similarity with Peter's romantic dreams. But Hawthorne's continual awareness of their fictionality distinguishes them from Peter's speculations. In "The Custom-House" Hawthorne writes of the "fantastic speculations" and "impracticable schemes" (*SL* 24) of transcendentalist reformers who, like Peter or Holgrave or Hollingsworth or even Hester, when she assumes a "freedom of speculation" (*SL* 156), would tear down inherited institutions to rebuild them on the shaky foundation of the self. His own romances, self-acknowledged products of his imagination, are similarly suspect. Yet Hawthorne seems to want to make a special claim for his romances, as if his awareness of their fictionality gives them a securer foundation, for it is also in "The Custom-House" that Hawthorne creates the myth of the truth-seeking artist, independent of everyday concerns. Because he writes his romances neither for wealth nor political favor, Hawthorne implies that the foundation for his fictions is the conscience so easily bartered away in Vanity Fair. The problem, as Hawthorne portrays it, is that those who refuse to trade their consciences become helpless victims to the power of the marketplace, prey to the maneuvers of politicians who gain power by serving the world of commerce and to the demands of readers who determine the sale of books.[23]

In *The House of the Seven Gables,* written after Hawthorne's recent success in the marketplace with *The Scarlet Letter,* the role of the artist is somewhat different. It is not the romancer who is linked to speculations for wealth but the town's most solid, practical citizen, Judge Pyncheon. In one sense, linking Judge Pyncheon with the type of economic speculations common at the time is historically accurate, since although they depended on fiction, they exerted real power. Indeed, the judge is fully aware of how to gain power by fictionalizing one's value. He describes to Hepzibah how his Uncle Jaffrey had concealed the "amount of his property by making distant and foreign investments, perhaps under other names than his own, and by various means, familiar enough to capitalists, but unnecessary here to be specified" (*HSG* 234). Wealth and value seem to be created on paper, and paper documents hold the greatest of power. But the judge's recognition of the power of documents turns against him, since it is a document that eventually exerts complete control over his dreams. Pursuing his uncle's missing property, he feels he must acquire the deed to the mythical land in Maine. From Clifford he demands the "schedule, the documents, the evidences, in whatever shape they exist, of the vast amount of Uncle Jaffrey's missing property" (235), but by the end of the romance these documents, like Peter's treasure, turn out to be utterly worthless.

In *The House of the Seven Gables* the romancer, unlike Peter, is not a victim of the new economy, for if the market economy is one in which value becomes fictional, who is better suited to control it than a writer of fictions? Appropriately, it is Holgrave, Hawthorne's representative writer of romances, who has all along known the secret whereabouts of the Indian deed that Judge Pyncheon spends so much effort trying to procure. This secret, which Holgrave claims is the "only inheritance that has come down to me from my ancestors" (316), was passed on by Thomas Maule, who, while seeming to serve the Pyncheons by building their house, actually gained power over them by hiding the deed in the structure of the house. The deed that gives the Maules power over the Pyncheons has remarkable similarities with a romance. Promising the Pyncheon family land "more extensive than many a dukedom, or even a reigning prince's territory, on European soil" (18), the Indian deed has more to do with dreams of castles in the air than with control over real land. Limited to the world of dreams, the deed, like a romance, seems to lack any authority and power. The narrator, for instance, lists the Maules' ability to exercise an "influence over people's dreams" among their other "good-for-nothing properties and privileges" (26). But just as a romance can influence people living in the real world – if it is believed – so the deed influences Judge Pyncheon, because he believes in its authority. Thus, the Maules' worthless, invisible property controls the Pyncheons' quest for visible property. No matter how haughtily the Pyncheons rule the "noonday streets of their native town," they are "no better than bond-servants to these plebeian Maules, on entering the topsy turvy commonwealth of sleep" (26). Hawthorne's representatives of the romance turn out to control those who control the paper economy, not vice versa.

Hawthorne arrives at such a vision through having managed some "pretty good business" of his own by peddling a paper document known as *The Scarlet Letter*. The money he earned from his fictional speculation freed him temporarily from both the worries of commerce and the "house" of his ancestors, as he escaped Salem to write his romance in a country house in the Berkshires, near to where the Pynchon family had moved. A romance in the America of Hawthorne's day does seem possible, at least for writers of romances. Its possibility seems to allow Hawthorne, like Holgrave, to live in harmony with the seemingly corrupt political and economic system within which he must function.

As a number of critics have pointed out, however, Hawthorne invites an ironic reading of his hopeful, romantic conclusion. According to this reading, to bring the book to a "prosperous conclusion" is in no way hopeful, given the dehumanizing role that wealth has played previously. In allowing Phoebe and Holgrave to inherit the judge's fortune as a result of the "misfortune" of his only son's sudden death at sea, Hawthorne seems to be setting the stage for his romantic couple to repeat the old generation's cycle of wrongdoing, as they set out to endow and plant a family in the house built from the judge's ill-gotten wealth.[24]

The ironic reading may undercut the hopeful reading of the book's conclusion, but it does not lead us back to a call for reform. Instead, it indicates the folly of human efforts to control the direction of history. Just as in exposing the sins of the Pyncheons Hawthorne repeats them, so does reformer Holgrave. If the happy ending makes reform unnecessary because true value is located in a private, imaginative world that escapes history, the ironic one makes reform impossible because the very effort to realize imaginative visions leads to a repetition of past sins.

At odds, the two readings of Hawthorne's ending also depend on one another. An escape to the romantic world of the imagination is the only humanly possible happy ending, because the everyday novelistic world cannot embody true value. But so long as true value remains consigned to a romantic realm outside of history, any attempt to embody it in the ordinary, novelistic world is doomed to failure. At the same time, precisely because private, imaginative visions cannot be realized within history, they too are suspect as being no more than castles in the air. The world of the novel exposes the false foundation of the world of the romance, and vice versa. Condemned to break from the sins of the past by escaping from history, humanity ends up repeating them, thus perpetuating the cycle of history.

In exposing the false foundation of the legal system, Hawthorne's narrative would seem to make the call for reform unavoidable. Instead, the flaws in the present system reinforce Hawthorne's belief that any man-made political system – past, present, or future – is doomed to make spurious claims to authority. As a result, Hawthorne ends by ruling out the probability of human-directed reform within the historical world. This is not to say that he is satisfied with the world as it is. He continues to hold out hope that "we are not doomed to creep on forever in the old, bad way, but that, this very now, there are harbingers abroad of a golden era, to be accomplished in [our] lifetime" (179). But whether or not that golden age occurs is beyond human control. For Hawthorne, as for America's romantic historians, the "ascending spiral curve" (259) of history will be directed by the hand of providence.[25]

If such a vision allows Hawthorne to close the book on human-directed reform, the reader can leave it open, for the very intrusion of history that Hawthorne fears will inevitably corrupt the innocence of his romantic vision lets us see its limitations. For Hawthorne, human history repeats the circular pattern generated by the form of the romance as he conceives it. But since that form is in part the product of the very historical forces from which it would escape, the circular narrative that it generates is not inevitable. Based on the same separation between public and private as the dominant legal ideology of the period, Hawthorne's romance can endlessly expose the limitations resulting from that separation but not transcend its constraints. In his penetrating criticism of the historical world, Hawthorne ultimately undermines his own authority to criticize, because any criticism he makes turns back on itself and becomes self-criticism. Just as he writes about Salem while escaping from it, so in his romance he opens us to a world of "forgotten events and personages, and to manners, feelings, and opinions, almost or wholly obsolete" (6), while claiming to confine himself to a world of the imagination. The impotency of that imaginative alternative is most clearly seen in Hawthorne's response to one of the most important legal issues of his day, an issue virtually absent from *The House of the Seven Gables:* slavery.

In his campaign biography of Pierce, Hawthorne writes that slavery is "one of those evils which divine Providence does not leave to be remedied by human contrivances, but which . . . by some means impossible to be anticipated, but of the simplest and easiest operation, when all its uses shall have been fulfilled, it causes to vanish like a dream." Like the evil Judge Pyncheon, slavery will magically be removed from the world.[26]

Slavery in Hawthorne's day did not magically vanish. It impinged on the world of *The House of the Seven Gables* in a way Hawthorne could never have imagined. *The House of the Seven Gables* was officially opened to the public on Wednesday, April 9, 1851. At the moment when the book appeared in Boston bookshops, the city was still abuzz with talk about Monday's trial of the alleged fugitive slave Thomas Sims. Twenty-one years after the White murder, the *Sims* case reenacted the confrontation between Robert Rantoul and Daniel Webster, as Rantoul defended Sims against provisions of the Fugitive Slave Act of 1850, a bill passed with Webster's blessing. Justice Story was no longer alive, but Lemuel Shaw, the Massachusetts judge who presided over the trial, had also been involved in the White affair. When the presiding judge, Isaac Parker, died of apoplexy during Frank Knapp's trial, Shaw was named to replace him as chief justice of the Supreme Judicial Court of Massachusetts. At first, Governor Levi Lincoln had offered the position to Story. Story had refused, however, citing fears that if he resigned from the U.S. Supreme Court, President Jackson would have the choice of his successor. Urged by Webster, Lincoln then decided upon Shaw. Reluctantly accepting the post he would occupy for thirty years, Shaw disqualified himself from sitting on the White trials because he had served as the attorney for one of those suspected before the Knapps and the Crowninshields were arrested.

Although Shaw did not participate in the trials associated with the White murder, he did preside over a murder trial that replaced the White affair as the most controversial one in America. On trial was Professor John W. Webster of Harvard, accused of killing George Parkman, one of the richest men in America. The Webster trial, which took place in 1850, shortly before Hawthorne started *The House of the Seven Gables,* might have been one factor turning his mind to the famous murder in his hometown of Salem twenty years earlier, especially since Shaw was accused of bias in favor of the rich Parkman family.[27] But by the time *The House of the Seven Gables* reached the streets, even the Webster trial was overshadowed by the controversy produced by the Sims arrest.[28] With the introduction of slavery into our narrative, it is time to turn to the legal fictions of Herman Melville, the writer who was Hawthorne's neighbor as he composed *The House of the Seven Gables* – the writer who in 1847 became the son-in-law of Chief Justice Lemuel Shaw.

Part II

Wage and Chattel Slavery

4

"Benito Cereno": Melville's Narrative of Repression

No other antebellum American writer treats legal issues with more complexity than Herman Melville. Part of that complexity can be measured by examining the role his father-in-law played in shaping American law. During his thirty years as chief justice of the Supreme Judicial Court of Massachusetts, Lemuel Shaw wrote approximately twenty-two hundred opinions. They included some of the most important in the formative era of American law. According to Professor Zachariah Chafee, "Probably no other state judge has so deeply influenced the development of commercial and constitutional law throughout the nation."[1] Justice Oliver Wendell Holmes, Jr., praised Shaw for his "appreciation of the requirements of the community" and declared that "few have lived who were his equals in their understanding of the grounds of public policy to which all laws must be ultimately referred."[2]

Shaw's connection with the Melville family began long before Herman married Elizabeth Knapp Shaw in 1847. In 1802, Shaw's pursuit of a career in law took him to Amherst, New Hampshire, where he studied in the office of David Everett, a friend of Fisher Ames and Robert Treat Paine, Jr. In Amherst Shaw fell in love with the daughter of Major Thomas Melvill, Herman's grandfather. Nancy Melvill died before the two could marry, but Shaw carried two love letters from her in his wallet for the rest of his life. Shaw was also best friends with her brother Allan and stayed in close contact with the Melvill family. When Allan Melvill died in 1832, Shaw acted as surrogate father to his sons Gansevoort and Herman. *Typee*, Melville's first book, is dedicated to "Lemuel Shaw, Chief Justice of the Commonwealth of Massachusetts."[3]

Melville wrote that dedication shortly before his marriage to Elizabeth and five years before Shaw's controversial fugitive slave law decision in 1851. In this chapter I want to examine the role that Shaw played in the fugitive slave law controversy as a way of analyzing his son-in-law's only direct treatment of slavery – "Benito Cereno." At the same time I will use Melville's fictional account of a slave uprising to reconstruct the logic underlying Shaw's fugitive slave law decisions. Those decisions reveal more about the American legal mentality than its specific response to the slavery issue. The strain that conflicts over slavery placed on American law exposed contradictions inherent within the entire system. Shaw's decisions and their legal precedents are some of the most sophisticated attempts to contain those contradictions.

Given the complicated historical reactions to the contradictions that the slavery issue brought to the fore, it is not surprising to find that Melville's stand on slavery is still debated. My purpose in comparing "Benito Cereno" with Shaw's and others' legal opinions on slavery is not to extract the long hidden, true meaning from Melville's story that will tell us whether Melville was pro- or antislavery. What I do hope to do is to explain historically why it is so difficult to pin down a definitive point of view within the story, an explanation that can help us account for a notable characteristic of Melville's later fiction – its ambiguity. In turn, the ambiguity of Melville's fiction helps confirm Jean-Paul Sartre's vision of history, a vision that insists on the "ambiguity of past facts," an ambiguity that results from a "contradiction which has never arrived at its point of maturity."[4]

Prior to the Fugitive Slave Act of 1850, Shaw had, with one important exception, decided cases in favor of blacks. For instance, in August 1836 he ruled on a case in which Massachusetts abolitionists tried to win freedom for a six-year-old black girl who had been brought into the state on a visit by the wife of her Louisiana owner. Ellis Grey Loring, along with Rufus Choate and Samuel E. Sewall, argued for the girl's freedom, whereas Benjamin R. Curtis, one of Joseph Story's pupils, and later to become a member of the U.S. Supreme Court, represented the owner. Story, following the case closely, wrote to Loring, "I have rarely seen so thorough and exact arguments as those made by Mr. B. R. Curtis and yourself."[5] Shaw was more impressed by Loring's argument and granted the girl her freedom. Ruling that the Fugitive Slave Law of 1793 did not apply because the girl was not a fugitive, Shaw agreed that the moment she entered Massachusetts she became free under Massachusetts law.

Shaw went even farther in the case of Robert Lucas, the slave of a purser on the U.S. Frigate *United States*. Lucas had been enrolled in the Navy in order to serve his master. One of Lucas's fellow sailors on the return voyage was Herman Melville, who later drew on his experiences to write *White-Jacket*.[6] When the ship docked at Boston, Lucas went ashore and asked for his freedom. Shaw granted it to him, arguing that since "slavery is local, the instant the frigate went out of Virginia, the slave became free." Furthermore, the contract entering Lucas into the Navy was void because the contract was made while Lucas was a slave, and "none but a free person can enter into a contract."[7] In short, Shaw freed Lucas from the claims that both the purser and the U.S. Navy had on him.

Shaw's desire to get around the Fugitive Slave Law if possible reflected his personal attitude toward slavery. In an 1811 speech, prior to his appointment to the bench, he had called slavery "one continued series of tremendous crimes" and had urged its abolition, to further the "cause of humanity." But Shaw was not always successful in making rulings consistent with his abhorrence of slavery. In the fall of 1842 he presided over a case that he felt necessitated application of the Fugitive Slave Law. On October 19, 1842, George Latimer was arrested and detained, charged by James B. Gray, a Norfolk slave master, with being a thief and fugitive slave. A heated controversy ensued, with abolitionists meeting in Faneuil Hall and Wendell Phillips delivering his famous curse on the Constitution. Much of the wrath of the abolitionists was directed against Shaw, who declared that, his personal sympathy for the prisoner aside, "This was a case in which an appeal to natural rights and the paramount law of liberty was not pertinent! It was decided by the Constitution of the United States, and by the law of Congress, under that instrument, relating to fugitive slaves. These were to be obeyed, however disagreeable to our own natural sympathies and views of duty!"[8] Despite Shaw's ruling, Latimer eventually achieved his freedom. While waiting for a federal court to convene, Latimer's supporters applied pressure on his jailors, assuring his temporary release. Gray, faced with the possibility that Latimer would escape, sold his claim to him, and Latimer was immediately granted his freedom.

Despite the Latimer decision, Shaw's reputation remained that of a staunch antislavery judge, so much so that in an 1845 decision Judge Nevius of New Jersey questioned whether Shaw's personal beliefs might have biased his opinions on slavery. "It is no matter of surprise that Chief Justice Shaw, entertaining the opinions he did upon the questions of slavery, should have found it repugnant to the spirit of the Constitution."[9] Given Shaw's antislavery reputation, it *was* a matter of surprise to some that he reversed himself and supported the new Fugitive Slave Act of 1850.

To the embarrassment of supporters of Daniel Webster in Massachusetts (Shaw was one), no fugitive slave had been returned from Boston before 1850. They were therefore determined that the new law, which was part of Webster's compromise designed to hold the country together, would be enforced in Massachusetts. Their first chance came in February 1851, when a black named Shadrach was apprehended in

Boston. But to the dismay of Southerners and Webster supporters, Shadrach escaped from the courthouse, aided by an unruly crowd of antislavery forces. Thus, on April 3, 1851, when Thomas Sims was taken into custody, officials made certain that he was brought to "justice." Curtailed by a state law from holding an accused runaway slave in a state jail, officials locked Sims in the federal courthouse and barricaded the door with chains. As abolitionists were quick to point out, the chains produced a highly symbolic scene the next day when Judge Shaw had to bow beneath them in order to enter a court of justice. In his decision Shaw himself felt fettered by the existing law of the land. When asked to rule on the constitutionality of the 1850 law, Shaw upheld it in a decision that for a decade was regarded as the highest authority on the issue. Free to proceed, the federal commissioner ordered the return of Sims to slavery, and, guarded by three hundred armed men, Sims was delivered to a ship and sent on his way south.

If Shaw's decisions in the *Latimer* and *Sims* cases seemed inconsistent with his antislavery decisions, he did not think they were. Shaw always maintained that he ruled according to the letter of the law. When the 1850 law tightened the loopholes that had earlier allowed him to decide in favor of blacks, he saw no recourse but to decide as he did. Furthermore, both the *Lucas* case (which freed a black) and the *Sims* case (which enslaved one) drew on the same legal precedent: Judge Story's decision in *Prigg v. Pennsylvania* (1842).

Prigg involved a runaway slave who had escaped from Maryland and lived in southern Pennsylvania. When she and her children were forcibly returned to Maryland five years later, her captors violated a Pennsylvania law requiring that they receive a certificate from a judge authorizing removal. When the case went to the U.S. Supreme Court, abolitionists hoped that the court would use the occasion to declare the 1793 Fugitive Slave Law unconstitutional. To the contrary, Story upheld the constitutionality of the Fugitive Slave Law and found the Pennsylvania law unconstitutional, concluding that the woman's removal had been legal. But Story did not stop there. Having antislavery views as strong as Shaw's, he made it clear that the return of fugitive slaves was strictly a federal matter. This ruling paved the way for the invalidation of state laws designed to aid owners in the recapture of fugitive slaves. His opinion also implied that state services need not be used to enforce a federal statute. As a result, many northern states, including Massachusetts, passed laws refusing to allow state jails and state police to help in the retention of accused fugitive slaves. These laws rendered the 1793 law ineffective and prompted southern calls for a more effective federal law. A major provision of the 1850 law was to provide for federal officers to enforce the law.

Story made another point disputed by proslavery people. Slavery, he declared, was protected exclusively by municipal, not international, law.

> By general law of nations, no nation is bound to recognize the state of slavery, as to foreign slaves found within its territorial dominions, when it is in opposition to its own policy and institutions, in favor of the subjects of other nations where slavery is recognized. If it does it, it is as a matter of comity, and not as a matter of international right. The state of slavery is deemed to be a mere municipal regulation, founded upon and limited to the range of territorial laws.[10]

So, despite abolitionists' anger over the decision, Story considered it a "triumph of freedom."[11] Indeed, the ruling that slavery was local gave Shaw a precedent permitting him to free Robert Lucas. At the same time, *Prigg* also justified Shaw's refusal to declare either the Fugitive Slave Law of 1793 or the Fugitive Slave Act of 1850 unconstitutional.

However much both Shaw and Story deplored slavery, they felt it was sanctioned by the Constitution and must therefore be accepted. Story wrote to a friend, "You know full well that I have ever been opposed to slavery. But I take my standard of duty as a *Judge* from the Constitution."[12] As early as 1820, Shaw expressed similar sentiments. Writing on the Missouri Compromise, he used strong language to denounce slavery but added that immediate emancipation might cause misery. Furthermore, he felt the most important consideration was the "moral" necessity of holding the Union together.

That Shaw saw maintaining the Union in moral terms helps clarify a common misunderstanding about the conflict between antislavery forces and their opponents. Persuaded by powerful antislavery rhetoric, we often see the conflict as one between defenders of rule by secular authority – man-made law manifested in positive law – and defenders of rule by sacred authority – divine law manifested in private conscience. To a certain extent this statement of the conflict is accurate, but it is important to recognize that Shaw and many members of the legal profession also saw their mission in sacred terms. Preserving the Union was a moral imperative because the United States was not merely one government among many but the hope of mankind: It, above all others, guaranteed the absolute and entire supremacy of law. If abolitionists claimed that the country was not worth saving because the passage of laws like the Fugitive Slave Act violated its sacred mission, Shaw felt that unless the Union were saved its sacred mission could never be fulfilled. To obey the act of 1850 would not only reaffirm the sacred principle of rule by law, which made the Union worth preserving; it would also support a law that everyone knew was designed to keep the country united. Thus, those who praised Shaw's *Sims* decision praised it because it made clear that rule by law would prevail over the violence that threatened to tear the country apart.

Associated with blackness, that violence could easily be linked with satanic forces.

Those in power feared a violent slave uprising that might threaten the peace of the country and the sanctity of the law; this is shown by the response to Shadrach's escape. The escape was reported as an example of "negro insurrection"; Secretary of State Webster labeled it a "case of treason"; President Filmore called a special cabinet meeting to discuss the crisis; and on the Senate floor Henry Clay asked whether "a government of white men was to be yielded to by a government of blacks."[13] For those so threatened, Shaw's decision in the *Sims* case signaled a victory for the forces of light over the forces of violence and darkness. The problem that the slavery issue posed for people who saw America's mission as furthering the cause of enlightenment – a group that, as I have argued, included both Shaw *and* antislavery factions – was that it was not clear which were the forces of light and which of darkness.

This is, of course, precisely the dilemma facing readers of "Benito Cereno." Published in 1855, soon after Shaw's next controversial upholding of the Fugitive Slave Act in the *Burns* case (1854), "Benito Cereno" confronts us with a story that starts as a world full of grays only to transform into a world divided into blacks and whites, where the whites who seem to be in power are not in power and where a violent slave uprising, masterminded by a black man described in satanic terms, is put down by an American captain, who, because he is oblivious, appears innocent. A history of conflicting interpretations has arisen because the story provides no authoritative point of view to help us determine whether the blacks, the whites, or neither fight for an enlightened cause. To be sure, the two points of view through which the events of the story are filtered would conventionally be accepted as authoritative: first, the personal authority of a ship's captain; second, the impersonal authority of a legal deposition. But the authority of both of these points of view is undercut. The deficiencies of the legal deposition prompt us to examine the nature of justice guaranteed by the rule of law held so sacred by Chief Justice Shaw. But first we need to review the limitations of Captain Delano's personal point of view.

Despite the many conflicting interpretations of the story, almost all recent readers agree that it exposes the narrowness of Captain Delano's innocent point of view. His innocent, straightforward reading of the events aboard ship turns out to be a complete misreading, a misreading that ironically saves him. As Don Benito Cereno tells him toward the end of the tale, if he had accurately interpreted the state of affairs aboard ship, he would have faced instant death. As a result, both he and Don Benito attribute his salvation to Providence; the reader, however, can see that Captain Delano's salvation results as much from his prejudice as from a providential concern for the innocent. Or, put another way, his innocence is riddled with prejudice. As kind as Delano seems to be to the Africans, he is unable to decipher the bizarre events aboard the ship because the possibility that Africans rather than Europeans could be in power is incomprehensible to him. When he sees blacks and whites, he immediately relegates blacks to a subservient role. He can think of blacks only as valets, hairdressers, or body servants. The true extent of Delano's kindness to blacks is apparent when we learn that "like most men of good, blithe heart, Captain Delano took to negroes, not philanthropically, but genially, just as other men to Newfoundland dogs."[14]

If the reader has not realized the limitations of Delano's point of view, they are further emphasized in the story's second half when the events are recounted from the point of view of the legal deposition. As opposed to Delano's partial account of events, the legal point of view purports to offer an impartial account. But there are hints in the text that even the legal point of view might be partial, although in a much more subtle manner than Delano's "innocent" prejudice.[15] First, the "document" that Melville includes from the proceedings has been "selected, from among many others, for partial translation" (BC 299). We do not receive all of the documents, or even a complete translation of the one we do receive. Second, the selected document contains Don Benito's deposition, including testimony originally "held dubious" (299) because of his "not undisturbed" (299) state of mind. Benito admits that "in some things his memory is disturbed, he cannot distinctly recall every event" (308). Third, the final decision on what evidence is accepted as authoritative is made by a tribunal none of whose members witnessed any of the events under litigation. Rather than bringing us closer to the actual events, the legal point of view in one sense removes us even farther from them. Finally, nowhere is the Africans' position voiced, a point I will return to later. But first I want to show how a close look at the deposition undercuts the authority it tries to assert.

Even though the African point of view is never given, it is sometimes referred to in order to confirm some of the most questionable parts of the deposition. For instance, the deposition records that

> the negresses of age, were knowing to the revolt, and testified themselves satisfied at the death of their master, Don Alexandro; that, had the negroes not restrained them, they would have tortured to death, instead of simply killing, the Spaniards slain by command of the negro Babo; that the negresses used their utmost influence to have the deponent made away with; that in the various acts of murder, they sang songs and danced – not gaily, but solemnly; and before the engagement with the boats, as well as during the action, they sang melancholy songs

> to the negroes, and that this melancholy tone was more inflaming than a
> different one would have been, and was so intended; that all this is
> believed, because the negroes said it. (310)

The Africans' confirmation does seem to heighten our belief, but it also
raises questions about those portions of the deposition that are not
granted such confirmation. Are they not to be believed because the Africans do not confirm them, or were they merely not incredible enough
to warrant confirmation, a situation that would ironically turn the most
incredible acts into the most believable ones? Or does the emphasis on
the blacks' confirmation serve the opposite purpose, making us suspect it
as a rhetorical ploy used to elicit our belief of incredible actions?

Even when we read the passage with confidence, it can raise unsettling
possibilities. Critics often cite it as an example of how the deposition
exposes Captain Delano's blindness concerning blacks. While on the *San
Dominick,* Delano sees a naked woman nursing her child and thinks,
"There's naked nature, now; pure tenderness and love" (268). The deposition shows how far from the truth Delano is about the African women.
Nonetheless, even while undercutting Delano's view, it gives part of it a
certain validity. Delano goes on to think how gratified he is that "like
most uncivilized women, they seemed at once tender of heart and tough
of constitution; equally ready to die for their infants or fight for them"
(268). The black women did indeed turn out to be ready to fight for their
infants. They might have been fighting for themselves, as well. The
deposition leads us to believe that their cruelty to the Spaniards grew out
of irrational barbarity, but sexual abuses to slave women were com-
monplace and were well publicized in antislavery tracts. The black wom-
en's hatred of the Spaniards might well have grown out of resentment
over how they were treated.

Although the objective style of the deposition seems to offer a definitive account of what actually happened on the *San Dominick,* thus closing
the case, it actually opens up the possibility of new speculative interpretations. As we have seen, what the deposition tells us could be true – and
still partial, since it may leave out significant details needed to explain
what it reports. Furthermore, even what it tells us is subject to question,
since much of it is not told neutrally but in order to make a point.

The final section of the deposition is said to be made up of "various
random disclosures," but the first set of these disclosures is "made to
show the court that from the beginning to the end of the revolt, it was
impossible for the deponent and his men to act otherwise than they did."
The next set of disclosures describes how the Americans, while boarding
the ship, mistakenly killed some of the Spaniards. Here too we learn that
such a mistake was "one impossible to be avoided" (311). The actions of

both the Spanish crew and the American crew are described as inevitable. But these two juxtaposed inevitabilities contradict one another.

The two Spaniards were killed, the deposition tells us, because the Americans mistakenly believed that the two men had taken the cause of the Africans. Hermenegildo Gandix was "killed by a musket ball fired through mistake from the boats before boarding; having in his fright run up the mizzen-rigging, calling to the boats – 'don't board,' lest upon their boarding the negroes should kill him; that this inducing the Americans to believe he some way favored the cause of the negroes, they fired two balls at him." Don Joaquin, Marques de Aramboalaza, was "shot for a renegade seaman" because "with hatchet tied edge out and upright in his hand" he was "made by the negroes to appear on the bulwarks" in a "questionable attitude" (311).

If the American crew could imagine that these two Spaniards had taken the cause of the Africans, then it is clear that the Spaniards could have responded to the African revolt other than the way they had. As the Americans feared, some could have sided with the enslaved Africans. An unthinkable possibility when describing the actions of the Spanish crew, it is readily seized upon to explain to the court the inevitability of the Americans' "mistakes."

Furthermore, as impossible as it seems, a similar possibility is considered by innocent Captain Delano when he tries to make sense of the strange actions on the *San Dominick*. Having seen a Spanish sailor secretly try to communicate something to him, Delano worries that the sailor might have been trying to warn him of a plot Cereno was hatching against the captain.

> Was it foreseeing some possible interference like this, that Don Benito had, beforehand, given such a bad character of his sailors, while praising the negroes; though, indeed, the former seemed as docile as the latter the contrary? The whites, too, by nature were the shrewder race. A man with some evil design, would he not be likely to speak well of that stupidity which was blind to his depravity, and malign that intelligence from which it might not be hidden? Not unlikely, perhaps. But if the whites had dark secrets concerning Don Benito, could then Don Benito be any way in complicity with the blacks? But they were too stupid. Besides, who ever heard of a white so far a renegade as to apostatize from his very species almost, be leaguing in against it with negroes? (270)

Not only does the deposition prove that the blacks were not too stupid to hatch plots; it also suggests that, the Americans, at least while they were boarding, suspected that some whites had joined with the Africans. It is even possible that the two Spaniards actually had leagued themselves with the Africans, that what appeared to the American crew to be their hostility actually was hostility, that the two Spaniards, both clerks, who were said to have been "degraded to the office and appearance of a common seaman" by the Africans, had actually been demoted before the revolt and, feeling resentment, cast their lot with the downtrodden slaves. Indeed, as Melville wrote his story, many people *had* heard of whites helping blacks to gain their freedom. There was even an account of such help being offered by whites serving on a slaver. In a case decided in 1855, the *Porpoise,* a New England ship chartered to a Brazilian, was tried for having operated as a slaver in 1845 between the African coast and Brazil while flying the American flag. Its slaving activities were revealed when three members of the crew informed naval personnel in the harbor of Rio de Janiero.[16]

Of course, such evidence by no means proves that the two slain Spaniards on the *San Dominick* were on the side of the Africans. Such a possibility could never be proved and should not be pushed too far. I have suggested it merely to make a point about the deposition. Trying to prove that the whites' reaction to the slave uprising was inevitable, the deposition raises the opposite possibility. Rather than close our interpretation of the story, it opens it.

The failure of the legal deposition to close the case on the events on board the *San Dominick* has its historical parallel in the failure of American law to close the case on slavery. The *Amistad* affair, which is sometimes cited as a source for "Benito Cereno," offers a perfect example. In 1839, forty-nine Africans bloodily seized control of the Spanish ship the *Amistad* and tried to return to Africa. The ship was captured off Long Island by the U.S. Navy. The lawsuit that followed involved two Americans filing salvage; the Spanish owners demanding the ship's cargo, including the Africans; and the Africans claiming their freedom. The U.S. government intervened on behalf of the Spaniards, citing a treaty between Spain and the United States promising to restore merchandise rescued from the hands of robbers or pirates. The Africans were defended by John Quincy Adams, who felt that there was an "immense array of power – the Executive Administration instigated by the Minister of a foreign nation – . . . on the side of *injustice.*"[17] Justice Story wrote the opinion of the U.S. Supreme Court that granted the Africans their freedom. Arguing that the treaty did not apply, because under Spanish law the Africans had been unlawfully enslaved, Story claimed that they were rightfully free men and thus not pirates or robbers. "We may lament the dreadful acts by which they asserted their liberty, and took possession of the *Amistad,* but they cannot be deemed pirates or robbers in the sense of the law of nations."[18]

Southerners were upset with Story's decision. Some blamed it for the rebellion on board the slave ship *Creole* in October 1841. Destined for New Orleans, where they would be sold, 19 of the 138 Virginia slaves rebelled. Following their leader Madison Washington, they killed one of the slave owners, wounded the captain and first mate, and forced the second mate to sail to the British-owned Bahamas. There the British freed the group of slaves and refused Secretary of State Webster's demand that they be sent back to the United States for trial as mutineers. Seeking legal advice, Webster asked Story in a letter whether the law of nations did not make a difference between ordinary fugitives from justice and that of persons committing offenses on the high seas. Story replied that he knew of no such distinction, except for piracy. Referring Webster to the *Amistad* and *Prigg* cases, he concluded that in the absence of treaty commitments, the United States had no basis for its claims.[19]

The *Creole* incident struck even closer to home for proslavery forces than the *Amistad* case because it involved people legally enslaved under American law. Story, no doubt, was pleased that he could refer to the principles he had set down in *Amistad* and *Prigg* to turn the *Creole* incident into an antislavery victory. He may also have been relieved that the British made it unnecessary for American courts to try the rebellious American slaves, for, as Story himself knew, the *Amistad* decision could be considered a victory for antislavery forces in only a very narrow sense.

If in granting the Africans their freedom Story's decision appeared to show the concern the American legal system had for blacks, it more accurately showed the pressures that slavery placed on America's rule by law. So many conflicts and contradictions became apparent that it was impossible to decide whether some laws and legal decisions were ultimately proslavery or antislavery. At first, abolitionists were delighted with Story's decision, but Adams was not. Story, speaking for a Supreme Court that included slaveholders, severely limited the topics he discussed in his opinion. Adams, to the contrary, had presented an argument that Story considered "extraordinary . . . for its power, for its bitter sarcasm, and its dealing with topics far beyond the record and points of discussion."[20] Topics beyond the points of discussion included questions of human liberty that had been involved in decisions of lower courts but avoided by the Supreme Court. If he had been forced to discuss such topics, Story would have had to admit that he could free the Africans and even guardedly justify their rebellion only because they had been illegally enslaved and because the rebellion took place on the high seas. If the rebellion had occurred within the United States, under American law, the legal questions would have been different. Thus Story carefully avoided an issue that Adams's "extraordinary" argument repeatedly raised. As far as slavery was concerned, Adams reminded the court, American law was more repressive than the "law of nations." Story's decision did nothing to remedy that discrepancy. Summarizing the effect of the *Amistad* case, Robert Cover concludes, "It more than any other case was a disturbing ideological monument to both antislavery and proslavery forces. For the slaveholder it was a Supreme Court declaration that in the natural order of things – even though not in the legal order – his slave had a right to kill him. For antislavery forces, the *Amistad* and *Creole* together were a confession in open court of the depths of the difference between the order of right and the order of law."[21]

Just as the legal deposition in "Benito Cereno" adds to the indeterminacy of the story's meaning, rather than provides a key to unlock it, so American legal decisions on slavery and the slave trade failed to resolve the conflict over slavery. Instead the decisions themselves became the subject of dispute and debate. If it was impossible to determine whether a judgment of court was ultimately pro- or antislavery, it is not surprising that it is difficult to determine what attitude Melville takes toward slavery in a story describing a slave uprising. Even the story's setting adds to its indeterminacy.

Because "Benito Cereno" is a fictional treatment of a legal tribunal in Peru ruling on a slave uprising on a Spanish ship in 1799, it might seem that the story has no bearing on how U.S. law dealt with slavery in the 1850s. No doubt Melville's setting and his turn-of-the-century dating helped him defuse the controversial nature of the story. Furthermore, even if the story recalls some of the most controversial legal rulings on slavery, its ocean setting seems to allow Melville, like Judge Story in the *Amistad* case, to avoid direct comment on the man-made laws that supported slavery on U.S. soil. At the same time, as the controversy over the *Amistad* and *Creole* shows, whether he intended to or not, in setting his slave rebellion on the high seas Melville gave his story a complex historical significance. Although critics of *Moby-Dick* and "Benito Cereno" have recognized that Melville's ocean settings place ships in direct contact with the state of nature, they have not noted that the "literary" idea that the sea was ruled by natural, not man-made, law had important legal consequences. As we have seen, a ship at sea carrying slaves was no ordinary ship.

Since, according to Story, slavery had no basis in natural law, only in man-made law, those who opposed slavery argued (as Shaw had in the *Lucas* case) that once a slave ship entered the high seas, any protection it might be afforded by local laws supporting slavery stopped. Pursuing this logic, an anonymous author – probably William Jay, the son of John Jay – wrote a series of articles in the New York *Herald* in response to Webster's demand that the mutinous slaves on the *Creole* be returned to the United

States. The author admitted that often voyages of slavers were successful from the master's point of view, but their success, he argued, depended solely on the master's security arrangements. The issue on the high seas was entirely one of superior force. If slaves should gain the upper hand, he argued, the master had no law to appeal to. "Resistance of . . . force . . . even unto death, cannot be called mutiny or murder – because they are violating no law by such resistance, but on the contrary vindicating their natural freedom – the gift of God alike to all."[22]

From the start of "Benito Cereno" Melville emphasizes that the action takes place in a territory where the customary controls of man-made law are absent. Seen from a distance, the *San Dominick* "showed no colors; though to do so upon entering a haven, however uninhabited in its shores, where but a single other ship might be lying, was the custom among peaceful seamen of all nations" (239). Some of Melville's contemporaries would have argued that in this setting, characterized by "lawlessness and loneliness," the Africans' revolt was justified by the law of nature. Others would have claimed that rebellious slaves were akin to pirates.

Like the setting, the name of the Spanish ship adds to the story's indeterminacy. The name *San Dominick* evokes associations with the bloody slave rebellion on the island of Santo Domingo. This association is heightened by Melville's dating of his story in 1799, the year of the rebellion, rather than 1805, the year in which the historical Captain Delano experienced a slave rebellion at sea.[23] Antebellum Americans had as much difficulty in agreeing on the significance of the Santo Domingo revolt as critics have today agreeing on the meaning of "Benito Cereno." For Southerners it was a reminder that to indulge in the lax discipline and naive trust in blacks that Melville reports on board the *San Dominick* was to encourage rebellion producing violence worse than that used to maintain slavery. For them, the Santo Domingo rebellion demonstrated the necessity to hold slaves in heavier bonds. For others, however, it proved the folly of trying to hold people in bondage. In his circuit court opinion in the *Antelope* case, Justice William Johnson argues that the lesson learned from Santo Domingo had more to do with Britain's abolition of the slave trade than with moral arguments. At first, Johnson claims, "British policy struggled against the effort to abolish it, and all the efforts of the Quakers, the Methodists and Mr. Wilberforce proved abortive until the horrors acted in St. Domingo opened the eyes of Government to consequences that it became political to guard against. From that time, philanthropy, like the pent up vapor, began freely to diffuse itself, and extended its spread even to the British Court of Admiralty."[24]

There was yet a third lesson to be learned from Santo Domingo. Antislavery defenders of rule by law could agree that the rebellion was the logical result of the evils of slavery. For instance, in his 1822 circuit court opinion on the slaver *La Jeune Eugenie,* Justice Story had offered an indictment of the slave trade that anticipates what some liberal critics argue is the lesson of "Benito Cereno."

> It breaks down all the ties of parent, and children. . . . It manacles the inoffensive females and starving infants. It forces the brave to untimely death in defense of their humble homes. . . . It stirs up the worst passions of the human soul, darkening the spirit of revenge, sharpening the greediness of avarice, brutalizing the selfish, envenoming the cruel, famishing the weak, and crushing to death the broken-hearted.[25]

People like Story could believe that slavery caused such evils, yet for them the violence of an event like Santo Domingo once again proved the necessity for maintaining rule by law. The abolition of slavery had to be accomplished in an orderly and legal fashion.

The historical complexity of Melville's allusions to Santo Domingo is supplemented by the use of Christopher Colon for the ship's figurehead. As H. Bruce Franklin notes, shortly after Columbus "discovered" Santo Domingo, Charles V turned the island into the New World's first site of large-scale black slavery.[26] Interweaving mention of Charles V with references to friars, monasteries, and Muhammedans, Melville adds further allusions to the origins of the African slave trade. According to George Bancroft, the history of African enslavement had to be understood in the context of the ancient Islamic–Christian conflict that finally ended with the Spanish triumph over the Moors in Granada, the same year Columbus set sail for America. The Moors, relocated in northern Africa, remained the object of Christian hatred. According to Bancroft, that hatred extended to all the people of Africa. Africans were doomed to bondage, because all Africans were considered Moors. The man who convinced Charles V to legalize the African slave trade was the Dominican priest Bartholomew de Las Casas. Thus Melville, in choosing *San Dominick* as the slave ship's name, mixes allusions to both Santo Domingo and the Dominican order. When Delano first sights the ship, it "appeared like a whitewashed monastery," with "dark moving figures" aboard "as of Black Friars pacing the cloisters" (240). (Black Friars are Dominicans.) The last scene of the story, Babo's execution, takes place in a plaza fronted by the Church of Saint Bartholomew, a name that suggests Bartholomew de Las Casas, the Saint Bartholomew Day massacres, and Bartholomew Barlo, the Spaniard whom Captain Delano has to restrain from stabbing a shackled black after whites had recaptured the ship.[27]

Within the context of the Islamic–Christian conflict, Bartholomew's action shows the deep historical roots of the cycle of repression, rebellion, and repression enacted on board the *San Dominick*. When Bar-

tholomew Barlo is freed from enslavement, he turns the cruelty he suffered onto the reenslaved African, just as Christians led by Bartholomew
de Las Casas advocated enslaving the dark Moors who had so long
dominated Christians on the Iberian peninsula.

Seeing the African slave trade in the context of the Islamic–Christian
conflict also contributes historical resonance to Melville's implied comparison between Babo and Iago. In the first scene of *Othello,* Iago, who
serves the black Moor, complains of the "curse of service" but concludes, "Why, there's no remedy." Asked why he continues to serve
Othello, he responds, "I follow him to serve my turn upon him. / We
cannot all be masters, nor all masters / Cannot be truly followed."[28] In
"Benito Cereno," the Iago-like servant is himself a black who serves his
turn on his white master. The cycle of repression is reenacted.

When Captain Delano prevents Bartholomew Barlo from performing
his resentful act of revenge upon the slave who had enslaved him, the
American seems to break the cycle of repression. Thus Melville's allusions would seem to confirm American claims that the historical role of
the United States was to offer an alternative to the Old World's repetition of hereditary wrongs. Unfortunately, the story's action suggests the
opposite. Although Delano seems to break the cycle of repression, he
actually perpetuates it, although in a new form.

For anyone who considers the United States a progressive country, there
is a certain irony in a plot in which Captain Delano, a representative of
the democratic United States, returns Africans to slavery after they have
achieved freedom from Benito Cereno, a representative of the decaying,
feudal power of Spain. Read as a political allegory, the story marks the
emergence of the United States to its role as the new, more effective,
imperialistic power. The moment of ascendancy occurs in the boat de-
parting from the *San Dominick* when Captain Delano uses his hand to
hold down Benito Cereno while simultaneously, with his foot, holding
down Babo, who is "snakishly writhing up from the boat's bottom"
(295), which recalls the symbolic stern piece, the story's emblem for
exploitation.

Occurring in 1799, the slave rebellion on Santo Domingo was linked
to the revolutionary spirit set ablaze by the French Revolution ten years
earlier. The tearing down of the Bastille had represented the destruction
of the feudal order in Europe and along with it the end of feudal institutions such as slavery and of feudal conflicts such as those between Christians and Moors. Old forms of authority sanctified by the Church were
to give way to republican forms of authority sanctified by the rule of
law. Nowhere was there more hope for the new mode of governing than
the United States, which had launched the age of revolution by declaring

its independence from Britain. But, as Melville's story suggests and people like John Quincy Adams pointed out, the new religion of the law in America continued to perpetrate the age-old institution of slavery, even while the Old World made slavery illegal.[29] Despite its policy on slavery – or perhaps partially because of it – the United States continued to progress as a world power.[30]

Melville's story even suggests one motive behind the rise of the United States to power. Boarding the ship to put down the black insurrection, the sailors of the *Bachelor's Delight* are spurred on by a promise that they will be economically rewarded, since Benito has declared the cargo lost and for their taking. One of the most valuable cargoes on ship is, of course, human beings. Thus, although they mistakenly kill two of the remaining Spanish crew members, the Americans take great care not to "kill or maim the negroes" (298).

When Captain Delano first sights the *San Dominick* he fears that the ship is "of a piratical character." Later he thinks of the Africans' uprising as a "ferocious piratical revolt" (295). In the *Amistad* case, the Spanish government had tried to get the court to rule that in seizing the ship the Africans had acted as pirates. Such a ruling would have allowed the Spanish to invoke a treaty with the United States in order to regain their lost cargo. Justice Story refused to so rule. In fact, in his earlier circuit court opinion in *La Jeune Eugenie* he had ruled that all slave ships were pirates. In its *Antelope* decision, however, the Supreme Court refused to uphold Story's ruling. In "Benito Cereno" neither the possibly piratical practice of the slaver nor the possibly piratical revolt of the Africans is successful. Instead, the victors turn out to be the Americans who seize control of the slaver and its cargo.

Melville suggests the piratical nature of the Americans' takeover by changing the name of the ship ruled by the historical Captain Delano from the *Perservance* to the *Bachelor's Delight,* the name of buccaneer William Ambrose Cowley's ship. He also tells us that the leader of the attack had been a "privateer's-man" (297). Of course, a privateer is not exactly a pirate. Carrying the commission of a sovereign power, a privateer was free to commit piratelike acts during a time of war. While Melville was writing "Benito Cereno," Western powers debated the status of privateers. On April 16, 1856, (after "Benito Cereno" was published) the Declaration of Paris abolished privateering. The United States, however, did not sign the declaration because the agreement did not include a provision exempting private property at sea from seizure by public armed cruisers as well as privateers. The government's official argument was that it was too difficult to distinguish volunteer warships from privateers, but very likely it was also concerned about the seizure of transported slaves by foreign powers. Both these concerns remind us how much the actions of the crew of the *Bachelor's Delight* resemble the acts of pirates. If Judge Story's legal identification of slavers as pirates had stood, when Melville wrote his story actions like the Americans' would have been considered aiding and abetting pirates. As it was, even though their taking of the ship is piratelike, since it was legitimized by the law it would not have been deemed piratical. And even if the courts had declared it piracy, we cannot be sure of the outcome. The slavery issue caused so much tension that at times it split the executive and judicial branches of the American government. Each administration until Lincoln's tried to find a way to compensate the Spaniards for the freed Africans on the *Amistad,* thus blatantly ignoring the law of the land as established by Story's decision.[31]

In his circuit court decision in the *Antelope* case, Justice Johnson declared, "That slavery is a natural evil no one will deny except him [he] who would maintain that national wealth is the supreme national good."[32] As slavery remained in force, more and more people complained that national wealth had become the supreme national good. Rather than control greed and encourage the flourishing of higher principles, the country's legal system legitimized an exploitative system that allowed some to increase their wealth. Considerations of economic value seemed to outweigh considerations of moral value. For instance, according to Conscience Whigs, the Fugitive Slave Act of 1850 was the product of an affiliation of the cotton spinners of the North and the cotton producers of the South, or, as Charles Sumner put it, "the lords of the loom and the lords of the lash."[33] In the name of national unity and of loyalty to the Constitution, Boston Cotton Whigs protected their financial interests. Indeed, some members of the Boston merchant class in the 1840s and 1850s were outright supporters of the South and its "peculiar institution."

That Judge Shaw's decisions upholding the fugitive slave laws aided the commercial interests of Boston merchants was readily noticed by his critics. After Shaw's *Latimer* decision, one abolitionist accused Shaw of being as morally reprehensible as a "slave pirate of the African coast." Probably more accurate, Richard Henry Dana wrote in his journal, after the *Shadrach* case, that Shaw's conduct "shows how deeply seated, so as to affect, unconsciously I doubt not, good men like him, is this selfish hunkerism of the property interest on the slave question."[34] Similarly, Captain Delano, a good, honest man serving on a merchant ship, aids – unconsciously, I do not doubt – in the exploitation of human beings for commercial reasons, thereby helping to make the new democracy of the United States, as exploitative as the feudal system it replaced. The exploitative power of the United States promises to be more difficult to unmask than even that of the cunning Babo, since it is disguised by the benevolence, goodwill, and spirit of equality embodied by Captain Delano.

Through his father-in-law Lemual Shaw, Melville would have known at firsthand how a man with as much benevolence, goodwill, and spirit of equality as Delano could contribute to exploitation while maintaining the law in the name of justice. Commenting on Shaw's stand on the fugitive slave laws, Benjamin Thomas remarked that Shaw was "so simple, honest, upright, and straightforward, it never occurred to him there was any way around, over, under, or through the barrier of the Constitution."[35] To be sure, it would be too crude to identify Judge Shaw with Captain Delano. Nonetheless, it is important to remember that these two good, fairminded men from Massachusetts both return to slavery blacks who had achieved freedom. In both cases, they are merely upholding existing laws. The final paragraph of "Benito Cereno" makes poignantly clear what kind of actions the authority of the law can legitimize.

Certainly, one of the most heinous acts that Babo commits is using Aranda's decaying body as the *San Dominick's* figurehead. But that act of violence is no worse than the one committed against Babo during his execution. "Dragged to the gibbet at the tail of a mule, the black met his voiceless end. The body was burned to ashes; but for many days, the head, that hive of subtlety, fixed on a pole in the Plaza, met, unabashed, the gaze of the whites" (315). Babo's bleached skull, like the bleached bones of Aranda, had been put on display to ensure obedience. The law, it seems, has the power to sanction an act that outside the law is censured as inhuman. Violence is justified when backed by the authority of the law, condemned as brutal and satanic when not.[36] Rule by law, supposedly the only safeguard against the irrationality of violence, depends upon violence or the threat of violence to maintain itself, whether it be the suppression of the Africans' revolt or the armed enforcement, by three hundred men, of Sims's return to slavery.

Through such details, Melville's story undercuts the authority of both points of view presented by the story: the personal and the legal. The effect of this undercutting would seem to be to invite us to read the story from a point of view not contained within its pages. That alternative perspective, it could be argued, of necessity goes beyond and challenges the two presented in the story. The problem with this argument is that not all readers construct an alternative perspective. Because Melville formulates no alternative himself, he allows readers either sharing Delano's prejudices or believing in the objectivity of legal documents to accept the version of the story closest to their perspective.[37] Even readers holding neither view can argue that because the alternative, antislavery point of view is not explicitly supplied by the story, it cannot be attributed to it. In fact, if readers insist on locating a point of view *within* the story, they can only conclude that Melville presented a story from a proslavery perspective. Although one reader can argue that it is precisely through presenting proslavery prejudices that Melville undercuts them, another can argue that Melville's technique reinforces them. Ultimately, then, "Benito Cereno" subverts its own power of subversion. Readers who see the text undercutting the proslavery perspectives within it cannot propose their antislavery perspective as an impartial and complete account of the text, because their perspective is based on an absence.

It comes as no surprise, then, that a major part of the critical controversy over "Benito Cereno" concerns Babo, the one major character whose opinion we never hear. Reacting to readings that turn Melville into a racist for portraying a black capable of such evil, critics have tried to fill the gap within the text by claiming that the story's ultimate point of view is the one absent from its pages. Indeed, when they tell the story from Babo's point of view, they eliminate the ambiguity of the story by turning it into an antislavery tract.[38] Forced into violence by oppressive conditions, Babo becomes a heroic rebel, Melville's counterpart to Frederick Douglass's Madison Washington, a character modeled on the leader of the slave uprising on the *Creole*. The problem with this reading is that it is precisely Babo's point of view that Melville does not offer. Instead, we are presented with Babo's mysterious silence.

Confronted by Babo's Iago-like silence, liberal critics, less sympathetic to violence as a way to right wrongs, cannot ignore Babo's capacity for evil. Nor can they ignore the evil perpetrated by the whites. Thus they try to reconcile the opposite interpretations of Babo. The point of the story for them is that all humans are potentially depraved. "'Snakishly writhing up' from the bottom of Delano's boat, [Babo] is far more than a homicidal black: he is the devilish symbol of *all* the depravity – black, white, male, and female – to be found aboard the *San Dominick*."[39]

I do not want to deny Melville's insight into the potential evil in all of us, but this attempt to reconcile critical differences about the story by universalizing its theme overlooks an important point that other critics recognize. Babo is black. Although it makes no more sense to argue that Babo's depravity proves that blacks alone are depraved than to argue that Iago's depravity proves that whites alone are depraved, it does make sense to point out that all of the blacks on the *San Dominick* follow Babo's lead and rebel. At the historical moment when Melville wrote his story, to make a black man a symbol of depravity is not a neutral act. It is the "negro" who casts a shadow over Benito at the end of the book, not humanity, and the shadow that Babo casts over Benito makes it even harder to discern Babo's dark meaning because that shadow reduces to silence the only character in the story capable of understanding him.

Babo's and Benito's silences give rise to yet another school of interpretation. Abandoning the task of trying to decide whether Melville is sympathetic toward Babo, critics of this school see Melville's silence as his comment on Babo. I tend to agree with this reading, but unlike those who are content to conclude that Melville's silence indicates that the story is about undecidability, I have tried to argue that the text's silences and ambiguities can be explained in terms of the historical contradictions that slavery presented to sympathetic whites such as Melville and Shaw.

The simplest explanation of Babo's silence is to see it in terms of the silencing of blacks throughout antebellum America. Not only were blacks generally repressed: The Fugitive Slave Act of 1850 specifically refused to permit testimony of accused slaves in proceedings against them.[40] But to see Babo's silence merely as Melville's comment on the silencing of blacks in American society would be far too simple. Psychological critics who see Babo as a frightening product of Melville's psyche, a character whose Iago-like silence indicates Melville's inability to comprehend him, are not irresponsibly imposing their own reading onto the text. Babo was indeed frightening to a white audience – and Babo was indeed created by Melville's imagination, an essential part of his imaginary narrative treating the complexity of the slavery issue.

But if Babo is part of Melville's imagined resolution, Melville's resolution is no resolution. Although rule by law seems to have settled all questions about the events aboard the *San Dominick* and transformed its violent chaos into rational order by eliminating Babo, Babo continues to cast a shadow over the world of the book, just as hints throughout the text continue to cast doubt on the accuracy of the legal deposition. As a true representative of the repressed, Babo cannot be contained.[41] He marks the return of the repressed not only in Freud's psychological sense but also in the political sense. At the same time that he is the embodiment of the dark, irrational forces repressed by Melville's psyche, forces that in the culture at large only the legal system seems able to control, he is also the repressed black, who, denied voice by that very legal system, has no way to speak but through violence. He is a figure whom Melville, in treating slavery, must represent, but for whom, as the alien other, Melville can provide no voice.

5

A Sentimental Journey: Escape from Bondage in *Uncle Tom's Cabin*

In representing Babo but not presenting his point of view, Melville's text reinforces Babo's existence as "other," denying Melville's contemporary white audience direct sympathy with him. In this respect "Benito Cereno" is in direct contrast to the period's most influential work of fiction dealing with slavery – *Uncle Tom's Cabin.* Harriet Beecher Stowe's work is designed to conflate the interests of white readers and black slaves. In her preface she writes, "The object of these sketches is to awaken sympathy and feeling for the African race, as they exist among us; to show their wrongs and sorrows, under a system so necessarily cruel and unjust as to defeat and do away the good effects of all that can be attempted for them, by their friends, under it."[1]

To awaken that sympathy, Stowe imagined a black character not as other, but self-consciously created in the image of the white man's spiritual leader and most celebrated victim – Christ. Because Uncle Tom's nobility lies in his strength as a victim, he has been subject to criticism from some twentieth-century blacks, who identify his passivity as too close to a white wish-fulfillment of how blacks should respond to their subservient position.[2] Unlike Babo, Tom seems to pose no threat to the order that exploits him. Critics have even read Babo as Melville's response to Stowe, who speaks of the "gentleness" of the Negro race, "their lowly docility of heart, their aptitude to repose on a superior mind and rest on a higher power, their childish simplicity of affection, and facility of forgiveness" (*UTC* 178).[3] Nonetheless, when we compare the effect of Melville's story with that of *Uncle Tom's Cabin,* an irony immediately comes to mind. Melville's story, which anticipates that the slavery issue could be resolved only by violence, had no effect in bringing about the war that finally freed the slaves. On the contrary, many feel that Stowe's novel, which celebrates Tom's nonviolence, raised enough consciousnesses on the slavery issue to help hasten the violence of civil war. The response to slavery in *Uncle Tom's Cabin* helps us better understand the ambiguities of Melville's portrayal of a slave rebellion in "Benito Cereno." It also shows how intricately the writer's response to slavery is interwoven with her entire social vision.

Because of the effect it had on the slavery issue, Stowe's book has been the subject of much criticism that tries to determine how accurately she portrays slavery and blacks.[4] From the start, the outraged response of many Southerners was to harp on what they regarded as Stowe's inaccuracies and falsehoods. Stowe defended the accuracy of her portrayal of "Life Among The Lowly" by publishing *A Key to Uncle Tom's Cabin*, documenting the historical occurrence of incidents similar to those in her fiction. Whatever the merits of Stowe's claim, her primary concern was not to represent the norm of southern life under slavery. She does not imply that Tom's fate was typical. She wanted to show that such horrible acts *could* occur and be supported by existing slave laws. For her, the slave code itself was an inexcusable evil.

In almost the middle of the book, Augustine St. Clare, the southern plantation owner who hates slavery, explains his hatred to his New England cousin Miss Ophelia. Calling it a "cursed business" that "comes from the devil," St. Clare cries out,

> "I defy anybody on earth to read our slave-code, as it stands in our law-books, and make anything else of it. Talk of the *abuses* of slavery! Humbug! The *thing itself* is the essence of all abuse! And the only reason why the land don't sink under it, like Sodom and Gommorrah, is because it is *used* in a way infinitely better than it is. For pity's sake, for shame's sake, because we are men born of women, and not savage beasts, many of us do not and are not, – we would *scorn* to use the full power which our savage laws put into our hands. And he who goes the furthest, and does the worst, only uses within limits the power that the law gives him." (*UTC* 221)

At this point in the book Stowe has shown evils in the slavery system, but they have been balanced to some extent by the kindness of slave owners like St. Clare, who care for Uncle Tom. By the novel's end, however, she exposes Tom to the full extent of what is allowed under the law. When St. Clare dies, Tom is left to be disposed of as part of St. Clare's estate. Stowe writes,

> We hear often of the distress of negro servants, on the loss of a kind master; and with good reason, for no creature on God's earth is left more utterly unprotected and desolate than the slaves in these circumstances.
>
> The child who has lost a father has still the protection of friends, and of the law; he is something, and can do something, – has acknowledged rights and position; the slave has none. The law regards him, in every respect, as devoid of rights as a bale of merchandise. (*UTC* 317)

Tom is sold to Simon Legree, who carries the logic of the slave code to its cruel extreme.

Stowe's portrayal of the inhumanity of the slave code can be better understood in light of Mark Tushnett's recent study, *The American Law of Slavery*. Tushnett is at pains to argue against a simple reflection model of the law that scholars such as Stanley Elkins have used to explain southern slave law. For Elkins, slave law merely reflected the interests of those who ruled southern society. He explained the southern slave law by the lack of any opposition to capitalism in the southern economy, such as there was, for example, in Latin America, where the Church opposed capitalism and thus affected the development of slave codes. For Tushnett, the reflection model is too simple. Drawing on the work of Eugene Genovese, he points out that the situation in southern slave society was not one of unopposed capitalism; the very logic of slavery is opposed to capitalism. Capitalist society conceives of social relations in individualistic terms. Rule of law defines a sphere of individual autonomy into which intrusions, whether by the state or other people, are prohibited. In contrast, slave society sees social relationships organically. Workers in capitalist society hire out their labor for a set amount of time, leaving the rest of the day "their own." Theoretically, the employer has no control over – or concern with – those hours of freedom. Slaves do not hire out a part of their lives. Instead, their entire lives are under the control – and care – of the slave owner. In this way, capitalist social relations are partial, slave relations total. So, although the South was in many respects a capitalist society, it also had remnants of a precapitalist mode of production and social structure. Social relations on the plantation were conceived in almost feudal terms, whereas social relations in the market were essentially those of a capitalist society.[5]

For Tushnett, these different social relations set up an opposition between sentiment and law as forces of regulation. The difficult task for the American law of slavery was "to draw a sharp line between regulation of the institution according to law, appropriate in market settings, and regulation according to sentiment, appropriate on the plantation." Thus, cases between master and master, dealing in the market for slaves, were regulated by the law, as any other trade would be. But in cases involving master and slave, living together in the master's domain, the law limited its regulatory power, leaving control to the paternal care of the owner, implicit in the master–slave relationship. In the cases he studies, Tushnett finds that the law–sentiment opposition parallels other oppositions enacted in the court's rhetoric. They are as follows:[6]

Law	Sentiment
Market relations	Slave relations
Duty	Feeling
Magistrate	Man

Tushnett's analysis offers a corrective to some of the abstract statements that Stowe lets her characters make about slavery. These statements indicate that Stowe agrees with Elkins's reflection model. For instance, she has St. Clare explain slavery simply in terms of the vested interests of "planters, who have money to make by it, – clergymen, who have planters to please, – politicians, who want to rule by it" (221). Slavery would seem merely to reflect the interests of the planters and their desire for profit.

Yet Stowe's dramatic portrayal of slave relations indicates how strongly she sensed the influence of sentiment as a regulatory force. What Stowe, a believer in sentiment, had to do in *Uncle Tom's Cabin* was to appeal to the sentiment of her readership by showing that slavery was such an evil that even sentiment, with all its influence, could not control the inhumanity of southern slave law. At the same time, she had to reconfirm the power of sentiment to do something about that state of affairs. Thus Stowe's presentation of slavery not only tells us something about a literary response to slavery quite different from Melville's; it also prepares us for a discussion of how Melville differs from writers of sentimental fiction and how those writers responded to the legal system.

To understand the opposition between law and sentiment in the South, we can turn to George Fitzhugh's work, the most sustained and consistent defense of slavery of the time. Few Southerners were as extreme in their defense of slavery as Fitzhugh, but the extremity of his position is useful in explaining the role of sentiment in the South.

Some Southerners defended slavery as necessary because of the peculiar conditions of the South; Fitzhugh argued that it was simply a better system of governance than any other. Defending slavery in terms of social relations, not profit, Fitzhugh found his model for society in the patriarchal household economy of precapitalist Europe. In the household economy, the family extended to include servants and a certain number of dependent laborers. The head of the household had absolute sovereignty over all members of the family. In return for their subjection to the rule of the father, all members of the family received his paternal protection.

> Wife and children, although not free, are relieved from care and anxiety, supported and protected, and their situation is as happy and desirable as that of the husband and parent. In this we see the doings of a wise and just God. The slave, too, when the night comes, may lie down in peace. He has a master to watch over and take care of him. . . . Here, again, we see harmonious relations, consistent with the wisdom and mercy of God.[7]

The patriarch does not govern selfishly. Because of the organic relationship among family members, the father's interests are inseparable from his family's. "His feelings and affections, as well as his interests, are so blended and interwoven with theirs, that whatever affects them, beneficially or injuriously, in like manner affects him. He is the natural head or ruler of his family, and their natural and faithful representative." In such a social structure, behavior is controlled not by law but by the sentiment that naturally develops from the interdependence of everyone's interests. "The mass of mankind cannot be governed by LAW. More of despotic discretion, and less of LAW, is what the world wants. . . . THERE IS TOO MUCH OF LAW AND TOO LITTLE OF GOVERNMENT IN THIS WORLD." Turning Thomas Jefferson's declaration of natural and inalienable rights on its head, Fitzhugh declared that "about nineteen out of every twenty individuals have 'a natural and inalienable right' to be taken care of and protected, to have guardians, trustees, husbands, or masters; in other words, they have a natural and inalienable right to be slaves."[8]

Fitzhugh's attack on Lockean notions of individual rights and on the doctrine of the supremacy of the law shows how incompatible any consistent defense of slavery was with the legal system accompanying the rise of capitalism. Capitalism replaced the traditional patriarchal relations between master and servant with contractual relations between free and independent citizens. Unlike many southern apologists for slavery, Fitzhugh saw this distinction clearly and saw free trade itself as a threat to slavery. Slavery could not serve capitalism because capitalism would ultimately destroy the set of social relationships necessary to maintain a slave society. "Its fundamental maxims, *Laissez-faire* and 'Pas trop gouverner,' are at war with all kinds of slavery, for they in fact assert that individuals and peoples prosper most when governed least."[9]

The problem with Fitzhugh's logic is that the South did not exist in feudal times, although its particular brand of romanticism, exalting Sir Walter Scott and chivalry, reveals how compatible its self-image was with an idealized version of the Middle Ages. But even Scott dealt with the impingement of capitalism and its code of law onto a feudal society. As Tushnett argues, the coexistence of the cult of sentiment and the code of law caused inevitable conflicts in judges' attempts to decide cases concerning slaves. One of the most important cases illustrating this conflict is *State v. Mann* (1829). In *A Key to Uncle Tom's Cabin,* Stowe treats *State v. Mann* at length. It is the case that, for her, best answers the question posed in her section "What Is Slavery?"[10]

State v. Mann arose when a woman hired her slave Lydia to John Mann for a year. Lydia committed a small offense, for which she was chastised. Lydia ran off, and Mann called for her to stop. When she did not, he shot and wounded her. Mann was charged with assault and battery. The jury, finding Mann's punishment "cruel and unwarrantable, and disproportionate to the offense committed by the slave," convicted him because he had only a "special property in the slave" (*Key* 77). Mann appealed, and the North Carolina Supreme Court reversed the lower court's verdict.

Judge Thomas Ruffin's opinion needs careful scrutiny. He begins with a lament that the courts must rule on such cases. He then describes the struggle "in the judge's own breast, between the feelings of the man and the duty of the magistrate" (*Key* 77). Nonetheless, he adds, it is useless to "complain of things inherent in our political state. And it is criminal in a Court to avoid any responsibility which the laws impose" (77). Robert Cover argues that Ruffin's language reveals a struggle between his private antislavery feelings and his duty to follow the law. But, as Tushnett remarks, "Judge Ruffin's problem was not that of an antislavery judge enforcing proslavery law; it was that of a proslavery judge looking into the heart of the law of slavery, and doing so unflinchingly despite what he saw there."[11]

He saw that, as far as the law was concerned, Fitzhugh's analogy comparing the slave to the child did not hold. "The difference is that which exists between freedom and slavery; and a greater cannot be imagined" (*Key* 78). The child is born to equal rights with the governor. If moral instruction fails to make a free individual act properly, "It is better to leave the party to his own headstrong passions and the ultimate correction of the law than to allow it to be immoderately inflicted by a private person" (78). Slavery is completely different. His description of slavery deserves lengthy quotation.

> The end is the profit of the master, his security and the public safety; the subject, one doomed, in his own person and his posterity, to live without knowledge, and without the capacity to make anything his own, and to toil that another may reap the fruits. What moral considerations shall be addressed to such a being, to convince him what it is impossible but that the most stupid must feel and know can never be true, – that he is thus to labor upon a principle of natural duty, or for the sake of his own personal happiness? Such services can only be expected from one who has no will of his own; who surrenders his will in implicit obedience to that of another. Such obedience is the consequence only of uncontrolled authority over the body. There is nothing else which can operate to produce the effect. THE POWER OF THE MASTER MUST BE ABSOLUTE, TO RENDER THE SUBMISSION OF THE SLAVE PERFECT. I most freely confess my sense of the harshness of this proposition; I feel it as deeply as any man can. And, as a principal of moral right, every person in his retirement must repudiate it. But, in the actual condition of things, it must be so. There is no remedy. This discipline belongs to the state of slavery. They cannot be disunited without abrogating at once the rights of the master, and absolving the slave from his subjection. It constitutes the curse of slavery to both the bond and free portion of our population. But it is *inherent in the relation* of master and slave. (78: Emphasis added by Stowe.)

For slavery to function, in the eyes of the law the power of the master must be absolute. But the voice of the law does not stop with that chilling pronouncement. In a passage that Stowe does not cite, Ruffin goes on to express pleasure that fewer and fewer cases like *Mann* come to the courts.

> The protections already afforded by several statutes, that all-powerful motive, the private interest of the owner, the benevolences towards each other, seated in the hearts of those who have been born and bred together, the frowns and deep execrations of the community upon the barbarian who is guilty of excessive and brutal cruelty to his unprotected slave, all combined, have produced a mildness of treatment and attention to the comforts of the unfortunate class of slaves, greatly mitigating the rigors of servitude and ameliorating the condition of the slaves.

Imagining a time when the harsh slave code can be relaxed, Ruffin is quick to warn that improvements will not be brought about by

> any rash expositions of abstract truths by a judiciary trained with a false and fanatical philanthropy, seeking to redress an acknowledged evil by means still more wicked and appalling than that evil.

For Ruffin, there are controls to cruelty in slave society; they simply do not fall under the province of the law, unless the legislatures see fit to enact them. As far as the courts are concerned, sentiment alone must remain the check on cruelty.[12]

Discussing Ruffin's decision, in *A Key to Uncle Tom's Cabin,* Stowe does not condemn him. She even admires him for his "fine and clear" expression, "so dignified and solemn in its earnestness" (78). Ruffin has "one of that high order of minds which looks straight to the heart of every subject which it encounters. He has, too, that noble scorn of dissimulation, that straightforward determination not to call a bad thing by a good name, even when most popular, and reputable, and logical. . . . There is but one sole regret; and that is, that such a man, with such a mind, should have been merely an *expositor,* and not a *reformer* of law" (78–9, emphasis in original). If Stowe feels "deep respect for the man," that respect makes her feel even more "horror for the system" (78). One of the worst crimes of slavery is that "like Judge Ruffin, men of honor, men of humanity, men of kindest and gentlest feelings, are *obliged* to interpret these severe laws with inflexible severity" (71, emphasis in original).

Stowe does not deny the existence of sentimental controls in the South, but she wants to show how they must be subordinated to the logic of slave law. In the first chapter of *Uncle Tom's Cabin* she writes,

> Whoever visits some estates there, and witnesses the good-humored indulgence of some masters and mistresses, and the affectionate loyalty of some slaves, might be tempted to dream the oft-fabled poetic legend of a patriarchal institution, and all that; but over and above the scene

there broods a portentous shadow – the shadow of law. So long as the law considers all these human beings, with beating hearts and living affections, only as so many things belonging to a master, – so long as the failure, or misfortune, or imprudence, or death of the kindest owner, may cause them any day to exchange a life of kind protection and indulgence for one of hopeless misery and toil, – so long it is impossible to make anything beautiful or desirable in the best-regulated administration of slavery. (*UTC* 8)

In the very next scene she shows how the unfeeling logic of the law and the market overwhelms the sentiment that derives from and holds together social bonds. Speculating "largely and quite loosely" (*UTC* 8), Tom's kind owner finds himself in debt to a slave trader. Forced by the laws of the market to come up with money, Mr. Shelby sells his most faithful slave. Whereas defenders of slavery argued that a slave society fosters a cohesive set of social relations, Stowe is at pains to illustrate that so long as the law considers a human being a commodity, the calculating world of the market will destroy any sentimental bonds between slave and owner and between slave and slave. The unsympathetic, almost inhumane, slave trader who separates husband from wife, mother from child, merely carries out the logic of this system. If St. Clare argues that slave owners do not use all the power granted to them by law because they are "men born of women" (221), Stowe's worst villain, Simon Legree, tries to deny the bond of even his mother's love.

As a southern reviewer noted, Legree's denial of sentimental bonds is appropriate because he is from the North.[13] His ruthlessness reminds us that Stowe criticized the North as well as the South. Written partially in response to the Fugitive Slave Act, the first serial installment of *Uncle Tom's Cabin* was printed shortly after the *Sims* case was tried. Stowe's sister-in-law had written to her in 1850, "If I could use a pen as you can, I would write something that would make this whole nation feel what an accursed thing slavery is."[14] In fact, Stowe's book is directed most powerfully at a northern audience, more specifically a northern, middle-class, Christian, predominantly female audience. She continually draws attention to how, despite the values of her audience, the North helps to perpetuate the slavery system. Imagining a response to her slave trader, she writes,

> "He's a shocking creature, isn't he, – this trader? so unfeeling! It's dreadful, really!"
>
> "O, but nobody thinks anything of these traders! They are universally despised, – never received into any decent society."
>
> But who, sir, makes the trader? Who is most to blame? The enlightened, cultivated, intelligent man, who supports the system of which the trader is the inevitable result, or the poor trader himself? You make the public sentiment that calls for this trade, that debauches and

depraves him, till he feels no shame in it; and in what are you better than he?

Are you educated and he ignorant, you high and he low, you refined and he coarse, you talented and he simple?

In the day of a future Judgment, these very considerations may make it more tolerable for him than for you. (130)

When Tom is put up for sale in the New Orleans market, a mother and daughter are also for sale. Their owner is a New Yorker who acquired them when the son of their former owner squandered his mother's fortune and ended in debt to the "respectable firm of B & Co., in New York."

> Brother B., being, as we have said, a Christian man, and a resident in a free state, felt some uneasiness on the subject. He didn't like trading in slaves and souls of men, – of course he didn't; but, then, there were thirty thousand dollars in the case, and that was rather too much money to be lost for a principle; and so, after much considering, and asking advice from those that he knew would advise to suit him, Brother B. wrote to his lawyer to dispose of the business in the way that seemed to him the most suitable, and remit the proceeds.[15]

Uncompromisingly, Stowe demonstrates that if the slave trade is controlled by the logic of the market, Northerners are implicated because the market system extends beyond the Mason-Dixon line and even has its financial centers in the North. As a result, she implicates Northerners in what, for her, most poignantly dramatizes the evils of slavery – the breakup of black families. As one critic puts it, for Stowe the "family, not the Constitution, was depicted as threatened by slavery."[16] By showing how slavery threatened the family, Stowe effectively fulfills the purpose of her book, striking a sympathetic chord with an audience that shared her belief in the sacredness of domestic values. If slavery violates those values, it must be evil.

The success Stowe had in appealing to the family to elicit sympathy from her northern audience introduces a different way to look at the law–sentiment opposition formulated by Tushnett. Tushnett emphasizes the coexistence of two social structures in the South: the market and the plantation, one controlled by law, the other by sentiment, yet a similar coexistence of contradictory social structures occurred in the North: the market and the domestic economy of the home.

The oppositions that Tushnett sets up for the South can be repeated and extended in the North:

Law	Sentiment
Market relations	Domestic relations
Public	Private
Duty	Feeling

Magistrate   Man
Male   Female

Like the plantation economy, the domestic economy of northern (as well as southern) families was a residual element of an older mode of production within a capitalist economy. As the family lost its central role in production, it shifted in character from a kinship network held together by common tasks to a nuclear family united by sentiment. According to Eric Hobsbawn, "The structure of the bourgeois family flatly contradicted that of bourgeois society. Within it freedom, opportunity, the cash nexus and the pursuit of individual profit did not rule."[17] The family, like the plantation economy, was supposedly the realm where integrated rather than individualistic relations fostered sentimental bonds. Presided over by women, even though men had legal authority, it was the private realm where moral values and religion were taught. Increasingly, it defined itself against the calculating, rational, public world of business presided over by men.

In *Uncle Tom's Cabin* the conflict between these two spheres is shown most clearly in the conflict between Senator and Mrs. Bird. Senator Bird, retreating home for a "little comfort" from the "tiresome business" of legislating, is surprised to hear his wife ask him about "what was going on in the house of the state" (75–6). Usually Mrs. Bird does not worry about what goes on in the public world. "Her husband and children were her entire world, and in these she rules more by entreaty and persuasion than by command or argument. There was only one thing that was capable of arousing her, and that provocation came in on the side of her unusually gentle and sympathetic nature; – anything in the shape of cruelty would throw her into a passion" (76). This evening Mrs. Bird has been thrown into a passion because she has heard that the legislature has passed a law forbidding citizens of Ohio to help fugitive slaves. When she protests to her husband, he replies, "Your feelings are all quite right, dear, and interesting, and I love you for them; but, then, dear, we musn't suffer our feelings to run away with our judgment; you must consider it's not a matter of private feeling, – there are great public interests involved, – there is such a state of public agitation rising, that we must put aside our private feelings" (77). Immediately thereafter, Eliza arrives with her son Harry, having escaped across the river and needing shelter. Senator Bird, whose "heart is better than [his] head, in this case" (84), casts off his public role and lends his help.

Earlier I related the conflict between heart and head to class conflict. Stowe's work demonstrates the need to consider the conflict in terms of gender and race. In the North, as in the South, sentiment/feeling is associated with the organic social structures linked to residual modes of production, whereas law/reason is associated with the business realm. For Stowe those most capable of feeling are associated with organic social structures – slaves and women. Significantly, in *Uncle Tom's Cabin* the major instance in which the opposition between feeling women and rational men breaks down occurs in the South, with Augustine St. Clare and his wife. St. Clare, the sentimental plantation owner, lacks a practical business mind, whereas his wife is almost completely void of sentiment, other than for herself, which is not to say that she is practical. Although Stowe attributes Augustine's sentiment to the influence his mother had over him, it is also possible for a rich southern man to be more sentimental than a rich northern man, since the southern economic system allows some men to afford a life of leisure not influenced by immediate business concerns. The leisure, however, has a damaging influence. It contributes to Augustine's passivity and spoils his wife. Furthermore, Augustine's leisure is a luxury allowed because of the business sense of his brother Alfred, who manages the family estate with logical and inhumane efficiency. According to Augustine, when the brothers inherited their father's property Alfred "told me that I was a womanish sentimentalist, and would never do for business life; and advised me to take the bank-stock and the New Orleans family mansion, and go to writing poetry, and let him manage the plantation" (*UTC* 230).

In these terms, Stowe's privileging of feeling and sentiment over reason and law indicates her resistance to the emerging capitalist order and its accompanying social relations, much in the way that in Cooper's *Pioneers* our feelings sided with Natty against the rational economic regulation of Judge Temple's laws. As Max Weber argued, there is an integral relation between the rise of capitalism and rational legal forms of political authority. Capitalism needs the uniformity and predictability that a code of rational laws provides. At the same time, as Stowe saw as clearly as Fitzhugh, capitalism threatens the organic structure of traditional social relations. When the logic of the market prevails without the check of sentiment, families are separated, and human beings are turned into commodities. Fitzhugh, however, rejects capitalism completely, whereas Stowe envisions a capitalist society in which sentiment tempers the cold logic of the market. If in the South sentiment cannot protect slaves, in the North, sentiment, embodied in women, can humanize a potentially heartless set of laws.

Although capitalism benefited from the triumph of a legal, rational system of government, the change was experienced by many as the triumph of an irrational cataclysm. Human will was subordinated to the whims of a market, illogical and uncontrollable. Forces associated with controlling

the market were not understood and were given such names as the
"Monster Bank." Eliza, trying to explain why Mr. Shelby had to sell
Tom and her son, lapses into mysticism. The slave trader, she tells a
fellow slave, "has the power over him" (*UTC* 37).

Not trained in the logic of business or the law, women felt especially
helpless when confronted by the power of the market. That helplessness
underlies the action of a book that almost matched *Uncle Tom's Cabin* in
popularity – *The Wide, Wide World* by Susan B. Warner. The book opens
with Ellen Montgomery learning that her father has lost a lawsuit, and
with it much of his fortune. Lacking sufficient funds to allow his daughter
to travel abroad with him and her mother as they search for new sources of
income and a region where Mrs. Montgomery's health will improve, Mr.
Montgomery leaves Ellen behind in the care of her Aunt Fortune. The
lawsuit itself is never explained, and from Ellen's point of view, details are
unimportant. She has no desire to understand the laws and economic
forces that dictate her life. Her task is to learn to submit to their uncontrollable power and respond with proper Christian humility and obedience. In this sense, her fate bears striking resemblance to Uncle Tom's
and reminds us of the extent to which a woman's role is like a slave's. Like
Tom, Ellen is separated from her family because of economic forces. Like
Tom, she has no control over her destiny as she drifts from one circumstance to another, completely dependent upon the sentiment of those who
control her life. Like Tom, she reaches heroic stature through staying true
to the higher laws of God while submitting to earthly authority.[18]

Tom's similarity to a nineteenth-century heroine has been pointed out
by Elizabeth Ammons, who emphasizes the extent to which Stowe's
book is about white women in the North as well as about slaves in the
South.[19] Both slaves and white women occupy subservient positions in
society, and both are associated with residual organic modes of production that are ruled by the dominant, market economy. In opposition to
the business and legal logic of most white men, Stowe has slaves and
women offer feeling, sentiment, emotion, and, significantly, Christian
faith. From their Christianity they learn the moral virtues of hope, charity, mercy, self-sacrifice, and submission to mundane authority. But
there is, ultimately, an important difference. Northern women are not
slaves, and for Stowe this distinction is crucial. Women who are free and
white are not helpless. Thus, in *Uncle Tom's Cabin,* a male slave enacts
the typical plot of a submissive woman, whereas Stowe offers models of
active and influential women.

Men who are born of women are shaped by their mothers' moral
influence. Augustine St. Clare's close identification with his mother
makes him a kindly slave owner. Even Simon Legree, who tries to cast
off his maternal bond, is haunted by his mother. The feminine influence

on men is so great in Stowe's world that the bond of slavery itself cannot destroy it. Cassie, the slave with whom Legree lived, had "always kept over Legree the kind of influence that a strong, impassioned woman can ever keep over the most brutal man" (368). If a slave woman can influence Legree, certainly free women can influence their more kindly, sensitive husbands.

The influence that Stowe attributes to women is an important corrective to the image of the submissive woman perpetuated by a writer like Warner. Indeed, some women acted as Stowe describes them, but ultimately Stowe uses her art for more than mimetic purposes. Her most important purpose is exhortative. She calls women to action. She tells her female readers that, even confined to a domestic sphere and denied legal means to effect political change, they can, like Mrs. Bird, do something about slavery by influencing their husbands. Just as her portrayal of Uncle Tom shows not what usually happens to a slave but what might happen to a slave, so her portrayal of women shows not how women usually act but how they might act to eliminate the suffering that slavery necessitates. If the first is a negative possibility, the second is a positive one. The effect of her work on the public testifies to how many heeded her call to positive action. As a number of recent critics have noted, in rallying readers to action Stowe's narrative has profound and subversive political effects. Stowe may accept the standard antebellum definition of woman confined to the domestic sphere, but she also displays a "facility for converting essentially repressive concepts of femininity into a positive (and activist) alternative system of values in which woman figures not merely as the moral superior of man, his inspirer, but as the model for him in the new millennium about to dawn."[20]

My position, however, is somewhat different. Granting Stowe's ability to show how women can use to their advantage the popular nineteenth-century ideology about domesticity and femininity, I want to emphasize how much women paid in making subserviency the price of influence. By showing the influence that women could have while confined to their limited role, Stowe makes it easier for women to accept that role. Furthermore, since Stowe granted moral superiority to the feminine values associated with the domestic sphere, she had to be very cautious about social transformations that would break down the separation between public and private. If the calculating logic of the public sphere were allowed to intrude into the private sphere, there would be no space where proper value could be cultivated. Denied a separate "world of their own," women would have been denied a space in which they could exert their moral influence. Thus, after the war, when radical American feminists began attacking Christianity and domestic virtue for restricting women, Stowe launched a counterattack. In *My Wife and I* she

dismisses an article by a radical feminist as exceeding the "wildest principles of modern French communism. [The article] consisted of attacks
directed about equally against Christianity, marriage, the family state,
and all human laws and standing order, whatsoever."[21] According to
Dorothy Berkson, although Stowe had been "advocating the feminization of politics and culture to create a new society in which women's
influence would permeate the world of business and government and
elevate those male bastions to a finer, more Christian practice, the radical
suffragists seemed to her to be agitating for a masculinization of culture –
for a world in which family, marriage, and morals were to be discarded
in favor of self-indulgence, selfishness, greed and opportunism."[22] For
Stowe, to give up Christianity, marriage, and the family was to give up
any hope of reforming the world.

In Stowe's fiction, women are not incapable of handling the business
and legal matters associated with the public sphere. When Mr. Shelby
dies suddenly, Mrs. Shelby, with the aid of her son, "applied herself to
the work of straightening the entangled web of affairs" (*UTC* 413).
More efficient than her husband, she puts the estate in order. Women,
then, are capable of handling business affairs when necessary, but someone like Mrs. Bird would normally prefer to remain within her domestic
realm. "It was a very unusual thing for gentle little Mrs. Bird ever to
trouble her head with what was going on in the house of the state, very
wisely considering that she had enough to do to mind her own" (76).
Only when men mismanage business affairs or violate a Christian moral
code do women enter – quite competently and intelligently – the public
realm. Otherwise, they are content to mind their private homes because,
as Stowe and some of the most important men of the period proclaimed,
the business of the domestic economy was the highest and most sacred
duty in society.

The 1850 Phi Beta Kappa address at Harvard gives us a sense of how
well Stowe's image of woman corresponded with that of powerful
northern men. It was delivered by Timothy Walker, who, along with
Stowe, had been a member of the Semi-Colon Club in Cincinnati, one of
the most famous literary societies in the West.[23] Walker had been one of
Joseph Story's first pupils at Harvard and had organized the law school at
Cincinnati College. He had also compiled a series of lectures entitled the
Introduction to American Law that went through thirteen editions between
1837 and 1905, and he was editor of the *Western Law Journal*. In his
address, entitled "The Reform Spirit of the Day," Walker considers the
demands of women reformers. Noting approvingly that a woman's legal
rights were beginning to be acknowledged and protected, Walker nonetheless complains that not all women are "satisfied with the gradual

amelioration of their *legal condition*." Some "sigh for *political rights*." No longer content with their "influence as wives, mothers, sisters, daughters, authors, teachers and companions, – an influence every day increasing, and where the sphere is boundless," some "seek to be voters, legislators, governors, judges, and, for aught I know, generals and commodores." Walker admits that the "number of aspirants" is small, but he fears that it is likely to grow:

> For when we come to the question of abstract natural right, I am unable to find a reason for excluding the better half of the human race from the transcendent right of political equality, against their will. But the question of expediency is a very different one, and may safely be left to the taste of the refined portion of the sex. I think that, if there were no constitutional exclusion, they would instinctively exclude themselves. I do not believe they wish to be unsexed, and turned into Amazons, by the rude and coarse encounters of the barroom, the hustings, the stump, the caucus, or even the senate, as senates are now. Think you that Otway, if he had often seen women in these manly predicaments, could have pronounced upon that sex the splendid panegyric found in Venice Preserved!
>
> O woman! lovely woman! Nature made thee
> To temper man; we had been brutes without you!
> Angels are painted fair to look like you;
> There's in you all that we believe of heaven; –
> Amazing brightness, purity, and truth,
> Eternal joy, and everlasting love!
>
> No, no when true women can be such "ministering angels" in private and domestic life, – so heightening all mortal joys, and lessening all mortal sorrows, – there is no danger of their descending from this blessed sphere into the foul arena of politicians and demagogues.[24]

Insofar as Walker argues against woman suffrage, Stowe would have disagreed. She felt that granting women the vote would have an important effect on moral issues. Insofar as Walker extols the moral virtue of women and warns of the danger of women becoming unsexed, Stowe would have agreed. The right to vote would allow women to have a more direct influence on political matters, but the moral worth of that influence would be endangered if women compromised their values by abandoning the private sphere from which they could influence public issues. Within this sphere, influence, for both Walker and Stowe, is "boundless." Women, however, chose to flee it. Why? Because for some this territory was neither blessed nor vast.

Diane Polan, writing on the legal effects of the public–private split for women, notes that it justified the courts' reluctance to examine activities within the "private" realm of the family.

By placing the operation of law squarely in the public realm and, at least rhetorically, removing itself from the private realm of personal life and the family, the legal system created a distinction between a public realm of life, which is a proper arena for legal or social regulation, and another, fundamentally different, personal sphere, which is somehow outside the law's or society's authority to regulate. Thus the legal system has functioned to legitimate that very distinction by asserting it as a natural, rather than socially imposed, ground for different treatment.

This courtly reticence resembles the stance that southern courts adopted toward master–slave relations. In both cases law, in effect, decreed that sentiment should rule. The result, according to Polan, diverges from Stowe's idealized vision, for the law has licensed "men's exploitation of women within the family unit. In essence, by purportedly withdrawing itself from regulation of the private sphere, the legal system has lent its actual support to male supremacy by permitting men to completely dominate and control family life. Even today, it is difficult to get courts to intervene in domestic violence situations because of a supposed deference to the privacy of the family."[25]

Stowe's image of the family in which the wife rules "more by entreaty and persuasion than by command or argument" is as much an apology for the harmony of domestic relations as Southerners' depictions of genteel plantation life was for master–slave relations. A "haven in a heartless world," the family sheltered men but exploited women. Men could retreat to the family from the world of work, but much of women's work occurred within the domestic sphere. To be sure, confined to domesticity, women were shielded from direct contact with the public sphere, but they were not shielded from a set of laws and social relations that perpetuated patriarchal rule.

Patriarchal rule is further perpetuated if, as in *Uncle Tom's Cabin,* women have a tendency to eschew reason as a way to exert influence. To be sure, when the exercise of reason rationalizes the subjection of slaves it is understandable that reason is rejected. For instance, when Senator Bird offers to reason with his wife about the slave law, she responds, "I hate reasoning, John, – especially reasoning on such subjects" (78). But Mrs. Bird's hatred of reasoning reinforces the stereotype of women as sensitive, emotional creatures incapable of reasoning, a stereotype resulting in part from women's confinement to the domestic sphere. If, in the ideal marriage between head and heart, the domestic sphere is associated with the heart and if women are perceived as sentimental creatures, it is only natural that women's natural place remains the home. To escape such logic involves more than the rejection of reason. It also involves understanding why men have been granted the power of reasoning, whereas women have been limited to the influence of emotion.

Moving between the public and private spheres, men are not confined to either logic or sentiment. Senator Bird is full of feeling, but expresses it in the privacy of home. He reserves his strongest sentiment for his dead son. When Eliza asks Mrs. Bird, "Have you ever lost a child?" (81), Mr. Bird the senator becomes Mr. Bird the father and cries in sympathy for her plight.

Like Senator Bird, the most important Whig lawyers of Stowe's day were capable of profound sentiment. Joseph Story wrote sentimental poetry about his family, including a poem on his daughter's death and one imagining his wife meeting his daughter in heaven. The latter was written while Story was hard at work preparing his *Commentaries* for the press. Similarly, few orators were better at appealing to sentiment than Daniel Webster or Rufus Choate. Webster's ideal was a harmonious marriage of logic and sentiment in which sentiment served rational ends, just as the woman served the man in the domestic sphere. For Choate, as we saw in the introduction to this volume, the opposition between head and heart was reflected in the different disciplines of law and literature. Both, however, had the common purpose of unifying the country behind the lofty ideals of a national purpose.

A Whig herself, Stowe accepted the separation of head and heart and the possibility of their harmonious marriage, except where laws supporting slavery existed. But so long as the North supported southern slavery and the South retained its slave code, there could be no marriage between law and sentiment. If laws embody logic and support slavery, then sentiment must rule and reason give way. Describing the harshness of American slavery laws in *A Key to Uncle Tom's Cabin,* Stowe writes,

> Slavery, as defined in American law, is no more capable of being regulated in its administration by principles of humanity, than the torture system of the Inquisition. Every act of humanity of every individual owner is an illogical result from the legal definition; and the reason why the slave-code of America is more atrocious than any ever before exhibited under the sun, is that the Anglo-Saxon race are a more coldly and strictly logical race, and have an unflinching courage to meet the consequences of every premise which they lay down, and to work out an accursed principle, with mathematical accuracy, to its most accursed results. The decisions in American law-books show nothing so much as this severe, unflinching accuracy of logic. It is often and evidently, not because judges are inhuman or partial, but because they are logical and truthful, that they announce from the bench, in the calmest manner, decisions which one would think might make the earth shudder, and the sun turn pale. (82)

Stowe's condemnation of slavery laws would seem to challenge the status accorded to Anglo-Saxon logic in legal circles. When Lemuel

Shaw died in 1861, he was praised for his "good, sound Anglo-Saxon common sense": "This it was which gave him such mastery over the rules and principles of the common law, that 'ample and boundless jurisprudence' which the experience and common sense of successive generations of men have gradually built up, and which came to us from our English ancestors, a precious inheritance of freedom and of the great principles of justice and right."[26]

But despite Stowe's seeming challenge to the celebration of Anglo-Saxon common sense, she does not blame logic in itself. In fact, she praises a judge like Ruffin for having the unflinching courage to let us see the cold logic of slavery law, making it clear and simple. The problem for Stowe is neither logic nor the law. It is slavery. Thus, although Stowe seems to challenge orthodox legal thought, she leaves its opposition between logic and feeling intact. Laws should be logical, but they should not support institutions whose logic makes it impossible to exert the influence of sentiment.[27]

Such strict opposition between logic and sentiment fosters essentialist thinking in regards to nationality, race, and gender. For example, when Stowe compares American slavery codes with those of other nations, she attributes the differences to the inherent temperament of nationalities. "The French and the Spanish nations are, by constitution, more impulsive, passionate and poetic, than logical; hence it will be found that while there may be more instances of individual barbarity, as might be expected among impulsive and passionate people, there is in their slave-code more exhibition of humanity. The code of the State of Louisiana contains more really humane provisions, were there any means of enforcing them, than that of any other state in the Union" (*Key* 82). The political constitutions of nations derive from their temperamental constitutions, not vice versa. A similar argument would assign women and men their political roles on the basis of their constitutions, rather than relating their constitutions to the roles assigned them. As for race, we learn that Africans have been misunderstood in America because they are an "exotic race, whose ancestors, born beneath a tropic sun, brought with them, and perpetuated to their descendants, a character . . . essentially unlike the hard and dominant Anglo-Saxon race" (*UTC* xvii).

But the moment I accuse Stowe of essentialism, I neglect one of the most effective ways in which she elicits sympathy for blacks from the "hard and dominant Anglo-Saxon race." Blacks, she shows, are really no different from whites. Contrary to white prejudices, blacks do have the same feelings as whites, caring especially about family members that the cruel institution of slavery separates from one another. If blacks sometimes seem unregenerate, the example of Topsy shows that inferior characteristics attributed to them by whites result from the system of slavery and the evils it perpetuates. Even the passage cited in the preceding paragraph is not pure essentialism. Although it relies on the standard argument that climate is responsible for the different characteristics of races, it attributes the Afro-American character to a character brought to America and *perpetuated* through cultural, not hereditary, transmission. Furthermore, as George Harris will acknowledge, the Afro-American race lacks the Anglo-Saxon race's hard dominance, because it had been "called in the furnace of injustice and oppression" (*UTC* 431). Its character has been shaped by its bondage in slavery.

To be sure, much of Stowe's work is aimed at showing how character is shaped by existing economic systems. St. Clare, for example, tells his New England cousin that their fathers were of the same character but developed different beliefs because of where they lived. "My father, you know, came first from New England; and he was just such another man as your father, – a regular old Roman, – upright, energetic, noble-minded, with an iron will. Your father settled down in New England, to rule over rocks and stones, and to force an existence out of Nature; and mine settled in Louisiana, to rule over men and women, and force existence out of them" (*UTC* 222). There is no difference between Northerner and Southerner. They merely take on different characters in different circumstances. Similarly, men as well as women are capable of feelings. Their roles as politicians, judges, or businessmen force them to choose head over heart.

Self-contradictory as Stowe's positions on racial and gender essentialism are, she could not eliminate these contradictions by adopting our twentieth-century prejudices about prejudice. In fact, her contradictions are one factor making her tale a highly effective antislavery work. On the one hand, blacks have the same feelings and emotions as whites. On the other, they are different, so different that the best solution to the slavery problem would be to allow liberated slaves to return (as good Christians, of course) to Africa and the tropical sun under which they were born. Stowe's audience could feel for blacks without feeling threatened.

Stowe did a great service by heightening Northerners' awareness that they indirectly supported slavery, but ultimately her criticism of slavery had influence because it adhered to an already existing set of beliefs within the North. Stowe used those beliefs subversively by replacing traditional masculine values with traditional feminine ones, yet her vision retains the oppositions between public and private, law and sentiment, masculine and feminine that grew out of and helped to sustain the dominant ideology of antebellum America. Furthermore, she strongly believes in the ideology of free labor that supported nineteenth-century market capitalism manifested in northern states.[28]

Responding to Stowe's representation of slavery, Southerners offered a bleak portrayal of life in the North. William J. Grayson wrote a long poem, *The Hireling and the Slave,* contrasting the patriarchal protection offered southern slaves to the miserable conditions of workers in the North. Cared for from birth until death, at all hours of the day and night, slaves were better provided for than northern workers, who sold their labor for a specified number of hours a day and then were left on their own, with no guarantee of protection by their employer. According to Grayson, the sentiment of the South's patriarchal society provided better care of its "children" than the laws of the North's market economy. Free under the law, a northern worker was not in fact free. If the South depended on black slaves, the North depended on "wage" slaves.

Stowe does not ignore the southern argument against wage slavery. In *Uncle Tom's Cabin* she gives it voice through Augustine St. Clare's brother. According to St. Clare, Alfred argues, "and I think quite sensibly, that the American planter is 'only doing, in another form, what the English aristocracy and capitalists are doing by the lower classes.'" When Miss Ophelia objects, "How in the world can the two things be compared? . . . The English laborer is not sold, traded, parted from his family, whipped," Augustine replies, "He is as much at the will of his employer as if he were sold to him. The slave-owner can whip his refractory slave to death, – the capitalist can starve him to death. As to family security, it is hard to say which is worst, – to have one's children sold, or see them starve to death at home." Ophelia does not counter this logic. She merely concludes, correctly, "But it's no kind of apology for slavery, to prove that it isn't worse than some other bad thing" (228).

As we have seen, Stowe's exposure of the cold inhumanity of the market economy seems to prepare her for a devastating criticism of the North as well as the South. In showing the interconnectedness between the northern and southern economies, she effectively implicates the North in the slave trade, but her critique of the northern market system stops the moment it does not involve slavery. Stowe offers the wage-slave argument without denying the exploitation that free laborers suffer, but she locates the exploitation in England, not America.[29] Representing an alternative to slavery, wage labor in America is idealized.

To show the waste produced by slavery, Stowe has George Harris hired out by his owner to a manufacturer, Mr. Wilson. George gains notice by inventing a machine for cleaning hemp. Jealous of George's success, his owner decides to put him in his place by returning him to work in the field, "hoeing and digging" (11). When the manufacturer's offer to raise George's wages cannot influence the slaveholder, we are left with the sense that if George had been a free man, able to bargain for his own wages, he would still be at work in the factory, helping to increase production. In contrast to the "vulgar, narrow-minded, tyrannical master," (11), Mr. Wilson, who is the only manufacturer depicted in the novel, is a kindly man who later lends George money to help him escape to the North. There is no suggestion that the demand for profit would make manufacturers exploit their workers to increase production, just as slave owners might exploit their slaves, yet, in fact there were manufacturers whose tyranny approached Simon Legree's.

Stowe, however, equates freedom with free wages. George Selby sets his slaves free, telling them, "You are now free men and women. I shall pay you wages for your work, such as we shall agree on" (436). Earlier, St. Clare laments the problems that emancipation would bring. "But suppose we should rise up to-morrow and emancipate, who would educate these millions, and teach them how to use their freedom? They never would rise to do much among us. The fact is, we are too lazy and unpractical ourselves, ever to give them much of an idea of industry and energy which is necessary to form them into men. They will have to go north, where labor is the fashion; – the universal custom" (313).

Stowe, like Augustine St. Clare, saw no solution for slavery within the South. The laws and values of its culture were too corrupted by slavery to reform. This hopelessness pervades the action of Stowe's second book on slavery, *Dred: A Tale of the Great Dismal Swamp*, even more than the action of *Uncle Tom's Cabin*.[30] The book's protagonist, Edward Clayton, a young southern plantation owner and lawyer, tries to find a solution to slavery within his own culture. To impress the reader with Clayton's difficulties, Stowe reconstructs a situation similar to *State v. Mann* and has the young lawyer, in his first trial, argue the case for the slave. Clayton builds his argument on an appeal to the southern belief in sentimental control. " 'No obligation,' he said, 'can be stronger to an honorable mind, than the obligation of *entire dependence*. The fact that a human being has no refuge from our power, no appeal from our decisions, so far from leading to careless security, is one of the strongest possible motives to caution, and to most exact care" (*Dred* 2:41). Pursuing the logic of patriarchal protection, he claims that the "good of the subject" is the foundation of the owner's rights over a slave. Thus, "When chastisement is inflicted without just cause, and in a manner so inconsiderate and brutal as to endanger the safety and well-being of the subject, the great principle of the law is violated. The act becomes perfectly lawless, and as incapable of legal defence as it is abhorrent to every sentiment of humanity and justice" (2:41). Clayton's argument, linking law to sentiment, carries the day, and he wins, but the case is appealed to the North Carolina Supreme Court, presided over by Edward's father.

Judge Clayton had watched his son win his first case with fatherly pride. Before the trial, though, when he was asked by Edward's sister if he thought Edward would win, he replied, "Not if the case goes according to law." Even so, he adds, "Edward has great power of exciting the feelings, and under the influence of his eloquence the case may go the other way, and humanity triumph at the expense of law" (2:40). The morning before he announces the North Carolina Supreme Court's decision reversing the lower court, Judge Clayton reveals similar thoughts to his wife. Admitting how much his decision goes against his feelings and sense of right, he defines his function as judge as being "not to make laws, nor to alter them, but simply to declare what they are. However bad the principle declared, it is not so bad as the proclamation of a falsehood would be. I have sworn truly to declare the laws, and I must keep my oath" (2:99–100).

The decision that Judge Clayton reads is almost word for word (except for some short deletions) from Judge Ruffin's decision in *State v. Mann*. Edward, hearing his father's voice, "so passionless, clear, and deliberate," declare the law that denies a victory for humanity, for the first time "fully realized the horrors of slavery" (2:105). Addressing the court, he announces,

> "I hope it will not be considered a disrespect or impertinence for me to say that the law of slavery, and the nature of that institution, have for the first time been made known to me to-day in their true character. I had before flattered myself with the hope that it might be considered a guardian institution, by which a stronger race might assume the care and instruction of the weaker one; and I had hoped that its laws were capable of being so administered as to protect the defenceless. This illusion is destroyed. I see but too clearly now the purpose and object of the law. I cannot, therefore, as a Christian man, remain in the practice of law in a slave state. I therefore relinquish the profession, into which I have just been inducted, and retire from the bar of my native state." (2:105–6)

Edward's rejection of law dramatizes Stowe's belief that so long as the institution of slavery existed, no legal remedy was possible in the South. As a conversation between Edward and his father, a few days later, makes clear, the law "cannot be repealed without uprooting the institution" (2:110). Someone willing to serve the law must be willing to serve the institutions it upholds. As Judge Clayton admits, "Human law is, at best, but an approximation, a reflection of many of the ills of our nature. Imperfect as it is, it is, on the whole, a blessing. The worst system is better than anarchy" (2:109). When Edward asks his father, as Stowe wondered of Judge Ruffin, "But, my father, why could you not have been a reformer of the system?" (2:109), the judge makes a long response that explains why reform in the South is impossible.

Reform is possible only if the South is willing to give up slavery. That will occur only when "there is a settled conviction in the community that the institution itself is a moral evil." Unfortunately, the judge sees no hope for such a change because of the failure of the southern clergy. "It is with them that the training of the community, on which any such reform could be built, must commence; and I see no symptoms of their undertaking it. The decisions and testimonies of the great religious assemblies in the land, in my youth, were frequent. They have grown every year less and less decided; and now the morality of the thing is openly defended in our pulpits, to my great disgust." Admitting that he himself lacks the talents of a reformer, he makes it clear to his son that he will not deny Edward's talents: "If you feel a call to enter on this course, fully understanding the difficulties and sacrifices it would probably involve, I would be the last one to throw the influence of my private wishes and feelings into the scale. We live here but a few years. It is of more consequence that we should do right, than that we should enjoy ourselves" (2:110).

Edward, an idealist, insists on attempting reform. Since reform of the legal system is impossible without changing settled convictions in the community supporting slavery, he decides to change community opinion by operating a model plantation that shows the evils, as well as the inefficiency, of the slave system. This solution, too, proves impossible. As his father had warned, "Your course . . . will place you in opposition to the community in which you live. Your conscientious convictions will cross self-interest, and the community will not allow you to carry them out" (2:108–9).

Almost systematically, then, *Dred* dramatizes Edward's inability to find alternatives to slavery within the South. Nonetheless, for Stowe there is always the hope of escaping the house of bondage and entering the promised land. The Fugitive Slave Act ruled out northern states as a location for Edward's community, but it did not rule out adopting the northern alternative in Canada. Relocating with some renegade slaves and his faithful unmarried sister, Edward forms a township that is a model of northern productivity. The surrounding whites, at first worried by the presence of blacks, eventually are "entirely won over," partly because the "value of improvements which Clayton and his tenants have made has nearly doubled the price of real estate in the vicinity." A school has been established and the previous slaves converted to "energy and thrift" as they acquire "property and consideration in the community" (2:331).

Similarly, the vision of African resettlement that Stowe offers in *Uncle Tom's Cabin* endorses capitalism and perpetuates the gender differentiation linked to nineteenth-century capitalism's separation of public and private spheres.[31] To be sure, corroborating Stowe's hope that traditional feminine values will gain ascendancy within a capitalist framework, George Harris's vision of the republic that he and other former slaves will form in Liberia offers an alternative to the "stern, inflexible, energetic elements" of the Anglo-Saxon race (*UTC* 431). The people populating his republic will be "essentially a Christian one. If not a dominant and commanding race, they are, at least, an affectionate, magnanimous, and forgiving one. Having been called in the furnace of injustice and oppression, they have need to bind closer to their hearts that sublime doctrine of love and forgiveness, through which alone they are to conquer, which it is to be their mission to spread over the continent of Africa" (431–2). Nonetheless, George goes instructed in proper New England, capitalist values. "I go to *Liberia,* not as an Elysium of romance, but as to a *field of work.* I expect to work with both hands, – to work *hard;* to work against all sorts of difficulties and discouragements; and to work till I die" (432). Whenever Stowe gives a positive image of a former male slave, she shows him to be an industrious worker or small businessman with a good business sense. Furthermore, it is George Harris, not Eliza, who will found Liberia. Eliza's role remains that assigned to women in the nineteenth-century market economy. George, confessing that the Saxon blood in his veins sometimes makes him unsuited for the task he has in mind, rejoices to "have an eloquent preacher of the Gospel ever by my side, in the person of my beautiful wife. When I wander, her gentle spirit ever restores me, and keeps before my eyes the Christian calling and mission of our race" (432). Apparently the Saxon blood in Eliza's veins will not affect her in the same way as it affects her husband.

Although Stowe was fully aware of problems of domination within capitalist society, she strongly believed in the private space within which it allowed women to exert a positive moral influence. Thus it remained an alternative to slavery, which was so exploitative that even the feminine values embodied in Eliza could not reform it. A major difference between Stowe's and Melville's reaction to slavery is that Melville lacks Stowe's faith that women can resist the exploitation of capitalist society and bring about constructive reform. Certainly Melville's representation of women has problems of its own. Nonetheless, it denies the simplistic alternative that Stowe offers to slave society. When Melville includes women in his work (which is not often) they are frequently victims or threats. If Stowe sees slavery as a form of social exploitation that cannot be reformed by feminine values fostered in the domestic sphere, Melville sees exploitation in all existing institutions, including the domestic family. Thus, for Melville the hopelessness that Stowe sees in the South is extended to the entire world.

Melville, lacking Stowe's faith in the possibility of a just northern alternative to slavery, also lacked Stowe's ground from which to launch an attack on slavery. As systematically as Stowe dramatizes the lack of alternatives to slavery within the South, Melville's works dramatize the limitations of her alternatives outside the South. Returning slaves to Africa might free America from the problem of slavery but would not necessarily signal an end to slavery. As Babo reminds us, slavery exists in Africa as well. If Stowe thinks that returning Christianized former slaves will civilize the African continent, in *Typee* Melville lays bare the imperialistic motives behind the introduction of Christianity to non-Western cultures, the savagery it causes rather than eliminates. Most important, if opponents of slavery think the eradication of slavery from America's shores will finally make America the land of the free, Melville's works offer example after example demonstrating exploitation in "free" states. The increased attention paid to the plight of the slave as a result of the Fugitive Slave Act of 1850 caused many Northerners to appreciate the superiority of their system over the slave economy of the South. For Melville, it seemed to heighten his awareness of the exploitation existing everywhere. As Ishmael wonders, "Who ain't a slave?"[32]

6

Exploitation at Home and at Sea

One of the best ways to understand why Melville's response to slavery in "Benito Cereno" is so different from Stowe's in *Uncle Tom's Cabin* is to look at two of his works that rarely mention slavery: *White-Jacket: or The World in a Man-of-War,* written before the passage of the Fugitive Slave Act, and *Pierre; or the Ambiguities,* written after. I will start with *Pierre*.

Pierre invites comparison with *Uncle Tom's Cabin* for a number of reasons. First, Melville started writing it while *Uncle Tom's Cabin* was being serialized. Second, Melville claimed to direct it toward the large female novel-reading public that Stowe had captured. Unlike Stowe's work, however, Melville's was a marketing disaster. Whether readers were too busy reading Stowe or sensed, as some critics have, that *Pierre* is an artistic failure, it seems possible that part of *Pierre's* failure in the marketplace was the result of its bleak attack on its audience's settled convictions, convictions to which Stowe was able to appeal in order to increase Northerners' moral sensitivity concerning slavery. Most important, Melville challenges his audience's faith in the sacredness of the domestic family. Melville's only extended treatment of the domestic family, *Pierre* shows that if the family is held together by private bonds of affection, those bonds duplicate the system of exclusions and repressions of the public sphere, rather than provide a haven from it. Constrained from following a higher moral law, Pierre renounces his family to follow a moral calling. But his quest does not lead to an escape from the constraints of the family. He merely finds himself ensnared in a wider web of unacknowledged family connections. Rather than find a private realm of freedom, he ends his life as a suicide in a public prison. The first complete book that Melville wrote after his father-in-law Lemual Shaw's decision in *Sims, Pierre* imagines the disastrous consequences to someone who decides to oppose his family and devote himself to a higher, moral cause.

Even in *Uncle Tom's Cabin* the family is not always a haven in a heartless world. Too often the protection the family promised was de-

stroyed by the forces of the heartless world. Melville, whose family
suffered the bankruptcy and resulting early death of Allan Melvill, knew
personally how pervasively uncertain economic conditions could pene-
trate the security of the family. There are numerous examples in his
fiction of a child deprived of the father's patriarchal protection. Death is
not the only cause of the father's absence. In *Moby-Dick,* a book written
soon after numerous fathers left their families to head west in search of
California gold, Melville offers a glimpse of how a desire for restless
questing could break the family circle. Ahab, intent on a mad quest after
the white whale, sees his wife and child in Starbuck's eye and thinks how
his wife is a "widow with her husband alive."[1] Earlier, Ishmael thinks
that "in all cases man must eventually lower, or at least shift, his conceit
of attainable felicity; not placing it anywhere in the intellect or the fancy;
but in the wife, the heart, the bed, the table, the saddle, the fire-side, the
country" (*MD* 533).

Seen from distant seas in *Moby-Dick,* the domestic circle is granted
pastoral qualities, but in *Pierre* its pastoral simplicity is questioned. *Pierre*
begins in pastoral harmony at Saddle Meadows, but as its hero penetrates
the facade of his family's respectability he confronts scandal, not purity.
Pierre's family is not a harmonious unit whose tranquillity is upset by the
cruel outside world. Instead the cruelty of the outside world can be better
understood by observing the workings of the domestic family. Disillu-
sioned by the bachelor deeds of his dead father and rejected by his hypocritical mother, Pierre vows, Hamlet-like, to pursue the cause of moral
righteousness and right the world's wrongs. The narrator's description
of his quest recalls Ahab's mad, avenging quest that caused him to aban-
don his family.

> There is a dark, mad mystery in some human hearts, which, some-
> times, during the tyranny of a usurper mood, leads them to be all
> eagerness to cast off the most intense beloved bond, as a hindrance to
> the attainment of whatever transcendental object that usurper mood so
> tyrannically suggests. Then the beloved bond seems to hold us to no
> essential good; lifted to exalted mounts, we can dispense with all the
> vale; endearments we spurn; kisses are blisters to us; and forsaking the
> palpitating forms of mortal love, we emptily embrace the boundless
> and unbodied air. We think we are not human; we become as immortal
> bachelors and gods; but again like the Greek gods themselves, prone we
> descend to earth; glad to be uxorious once more; glad to hide these god-
> like heads within the bosoms made of too-seducing clay.
>
> Weary with the invariable earth, the restless sailor breaks from every
> enfolding arm, and puts to sea in height of tempest that blows off shore.
> But in long night-watches at the antipodes, how heavily that ocean
> gloom lies in vast bales upon the deck; thinking that that very moment
> in his deserted hamlet-home the household sun is high, and many a sun-

eyed maiden meridian as the sun. He curses Fate; himself he curses; his senseless madness, which is himself. For whoso once has known this sweet knowledge, and then fled it; in absence, to him the avenging dream will come. (*Pierre* 180–1)

Abandoning his beloved bonds in Saddle Meadows for a more "exalted mount," Pierre is subject to the avenging dream of the household sun that he abandoned. Pierre's quest to create a world commensurate with his dream of what the world should be might take him away from his only possibility of realizing his dream. The ambiguity in the book's title has to do with the meaning of that quest. Is the quest a madness leading toward destruction, or is it necessary because of the corrupt state of the world? If, as it seems in *Pierre*, allegiance to the domestic family rules out allegiance to the family of man, Pierre's abandonment of his "most intense beloved bond" (5) to pursue righteousness would seem justified. But, if Pierre's sense of a just world is merely an illusion, his abandonment of his familial bonds in order to embrace the common bonds of humanity would cause domestic strife for a utopian product of his imagination, a utopia shaped by his experience of domestic tranquillity at Saddle Meadows.

As Michael Rogin has demonstrated, Melville's fictional portrayal of familial conflict has national significance. Domestic imagery dominated the rhetoric used to try to hold the nation together as the slavery issue threatened to tear it apart. The Union was compared to the family, the division between North and South described in terms of family strife. Melville's connection to Lemuel Shaw helped to make literal the familial rhetoric applied to the Union. Nationally, to follow radical calls to abolish slavery, despite provisions in the Constitution making it legal, would be to risk violence and the destruction of what Shaw once called the "federal family."[2] Personally, for Melville to have written a book favoring antislavery opinions would have been to announce publicly his disagreement with the head of his own family, the man who had recently returned Thomas Sims to slavery.

In *Pierre* what he writes instead is a book in which his hero's quest to right the wrongs of society takes the form of adopting the cause of Isabel, who is probably the illegitimate daughter of Pierre's father. Appropriately, the exact bond between Pierre and Isabel is never certain. It might be the product of his imagined effort to fill that "one hiatus" that he discovered in the "sweetly-writ manuscript" of his life: "A sister had been omitted from the text" (*Pierre* 7). In taking up Isabel's cause, Pierre may be breaking from his acknowledged family for the doomed effort of writing a utopian text of his life that nature does not allow.

Recent scholarship suggests that even this fictionalized version of domestic strife caused strife within Melville's family. A letter from

Melville's uncle to Lemuel Shaw indicates that Melville's father, like Pierre's, might have sired an illegitimate daughter. Years after the publication of *Pierre,* Melville's daughter asserted that her cousin's husband thought the book referred to "family matters." Melville's granddaughter and biographer, Mrs. Eleanor Metcalf, noted in her copy of *Pierre* that the description of Glen Stanly's house in New York resembled the Shaw home in Boston and that Mr. Falsgrave's delicate hands recalled those of Lemuel Shaw and his son Samuel. Such allusions might have been partially responsible for a letter from Lemuel Shaw, Jr., to his mother in 1852 expressing the wish that Melville "could be persuaded to leave off writing books for a few years."[3] But if *Pierre* caused Melville's family uneasiness, it could be reassured that the significance of his veiled allusions would remain a family matter. This would not have been the case if Pierre had embraced the cause of a black slave, rather than a white woman. Nonetheless, there are similarities between the fate of Melville's dark lady, Isabel, and his rebellious slave, Babo.

Mysterious Isabel, like Babo, has been disinherited from the patriarchal protection of the legal system. In "Benito Cereno," of course, no white "brother" comes to the aid of Babo, whereas in *Pierre* the hero tries to represent the unrepresented claims of what he takes to be his unacknowledged sister. Nonetheless, trying to right the wrongs inscribed in the social system, aspiring reformer and writer Pierre cannot offer a romance of hope for the future but becomes entangled in an intricate web of preexisting social codes, turning his attempt to re-write and re-form society into a life of duplicity and role playing. Like Babo's attempt to gain freedom, Pierre's attempt to represent the disinherited Isabel leads to a masquerade of existing social forms. Pierre pretends to be married to Isabel. Babo pretends to be the obedient slave. Their masquerades show the extent to which those accepted social relations depend on role playing. Yet, although they undermine the existing set of social relations, the masquerades cannot offer a more liberating set of relations in their place. In both stories, attempts to break away from the existing forms and usages of society end in destruction and violence. *Pierre* ends with "brother" and "sister" dead, just as "Benito Cereno" ends with "master" and "servant" dead. If the quest to transcend the normal set of social relations causes such violence, perhaps Starbuck's warning to Ahab to return home to the domestic circle should be heeded. But, as the action of *Pierre* emphasizes, it is the family's duplication of society's repressions that force Pierre to rebel in the first place.

In comparing "Benito Cereno" with *Pierre* in this way, I am not trying to argue that Melville's real allegiance was to Babo and to Isabel and that familial pressures kept him from openly expressing that allegiance. Starting with the title page, Melville views Pierre's disruption of the family ambivalently. Although Melville has obvious sympathy for his hero, he also shows how Pierre's actions lead to destruction. Even the rebel Pierre is concerned with protecting his family. He refuses to recognize Isabel publicly as his sister because he does not want to disgrace his family. His attempt to preserve his family's reputation leads him to hide his acknowledgment of Isabel behind the socially accepted form of marriage, just as four years later any recognition that Melville might give to Babo's claim to brotherhood is hidden behind a narrative mask, cunning enough to get a story about slavery published in *Putnam's*, a journal that, although a voice for moderate antislavery views, had an editorial policy of avoiding controversial issues. Furthermore, that narrative mask is more than a pose. If the narrative point of view hides Melville's sympathy for Babo so well that only a few clever readers can detect it, it also reveals a sympathy for Benito when he is held hostage by his black "brother." To be sure, the shadow that Babo casts upon Benito, causing his silence at the end of the story, might signify more than Benito's fear and terror or even his recognition of the irrational potential in man. Like most actions and nonactions taking place in the shadowy realm of Melville's fiction, Benito's refusal to face Babo at the trial, or even to identify him, might be more complicated than critics usually allow. Having himself been forced to play the role of slave by Babo, Benito might have identified with Babo enough to understand why Babo acts as he does. Perhaps, just as Captain Vere dies thinking of Billy Budd, so Benito dies thinking of Babo, feeling a pang of guilt and betrayal at not having testified to the horrors of enslavement. Perhaps that guilt was shared by Melville, who refuses openly to acknowledge any sympathy for Babo. But if there is sympathy for Babo, it is mixed with fear of his dark violence, just as Pierre's sympathy for Isabel is mixed with fear of her dark sexuality and the disorder she seems to spread through the seemingly ordered world of light at the beginning of the book. If Stowe's Uncle Tom can be likened to a woman because he is a victim, Melville's Isabel can be likened to a slave because she is a threat.

In comparing "Benito Cereno" with *Pierre,* I am also not suggesting that family circumstances made it impossible for Melville to write the book on slavery that he wanted to write in 1851–2 and that therefore we should read *Pierre* as an allegory whose real topic is slavery. Lemuel Shaw's role in the *Sims* controversy may indeed have emphasized to Melville that his family situation restricted what he could write, but Melville's awareness of how his family situation could exercise control over him helped to distinguish his attitude on slavery from Stowe's. If Stowe saw the values fostered within the family as a moral force to counter the effects of slavery, Melville saw the family as potentially enslaving. If the history of Pierre's family is a national history, it reminds us that national acts of exploitation were accomplished by numerous individuals and families.

In *Pierre,* as in *The Pioneers* and *The House of the Seven Gables,* the story of how the book's central family acquired its land has national significance. What appears to be the harmony of Saddle Meadows at the start of the book is the result of a series of conflicts that gave the Glendinning family ownership of its property. "The Glendinning deeds by which their estate had so long been held, bore cyphers of three Indian kings, the aboriginal and only conveyancers of those noble woods and plains" (*Pierre* 6). The orderly legality of these deeds conceals the bloody deeds that helped to secure them. Idyllic Saddle Meadows was once the site of a battle with the Indians. Not far away, Pierre's grandfather had defended his land against the "repeated combined assaults of Indians, Tories, and Regulars" (6). Before the Revolutionary War, the same grandfather had "annihilated two Indian savages by making reciprocal bludgeons of their heads" (29–30). The Glendinnings' acquisition of Saddle Meadows mirrors the violence involved in the acquisition of land by the nation as a whole.

Even Pierre's name invites a reading rooted in America history. Nineteenth-century conservatives were embarrassed by the revolutionary fathers' reliance on the French to overthrow the tyranny of the British fathers. They wanted to keep the Revolution Anglo-Saxon. For instance, an article that appeared in the *North American Review* in the 1840s discounts the aid of the French as "little else than a love of military adventure. . . . Excepting this attraction, Anglo-Saxon, Puritan America not only had no bond of union with France, but there was a positive antipathy between the inhabitants of the two countries." For this writer, "The truth is incontestable, and we mean only to state it, that the Revolution was *our own,* – and such is our pride in this distinction, that we sometimes feel a shade of regret, as a matter of historical association, at even the French alliance."[4]

The regret the author feels over the French alliance results from his attempt to distinguish the American Revolution from the radicalism of the French Revolution that followed. Read allegorically, then, Pierre's taking the cause of his unacknowledged half-sister, born from the illicit liaison between his father and a Frenchwoman, emphasizes the extent of Pierre's radicalism. Like his own name, his championing her is a reminder of the French connection that America's conservatives tried to repress. (And what, after all, would Pierre's mother have made of her son's name, if her husband did have a premarital affair with a Frenchwoman?) To be sure, Melville draws on the name of his cousin Pierre Thomas Melvill for his fictional character's name. But for Melville, the fact that his uncle, born in 1776, married a Frenchwoman who gave birth to children named Francoise, Pierre Thomas, and Napoleon might well have served as a reminder of France's role in American history.

Pierre, the narrator reminds us, sprang on both sides of his family from heroes. He has a "double revolutionary descent" (20). But when he stays true to the revolutionary spirit of his ancestors that led them to side with France, he disrupts the harmony of Saddle Meadows.

To stay true to the revolutionary spirit that informed the French Revolution is to violate the doctrine of "Chronometricals and Horologicals," which is centrally located in Melville's narrative and offers a way to guarantee harmony in Saddle Meadows and the nation. Part of the philosophy of Plotinus Plinlimmon, "Chronometricals and Horologicals" takes as its subject the conflict between God's Truth and man's truth. The sum of its teaching is "that in things terrestrial (horological) a man must not be governed by ideas celestial (chronometrical)" (214).

Imagined so soon after Chief Justice Shaw's *Sims* decision, this doctrine can be read as Melville's ironic comment on his father-in-law's argument that man-made rather than higher laws must be followed. But as appropriately as the doctrine of "Chronometricals and Horologicals" comments on the slavery issue, it has a much wider application. As Sacvan Bercovitch has argued, it is Melville's ironic comment on a rhetorical strategy that pervades American culture.[5] It is a logic that has allowed conflicts within American society to be absorbed by a consensus that claims to represent the interests of all the people in the nation. As a nation we stay true to our divine mission precisely through our ability to compromise. For northern Whig lawyers like Lemuel Shaw, Joseph Story, and Daniel Webster, the Constitution was the perfect example of how practical, consensus politics produced a document regarded with sacred respect.

On December 21, 1843, Joseph Story delivered to his law class an eloquent appeal for a full commitment to the Constitution. The Constitution, he felt, was the product and spirit of compromise, and it would end when that spirit died in the hearts of the people. If the many interest groups making up the Union disregarded those provisions with which they disagreed, the Union would disintegrate or become the instrument of a despot. True lovers of liberty would condemn "those mad men who even now are ready to stand up in public assemblies and in the name of conscience, liberty, or the rights of man, to boast that they are willing and ready to bid farewell to that Constitution under which we have lived and prospered for more than half a century."[6]

The madmen whom Story refers to are most likely abolitionists who protested his decision in *Prigg*. Although slavery was the immediate issue, Story wanted to emphasize to these future lawyers that a larger principle was at stake. In 1834 Story had written a monumental treatise, his *Conflict of Laws*. In it he tried to answer the question of what to do when laws of different sovereignties come into conflict.

According to Story, "It is an essential attribute of every sovereignty that it has no admitted superior, and that it gives the supreme law within its own domain on all subjects appertaining to its sovereignty. What it yields, it is its own choice to yield; and it cannot be commanded by another to yield it as a matter of right." Therefore, a court "may with impunity disregard the law pronounced by a magistrate beyond his territory."[7] Put in terms of "Chronometricals and Horologicals," Story's doctrine reads: The various horological differences to be found on earth are not to be resolved by an appeal to the chronometrical. Instead, each sovereign must respect the sovereignty of another country.

As any student of American jurisprudence knows, the American federal system presents a special problem in regard to the conflict of laws. The peculiar circumstances of American history had allowed each colony to adopt British common law, only to have each one make slight or sometimes major variations in the interpretation of it. Along with different constitutions framed by each colony and different statutes enacted, this meant that the thirteen colonies federated into the United States had different legal systems. The strength of the Constitution was that it both recognized the potential conflicts among the states and offered a way to reconcile those conflicts. Given this system, it is understandable that defenders of the Constitution denounced the madmen who disregarded it, since the Constitution alone seemed to act as a barrier to an inevitable series of conflicts among the states. By reconciling the conflicting claims of its citizens, it guaranteed national prosperity and allowed the country to pursue its sacred mission. A practical document embodying lofty ideals, it became the country's sacred text, serving as the Bible had in the Puritan's covenant theology. If abolitionists saw the Constitution as opposed to higher law, its supporters saw it as reconciling Chronometricals and Horologicals.

As Melville's ironic treatment of Chronometricals and Horologicals indicates, however, in reconciling the conflicting claims of many of the country's residents the covenant excludes those of others. Slaves were those most obviously excluded, but the events of *Pierre* point out that some whites were excluded as well. Foremost, of course, is illegitimate, French-descended Isabel, who threatens the harmony of Saddle Meadows. But the harmony of Saddle Meadows has been threatened even before Isabel is introduced. Immediately to the west, "magnificent Dutch Manors" are occupied by thousands of farmer tenants held in subservience by rent-deeds that were to hold "so long as grass grows and water runs; which hints of surprising eternity for a deed, and seems to make lawyer's ink unobliterable as the sea" (*Pierre* 11).

This allusion to the antirent movement in upstate New York draws attention to the power that lawyer's ink has to hold citizens in almost feudal bondage and the threat to social order that occurred when the tenants disregarded the lawyers' contracts. This threat to law and order roused the military might of the state. "Regular armies, with staffs of officers, crossing rivers with artillery, and marching through primeval woods, and threading vast rocky defiles, have been sent out to distrain upon three thousand farmer-tenants of one landlord, at a blow" (11).

Melville's allusion to the antirent movement is particularly telling, for it suggests that the North is as capable as the South of using a legal code to maintain oppressive social relations. In contrast to the South's slave economy based on totalized social relations, the North had a wage economy based on a legal contract between employer and employee. The contract system seemed to offer much more freedom because it was freely entered into by both parties and could be freely dissolved by either of them, but the contract was given more power by the legal system than we might suppose. Contracts, the Constitution declared and the courts confirmed, could not be impaired. A contract written in lawyer's ink involved an eternal obligation. When James Fenimore Cooper wrote the Littlepage trilogy in response to the antirent movement, he took the side of the landlords. To those who argued that it is against the spirit of American institutions to enforce leases that bind generation after generation of tenant families to terms agreed upon prior to the Revolution, Cooper responded, "These tenures existed when the institutions were formed, and one of the provisions of the institutions themselves guarantees the observance of the covenants under which the tenures exist."[8] Defenders of the Constitution used a similar argument against southern threats of secession. The obligation of the constitutional contract could no more be impaired than the obligations of private contracts. Both were sacred covenants that could not be violated.

Melville's treatment of the antirent movement in *Pierre* suggests, however, that such rhetoric made "these far-descended Dutch meadows along the Hudson" (11) a perfect example of how America's democratic institutions did not bring about the revolution hoped for by some and feared by others. "The monarchical world very generally imagines, that in demagoguical America the sacred Past hath no fixed statues erected to it, but all things irreverently seethe and boil in the vulgar caldron of an everlasting uncrystalizing Present. This conceit would seem peculiarly applicable to the social condition. With no chartered aristocracy, and no law of entail, how can any family in America imposingly perpetuate itself?" (8). These Dutch manors, with their "eastern patriarchalness," show how "such estates seem to defy Time's tooth, and by conditions which take hold of the indestructible earth seem to contemporize their fee-simples with eternity" (11).

Yet there is an irony to this last sentence, indicated by its double use of the word "seem." When Melville wrote *Pierre,* a convention to amend the constitution of New York State had already met, partially in response to the antirent agitation. Compromises were reached, and the old patroon system lost more of its power. Nonetheless, the contract ideology of the North remained. Its power was felt most strongly in the cities. Therefore, if the northern defense of contract ideology were valid, cities would be the most democratic places in the country. "In our cities families rise and burst like bubbles in a vat. For indeed the democratic element operates as a subtile acid among us; forever producing new things by corroding the old" (9). But as Pierre discovers when he moves to the city, the new forms of social relations developing in northern cities are far from democratic. Radical Pierre himself becomes one of those excluded from the American covenant.

Pierre's fate demonstrates the contradictory logic of consensus politics. On the one hand, through compromise, consensus politics claims to transform the conflicting interests of different people into a harmonious balance that ensures national prosperity. On the other hand, the one conflict that the consensus cannot tolerate is the one caused by those who challenge its claim to represent all of the people by pointing to those who do not benefit from the national prosperity. Such madmen serve no purpose other than to threaten the delicate harmony essential to the national good. Thus, in the name of the people, the consensus has to exclude those radical voices that speak for those excluded.

This theme of political exclusion is intricately related to another of *Pierre*'s themes: its reflection upon the writing of fiction. By the second half of the book we learn that Pierre's radical quest is coupled with his desire to write a great American novel. The exclusions caused by America's consensus politics help to explain why Pierre's aesthetic efforts will inevitably fail, just as Melville's aesthetic "failure" helps expose the system's political exclusions. The great American novel would be one that could harmoniously unite Chronometricals and Horologicals. What Melville shows instead is that any effort to reconcile the two leads to exclusions, including that of the serious artist.

Pierre's exclusion from American society clearly parallels the exclusion that Melville increasingly felt as an artist, an exclusion brought about by the impossible task Melville set for himself. On the one hand, he needed to market his books. When he was starting *Pierre,* Melville "knew that he had overdrawn his account with his publishers and needed a new book which would sell well enough to carry him over the next winter."[9] On the other hand, he truly desired to challenge his audience's settled convictions. The impossibility of accomplishing both is demonstrated by a passage in *Pierre*.

> If a man be told a thing wholly new, then – during the time of its first announcement to him – it is entirely impossible for him to comprehend it. For – absurd as it may seem – men are only made to comprehend things which they comprehended before (though but in the embryo, as it were). Things new it is impossible to make them comprehend, by merely talking to them about it. True, sometimes they pretend to comprehend; in their own hearts they really believe they do comprehend; outwardly look as though they did comprehend; wag their bushy tails comprehendingly; but for all that, they do not comprehend. Possibly, they may afterward come, of themselves, to inhale this new idea from the circumambient air, and so come to comprehend it; but not otherwise at all. (209)

For a writer hoping to market a book that would help bring about real reform and profit, the lesson is all too clear. Works that truly challenge the audience's beliefs will be ineffectual because they will never be understood and thus will never have a chance of wide consumption. Works that have the potential for effective influence because they are widely consumed cannot challenge the audience's settled convictions because they are either misunderstood or reflect back what the audience was prepared to believe in the first place.

According to these criteria *Pierre* had the potential to be a book radically subversive of the beliefs of the reading public. As we have seen, the success of *Uncle Tom's Cabin* in the marketplace was partially owing to its adherence to a value system that the northern public believed in, even if it was not always followed. By appealing to this value system, Stowe raised people's consciousness on the issue of slavery. In contrast, *Pierre* did not raise the public consciousness so much as challenge it. Most important, it challenged the foundation for Stowe's attack on slavery by undercutting the distinction she maintains between the private and the public. In *Pierre* there is no purely private realm of the moral domestic family separated from the public. Ironically, in demonstrating the fictional basis of the split between public and private, Melville avoids the period's most pressing "public" issue – slavery – whereas Stowe addresses it directly and helps to effect change. But she can affect the slavery issue only by leaving intact the more inclusive network of exploitation exposed in *Pierre*. Thus, by reading *Pierre* in conjunction with the slavery controversy we can see more clearly how Stowe's attack on the institution of slavery is strengthened by ideological assumptions supporting the social system of the North.[10] To turn to *White-Jacket* is to see how the slavery controversy could make a writer like Melville aware that the very idea of America, as envisioned by northern unionists, spawned contradictions.

Very different in tone from *Pierre*, *White-Jacket*, written before the passage of the Fugitive Slave Act, is, like *Uncle Tom's Cabin*, an explicit call for reform. Whereas Stowe demands the abolition of slavery, Melville demands the abolition of corporal punishment in the Navy. For Melville it is an outrage that the United States Navy uses essentially the same code of discipline found in the Russian navy. The laws supporting flogging directly contradict America's republican institutions, which "claim to be based upon broad principles of political liberty and equality" (*WJ* 144). Indeed, many Northerners related the campaign to abolish flogging, of which *White-Jacket* is a part, to the campaign to abolish slavery, that other "feudal" institution in America. Involving a dispute over social discipline, the antiflogging campaign became a sectional dispute between North and South. To emphasize the "unrepublican" nature of flogging, opponents in the Senate, led by New Hampshire senator John Parker Hale, argued that flogging, like slavery, was a "relic of feudalism and barbarity," a "stumbling block to an enlightened humanity." Republicans, like Hale, favored voluntary restraint over the external coercion of corporal punishment. As Myra C. Glenn argues, the republican attitude toward discipline is related to the ideology of free labor, which viewed an individual's freedom from economic or political constraints as essential for economic growth and personal liberty.[11] In the North, imposed self-restraints were, according to Eric Foner, the "web of civilized society."[12] Many Southerners, on the contrary, felt that corporal punishment was necessary to maintain social order.

In attacking flogging, Melville would seem to side with the North against the South. Echoing Hale and his Senate followers, Melville writes,

> We assert that flogging in the navy is opposed to the essential dignity of man, which no legislator has the right to violate; that it is oppressive, and glaringly unequal in its operations; that it is utterly repugnant to the spirit of our democratic institutions; indeed that it involves a lingering trait of the worst times of a barbarous feudal aristocracy; in a word we denounce it as religiously, morally, and immutably *wrong*. (*WJ* 146)

As this quotation illustrates, Melville borrows from abolitionist rhetoric to denounce flogging.

> No matter, then, what may be the consequences of its abolition; no matter if we have to dismantle our fleets, and our unprotected commerce should fall a prey to the spoiler, the awful admonitions of justice and humanity demand that abolition without procrastination; in a voice that is not to be mistaken, demand that abolition to-day. It is not a

dollar-and-cent question of expediency; it is a matter of *right and wrong*. (146)

Like the abolitionists, Melville appeals to the law of nature as authority, even adding the weight of Blackstone's *Commentaries*. "Now, in the language of Blackstone, again, there is a law, 'coeval with mankind, dictated by God himself, superior in obligation to any other, and no human laws are of validity if contrary to this.' That law is the Law of Nature; among the three great principles of which Justinian includes 'that to every man should be rendered his due'" (145). Just as abolitionists appealed to the Declaration of Independence to justify their position, so does Melville. So long as a sailor is allowed to be flogged, "for him our Revolution was in vain; to him our Declaration of Independence is a lie" (144).

But although Melville sounds like an abolitionist, he is writing about flogging, not slavery. To be sure, like other opponents of flogging he compares the life of sailors to the life of slaves: "The American Navy is not altogether an inappropriate place for hereditary bondmen" (378). Nonetheless, *White-Jacket* does not express unequivocal sympathy for the plight of Guinea, the enslaved sailor modeled on Robert Lucas. Allowed to "freely circulate about the decks in citizen's clothes, and, through the influence of his master, almost entirely exempted from the disciplinary degradation of the Caucasian crew" (379), Guinea becomes an object of envy to the crew. Melville does not use him to exemplify the horrors of slavery but to emphasize the horrible conditions under which American sailors work. In fact, *White-Jacket* is full of praise for Guinea's owner, the purser, and expresses sympathy for this fictional counterpart of the Virginia officer whose slave was ruled a free man by Lemuel Shaw. "From his pleasant, kind, indulgent manner toward his slave, I always imputed to him a generous heart, and cherished an involuntary friendliness toward him. Upon our arrival home, his treatment of Guinea, under circumstances peculiarly calculated to stir up the resentment of a slave-owner, still more augmented my estimation of the Purser's good heart" (379).

Melville's expressions of sympathy for Southerners in *White-Jacket* did not go unnoticed. Southerners did not feel that Northerners had a monopoly on self-restraint. Quite the contrary. Slavery worked, they argued, because owners continually exercised restraint, despite being in a position of absolute power. Raised in positions of authority, they knew how to use it. In his review of *Uncle Tom's Cabin,* George F. Holmes points to Simon Legree as a perfect example of a New Englander who does not know how to govern. Holmes claims that "it is well known in the Southern States that of all tyrants in the world, a New England slave-driver is the most cruel and remorseless."[13] New England masters err in being either too kind or too harsh. As proof that Southerners know how to administer corporal punishment properly, Holmes quotes Melville in *White-Jacket*. "It is a thing that American man-of-war's men have often observed, that the Lieutenants from the Southern States, the descendents of the old Virginians, are much less severe, and much more gentle and gentlemanly in command, than the Northern officers, as a class" (146).

Another Southerner who drew attention to Melville's attitude toward slavery was William Gilmore Simms. In a review of *White-Jacket*, Simms was more critical than Holmes. He juxtaposed Melville's favorable comments about Southerners with his mention of a "slave-driving planter" (385) and accused Melville of reflecting the "stereotyped prejudices of his region." Simms's review appeared in July 1850, the same month in which Melville read Hawthorne's *Mosses from an Old Manse*. Melville signed his own review of Hawthorne's stories "By a Virginian Spending July in Vermont." In the year in which the new Fugitive Slave Act was passed, that signature might well have been politically motivated, although its exact meaning is impossible to pin down. On the one hand, Melville might have been trying to announce his sympathetic understanding of the southern point of view. On the other, he might have indulged in a double masquerade, pretending to express sympathy to the South while remaining a Northerner nonetheless. [14]

However sympathetic Melville actually was to the South, we should not interpret that sympathy as support of slavery. His abhorrence of slavery can be documented. [15] Nonetheless, he might have looked with suspicion at those Northerners who monomaniacally traced the source of all evil and suffering to slavery, while overlooking nonrepublican behavior accomplished by those above the Mason-Dixon line. For Melville, slavery was only one case, if the most obvious, of America's failure to live up to the promises inscribed in the Declaration of Independence to offer liberty to all of its people. We can see the difference between Melville's sense of what needed reforming in America and that of northern reformists by comparing his use of the ship of state metaphor with Henry Wadsworth Longfellow's and by looking at one of the period's sources for that metaphor – the actions and writings of Alexander Slidell Mackenzie.

In *White-Jacket* Melville self-consciously draws on the ship of state metaphor that was becoming widely used to describe the Union. Its most famous literary use in antebellum America was in Longfellow's "Building of the Ship," written in 1849. Explicitly comparing the building of the Union with the building of a ship, in its famous line "Sail on, O UNION, strong and great!" the poem was hailed in the North for its patriotism. Lincoln reportedly was moved to tears by it. Schoolchildren recited passages from it under the title "Ode to the Union." Fanny Kemble recited the entire poem to an enthusiastic Boston audience of more than three thousand. Longfellow's poem was written during the height of the Free-Soil controversy. According to Richard Henry Dana, Longfellow decided to write a "new and more stirring ending" on the night before the November election, after dinner with his friend and Free-Soil supporter Charles Sumner. Always implicit in the poem's construction, the ship of state metaphor then became explicit with a political message to preserve the Union, a message relying on rhetoric claiming that America is divinely sanctioned and follows higher law.[16]

Similarities between Longfellow's use of the metaphor and Melville's in *White-Jacket* are striking. Toward the end of his poem Longfellow writes, "Like unto ships far off at sea, / Outward or homeward bound are we."[17] The last chapter of *White-Jacket* starts: "As a man-of-war that sails through the sea, so this earth sails through the air. We mortals are all on board a fast-sailing, never-sinking world-frigate, of which God was the shipwright; and she is but one craft in a Milky-Way fleet, of which God is the Lord High Admiral" (*WJ* 398). The book ends, "For the rest, whatever befall us, let us never train our murderous guns inboard; let us not mutiny with bloody pikes in our hands. Our Lord High Admiral will yet interpose; and though long ages should elapse, and leave our wrongs unredressed, yet shipmates and worldmates! let us never forget, that, 'Whoever afflict us, whatever surround, / Life is a voyage that's homeward-bound!' " (*WJ* 400).

At the end of *White-Jacket* Melville pleads against strife within the American ship of state, because for him America serves a divine purpose. In an often-quoted passage, Melville proclaims that with America, the "political Messiah" has come, "if we would but give utterance to his promptings. And let us always remember that with ourselves, almost for the first time in the history of earth, national selfishness is unbounded philanthropy; for we can not do a good to America but we give alms to the world" (*WJ* 151). That America could be the "political Messiah" does not mean that all is well within the ship of state. Actual practices within America do not always live up to the ideal America. Precisely because America represents so much, institutions and laws that are tolerated in other countries should not be tolerated in the United States. Corporal punishment in the navy is the most obvious example. A look at Comdr. Alexander Mackenzie's importance for the North's defense of the Union indicates that an even larger issue is at stake.

Mackenzie was commander of the *USS Somers,* a training ship for young midshipmen. While the ship was at sea in the fall of 1842, Mackenzie suspected three crew members of organizing a mutiny and convened an informal officers' court. The court convicted all three of mutiny, and Mackenzie had them hanged at sea. Melville's cousin Lt. Guert Gansevoort served as second-in-command on the *Somers*. It was Gansevoort who relayed the threat of mutiny to Mackenzie, presided over the trial, and gave the hanging order. When the ship landed in New York City, the *Somers* affair started a national controversy. Mackenzie was court-martialed and acquitted, in a widely publicized trial.[18]

Much has been made of the *Somers* affair in Melville criticism because it is an obvious source for *Billy Budd*. I will return to it in detail in discussing *Billy Budd,* but for the moment it is merely important to note that many Northerners, including Longfellow, Sumner, Dana, and Story, offered Mackenzie their total support. Concluding his account of the affair, Mackenzie wrote, "The nominal party sinks into comparative unimportance, and the American nation rears her august form, entreating that her youngest, her favourite offspring, may be saved from its worst enemy, – that it may be saved from the demoralizing, destructive principle of insubordination."[19] Mackenzie's influential New England supporters agreed with him about the national significance of his individual act. They believed that such fidelity to one's duty was necessary to hold the ship of state together, as sectional factions threatened to tear it apart.

Longfellow, especially, was a personal supporter of Mackenzie. During Mackenzie's trial the poet wrote to him, "The voice of all upright men – the common consent of all the good – is with you."[20] Longfellow had met Mackenzie years earlier while traveling in Spain, and the poet owned a copy of Francis Lieber's *Encyclopedia Americana,* to which Mackenzie had contributed three articles, "Navigation," "Navy," and "Ship." When Longfellow started his patriotic poem in 1849, the year after Mackenzie died, he turned to these writings, notably "Ship," to construct the details of his own "Ship." The power of Longfellow's poem rests on its ability to combine the concrete details of shipbuilding with the message that the good in man, as embodied in people like Mackenzie, had gone into constructing a noble ship of state, a ship that must be protected from all evil attempts to destroy it. In a rough version, Longfellow had written,

> A goodly frame, a goodly frame,
> And the UNION shall be her name!
> And foul befall the traitor's hand
> That would loose one bolt, or break one band
> Of this gallant ship, or this goodly land!

In his "Ship" article Mackenzie writes, "Are we not justified in expressing our admiration at this great achievement of man – the production of this wonderful machine – the most complicated, most perfect, sublimest of all the works of art? If it be well said that man is the noblest work of God, it may with equal truth be asserted that the ship is the noblest work of man."[21]

But if the ship is the noblest work of man, it is ruled like a monarchy, not a republic. In a *North American Review* essay Mackenzie had written, "A ship indeed, with its captain, officers, and seamen, forms no imperfect miniature of a monarchy, with its king, nobles, and third estate."[22] That a ship was in practice governed like a monarchy did not seem to disturb Longfellow in his use of the ship of state metaphor, but it complicated Melville's use of the metaphor. If, on the one hand, the ship in *White-Jacket* generally suggests America on a voyage to manifest its destiny, on the other it is a specific ship whose mode of governance clearly contradicts America's national principles.

> For a ship is a bit of terra firma cut off from the main; it is a state in itself; and the captain is its king.
>
> It is no limited monarchy, where the sturdy commons have a right to petition, and snarl if they please; but almost a despotism, like the Grand Turk's. The captain's word is law; he never speaks but in the imperative mood. When he stands on his Quarter-deck at sea, he absolutely commands as far as eye can reach. Only the moon and stars are beyond his jurisdiction. He is lord and master of the sun. (*WJ* 23)

Melville admits that a ship could never be governed strictly according to republican principles; nonetheless, he argues that it should not violate the spirit of the institutions it is supposed to protect. "Certainly the necessities of navies warrant a code for its government more stringent than the law that governs the land; but that code should conform to the spirit of the political institutions of the country that ordains it" (144). The power entrusted to a naval captain clearly violates that spirit. "If there are any three things opposed to the genius of the American Constitution, they are these: irresponsibility in a judge, unlimited discretionary authority in an executive, and the union of an irresponsible judge and unlimited executive in one person" (143). Even so, by virtue of the Articles of War enacted by Congress, "The Captain is made legislator, as well as a judge and an executive" (143). Although for Longfellow, Sumner, and Dana Mackenzie's hanging of three suspected mutineers to save his ship represented the kind of action necessary to preserve the American ship of state, for Melville it was an example of how practices on an individual ship can contradict national principles. Melville goes so far as to justify the right to mutiny. So long as the nation remains true to the legal principles on which it was founded, "Every American man-of-war's-man would be morally justified in resisting the scourge to the uttermost; and, in so resisting, would be religiously justified in what would be judicially styled 'the act of mutiny' itself" (*WJ* 145).

As radical as *White-Jacket*'s defense of the right to mutiny may seem, it is important to remember that at the same time that Longfellow, Sumner, and Dana were defending Mackenzie for containing a potential mutiny on the *Somers,* they used rhetoric similar to Melville's to justify the right of Africans to mutiny on the *Amistad* and *Creole.* Melville, in echoing antislavery rhetoric to justify the mutiny of American sailors, consciously or unconsciously points to the inconsistency of the antislavery position.

Dana, for one, was aware of the inconsistency and tried to explain it. Making a distinction between the slaves' right to rebel and that of sympathetic freemen to rebel on their behalf, Dana argues that because slaves have no rights under the law they are not bound to respect it. On the contrary, because whites have rights, they have a corresponding obligation to respect the law. When the Fugitive Slave Act was passed, Dana argued that "we are not subjects of a monarchy, which has put laws upon us that we had no hand in making. I do not hesitate to say, here, that if the Act of 1850 had been imposed upon us, a subject people, by a monarchy, we should have rebelled as one man."[23] Dana would have agreed with Melville that "the Declaration of Independence makes a difference," but the difference it made was quite different. Even though, for both, the ideals embodied in the Declaration of Independence pointed to the inadequacy of some American laws, Dana felt that once the colonies had established the authority to make their own laws, American citizens could no longer point to the law's inadequacy to justify rebellion. To the contrary, on the flogging issue at least, Melville thought that the Declaration of Independence was the authority justifying mutiny against unjust laws.

This distinction is crucial, for it points to the essential element of the northern legal mentality. For people like Dana – those whom William M. Wiecek calls "antislavery constitutionalists"[24] – slavery was an evil precisely because it denied blacks the rights guaranteed by republican laws. For them the fugitive slave laws were appalling because they denied blacks who escaped to the North the protection of northern laws. Their criticism, therefore, assumes that northern laws will treat blacks fairly. To be sure, blacks had more rights under northern than southern law, but a case decided by Lemuel Shaw in 1849 shows that the republican North was not as republican as it claimed with respect to people of color.

In *State v. Mann* Judge Ruffin openly admits that a slave cannot seek patriarchal protection under law. In the North, however, Ruffin's Massachusetts counterpart, Chief Justice Shaw, emphasized that all citizens of the Commonwealth were "entitled to the paternal consideration and protection of the law." Shaw offered this assurance in *Roberts v. City of*

Boston (1849), a case involving the right of black children to attend all-white schools. Rather than guarantee this right, Shaw legitimized segregation in Boston's public schools by laying the foundation for the separate-but-equal doctrine that was adopted by the federal courts until it was overruled in 1954. According to Shaw, the rights that the law protected could vary according to a person's race, gender, or age. In his decision, Shaw agrees that the "great principle" that "all persons without distinction of age or sex, birth or color, origin or condition, are equal before the law . . . pervades and animates the whole spirit of our constitution of free government." When this principle is applied to the "actual and various conditions of persons in society," however, it does not mean that all citizens are "legally to have the same functions and be subject to the same treatment." All it means is that the "rights of all, as they are settled and regulated by law, are equally entitled to the paternal consideration and protection of the law. . . . What these rights are . . . must depend on laws adapted to their respective relations and conditions."[25]

Although all citizens are entitled to the paternal consideration and protection of the law, Shaw has to admit that for some citizens the law can offer only limited protection. Prejudice, he declares, is "not created by law, and probably cannot be changed by law." Thus, in this case involving a free black, one of the North's major advocates of the supremacy of law comes to the same conclusion that Stowe did when confronted with slave law. Law does not have the power to reverse community opinion. And, as *Roberts* makes clear, community opinion in the North was as prepared as its counterpart in the South to support institutions perpetuating inequality. It was the fate of this northern black that even his generous defender Charles Sumner betrays the sort of prejudice that Shaw felt could not be changed by the law. Concluding his defense, Sumner pleads,

> The vaunted superiority of the white race imposes corresponding duties. The faculties with which they are endowed, and the advantages they possess, must be exercised for the good of all. If the colored people are ignorant, degraded, and unhappy, then should they be special objects of care. From the abundance of our possessions must we seek to remedy their lot. And this Court, which is parent to all the unfortunate children of the Commonwealth, will show itself most truly parental, when it reaches down, and, with the strong arm of Law, elevates, encourages, and protects our colored fellow-citizens.[26]

Sumner's condescending, paternalistic attitude, typical of most well-intentioned whites who opposed slavery, including Shaw, is similar to the attitude Melville exposes in Captain Delano, his Massachusetts captain in "Benito Cereno." There is, of course, a major difference between Delano, who betrays his condescending attitude by beating slaves into submission, and Sumner, who makes a noble attempt to use the "strong arm of the Law" to elevate black citizens. Nonetheless, the case poignantly illustrates that if even reformers of the law cannot escape their community's prejudices, law itself cannot guarantee the absence of exploitation. Indeed, a writer did not need to be familiar with *Roberts v. Boston* to realize that Stowe's attitude toward slave law in the South could be adopted toward northern law as well, to realize that in the North as well as the South exploitation took place; that in the North as well as the South law failed as a guardian institution; that to eliminate exploitation, legal reform was not enough, because true reform was impossible without uprooting the institutions legitimized by the law; and that such uprooting was impossible so long as those institutions were supported by the settled convictions of the community. Furthermore, in one important aspect, at least, the northern legal system was potentially more repressive than the southern. As northern defenders of the law themselves admitted, those excluded by the law were granted one right denied those recognized by it: the right to rebel.

The North's potential for perpetuating repression under the guise of republican principles is illustrated by the northern captains of Melville's ships. A prime example is Captain Delano. Expressing the republican belief that authority should be earned by an individual, not granted by birth, Delano knows of "no sadder sight than a commander who has little of command but the name" (*BC* 253). Benito Cereno, he infers, had "not got into command at the hawse-hole, but the cabin window" (251). In *White-Jacket,* however, just before remarking that southern officers are more gentle than northern, and just after remarking that English officers are less disliked by their crews than American, Melville speculates, "The reason probably is, that many of them, from their station in life, have been more accustomed to social command; hence, quarter-deck authority sits more naturally on them. A coarse, vulgar man, who happens to rise to high naval rank by the exhibition of talents not incompatible with vulgarity, invariably proves a tyrant to his crew" (*WJ* 141). Delano is not coarse and vulgar, and he is not a tyrant to his crew. Nonetheless, the qualities of the self-made man, which he praises, are not incompatible with vulgarity. Furthermore, the effective manner in which he puts down the Africans' rebellion shows that the republican principles he embodies are not incompatible with tyranny.

Of course, Melville's most fully drawn despotic captain is Ahab. If we read *Moby-Dick* in terms of the slavery controversy, Ahab's status as a Northerner invites conflicting interpretations about the meaning of America. In *White-Jacket* Melville emphasizes a discrepancy between what America stands for and what actually occurs within the American

ship of state. Nonetheless, he seems to maintain faith in America's ability
to represent higher principles. In works after *White-Jacket,* however, precisely what America represents becomes less certain. This increased uncertainty over the meaning of America in Melville's works corresponds
with the increased uncertainty over what America stood for that accompanied the passage of the Fugitive Slave Act. Longfellow, writing "The
Building of the Ship" in 1849, made a powerful appeal for the preservation of the Union. A year later it was preserved, but only by compromising on the issue of slavery, an issue that Longfellow and his friends felt
should never be compromised. One way to read *Moby-Dick* is to see its
portrayal of the *Pequod*'s voyage in the light of the uncertainty about the
meaning of the Union generated by the events of 1850.

A book that some critics claim was radically rewritten starting in
September 1850, the month when the Fugitive Slave Act took effect,[27]
Moby-Dick suggests that the *Pequod* represents the American ship of state
when its crew is described as thirty isolatoes "federated along one keel"
(*MD* 166). Through Father Mapple's sermon Melville even evokes
Longfellow's "Building of the Ship."[28] Mapple is a counterpart to Longfellow's "worthy pastor –/ The shepherd of that wandering flock, / that
has the vessel, for its fold" (254). In both instances a man of religion
preaches about the necessity of the ship's following higher law. Describing Mapple's pulpit, Melville writes, "What could be more full of meaning? – for the pulpit is ever the earth's foremost part; all the rest comes in
its rear; the pulpit leads the world. From thence it is the storm of God's
quick wrath is first descried, and the bow must bear the earliest brunt.
From thence it is the God of breezes fair or foul is first invoked for
favorable winds. Yes, the world's a ship on its passage out, and not a
voyage complete; and the pulpit is its prow" (*MD* 69–70). Although
echoing Longfellow's and his own association of the ship of state with
higher law, Melville uses Mapple's sermon to remind the reader that in
Moby-Dick, unlike *White-Jacket,* the ship's voyage is outward, not homeward, bound. According to Charles Foster, he may also be using it to
challenge Daniel Webster's and Lemuel Shaw's stand on the 1850
Fugitive Slave Act.

Foster has suggested that Melville added material to *Moby-Dick* after
the *Sims* decision.[29] As an example he points to Mapple's pronouncement, "Delight is to him, who gives no quarter in truth, and kills, burns,
and destroys all sin though he pluck it out from under the robes of
Senators and Judges" (*MD* 80). If this was added late, it would seem to
allude to Massachusetts's most famous living senator and judge (Webster
and Shaw) and rebuke them for supporting the Fugitive Slave Act and
thus straying from the nation's higher purpose. Indeed, Mapple's entire
sermon about Jonah can be read as a pointed attack on Webster. Like

Webster, Jonah tries to shirk his duty to God by opting for a duty to the state. "He thinks that a ship made by men, will carry him into countries where God does not reign, but only the Captains of this earth" (72). Ultimately Jonah's sin was to try to escape his duty as an "anointed pilot-prophet, or speaker of true things" (79). Bidden "by the Lord to sound those unwelcome truths in the ears of a wicked Nineveh, Jonah appalled at the hostility he should raise, fled from his mission, and sought to escape his duty and his God by taking ship at Joppa" (79). Jonah, like Webster (and like Melville?) fails in his role as a spokesman for God's truth.

If we continue with Foster's argument and see Pip's abandonment at sea as an allusion to the North's abandonment of fugitive slaves, we can understand why Foster reads the sinking of the *Pequod* as Melville's indictment of the United States for straying from its higher purpose. Ahab, in trying to rule the *Pequod* solely by human authority and without higher sanction, causes the ship to be destroyed by the forces of nature that it violated.

Foster's reading gains an added resonance when we compare the rhetoric of Mapple's sermon with that which Webster himself used to call all citizens to do their duty. One of the period's favorite set pieces on duty came from Webster's address to the jury in the White murder trial. Memorized by New England schoolchildren, the passage employs imagery very similar to that used by Father Mapple:

> A sense of duty pursues us ever. It is omnipresent, like a Deity. If we take to ourselves the wings of the morning and dwell in the utmost parts of the sea, duty performed, or duty violated, is still with us, for our happiness or our misery. If we say the darkness shall cover us, in the darkness as in the light, our obligations are yet with us. We cannot escape their power, nor fly from their presence. They are with us in this life, will be with us at its close; and, in that scene of inconceivable solemnity, which lies yet farther onward, we shall still find ourselves surrounded by the consciousness of duty, to pain us whenever it has been violated, and to console us, so far as God may have given us grace to perform it.[30]

If Mapple's sermon was intended as a rebuke to Webster, it would be even more poignant to anyone aware of Webster's reputation as a defender of duty. But the similarity between Mapple's and Webster's rhetoric raises another possibility. Most likely the two echo one another because they both rely on standard rhetoric of the time. Almost universally the culture agreed on the importance of duty. The slavery issue caused such havoc because the correct choice of duty was no longer clear. The uncertainty that people faced in choosing their duty to God complicates Foster's antislavery interpretation.

The failure of the *Pequod* to return home can be read as having exactly the opposite meaning that Foster gives it. Instead of comparing Ahab to Webster, we can compare him to abolitionists who would suspend established rule by law in order to pursue their own transcendental dreams and take revenge on what they saw to be the seat of sin. Abolitionists so hated slavery that someone's failure to condemn it could lead them to blasphemy. For instance, Henry D. Thoreau reports the response of the editor Nathaniel P. Rogers to the argument that Jesus Christ never preached abolitionism. Claiming first that the precept "Whatsoever ye would that men should do to you, do ye even so to them" was abolitionist, Rogers went on to add that nonetheless, if it had been the case that the son of God "did not preach the abolition of slavery then I say, '*he didn't do his duty.*'" Appropriately, Thoreau, in describing Rogers doing *his* duty, uses the ship of state metaphor. Comparing Rogers's *Herald of Freedom* to an ordinary newspaper, "with its civil pilot sitting aft, and magnanimously waiting for the news to arrive," Thoreau praises Rogers as "wide awake, and standing on the beak of his ship; not as a scientific explorer under government, but a yankee sealer, rather, who makes those unexplored continents his harbors in which to refit for more adventurous cruises."[31] The sinking of the *Pequod* might be Melville's warning that the abolitionists' voyage into unexplored continents does not herald freedom but disaster. Rather than affirm Melville's faith in appeals to higher law, the slavery controversy might have forced him to question that faith. If natural law is not benevolent, appeals to it can lead to violence and destruction.

Of course, most critics do not read the ending of *Moby-Dick* in terms of the fugitive slave controversy at all. The danger of Foster's interpretation is not only that it simplifies Melville's response to the events of 1850 but also that it reduces *Moby-Dick* to a response to the slavery issue. If I am correct, Melville never treated slavery as an isolated issue.[32] It is inseparable from his entire vision of America. In this respect, the importance of the passage of the Fugitive Slave Act is that it seems to have contributed to Melville's awareness that more was amiss with America than a temporary discrepancy between what the country stood for and present practices. For in achieving national unity by sacrificing the freedom of fugitive slaves, the Compromise of 1850 suggested that maintaining the American ship of state inevitably involved the exploitation and exclusion of some human beings who lived within its boundaries. To recognize this inevitability is not necessarily to advocate a radical overthrow of existing laws and institutions. As we saw in the case of *Pierre,* radical attempts to represent the unrepresented can lead to disaster. Nonetheless, it is to recognize that the rhetoric holding the American ship of state together is riddled with contradictions. But if the events of

1850 emphasized those contradictions, they were already implicit in Melville's earlier use of the ship of state metaphor in *White-Jacket.*

In *Whitè-Jacket* a captain can, as Ahab does, use his absolute authority in a despotic way. In *White-Jacket* the possibility is suggested, as it is made clear in *Moby-Dick,* that a ship may not serve the purpose it claims to serve. Moreover, as we saw, if *White-Jacket*'s campaign against flogging is read in light of the slavery controversy, the book alerts us to the possibility that those who seemed most concerned about granting legal rights to slaves could point to the freedom of white sailors to deny the sailors the right to mutiny granted to black slaves. If this and other contradictions are not explicitly raised in *White-Jacket,* the potential for questioning them is there, as revealed in an oft-quoted passage. "Outwardly regarded, our craft is a lie; for all that is outwardly seen of it is the clean-swept deck, and oft-painted planks comprised above the waterline; whereas, the vast mass of our fabric, with all its store-rooms of secrets, forever slides along far under the surface" (*WJ* 399). Increasingly Melville's works suggest the masquerade that constitutes the ship of state, until by the time he crafts *The Confidence-Man,* everything has become masquerade, and the ship of state becomes the ship of fools. I will conclude this chapter by looking at a short passage from *The Confidence-Man,* because it economically summarizes a point I have tried to make by analyzing *Pierre* and *White-Jacket* together: Although the American political system is based upon a consensus politics that promises to serve the interests of all the people, paradoxically, lawful reform serving the interests of those most in need of representation is difficult precisely because the system is too responsive to various interest groups. Speaking directly to the issue of slavery, the passage illustrates how the injustices of that institution could lead Melville to recognize the injustices perpetuated by less obviously exploitative institutions within America.

In one of the book's many episodes, a character named Pitch searches for a machine to replace untrustworthy boy-laborers. An herb-doctor asks him if he has "philanthropic scruples" about going to New Orleans to buy a slave. Pitch responds with the standard wage-slave argument, accompanied by standard racial prejudice. " 'Slaves?' morose again in a twinkling, 'won't have 'em! Bad enough to see whites ducking and grinning round for a favor, without having those poor devils of niggers congeeing round for their corn. Though, to me, the niggers are freer of the two. You are an abolitionist, ain't you?' " (*CM* 154–5). Recognizing the need for tact, the herb-doctor returns, "As to that, I cannot so readily answer. If by abolitionist you mean a zealot, I am none; but if you mean a man, who, being a man, feels for all men, slaves included, and by any lawful act, opposed to nobody's interest, and therefore, rousing nobody's enmity, would willingly abolish suffering (supposing it, in its degree, to exist) from among mankind, irrespective of color, then am I what you say" (155). Pitch responds, "Picked and prudent sentiments. You are the moderate man, the invaluable understrapper of the wicked man. You, the moderate man, may be used for wrong, but are useless for right" (155).

Written about the same time Stowe was writing *Dred,* this passage satirically acknowledges, as much as Stowe does, that slavery is so bound up with powerful interests within the country that legal reform is impossible. It also emphasizes, as she does not, that suffering is not color-bound and that to eliminate other forms of suffering might also be impossible within a legal framework responsive to interest groups. Equally important, it shows how the understanding that suffering extends beyond the peculiar institution of slavery can be put to conservative as well as radical use. In his carefully worded response to Pitch, the herb-doctor sounds remarkably like the conservative lawyer-narrator of "Bartleby, the Scrivener." The first story Melville wrote after *Pierre,* his tale of a reckless breaker of man-made laws, "Bartleby" is about a moderate man who serves the law. If Pierre's radical sentiments take the cause of right yet lead him to do wrong, the lawyer's "picked and prudent sentiments" might well be "useless for right" but "used for wrong."

A philanthropic, humane man, who, like the herb-doctor, hates suffering of all sorts, the lawyer serves a system that perpetuates suffering. Promoting commerce as essential for the country's health, just as the herb-doctor promotes his medicine as essential for an individual's health, the lawyer's Wall Street, like the herb-doctor, is concerned with profit. Since profit can be maximized by increasing productivity and cheapening labor, human labor becomes a commodity, and laboring human beings are replaceable by machines. Just as Pitch looks for a machine to do work that boys do inefficiently, so the lawyer staffs his Wall Street office with human beings assigned machinelike tasks. If Pitch is baffled by boys who refuse to be turned into machines and loses faith in boys' nature, the humane lawyer tries to ease his conscience by treating with kindness the man he turns into a machine, failing to see that kindness is at odds with the logic of the system he serves. It is in "Bartleby," then, that we find Melville's most poignant and bizarre account of how lords of the loom and their commercial friends on Wall Street held their workers in bondage, just as the lords of the lash held their slaves.

Like "Benito Cereno," "Bartleby" is haunted by a figure whose silence – although different from Babo's – has produced endless critical controversies. Once again that silence can help us discover contradictions in the legal ideology of the period as embodied in the opinions of Chief Justice Shaw, at the same time that Shaw's legal ideology can help us understand the causes of that silence. If in "Benito Cereno" we saw how a general belief in the paramount necessity of rule by law could have led those theoretically sympathetic to blacks to support the slave economy of the South, in "Bartleby" we will see more fully how the specific individualistic basis of Shaw's legal system could have led those full of benevolence and charity to support the wage-slave economy of the North. We will also see the dilemma of a writer who senses the injustice of that system but does not feel capable of offering alternative, affirmative visions to combat its injustice. If neither Pierre's radical activism nor the lawyer's prudent moderation helps remedy the suffering of the world, neither does Bartleby's negative passivity.

7

"Bartleby, the Scrivener": Fellow Servants and Free Agents on Wall Street

To say that "Bartleby" is Melville's account of how the lords of the loom held their workers in bondage demands immediate qualification. To be sure, the story is about the relationship between an employer and his employee, but it fits few of the stereotypes associated with anticapitalist literature. "Bartleby" is no more a direct indictment of wage slavery than "Benito Cereno" is of chattel slavery. Just as a comparison between Melville's source for "Benito Cereno" seems to indicate that he weights the evidence against the Africans – they are more violent, Delano kinder in the fictional account – so it seems that Melville weights the evidence against his scrivener.[1] By making his lawyer-narrator a kind and accommodating employer, Melville gives us a character familiar to readers of the period's popular fiction: a well-to-do, amiable New York lawyer or bachelor who intervenes in the affairs of misused young people. For instance, in *The Lawyer's Story: Or, The Wrongs of the Orphans, By a Member of the Bar,* which was serialized in New York newspapers in 1853, a lawyer temporarily employs a young scrivener who appears plagued by a constitutional melancholy. Through the lawyer's intervention, the youth is reunited with his sister, his only friend and relative. The brother and sister turn out to have royal blood and, with the aid of the lawyer, receive their proper inheritance.[2]

Clearly Melville's story is at odds with the sentimentality of this happy ending. But if anyone is to be blamed for "Bartleby"'s unhappy ending, it is Bartleby, not the lawyer. By making Bartleby follow a logic alien to the reader, Melville creates a distance between the reader and the scrivener. Indeed, to some Bartleby appears to be an unmotivated, ungrateful worker with only himself to blame for not taking advantage of the lawyer's kindness.

Thus, "Bartleby" distinguishes itself from standard social-protest literature as well as popular, sentimental fiction. In a literature sympathetic with the worker's plight, the employee's alienation would result from social conditions, unfair laws, or a cruel boss. For instance, in a poem by George Greenville, published in 1851, directed against debtor laws – "Death of a Poor Debtor in Boston Jail" – a man wastes away in a "prison dark and dreary" with "no loved one by his side." Asking what sin condemned him to die "in woe and sorrow," the poet replies,

> *None:* except the crime of being
> Poor, and wasting with disease,
> That was hasting fast to free him
> From life's troubles, toils and cares:
> Yet men stern and iron hearted,
> Could *in jail* a brother hold,
> Till the breath of life departed,
> For a paltry sum of gold!

The poem ends by exorting legislators to "blot a statute so infernal / From your books of boasted Right."[3]

"Bartleby" makes no plea to alter existing laws. Bartleby's malady seems to be metaphysical or psychological, not social, in origin. Indeed, Melville's insistence on leaving the causes of Bartleby's malady unaccounted for is what makes the story so interesting for critics. We will no more successfully discover what Melville thought to be the causes of Bartleby's alienation than we can discover Melville's true position on slavery in "Benito Cereno." Nonetheless, just as reading "Benito Cereno" in light of the conflicts over slavery allowed us better to understand the historical conditions that made it possible for Melville to imagine a figure like Babo, so by reading "Bartleby" in light of the changes occurring in the legal system we can better understand the conditions that made it possible to imagine such an *unheimlich* character. Further, we can see how Bartleby's persistent "I would prefer not to" enables us to distance ourselves from the lawyer's familiar point of view and see its limitations. In other words, rather than argue that the key to the story is that Bartleby is an alienated worker, we can argue that Bartleby functions in the story to alienate us from – make strange – the type of thinking that in retrospect we can recognize as legitimizing the existence of an alienated work force.[4]

To understand the logic of the lawyer's point of view we can once again turn to the legal opinions of Melville's father-in-law. Of special interest for "Bartleby" are Lemuel Shaw's economic opinions, which reveal the extent to which Shaw served the interests of Wall Street. This is not to suggest that we should identify the lawyer in the story with Shaw, even though there are similarities, which we will come to. But Shaw's opinions give us access to a way of thinking familiar to Melville, a way of thinking that helped to shape American law as it transformed itself to meet the needs of a rising market economy. To look at Shaw's opinions is to see the double-edged nature of the period's legal philosophy. On the one hand, Shaw was a powerful advocate of laissez-faire. On the other, he was the patriarchal protector of the Commonwealth, expanding the powers of the state to protect its citizens. Shaw's role as a patriarchal protector is strongly emphasized in Leonard Levy's influential *Law of the Commonwealth and Chief Justice Shaw,* a study itself influenced by the implicit aim of New Deal historians to show that the regulatory state had its roots in the antebellum period. Thus, Levy sees the major theme of Shaw's work as the "perpetuation of what Oscar and Mary Handlin have called 'the commonwealth idea' – essentially a quasi-mercantilist concept of the state within a democratic framework." According to Levy, "The Commonwealth idea precluded the laissez-faire state, whose function was simply to keep peace and order, and then, like a little child, not be heard. The people of Massachusetts expected their Commonwealth to participate actively in their economic affairs. . . . As the Handlins say, 'Massachusetts observors conceived of the beneficient hand of the state as reaching out to touch every part of the economy.' "[5] As employed by Shaw, the commonwealth idea led to laws of public interest by which the power of the state to govern the economy was judicially sustained. Foremost were Shaw's decisions on the law of eminent domain and the expansion of police power.

For Levy, Shaw's notion of the commonwealth served the interests of the entire community. "In Europe, where the state was not responsible to the people and was the product of remote historical forces, mercantilism served the ruling classes who controlled the state. In America men put the social-contract theory into practice and actually made their government. The people were the state; the state was their Common Wealth." Shaw so ably served as a patriarchal protector of the Commonwealth because he complemented his economic decisions with a belief that it was his greatest duty to "apply the sustaining arm of the law to the support of right, liberty, and justice, to every individual, however humble."[6]

There is no doubt that Shaw based most of his decisions on the commonwealth idea. But as Morton Horwitz has argued, it is not enough to show that Shaw made decisions in the name of the welfare of the Commonwealth. Instead we need to ask whose welfare those decisions served. More often than not Shaw's economic decisions did not really make wealth common. Furthermore, as Horwitz also points out, Levy's emphasis on Shaw's commonwealth ideal leads to a striking contradiction, since Levy invokes the Handlins' conception of the Commonwealth during a period when the Handlins themselves sought to show that the commonwealth idea was disintegrating. In fact, through some of his decisions supporting the rising market economy, Shaw himself contributed to the disintegration of the commonwealth idea that the rhetoric of his opinions continually invoked.[7]

On the whole, Shaw's decisions favored rising commercial interests. There are, to be sure, exceptions. In the early nineteenth century, union activities and strikes were considered illegal, because according to common law they amounted to criminal conspiracy. In *Commonwealth v. Hunt* (1842) Shaw ruled that it was not unlawful for workers to form a union that established a closed shop. A major debate has arisen over the motivation for Shaw's decision. Without claiming to resolve the debate, I can point to it to prove Shaw's normal ideological position. What puzzles legal scholars is why he favored labor in this particular opinion, since in almost every other major opinion he favored commercial capitalism.

Shaw never saw his support of commercial interests, especially expanding industries, as a bias. For him, to encourage the growth of industry was to promote common prosperity. But the aid he lent to commercial powers often indirectly resulted in hardship for citizens he promised to protect. For instance, one of his most famous formulations – the *fellow-servant rule* – helped relieve industrial owners of unwanted expenses by helping to legitimize cost-efficient but unsafe working conditions.

The common law, developed in a feudal economy, was not prepared to deal with the increasing number of industrial accidents in a technological society. The common law had furnished the *master–servant rule,* which stated that masters were liable for their servants' actions. Conceivably this rule could have been applied to employer–employee relations, making employers responsible for damages caused by their employees on the job. Instead, Shaw proclaimed the fellow-servant rule, relieving employers of any responsibility for accidents caused by their employees.[8]

Even though it contravened common-law tradition, Shaw's decision was commended throughout the land for its sound reasoning and was at least partially responsible for delaying workmen's compensation laws until 1910. It gave extraordinary support to industry. Henceforth the burden of industrial accidents was borne by the individual or by charity, rather than by developing companies in a country poor in capital. The almost universal agreement that other courts accorded to Shaw's doctrine shows how deeply ingrained the ideology that informed it was in the first half of the nineteenth century.

The fellow-servant rule was based on the assumption that employees were "free agents" able to enter into a job market that offered an unlimited supply of work. When they consented to employment, they entered into what Roscoe Pound called the "free contract of a free man."[9] Thus, as Shaw argued, when employees signed a contract for employment they knowingly assumed the "ordinary risk" of the job, since common sense dictated that more dangerous jobs would be less attractive and would therefore need to offer a higher salary. In the words of another judge, "No prudent man would engage in any perilous employment, unless seduced by greater wages than he could earn in a pursuit unattended by any unusual danger."[10] Because workers assumed "ordinary risk" in making a contract, they were eligible for compensation only from injuries stated explicitly in the contract of employment. According to Horwitz, Shaw's formulation of the fellow-servant rule marked the "triumph of contract" in nineteenth-century law.

> The contractarian ideology above all expressed a market conception of legal relations. Wages were the carefully calibrated instrument by which supposedly equal parties would bargain to arrive at the proper "mix" of risk and wages. In such a world the old ideal of legal relations shaped by a normative standard of substantive justice could scarcely coexist. Since the only measure of justice was the parties' own agreement, all preexisting legal duties were inevitably subordinated to the contract relation.[11]

What this ideology does not recognize is that employee and employer are not equal bargaining partners. It ignores the economic compulsion that left a worker employed in a dangerous job no choice except starvation or equally dangerous employment. In 1888 an English judge echoed Shakespeare in *Romeo and Juliet,* remarking that when a worker consented to a contract of employment, more often than not, it was "his poverty and not his will which consented."[12]

The fellow-servant rule is a perfect example of how Shaw's well-intentioned desire to encourage progress and prosperity conflicted with his desire to be the patriarchal protector of all of the citizens of Massachusetts. Another example is his formulation of the doctrine of negligence. According to Shaw, a plaintiff could win a suit for damages resulting from negligence only if the defendant had used less than ordinary care. Ordinary care, he declared, "means that kind and degree of care, which prudent and cautious men would use." Shaw's definition of negligence, like the fellow-servant rule, served commercial interests by making it difficult for workers injured on the job to sue for damages, for a worker could prove an employer liable for not providing safe working conditions only if the employer was "chargeable with some fault, negligence, carelessness, or want of prudence."[13] Shaw's application of the doctrine of prudence poignantly illustrates why people like Pitch, in *The Confidence-Man,* can assert that moderate men "may be used for wrong, but are useless for right."

As John Stark has noted, Shaw's emphasis on prudence in defining negligence links an important part of his legal philosophy with that of the lawyer-narrator in "Bartleby." Early in the story the lawyer records the "fact" that John Jacob Astor considered his "first grand point" to be "prudence," his next "method." Throughout the story the lawyer returns to the necessity to remain prudent. Certainly, according to Shaw's criteria, it would be difficult to prove the lawyer negligent, and yet we also see how his prudence (like Shaw's) makes him a successful lawyer in the service of commercial interests on Wall Street, interests that helped to support a system that neglected the welfare of its workers. The doctrine of prudence that makes men of capital call the lawyer an "eminently *safe* man" (*B* 40: emphasis in original) made it difficult to guarantee safe working conditions for men of labor.[14]

Of course, the moment I mention safe working conditions I expose the limitations of applying Shaw's decisions too literally to "Bartleby." Bartleby's physical safety is never threatened – in fact, there is even doubt about his corporal existence. To be sure, the emphasis on the psychological nature of Bartleby's malady raises another interpretive possibility. In describing the confined working conditions on Wall Street and in suggesting that Bartleby's affliction grows out of his employment in the Dead Letter Office, Melville could be said to expose the psychological as opposed to physical damage inflicted on white-collar workers and on people – like himself – whose attempts to use the written word to establish communication with other isolated souls were thwarted by the market economy. As Hershel Parker persuasively argues, however, even the Dead Letter Office explanation is too simple to account for Bartleby's behavior.[15] Bartleby's malady remains a mystery. My aim is not to offer a definitive explanation of that mystery but instead to show how the lawyer's failure to understand Bartleby reveals contradictions within his legal philosophy, for although the lawyer's methodological prudence may be extremely effective in managing rich men's money, it cannot manage his lowly scrivener.

One of the most important parts of the lawyer's world view undercut in "Bartleby" is his philosophy of charity. Always practical, the lawyer views charity as a happy meeting place of allegiance to higher values and self-interest. "Aside from higher considerations, charity often operates as a vastly wise and prudent principle – a great safeguard to its possessor. Men have committed murder for jealousy's sake, and anger's sake and hatred's sake, and selfishness' sake, and spiritual pride's sake; but no man, that I ever heard of, ever committed a diabolical murder for sweet charity's sake. Mere self-interest, then, if no better motive can be enlisted, should, especially with high-tempered men, prompt all beings to charity and philanthropy" (*B* 64). The lawyer's mind is so taken up with the practical concerns of the world of business that he phrases his self-considerate generosity to Bartleby in terms of buying and selling. "Yes. Here I can cheaply purchase a delicious self-approval. To befriend Bartleby; to humor him in his strange willfulness, will cost me little or nothing, while I lay up in my soul what will eventually prove a sweet morsel for my conscience" (50–1).

Although it is open to an ironic reading, the lawyer's doctrine of charity may seem to have little to do with the legal philosophy of the time. But a look at a celebrated antebellum case indicates how it supported orthodox legal thought. The case was not decided by Melville's father-in-law but by Massachusetts's Joseph Story. It involved the will of Stephen Girard, reputed to be the wealthiest man in America. French-born Girard had gone to sea as a boy. He settled in Philadelphia during the Revolution and made a fortune in shipping and banking. A sympathizer with the French Revolution and radical causes, he dismayed his nieces and nephews when, dying a childless widower, he gave the bulk of his estate of seven million dollars to the city of Philadelphia to establish a school for poor, white orphan boys. In the will he required that "no ecclesiastic, missionary, or minister of any sect whatsoever, shall ever hold or exercise any station or duty whatever in the said college." Girard made this restriction not to "cast any reflection upon any sect or person whatsoever" but to "keep the tender minds of the orphans . . . free from the excitement which clashing doctrine and sectarian controversy are so apt to produce." He urged the college to "instill in the minds of the scholars the purest principles of morality, so that, on their entrance into active life, they may, from inclination and habit, evince benevolence towards their fellow-creatures, and a love of truth, sobriety and industry."[16]

Girard's relatives challenged the will, and after a long delay the case was heard by the U.S. Supreme Court in February 1844. Horace Binney defended Girard's bequest; Daniel Webster represented the relatives. Webster argued that the will was contrary to common law because its exclusion of the clergy from the school was anti-Christian, a "cruel experiment" calculated to ascertain whether orphans can be brought up without religion. Webster's defense of Christianity brought tears to many present, especially when he recalled that Jesus had proclaimed, " 'Suffer little children to come unto me!' Unto *me;* he did not send them first for lessons in morals to the schools of the Pharisees." Churchmen asked Webster to prepare part of his address for publication as a demonstration of the "vital importance of Christianity to the success of our free institutions, and its necessity as the basis of all useful moral education."[17]

Webster was not successful in convincing his friend Joseph Story, who presided over the trial. Story considered Webster's argument an "address to the prejudices of the clergy" and not to the law of the case. Story upheld the will and denied Webster's claim that "Christianity, general, tolerant Christianity, Christianity independent of sects and parties, that Christianity to which the sword and the fagot are unknown, general, tolerant Christianity, is the law of the land."[18]

Liberal opinion today almost certainly sides with Story against Webster in this split between two defenders of the conservative faith. Indeed, the genuineness of Webster's Christian motives was questioned. Despite his emotional defense of *caritas* against "vulgar deism and infidelity," if he won the court would have deprived deserving Philadelphia orphans of education and care and given Girard's money to a few who were already rich. According to John Quincy Adams, Webster himself would have pocketed fifty thousand dollars for "his share of the plunder."[19]

Nonetheless, the decision of the court was not unreservedly progressive. According to Maurice Baxter, the *Girard Will* decision marked the triumph of a "liberal law of charity. . . . [It] was a large forward step in encouraging the whole field of philanthropy that would be significant throughout the next century."[20] But the forces making the law of charity necessary were not so charitable. As the case indicates, in some realms of law the courts expanded their influence to replace traditional social organizations like the church and family as a patriarchal protector. For instance, in deciding against Girard's relatives, the court went against a desire that James Kent felt was "very prevalent with mankind" and "deeply seated in the affections," the desire to "preserve and perpetuate family influence."[21] The influence exerted by family blood in questions of inheritance is one of the major themes of Hawthorne's *House of the Seven Gables*. But Hawthorne's work also records the strain put on the traditional family-based and church-based patriarchal order. More and more, the legal order, not the church, proclaimed to its citizens, "Suffer little children to come unto me." As Michael Grossberg argues, "This transfer of power from the male parent to the male jurist made judges a new kind of patriarch, one invested with a power over some families that came to rival their male predecessors'."[22] The expansion of court power was a necessary reform to prevent abuses by the old patriarchal system, but, as the powerful image of the patriarchal judge reminds us, it was a double-edged reform. It did not challenge patriarchal rule; it merely relocated it. In doing so, it inscribed the dominant patriarchal beliefs more deeply into the law.

In addition, one reason that the law had to take over a patriarchal function in areas that used to be reserved for the family and the church was that the new economic system was destroying the cohesion of old social bonds. That economic system was aided by the increasing reluctance of the courts to interfere with the "natural" laws of the market. Thus, at the same time that judges moved away from their earlier patriarchal function of ensuring equity in the economic sphere, they increased their patriarchal function in the domestic sphere. As we have seen, few judges embodied these contradictory tendencies more than Melville's father-in-law. Part of the complexity of "Bartleby" arises from similarly contradictory tendencies within the lawyer in the story. On the one hand, the lawyer is a kind, patriarchal figure. On the other, he serves Wall Street. That contradiction is emphasized by his position as master of chancery, a position that necessitated the hiring of Bartleby in the first place.

Unique to Anglo-American law, courts of chancery descended from the lord chancellor of the king of England. The task of a master of chancery was to mediate disputes in "matters of equity for which the narrowness of the law courts provided no relief."[23] Equity, as defined by Aristotle, is "that idea of justice which contravenes the written law."[24] In England, where common law was bound by precedent, courts of equity were concerned with the ideal application of justice. Thus, courts of chancery helped the legal system fulfill its patriarchal function. Elitist, in that they derived their authority from the king, they also provided remedies beyond the power of ordinary courts.

Imported to the colonies, they survived the Revolution. In my brief look at the career of James Kent, I noted that his position as chancellor in New York state indicated the extent to which he continued to maintain a traditional notion of the paternal function of the courts. I also noted that under Kent chancery lost some of its protective role, because he increasingly subverted its regulatory power. Not only was the power of equity undermined but in New York's constitutional convention of 1846 the office of chancellor was actually abolished, a move heralded by those intent on eliminating the last vestiges of aristocratic rule but also one that marked diminished patriarchal control over the market. Finally, with the New York Field Code of 1848, law and equity were merged, a merger that, according to Horwitz, signaled the "final and complete emasculation of Equity as an independent legal standard."[25] In the eighteenth century, equity consisted of a system of substantive rules that could be appealed to to ensure "natural justice." In the nineteenth century the concept of equity was positivized so that it was turned into a set of procedural remedies. For example, in the eighteenth century, if the price specified in a business contract did not correspond to a "just price," it could be nullified by a court of chancery. In the nineteenth century the doctrine of *caveat emptor,* or "Buyer beware," replaced the just-price doctrine. The courts interfered less and less with a contract agreed upon by two "free agents," even if the contract seemed grossly unfair.

Thus, by making the lawyer-narrator of a story published in 1853 a master of chancery, Melville associates him with an outdated, paternalistic notion of law. By making him a Wall Street lawyer, Melville also suggests the forces leading to equity's demise. The man supposed to ensure equity does not control market transactions but instead serves Wall Street. Indeed, some of the most powerful irony directed against the lawyer comes from the description of his job as a master of chancery. Nostalgically describing the position as the "good old office, now extinct in the State of New York," the lawyer admits, "It was not an arduous office, but very pleasantly remunerative" (40). Angered at the loss of this easy income, he temporarily loses his prudent self-control. "I seldom lose my temper; much more seldom indulge in dangerous indignation at wrongs and outrages; but I must be permitted to be rash here and declare, that I consider the abrogation of the office of Master of Chancery, by the new Constitution, as a ——— premature act; inasmuch as I had counted upon a life-lease of the profits, whereas I only received those of a few short years. But this is by the way" (40).

This outburst is not "by the way" at all, for it is one of the clearest examples we have of how this humane lawyer indirectly makes a profit from the sufferings of others. Many of the cases that a master of chancery heard involved personal injury. The lawyer's job was to prescribe a remedy for those injuries, a job that rewarded him with a tidy profit. It is this same man who offers charity to Bartleby, hoping to reap a spiritual profit.

The similarities between the narrator's use of the doctrine of equity and the doctrine of charity indicate that it was not a coincidence that the liberal law of charity set forth in the *Girard Will* case developed precisely as the traditional concept of equity declined. For example, with the demise of equity a worker injured on the job and denied damages under Lemuel Shaw's fellow-servant rule had nowhere to turn for a remedy but to private charity and philanthropy. In fact, legally it was courts of chancery that provided a "remedy," whereas courts of law assessed damages. Unfortunately, the lawyer's charity is as unsuccessful in providing a remedy for Bartleby as Shaw's fellow-servant rule was in aiding workers injured on the job.

This is not to argue that "Bartleby" is Melville's plea for workmen's compensation. But Bartleby's passive resistance shows the limitations of the lawyer's doctrine of charity. One of the most subtle occasions on which this occurs is a scene that would seem to make readers sympathize with the lawyer while alienating them from Bartleby. The lawyer, having tried all he could with his scrivener, kindly offers to find him another "sort of business" (*B* 69). One by one, Bartleby prefers not to reengage in copying for someone else, to take a clerkship in a dry-goods store, or to become a bartender. Bartleby's refusals seem the height of ingratitude. Nonetheless, the lawyer's next offer suggests one possible reason why

Bartleby prefers "not to make any change." "Well, then, would you like to travel through the country collecting bills for the merchants? That would improve your health" (69). The lawyer's charitable offer is for Bartleby to improve his health by helping merchants collect their profits. Bartleby's refusal to become a bill collector does not mean that his social conscience dictates his passive resistance. Nonetheless, his refusal to accept the position invites us to stop and ponder what the consequences of such a job would be. When we do, we see that a charitable action toward one person can indirectly involve uncharitable acts toward others. As such, charity proved ineffective in remedying social and psychological ills on anything but an individual level. But if charity proved ineffective in helping those who suffered under market conditions, it proved an effective ideological tool for those who benefited from the rise of the market. Through charity the rich could purchase a good conscience and elicit the gratitude of the poor while they continued to perpetuate a system that made charity necessary in the first place. In refusing to be grateful for the lawyer's charity, Bartleby helps to expose its ideological function.

The point here is not that in acting charitably toward Bartleby the lawyer is an evil man. What else could he do – prefer not to? The point is that precisely his good points – his assets – make him an effective lawyer, serving an economic system that undermines his efforts to be kind. Refusing to be grateful, refusing to be routinized, Bartleby disrupts the "cool tranquillity" of the lawyer's "snug retreat," where he does a "snug business among rich men's bonds, and mortgages, and title-deeds" (B 40). As psychoanalytical critics have argued, this disruptiveness of Bartleby's mere presence suggests that he is a bizarre representative of an unconscious force that the lawyer tries to repress.[26]

Indeed, Bartleby's power over the lawyer results from the inability of the lawyer's conscious assumptions to account for him. In a telling moment in the story, the lawyer attempts to "assume" Bartleby away by adopting an orderly and decorous manner.

> The beauty of my procedure seemed to consist in its perfect quietness. There was no vulgar bullying, no bravado of any sort, no choleric hectoring, and striding to and fro across the apartment, jerking out vehement commands for Bartleby to bundle himself off with his beggarly traps. Nothing of the kind. Without loudly bidding Bartleby depart – as an inferior genius might have done – I *assumed* the ground that depart he must; and upon that assumption built all I had to say. (B 61)

But Bartleby cannot be assumed away.

The lawyer's inability to assume Bartleby away has led critics to associate the scrivener with Henry D. Thoreau. Leo Marx writes, "Bartleby represents the only real, if ultimately ineffective threat to society; his experience gives some support to Henry Thoreau's view that one intransigent man can shake the foundations of our institutions."[27] Bartleby does question the foundation of institutions served by the lawyer. But Marx's admission that Bartleby's threat is ultimately ineffective is revealing, because it indicates that in addition to exposing the limitations of the doctrine of prudent expediency, "Bartleby" exposes a flaw in Thoreau's challenge to it. Despite the subversive nature of Thoreau's philosophy, it adheres to a belief in free agency – a doctrine as widespread in the nineteenth century as that of charity. Melville's story questions the free agency of both his employee and employer.

Like Thoreau's passive resister, Bartleby undermines the authority of someone he seems to serve. Bartleby, the lawyer laments, is "denying my authority; and perplexing my visitors; and scandalizing my professional reputation" (*B* 65). The lawyer's concern with maintaining his professional reputation conflicts with his desire to help the scrivener and shows how little control he has over his own actions. Wanting to be charitable, he is forced by his social position to act uncharitably. "At length, necessities connected with my business tyrannized over all other considerations. Decently as I could, I told Bartleby that in six days' time he must unconditionally leave the office" (60). Despite this warning, Bartleby remains, forcing the lawyer to effect a compromise by allowing Bartleby to stay if he causes no trouble. But the lawyer cannot maintain this compromise because of pressure from his business associates. "I believe this wise and blessed frame of mind would have continued with me, had it not been for the unsolicited and uncharitable remarks obtruded upon me by my professional friends who visited the rooms. But thus it often is, that the constant friction of illiberal minds wears out at last the best resolves of the more generous" (65).

Thoreau too shows that those in positions of authority are not free because they are controlled by the institutions they serve. He finds this especially true of politicians. "Statesmen and legislators, standing so completely within the institution, never distinctly and nakedly behold it. They speak of moving society, but have no resting-place without it." This Archimedean allusion leads Thoreau to a consideration of Daniel Webster's limitations. "Webster never goes behind government, and so cannot speak with authority about it. His words are wisdom to those legislators who contemplate no essential reform in the existing government; but for thinkers, and those who legislate for all time, he never once glances at the subject." For Thoreau, only those who are able to escape the practical constraints of society can find true freedom. Admitting that, even so, Webster is "always strong, and original, and, above all, practical," Thoreau goes on to assert, "Still his quality is not wisdom, but prudence. The lawyer's truth is not Truth, but consistency, or a consistent expediency. Truth is always in harmony with herself, and is not concerned chiefly to reveal the justice that may consist with wrong-doing."[28]

For Thoreau the truly free individual is the one who can find a space of freedom outside of society in order to inhabit this realm of Truth. His belief in such a possibility allows him to imagine that each individual is a free agent with equal bargaining power with the state or any other form of authority. Each citizen is free to withdraw from the contract he or she has entered into with the state. In "Slavery in Massachusetts," Thoreau declares, "Let each inhabitant of the State dissolve his union with her, as long as she delays to do her duty." In "Resistance to Civil Government" he proclaims, "If ten *honest* men only – aye, if *one* HONEST man, in this state of Massachusetts, *ceasing to hold slaves,* were actually to withdraw from this copartnership, and be locked up in the county jail therefor, it would be the abolition of slavery in America."[29]

"Bartleby" challenges this transcendental doctrine. If Bartleby's passive resistance has the power to expose the limitations of the lawyer's prudent assumptions, its power is purely negative. Bartleby's only freedom is to refuse to comply with the assumptions of the world into which he is thrust, a refusal that in no way turns him into a free agent. Bartleby's withdrawal from the social system does not lead to freedom but to imprisonment and death. In fact, "Bartleby" empties of meaning the phrase "withdrawal from the social system." Whereas Thoreau celebrated his night in prison as a night of freedom in which he could obey his own law, not society's, Melville lets us see that confinement to prison is not a withdrawal from society but an entrance into yet another social institution.

A number of critics have perceptively noted that "Bartleby" offers another instance of Melville's fascination with the conflict between horological and chronometrical characters.[30] In *Pierre* we learn that

> if a man gives with a certain self-considerate generosity to the poor; abstains from doing downright ill to any man; does his convenient best in a general way to do good to his whole race; takes watchful loving care of his wife and children, relatives and friends; is perfectly tolerant to all other men's opinions whatever they may be; is an honest dealer, an honest citizen and all that; and more especially if he believes that there is a God for infidels, as well as for believers, and acts upon that belief; then, though such a man falls infinitely short of the chronometrical standard, ... [he] need never lastingly despond, because . . . he is a man and a horologe. (213–14)

This certainly describes the lawyer and his charitable disposition toward Bartleby. It also helps to emphasize the contradictions inherent in the lawyer's self-considerate generosity. Those contradictions might lead us to conclude that Bartleby is a chronometer. To be sure, Bartleby perfectly illustrates *Pierre*'s conclusion that someone who seeks to regulate his daily conduct by chronometrical time "will but annoy all men's earthly timekeepers against him, and thereby work himself woe and death" (212). But it is important to remember that such a character does not actually exist in a chronometrical realm. He merely strives to. Bartleby's disruption of the lawyer's horological philosophy does not place him in a higher realm. If Bartleby does not adhere to horological time, neither does he adhere to chronometrical time. In Melville's story there is no realm in which, as Thoreau would have it, Truth is always in harmony with herself. Rather than suggest the existence of a higher, transcendental world as an alternative to a world in which the majority of men live lives of quiet desperation, "Bartleby" suggests the existence of a world that the lawyer tries to repress. One characteristic of that world is that people are turned into objects. Compromising with Bartleby, the lawyer decides to let the scrivener stay, so long as he causes no more trouble than a piece of furniture. "Yes, Bartleby, stay there behind your screen, thought I: I shall persecute you no more; you are harmless and noiseless as any of these old chairs" (*B* 65). A possible reason for the lawyer's keeping Bartleby out of sight is that the scrivener's existence as thing might remind the lawyer of his own. In keeping money and bonds safe, the methodically prudent lawyer takes on the function of a secure, locked container. No wonder he is considered "an eminently *safe* man" (40).

Allotted machinelike roles, neither the lawyer nor the scrivener is a free agent. Nonetheless, they receive unequal rewards for fulfilling their tasks. Bartleby's job implicitly links him to the world of exploited workers produced by the same market system that allows the lawyer to live a comfortable life serving the rich. Thus, another possible reason for the lawyer's keeping Bartleby out of sight is that he is trying to repress his awareness of the existence of this repressed labor force. But if the lawyer is to be accused of repressing the existence of this "underworld," Melville should be as well, for it is never explicitly named in the story. To see Melville's presentation of it and its relationship to the comfortable life of lawyers, we have to turn to a story he wrote soon after "Bartleby": "The Paradise of Bachelors and the Tartarus of Maids."

This story consists of two sketches, one of the luxurious life of bachelor lawyers near the Temple Bar in London, the other of the deprived life of women in a Berkshire paper factory. The second half vividly presents a picture of what Lemuel Shaw's support of industry meant for some citizens of the Commonwealth. Indeed, the antebellum celebration of machines and technology so ably documented by Leo Marx pervaded the legal mentality. For instance, the response to Carlyle's attack on machinery quoted at length by Marx was written by Joseph Story's student Timothy Walker.[31] Story himself delivered a lecture entitled "Developments of Science and Mechanic Arts."[32] In 1823, on his way to visit Story in Cambridge, James Kent observed the new factory system in Lowell, completely fascinated by the power and efficiency of the machinery and recording no awareness of the condition of the women workers.[33] As any reader of Melville's tale knows, part of the thrust of the story is to undermine this celebration of machines at the expense of the women who serve them. The story is about sexploitation as well as exploitation.

The women working in the factory are stationed in front of machines "like so many mares haltered to the rack. . . . Before each was vertically thrust up a long, glittering scythe, immovably fixed at bottom to the manger-edge" (*PB/TM* 217). This phalliclike scythe resembles an erected sword, and the machinery that makes the liquid to be turned into paper is described as "two great round vats . . . full of a white, wet wooly-looking stuff, not unlike the albuminous part of an egg, softboiled" (218). Calling the boy who oversees the women Cupid, Melville evokes the sterility of labor under the factory system. The girls are called "maids" because they are unmarried, for marriage might produce a child and disrupt the work routine. Instead, they are wedded to their machines, which in nine minutes gestate blank sheets of paper.

Melville's association of exploitation with male sexual dominance distinguishes his story from simpleminded tracts against technology. That association is heightened when we compare the second part of the story with the first, a comparison implicating the bachelor lawyers in the exploitation of the women. Forming one narrative unit, Melville's two sketches should not be read separately. Although there is a spatial gap between his seemingly unrelated sketches, Melville creates a tale in which the gap becomes an important part of the narrative. In fact, the gap becomes the most subversive element of the story, because it challenges the narrative logic that underlies the contractarian ideology. One reason that this ideology was so convincing was that it adhered to the narrative form that also underlies the middle-class novel, a narrative in which society is generated by the interaction between autonomous free agents. This narrative traces the causes of negligence or exploitation to morally free agents. In the standard literature of the time – one thinks of Dickens – there is a cruel capitalist to blame. But as Melville's story suggests, such a narrative model is no longer adequate to explain the forces of exploitation. Under the new market conditions, it is not enough to explain exploitation in terms of face-to-face relations between employer and employee. Instead, exploitation results from an extensive interconnected system in which people are not even aware of those who contribute to their exploitation because they live thousands of miles away and have no direct contact with them. In such a world the hellish poverty of women in a paper factory is related to the leisurely splendor of bachelor lawyers in London, lawyers who are by no means cruel but who nonetheless benefit from and help perpetuate an exploitative system. Significantly, it is the paper manufactured by the women that helps the lawyers maintain their comfortable lives, for it is on those blank sheets of paper that lawyers can draw up contracts that hold in bondage women they do not even know. In the new market economy, Melville suggests, the most exploitative screwing is committed on paper. So long as the contractarian ideology ruled, many employees suffering injury or neglect could not turn to courts for help because the narrative model adopted by the courts was incompatible with the story they had to tell. The Shaw court provides a telling example.

In 1850 a spinner in a large textile mill brought suit against her employer to recover damages for an injury that she claimed was caused by the gross negligence of the general superintendent in charge of production and personnel. Shaw denied her damages, claiming that she and her *superintendent* were fellow-servants. Five years later, she brought suit against the superintendent who had directly caused her injury. Once again she was denied damages, the court ruling, and Shaw concurring, that because the superintendent had a contract only with his employer, he was responsible only to him. "She therefore can have no legal right to complain of his carelessness or unfaithfulness; for he had made himself, by no act or contract, accountable to her."[34]

The second of these cases occurred in 1855, after "Bartleby" and "The Paradise of Bachelors and the Tartarus of Maids" were written. My point is not that Melville was familiar with the cases; it is that his stories counter the narrative used by the legal system to legitimize the conditions of employment at that time, conditions that created an anonymous world of workers forced by poverty to work for low wages, wages sanctified as just by the sacredness of contract.

Although this world was legitimized, it was also, if possible, kept out of sight. Cities were arranged to keep the hellish world described in "The Tartarus of Maids" separate from the world of respectable society. This spatial separation corresponds to the ideological separation of public and private spheres in which the public was the realm of business and the head, the private the realm of charity and the heart. Expressed in the very form of "The Paradise of Bachelors and the Tartarus of Maids," this split is suggested by the metaphor of the wall in "Bartleby."[35] The story's walls and screens show how partitions served to repress workers both literally and metaphorically. In keeping workers out of sight, the partitions also placed them in a confined space, yet the narrative of "Bartleby" demonstrates how walls are not always successful in keeping spheres separate. Unlike "The Paradise of Bachelors and the Tartarus of Maids," where the underworld is spatially separated from the lawyers' quarters, "Bartleby" shows that the underworld exists within the world of Wall Street itself. To be sure, that world is present in the story before the arrival of Bartleby, in the person of the lawyer's three other employees, but their ultimate submissiveness allows the lawyer to continue to repress his awareness of its existence. Even their eccentricity serves an important function, for it lets the lawyer congratulate himself on his humanity. Bartleby's eccentricity does not. Hauntingly present, Bartleby becomes a bizarre representative of the existence of an underworld of workers that the lawyer and his class tried to ignore.

But if Bartleby, like Babo, is a representative of the repressed world that refuses to remain repressed, his silence also functions like Babo's to ensure that the world he represents remains a repressed element in Melville's story as well. The silence resulting from Bartleby's refusal or inability to express the causes of his curious behavior evokes an air of mystery similar to that surrounding the silent philosopher Plinlimmon in *Pierre*. One need not take the extreme position that historical forces provide the complete answer to the "mystery of the human condition" to recognize that Melville's continual suggestion of metaphysical mysteries is his own strategy of containment, a technique by which readers, like the lawyer, can avert their attention from the underworld from which Bartleby emerges. To offer a sociohistorical explanation for Bartleby's silence seems to reduce his mystery. But then, so do all other readings. If reference to sociohistorical conditions does not prove the key to unlocking Bartleby from his mysterious prison, it can help account for Melville's fictional strategy that creates silent figures like Bartleby, Benito Cereno, and Babo, a fictional strategy that in turn enables us to see the contradictions within the orthodox legal ideology.

As with "Benito Cereno" and *Pierre*, Melville's family situation in part explains why his attitude toward the law appears in "Bartleby" in psychological terms. As we have seen, during Melville's lifetime American culture experienced a transfer of power from male parent to male jurist. Melville experienced that transfer of power in a very personal way. Orphaned by the death of his father early in his life, Melville was provided patriarchal protection by his father's friend, the onetime suitor of Melville's aunt. As chief justice, that father figure, who later became Melville's father-in-*law*, became the paternal protector of all of the citizens of the Commonwealth. Considered by many the model of a patriarchal judge, Shaw was also a model patriarchal protector in his role as father-in-law. He helped finance trips for Melville abroad, lent him money to buy Arrowhead, and relieved him of financial debts.

Nonetheless, Melville's own economic hardship, resulting from his increasing failure to market his books, put him in a position to realize that all the personal kindness that his father-in-law could offer was no remedy for people devalued by the laws of the marketplace. As his own value as a writer waned and he was forced to sign less and less favorable contracts (contracts negotiated by his brother Allan), Melville experienced what could happen to free agents operating within the contractarian ideology. Their value was determined by market conditions, and writers were marketed like any other commodity. At the same time, Melville could not help but realize that it was his own stubborn refusal to comply with the demands of the market that contributed to his failure. For instance, Melville quite likely made revisions to *Pierre* in response to his disappointment over the niggardly terms of the contract he was forced to accept for the book. These revisions helped to guarantee the book's failure with the public.[36] Thus, Melville, as much as Bartleby, seems responsible for his own fate, and his refusal to write what was necessary to succeed in his profession could be interpreted as an ungracious response to his father-in-law's support. It is not farfetched to see Melville's ambivalent attitude toward his father-in-law's charity as contributing to his composition of "Bartleby." Nor is it farfetched to see Shaw playing a role in another fictional strategy at work in "Bartleby."

Richard Chase has remarked that "Bartleby" is a parable of the artist. Bartleby "insists on writing only when moved to do so. Faced by the injunction of capitalist society that he write on demand, he refuses to compromise, and rather than write on demand writes not at all, devoting his energies to the task of surviving in his own way and on his own intransigent terms."[37] That the decisions of Melville's father-in-law helped to legitimize that capitalist system adds another dimension to the parable of the artist. Melville's personal situation, in exaggerated relief, shows how the culture's general tendency to silence oppositional voices gets inscribed into everyday, personal relationships. For if Melville had openly criticized Shaw's beliefs, he would have been criticizing the beliefs of a man who had given him constant support. It may not have been only an unresponsive reading public and the editorial policies of *Harper's* and *Putnam's* that forced Melville to veil in allegory the "hidden meanings" of his short works. There was a force of censorship much closer to home, since Melville could easily see that kind and benevolent, paternal guardian of the law, who also happened to serve Wall Street and be his father-in-law, as secretly willing his silence.

The artist's position is even more complex, however, because it would seem on the surface that far from willing Melville's silence as a writer,

Shaw made it possible for him to speak. It was, after all, Shaw's financial support that allowed his son-in-law to pursue his career as a writer. Thus Melville is not immune from his own veiled criticism of the Wall Street world, since his avocation as a writer was intricately connected with and dependent upon the system he questioned. Lawyers are not the only ones making money by writing on paper. Reading "The Paradise of Bachelors and the Tartarus of Maids," we should remember that the very pages we are holding might have been produced by an exploitative system. Furthermore, Melville did not always do his own writing. Often copies of his creative works were copied for him by his wife Elizabeth, who served as his personal scrivener.

Given this situation, Melville's only choice as a writer would seem to have been to copy out the existing codes of the world he lived in – to be no more than a scrivener in service to Wall Street – or to prefer not to write at all. Instead Melville preferred to write a story about his dilemma, and what the story demonstrates is that Bartleby the scrivener and the lawyer-narrator are not the only ones who are not free agents; Melville, the writer, was not one either. However much freedom writers might seem to have to fill up the blank sheets in front of them with what they want, they cannot transcend the sociohistorical conditions of their time. The writers' complicity with the system that is the object of their criticism becomes one of the most important themes of Melville's final attempt to write a full-length novel: *The Confidence-Man*. Published four years after "Bartleby," on April Fools' Day, 1857, *The Confidence-Man* takes place on a riverboat floating down the Mississippi. For the first part of the book, a free state is on one shore, a slave state on the other. Wage and chattel slavery exist side by side and at times become indistinguishable.

8

Contracts and Confidence Men

One of Melville's most extensive meditations on the role allotted a writer in the market economy, *The Confidence-Man* is full of reflexive comments on the nature of writing. These comments have led some recent critics to read the book as an early example of a modernist text that self-consciously announces its status as a fictional construct separated from empirical reality. Paradoxically, however, the novel can also be read as Melville's most realistic response to the conditions of the rising market economy. According to Morton Horwitz, one of the most pressing issues faced by antebellum law was how to distinguish legitimate buying and selling from illegitimate swindles. More than any other antebellum book, *The Confidence-Man* indicates how arbitrary that distinction is.

Although these two ways of reading the book appear to conflict, they need not. A common theme underlying its many incidents and anecdotes is that things are not what they are advertised to be. This is especially true of the promises made by the country's system of justice, as we learn from a number of characters who have suffered because of its judgments. These explicit examples of injustice are supplemented by numerous examples of people who promise fellow passengers charity and then treat them uncharitably. If Melville's dramatization of the untrustworthiness of the phrase "Charity never faileth" is not an explicit comment on the failure of the legal system, charity did indeed fail as an adequate response to the injustices perpetuated by the legal system's free-agent ideology.

The theme that things are not what they seem to be also underlies Melville's self-conscious reflections on the general nature of fiction. A work of fiction presents itself to the public as a reality it is not. In *The Confidence-Man* Melville himself reflects upon fictionality by adopting a technique of ironic subversion that, in turn, functions by saying one thing while meaning another. Melville's concern with the counterfeit nature of writing helps us to see how his works question the dominant legal ideology of the time; in a world in which social relations are defined

183

by written contracts, to explore the nature of writing is to understand better the society in which that writing takes place. Like "Bartleby," *The Confidence-Man* comments on the craft of writing at the same time that it documents how the legal system was bound to the market economy and how questions of justice are circumscribed by contract ideology. In this chapter I will start by looking at the legal implications of Melville's self-reflexive commentary on the nature of writing and what it reveals about the failure of charity and the American dream of justice. I will then turn to Tom Frye's story, which explicitly condemns the judicial system while suggesting the difficulties Melville faced as a writer who had to deal with an uncharitable public. I will conclude by looking at a historical case similar to Frye's, one taking us closer to Melville's fictional world of *Billy Budd, Sailor*.

Many agreements in *The Confidence-Man* are oral, but one that is not poignantly illustrates what is at stake when we trust writing by drawing up a contract. Late in the novel, the Cosmopolitan, an avatar of the Confidence Man who dominates the second half of the book, enters the ship's barbershop. The barber, having learned from experience that when he grants credit his labor often is not rewarded, has posted a sign saying, "No Trust." This policy greatly disturbs the Cosmopolitan, who asks the barber for a shave. After a long discussion about the value of confidence, the Cosmopolitan convinces the barber to "try, for the remainder of the present trip, the experiment of trusting men." Playing with the financial implications of the free-agent ideology, Melville goes on to give the barber's qualification to this experiment in trust. "True, to save his credit as a free agent, he was loud in averring that it was only for the novelty of the thing that he so agreed, and he required the other, as before volunteered, to go security to him against any loss that might ensue. . . . Still the more to save his credit, he now insisted upon it, as a last point, that the agreement should be put in black and white, especially the security part."[1]

Drawing up the contract, the Cosmopolitan questions the necessity for putting the agreement "in black and white." "'I shall make a poor lawyer, I fear. Ain't used, you see, barber, to a business which, ignoring the principle of honor, holds no nail fast till clinched. Strange, barber,' taking up the blank paper, 'that such flimsy stuff as this should make such strong hawsers; vile hawsers, too'" (*CM* 324). But the barber insists that the contract be written and signed and then taken to the captain for safekeeping, "because the captain was necessarily a party disinterested, and what was more, could not, from the nature of the present case, make anything by a breach of trust" (324). Appalled at such a lack of trust, the Cosmopolitan refuses to leave the contract with a third party and gives it to the barber to hold. Predictably, when the barber asks for an advance to cover losses, the Cosmopolitan refuses, arguing that it is written in the contract that he will cover any losses. Finally, when the barber asks merely to be paid for the Cosmopolitan's shave, the Cosmopolitan refuses, again pointing to the contract that obliges the barber to accept credit for the remainder of the trip. When the Cosmopolitan leaves, the barber tears up the contract and replaces his sign: "No Trust."

Within the context of *The Confidence-Man,* where every transaction is a potential swindle, there is little doubt that the Cosmopolitan has used the contract to cheat the barber. For our purposes, however, it is important to imagine what would happen if the barber tried to take the case to court to recover his losses. In the eyes of the law it would be the barber, not the Cosmopolitan, who had broken the terms of the contract. Rather than live up to its conditions, the barber tears it up and restores the sign he agreed to remove, all the while having no concrete proof that the Cosmopolitan will not live up to the terms he agreed to. But if the barber's lack of trust virtually guarantees that he will not be able to seek remedy in court to be compensated for his labor in shaving the Cosmopolitan, it will guarantee payment from future customers. Given the world he lives in, the barber cannot afford the luxury of trust, since, as he says (if we can trust him), "I have a family" (318).

This bizarre yet plausible encounter in which a written contract is drawn to require someone to have confidence in his customers' word by removing a written sign announcing a lack of trust emphasizes the powerful authority our society grants to the writing on pieces of paper. As such, it forces us to reexamine the notion, quite fashionable in literary criticism today, that Western culture privileges the spoken word over the written word.[2] To be sure, we often betray a nostalgia for a lost world in which the fullness of the spoken word reigned, in which someone's word was binding, a nostalgia that the Cosmopolitan continually exploits. But that nostalgia itself indicates how little legal authority our culture actually grants to the spoken word. Far from being misled by a naive belief in the presence of the spoken word, those familiar with the laws regulating the market economy know that it cannot be trusted in business transactions. If they indulge in a mystification, it is a mystification of the written word, for, as the phrase "Put it in writing" illustrates, in a world ruled by the contractarian ideology, texts constitute binding authority.

The authority granted to written contracts is closely related to the transformations taking place in the marketplace. As Michael Rogin writes,

> Status, family, historically rooted relationship, and the insignias of dress marked a person's identity in traditional, stable societies. Modern strangers who came together to buy, to sell, and to persuade revealed

themselves by their performances. The performing self in public was not expected to act like the natural self at home. Nevertheless, relations of exchange among strangers in public required confidence in the reliability of appearances; there were good reasons, in antebellum America, not to have it.[3]

The written contract promised to fix the uncertainty caused by the new market conditions. It was hoped that if potential confidence men inscribed their words in a written contract they would be forced to stick to their promises. But, as the Cosmopolitan shows, contracts can be as untrustworthy as the spoken word. The reasons why are many.

For one, the contracts used to stabilize the unstable conditions brought about by an increasingly impersonal market economy contributed to its impersonality. As Peter Coleman puts it, "Customers became names on pieces of paper rather than faces and personalities."[4] Thus, paper contracts, along with paper money, were attacked by some for causing the instability that pervaded most Americans' lives.

Although part of the distrust of the paper economy grew out of a nostalgia for traditional face-to-face relations, part of it grew out of an unarticulated awareness of one of the paradoxical characteristics of writing. To fix words on a piece of paper is not to guarantee a stable meaning: quite the contrary. As both lawyers and literary critics know, finding the "true" meaning of a written text is no easy task. Separated from their author the moment they are put on paper, written words seem to take on a life of their own and allow many possible interpretations. Only through establishing a socially agreed upon mode of interpretation can their meaning be fixed. Yet it is a distinctive fact of the antebellum period that the legal guidelines on how to interpret contracts continually fluctuated. In a debate familiar to literary critics, jurists had to decide whether a contract expressed the intent of the parties involved or whether its words had an objective meaning independent of the parties' intentions.[5] The fluctuating criteria for the interpretation of contracts help to suggest the arbitrariness of the authority granted to them.

The distance between the words of a written document and their source not only makes their meaning impossible to pin down; it also renders them far easier to counterfeit than spoken words. The counterfeiting of paper documents and paper money so prevalent in *The Confidence-Man* threatened to disrupt the entire economic system of antebellum America. As Hugh Kenner points out in *The Counterfeiters*, to counterfeit something is not necessarily to indulge in an act of imitation.[6] For example, many counterfeit documents bring a completely new document into existence rather than copying an already existing one. The counterfeit imitates not an object but an invisible authorizing act that grants a document legitimacy. Not surprisingly, with the rise of the market economy the penalty for counterfeiting dramatically increased, for to counterfeit is to undermine a society's accepted criteria of legitimacy, criteria established in America by a legal system that expresses its authority in yet more documents.

The authority accorded documents in American society raises another possibility for counterfeiting. Ruled by law, not men, Americans submit to the authority of documents that ostensibly have the "people" as their author. The Declaration of Independence, the Constitution, the laws of the land are legitimized because they "represent" the people. But there are hints throughout *The Confidence-Man* that those who claim to represent the people may be indulging in an elaborate masquerade. Tracing Melville's use of the image of a "federated" people from *Redburn* to *The Confidence-Man*, we can see that the authority granted the laws of the land in the name of the people may be a counterfeit of the highest order.

Sailing from America to England, the title character of *Redburn* encounters "Dock-Wall beggars" when he lands in Liverpool. Realizing that some of these poor are destined for America, Redburn contemplates their fate while affirming his belief in the promise of the New World. "We are the heirs of all time, and with all nations we divide our inheritance. On this Western Hemisphere all tribes and people are forming into one federated whole; and there is a future which shall see the estranged children of Adam restored as to the old hearth-stone in Eden" (*R* 169). In a famous passage in *Moby-Dick,* the *Pequod* is described as "federat[ing] along one keel . . . an Anacharsis Clootz deputation" (*MD* 166). In *The Confidence-Man* the ship forms an "Anacharsis Cloots congress of all kinds of that multiform pilgrim species, man" (*CM* 14). If the *Fidèle's* congress of humankind is not led on an apocalyptic voyage of destruction by a mad captain, its fate is no more reassuring. The mixture of all the tribes and people assembled on Melville's Mississippi riverboat results in a world in which the gaudy Cosmopolitan can flourish. "A cosmopolitan, a catholic man; who, being such, ties himself to no narrow tailor or teacher, but federates, in heart as in costume, something of the various gallantries of men under the suns" (*CM* 186).

The Cosmopolitan's boast reminds us of the spurious nature of the country's claim to be a melting pot federating the various people of the earth. Like glorified American rhetoric, the Cosmopolitan's ostentatious display of color serves to blind us to the dark side of American life constituted by those excluded from or repressed by the sacred covenant. That underworld is suggested on the *Fidèle* by the emigrants' quarters. Rather than entering the promised land imagined for them by Redburn, emigrants are confined to quarters described as "purgatory" (*CM* 100). Dimly lit, "designed more to pass the night in, than the day" (99), these quarters crowd together as many beds as possible. Beds "devised by some sardonic foe of poor travelers, to deprive them of that tranquillity which should precede, as well as accompany, slumber, – Procrustean beds, on whose hard grain humble worth and honesty writhed, still invoking repose, while but torment responded" (99–100). Decrying these conditions, a decidedly uncynical narrative voice cries, "Ah, did any one make such a bunk for himself, instead of having it made for him, it might be just, but how cruel, to say, You must lie on it!" (100).[7]

The narrator's response draws attention to the inadequacy of the standard free-agent argument that an individual is responsible for the conditions in which he or she lives. It therefore lets a modern reader see the discrepancy between justice and humane treatment that existed in antebellum society. Justice on board the *Fidèle* can indeed be cruel, because it was emigrants like those who will crowd these quarters on the return trip who provided the land of the free with a continuous surplus of cheap labor, a surplus that helped "self-made" capitalists reap extensive profits, a surplus that undermined the judicial system's definition of a fair contract between employer and employee. The emigrants arriving were not free agents capable of shaping their own conditions of life. When they arrived they were forced to lie in beds already made for them.

Pitch, searching for a servant, meets the representative of a "Philosophical Intelligence Office" (PIO). "Intelligence office" was the name for a domestic employment agency. The PIO man is upset to hear Pitch praise machines – "things incapable of free agency" (*CM* 161) – at the expense of human beings.[8] Yet when the PIO man humanely defends human beings as free agents, he disguises the fact that in reaping a profit by selling human labor he deprives his boys of any possibility of free agency. One of the most disturbing aspects of *The Confidence-Man* is that the most humane and democratic rhetoric ends up serving inhuman and undemocratic ends.

Like myself, Michael Rogin tries to account for this counterfeit rhetoric by pointing to the dominance of the contractarian ideology in America's market economy. "The marketplace was the arena of masquerade, where values fluctuated, and nothing was as it seemed. There each bourgeois hid his own self-aggrandizing purpose behind a confidence-inspiring exterior. There contractual relations replaced the claims of the heart."[9] I would state this somewhat differently, since it is doubtful that before the rise of the mass market the claims of the heart ruled society. Contractual relations did not so much replace the claims of the heart as alter their status. As the phrase "Charity never faileth" reminds us, the market operates by playing on the feelings of the heart. The feelings of the heart have not been banished from the marketplace; they are everywhere in evidence. In fact, while critics usually emphasize Melville's cynicism, it is important to remember that if the *Fidèle* is full of confidence men, it is also full of people with charitable intentions. The pathos of the book lies in the discrepancy between those intentions and what they achieve, for somehow what could be called a surplus of charity seems incapable of eliminating the world's suffering.

This failure is often explained by the hypocrisy of those with even the most charitable intentions. But, as we saw with the lawyer in "Bartleby," this individualistic explanation is too simple. This is not to argue that individuals do not indulge in hypocritical acts when they come into contact with the Confidence Man, nor that humans have a presocial urge to do good that is corrupted by society. But it is to argue that socially defined actions can be charitable as well as malevolent in spirit. What Melville's work dramatizes is not the replacement of claims of the heart by contractual relations but how the present system of contractual relations creates the conditions whereby charitable acts are intricately linked with hypocrisy.

This link is humorously illustrated when Melville introduces us to a character in the "charity business" (*CM* 54) who proposes to solve the world's suffering by reforming existing charitable organizations to conform with the "Wall Street spirit" (57). When his listener expresses doubt about mixing business and charity, he responds with the practicality of a horologe.

> If, confessedly, certain spiritual ends are to be gained but through the auxiliary agency of worldly means, then, to the surer gaining of such spiritual ends, the example of worldly policy in worldly projects should not by spiritual projectors be slighted. In brief, the conversion of the heathen, so far, at least, as depending on human effort, would, by the world's charity, be let out by contract. So much by bid for converting India, so much for Borneo, so much for Africa. Competition allowed, stimulus would be given. There would be no lethargy of monopoly. We should have no mission-house or tract-house of which slanderers could, with any plausibility, say that it had degenerated in its clerkship into a sort of custom-house. But the main point is the Archimedean money-power that would be brought to bear. (57–8)

Using contracts to accumulate capital in large sums, he would create a corporate charity that could deal with suffering "once and for all and have done with it" (58).

Although this scheme is absurd, its very absurdity shows to what extent charity as it exists on board the *Fidèle* is subordinated to and in part produced by the contractarian ideology. Rather than stand in a dialectical opposition to the conditions that make the Confidence Man's ploys so effective, charity is defined by them. In a world where charity is continually evoked to secure a profit – "real" or "spiritual" – there can be no such thing as pure charity, and in a world where sincerity is potentially counterfeit nothing remains pure, not even counterfeiting itself.

A counterfeit is defined in opposition to what is real, what is authentic. Yet the action of *The Confidence-Man* reminds us that counterfeits themselves can be real. For instance, according to the man from the Black Rapids Coal Company, a depression like that of the panic of 1837 was brought about by "bears" – "destroyers of confidence," who, "whether in stocks, politics, bread-stuffs, morals, metaphysics, religion – be it what it may – trump up black panics in the naturally quiet brightness, solely with a view to some sort of covert advantage" (68). In questioning the "natural" bright view of the world, these bears are "hypocrites by inversion; hypocrites in the simulation of things dark instead of bright; souls that thrive, less upon depression, than the fiction of depression; professors of the wicked art of manufacturing depressions; spurious Jeremiahs; sham Heraclituses" (67–8). Fictional as they might be, these depressions, nonetheless, take place. They can be manufactured because the economy depends on confidence as well as a material base. "Confidence is the indispensable basis of all sorts of business transactions. Without it, commerce between man and man, as between country and country, would, like a watch, run down and stop" (178).

True as this statement is – without confidence in the value of paper currency or the authority of paper contracts the economy would come to a halt – it is ironic that it is made by an avatar of the Confidence Man, who hypocritically profits by gaining people's confidence. Just as the man from the Black Rapids Coal Company admits that destroyers of confidence, "though false in themselves are yet true types" (68), so the Confidence Man, false as he might seem, conveys truth about the world he inhabits. But although there is truth in the Confidence Man's argument for the necessity of confidence, it does not mean that we should trust him. The economy is not generated by confidence alone. It also depends on a material base.[10] If lack of confidence can cause a "fictional" depression, too much can lead to overspeculation and a "real" depression, the difference between the "fictional" and the "real" remaining indistinguishable once a depression occurs.

One way to interpret this inability to distinguish the counterfeit from the real is to argue, as Michael Rogin does, that Melville's fictional world "calls attention to the fictionalized, self-constructed character of American life. The confidence man exposes the absent core of marketplace reality itself."[11] But it could also be argued that in its reliance on written contracts and printed money the new market economy merely draws attention to an absent core that always existed in human relations. The separation between authors and their words so apparent in written documents heightens our awareness of the absences within any system of signs, an absence as constitutive of spoken language as of written, since, as Ferdinand de Saussure has shown, all language consists of differences and separations. Thus, marketplace reality is not the only reality absent at the core.

In fact, insofar as our identity is in part constituted by language, we are all potential confidence men, masquerading as having a secure identity, whereas our identities are actually established through differentiation. This is brought home when we link Pitch's comment to the PIO man – "Ah, you are a talking man – what I call a wordy man. You talk, talk" (*CM* 173) – with Black Guinea's claim "dat dis poor ole darkie is werry well wordy of all you kind ge'mmen's kind confidence" (20). Despite verbal similarities, a "wordy" man is not a "worthy" man, not at all worthy of trust. In turn, Guinea's own series of masquerades, in which he takes on identities of both whites and blacks, recalls the barber's demand that the Cosmopolitan's word be put in "black and white." The black and white of writing emphasizes the differentiation that inevitably occurs in the establishment of identity.

Combined with the book's rich mythological allusions, embracing Eastern and Western cultures, Melville's exploration into the nature of writing seems to suggest a world in which history itself becomes an elaborate masquerade. For instance, slavery, one of the most controversial economic issues of the time, which threatened the authority of the country's entire legal system, was intricately connected with the question of separating people into blacks and whites. The movement in "Benito Cereno" from the story's opening grays to the blacks and whites that Delano notices the moment he boards the slave ship can be seen as slave society's reenactment of the eternal problem involved in establishing identity.[12]

But if issues like slavery seem to be absorbed by an ahistorical problematic, it is the interweaving of Melville's metaphysical speculations with historical specificity that makes *The Confidence-Man,* indeed all of his works, so complex. *The Confidence-Man* may speculate on the counterfeit nature of all identities, but that speculation has profound implications for a legal system that places so much confidence in the secure identity of free agents. In turn, Melville's speculations on identity were influenced by a world in which counterfeiting and imposture became widespread as the result of conditions linked to the establishment of free-agent ideology in the law – identity itself being in part a legal definition. Finally, as the reflexiveness of the book illustrates, Melville himself cannot escape the conditions he describes. Presenting himself to the public as a wordy man, Melville becomes the supreme confidence man, trying to pawn off a counterfeit world of fiction on a reading public whose confidence he must win if he is to reap a profit. Although the book's reflex-ivity invites a reading that turns the techniques of metafiction into meta-physical principles, it also opens us up to the world that helped to produce such explicitly self-reflexive techniques.

Michael Rogin argues that "the ur-story underneath *The Confidence-Man* is the bankruptcy, madness, and death of Allan Melvill. He is the missing person behind the novel's confidence games." It seems to me, however, that the story of Melville's own failure in the literary mar-ketplace is a much more obvious influence on his portrayal of the market economy, although neither that story nor the one of his absent father, will, as Rogin claims, make the "fictional fragments of *The Confidence-Man* whole."[13] Nonetheless, it does give added resonance to the story of Thomas Fry, the book's most outspoken critic of how the legal system favors the rich. In turn, Fry's story illustrates how Melville's failure in the marketplace is related to his awareness of the counterfeit nature of the American federal republic's claim to provide justice for all.

Fry, so he tells the herb-doctor, was a hardworking cooper in New York City until his twenty-third year. A great patriot at the time, he attended a political meeting one night where he witnessed a scuffle "between a gentleman who had been drinking wine and a pavior who was sober. The pavior chewed tobacco, and the gentleman said it was beastly in him, and pushed him, wanting to have his place. The pavior chewed on and pushed back. Well, the gentleman carried a sword-cane, and present-ly the pavior was down, skewered" (*CM* 132). The pavior died, and Fry, as a witness was taken with the gentleman to the Tombs. The gentleman came up with bail, but Fry could not and was forced to wait for the trial in jail, where the dampness crippled him. At the trial, even though the pavior had merely been trying to "maintain his rights" and despite Fry's testimony that he saw the gentleman's "steel go in, and saw it sticking in" (133), the gentleman was acquitted because of the influence of his rich friends. The gentleman and his friends celebrated his victory in a park, but Fry had nowhere to go and was sent to the Corporation Hospital, where his health further deteriorated. After three years, he left the hospi-tal, a hopeless invalid, reduced to begging.

The herb-doctor, considering Fry's story in the light of what he be-lieves to be the "system of things," finds it "so incompatible with all" (135) that he refuses to believe it. According to him, the law must be fair. "It is never to be forgotten that human government, being subordinate to the divine, must needs, therefore, in its degree, partake of the charac-teristics of the divine" (137). If, as in Fry's case, it seems that the law has acted unfairly, the herb-doctor reassures him that to "one who has a right confidence, final benignity" is certain (137). Thus, when Fry throws out "unhandsome notions" about "free Ameriky" (136), the herb-doctor asks him, "Where is your patriotism? Where your gratitude?" (136).

Fry has faced an audience like the herb-doctor before and knows that it is useless to argue. To argue, after all, brings him no money. To transform his misery into cash, he cannot offer the public a story that clashes with its belief in the "system of things," a system that the public thinks is ultimately just. Accordingly, adopting the costume of a war veteran, he tells the ship's passengers that he was crippled while serving in the glorious Mexican War and is promptly rewarded with handouts.

Rufus Choate, proposing that writers of fiction should select positive aspects of American history for their topics, in order to "impress the facts, the lessons of history, more deeply, and incorporate them more intimately into the general mind and heart, and current and common knowledge of the people," had imagined that "they would melt down, as it were, and stamp the heavy bullion into a convenient, universal circulating medium."[14] In *The Confidence-Man* Melville shows to what extent the melted-down bullion of history circulated in America is counterfeit and how any version of American history that does not conform to this counterfeit version will find little circulation. Certainly, Fry's necessity to replace his unsettling story about "free Ameriky" with a patriotic one, in order to earn a living, recalls Melville's inability to market stories that suggest flaws in the American "system of things."

Melville's inability to market works that would expose the inequities of the legal system provides a link between the two aspects of *The Confidence-Man* with which this chapter began; the book's modernism and its response to market conditions supported by the American legal system. Modernist techniques are often considered to result from artists' reflection upon purely aesthetic matters, but the legal issues with which Melville deals in his most "modern" texts allow us to see some of the social and political preconditions for such reflections. Melville's reflection upon his role as artist and the nature of fiction is in part a response to his failure in the marketplace, which in turn is in part the result of his desire to expose the counterfeit claims of America's republican rhetoric, a rhetoric most obviously exposed in the false promise of its legal system to provide justice for all. As Fry's story suggests, the fate of someone who bears witness to such injustice is social estrangement. His alleged imprisonment in the Tombs recalls Bartleby's fate. Bartleby, however, refuses to play the role of Happy Tom by telling a happy story.[15]

After *The Confidence-Man,* Melville himself seems to have adopted Bartleby's option. For almost thirty years he preferred not to write any more prose fiction and turned to writing poetry for a small audience. When he finally returned to prose fiction, the most important story he produced was *Billy Budd, Sailor,* a work that will allow us further to explore the preconditions of a modernist aesthetic. Like *The Confidence-Man, Billy Budd* is considered a proto-modernist text because of its reflection on its own forms. Also like *The Confidence-Man, Billy Budd* is concerned with a possible discrepancy between what appears just and what is. If in *The Confidence-Man* a murder trial is only one of many incidents, in *Billy Budd* it is central to the book's action.

Before turning to Melville's final fictional treatment of the law, I will end this chapter with an account of a murder case that provides a historical connection between Melville's cynical vision of American justice in *The Confidence-Man* and what has been termed his tragic vision of justice in *Billy Budd.* Surrounded by accusations that the judiciary had exhibited class bias, the case has many similarities with the one narrated by Fry. Resulting in the death of a youthful hero and taking place in the context of political strife in which Americans accused one another of sympathizing with Jacobin rebels or British monarchists, it has many similarities with the action of *Billy Budd.* Occurring before Melville was born but related to him through family history, it also introduces us to connections between Melville and an important naval family that produced a Captain Vere-like officer who disputed Melville's vision of the system of things.

Benjamin Austin was the cousin of William Austin, the lawyer-author of "Martha Gardner" and a partisan Jeffersonian editor of the *Boston Chronicle.* He was well known as "Honestus," who, at the height of Shays' Rebellion, in 1786, had written a series of newspaper essays calling for the annihilation of the legal order. Like many anti-Federalists of his day, he distrusted lawyers as defenders of Federalist policy and sympathizers with the British monarchy. Federalists responded by calling anti-Federalists Jacobins.

On the thirtieth anniversary of the Declaration of Independence, Austin helped to sponsor a large public dinner. Later a dispute arose as to payment of the bill. Thomas O. Selfridge, a prominent Federalist lawyer in his thirties, helped bring suit to recover payment. When the bill was paid, Benjamin Austin stated that "everything would have been all right if it had not been for the interference of a damned Federal lawyer." Selfridge demanded a retraction of Austin's statement. Austin made inquiries and did correct his statement to those who had heard him, but Selfridge demanded a written retraction. Austin refused, and Selfridge wrote an insulting letter and published an advertisement in the *Boston Gazette:* "I hereby publish said Austin as a coward, a liar, and a scoundrel; and if said Austin has the effrontery to deny any part of the charge he shall be silenced by the most irrefragable proof."[16]

Fearful of a personal attack, the aging Austin told a friend of Self-ridge's, "If Mr. Selfridge attacks me, I hope to have such support from friends at hand as shall be able to avoid any injury" or, as testified by another witness, "he should not meddle with Selfridge himself, but some person on a footing with him should take him in hand."[17] Selfridge heard Austin's comment and took it as a threat. Austin's son, an eigh-teen-year-old Harvard student and a universal favorite with remarkable promise, had read Selfridge's advertisement in the *Gazette*. Seeing his father's enemy in downtown Boston, Austin approached him, carrying a long hickory cane. Exactly what happened then is unclear. Selfridge claimed that when Austin struck him a heavy blow on the head, he responded by shooting him with a pistol he had pocketed on leaving his office. Austin's supporters claimed that Selfridge fired first and that Aus-tin struck him repeatedly as he fell to his death. At any rate, Selfridge quickly surrendered himself to civil authorities in order, as he put it, "*to escape into prison* to elude *the fury of democracy.*"[18]

Anti-Federalists were indeed furious. The *Chronicle*'s obituary lamented the premature loss of a young man with "beauty of youth . . . excellent in virtue, and rich in expectation." According to the paper, it was young Austin's "filial piety" that "received the fatal ball which probably had been prepared for the fond bosom of his father!" When the coroner's jury declared Selfridge's act "willfull murder," anti-Federalist papers called it a "Federal murder." They were even more outraged when the grand jury, headed by a prominent Federalist mer-chant, neglected to consult anti-Federalist Attorney General Sullivan and brought in an indictment for manslaughter only. They were guided in their decision by Chief Justice Theophilus Parsons's explanation, in his charge to the jury, of the differences between murder, manslaughter, and justifiable homicide. "If the party killing had reasonable ground for be-lieving that the person slain had a felonious design against him and under that supposition kills him, although it should appear that there was no such design, it will not be murder but it would be either manslaughter or excusable homicide, according to the degree of caution used and the probable ground of such belief."[19] Parsons's charge carried the day, but it neglected important considerations. As the biographer of James Sul-livan notes, "In laying down the law of murder and manslaughter, Par-sons omitted certain maxims of general recognition bearing on the case. . . . One of the rules thus omitted was that the party justifying killing from necessity must be himself wholly without fault; another, that he had no possible, or at least probable means of escape; a third, that the crime prevented by the killing would have been itself capital; and a fourth, that no provocation will avail, if sought."[20]

When the actual trial for manslaughter began, Parsons pled illness and

assigned newly appointed Isaac Parker to sit. Later to become chief justice, Parker was the judge who died during the White murder trials,
making way for Lemuel Shaw to become chief justice. Selfridge's attorney, Samuel Dexter, played to the jury by supplementing Selfridge's
claim of self-defense with the argument that a man's honor was as sacred
as a woman's virtue and that Selfridge was justified in killing Austin to
save his honor. Attorney General Sullivan responded,

> Is there any distinction between the would-be nobleman and the
> chimney-sweep? . . . Is there a distinction between them as to their
> privilege of self-defense? Is the push of the sweep, or a stroke with his
> scraper at the head of his comrade, to be a murder in him, whilst the
> other shall be allowed, with his gold-headed cane, or his elegantly-
> mounted pistol, in defense of his honor, to play a secure but mortal
> game, and be justified in killing, on a like provocation, either his friend
> or his foe, or, as in this case, a man he is hardly said to know? You are
> not, then, to determine his case by the circumstances attending it, but
> by the nice sense of honor of the gentleman, or the distinction and
> dignity of his station. What, then, has become of that part of the con-
> stitution which declares ours to be a government of laws, and not of
> men?[21]

But the jury paid no heed to Sullivan's plea. Like the gentleman in Fry's
story, Selfridge was acquitted.

Anti-Federalists attributed Selfridge's acquittal to the Federalist bias of
Selfridge's friends in the judicial system. "Murder is no crime in a
Federal lawyer," exclaimed some. Others hanged Selfridge and Parsons
in effigy. Dr. Nathaniel Ames called the agitation a response to the
"reign of Pettifogarchy."[22] Federalists, however, denied any political
bias in the decision. In his charge, Judge Parker, like Parsons a Federalist,
had remarked on the political atmosphere surrounding the trial, but
assured all that he did not believe that "any general apprehension is
entertained that a man accused of crime is to be saved or destroyed
according to the political notions he entertains." In a pamphlet explaining his side of the case, Selfridge claimed, "Nothing of a political nature
ought, even in the remotest degree to have been connected with the
transaction, for it was a mere personal controversy."[23]

Anti-Federalists were not convinced. According to Charles Warren, it
took many years for Boston society and politics to recover from the
influence of the "partisan dissensions and the personal passions which
[the case] evoked. . . . for, without question, part of the confirmed bit-
terness of the leaders of the opposing political parties is traceable directly
to the supporters of the two figures in this murder."[24] Significantly,
Melville had relatives who had served as witnesses for both parties.

Testifying on behalf of Selfridge's character was a young Federalist lawyer named Lemuel Shaw. Shaw's father, the Reverend John Shaw, had run a school in Haverhill, Massachusetts, attended by Benjamin Austin's cousin William in preparation for Harvard. Lemuel's mother, the sister of Abigail Adams, was related to the Austin family by marriage. Shaw had known Selfridge, a regular contributor to the *Gazette,* a Federalist paper, and it was through Selfridge that Shaw was asked to write for the paper. They got along well enough for Shaw to leave his old law office and enter that of Selfridge. From the first, Shaw believed in his friend's innocence.

Called to testify for the prosecutor was Major Thomas Melvill, Herman's grandfather, the man who would be memorialized in a poem by Oliver Wendell Holmes as the last person in Boston to wear a three-cornered hat (the last but one to do so was Benjamin Austin). Melvill's testimony contributed to the trial's "most remarkable discrepancy." One of two customers in a barbershop on State Street, outside of which the homicide took place, Melvill was reported to be one of the first to reach Selfridge after the incident. At the trial the major was asked to confirm the barber's testimony that he was standing at the door of the shop and saw Selfridge shoot before Austin struck him. Melvill confirmed that the barber was at the door. The other customer claimed that he was seated inside and did not move to the door until the shot was fired. If the barber's testimony had been accepted, Selfridge would have been convicted of manslaughter. As it was, the jury discounted the barber's testimony, along with that of Melville's grandfather. According to reports after the trial, the barber was so shaken by the jury's having doubted his testimony that he, like Melville's fictional witness Thomas Fry, suffered impaired health, whereas Federalist lawyer Selfridge gained his freedom.[25]

Despite the similarities between the *Selfridge* case and the case narrated by Thomas Fry in *The Confidence-Man,* we will never know how much – if anything – Melville knew about this controversial incident involving two of his relatives. We do know that it was possible for Melville to have remained aware of the Selfridge family throughout his life. While at work on *Billy Budd,* Melville could have read about the court-martial of Selfridge's grandson, Rear Adm. Thomas O. Selfridge, Jr., for firing in Japanese waters. Just as his grandfather was acquitted for killing an innocent youth at the turn of the century, so Selfridge was acquitted of all charges against him. This same naval commander was a Civil War hero, having saved the flag of the *Cumberland* when it was sunk by the *Merrimack,* a battle commemorated by Melville in his poem "*The Cumberland*" in *Battle-Pieces.*

Years earlier, Melville had raised the ire of this hero's father, who was also Rear Adm. Thomas O. Selfridge. The son of the former friend of Shaw was upset at Melville's publication of *White-Jacket.* A pious, temperate man and a strict disciplinarian, who had served as a midshipman on the *United States,* Selfridge wrote a twenty-one-page memorandum taking issue with Melville's fictional account of the forms and usages in the navy. Although his criticism of Melville was not published in his lifetime, Selfridge sounds a bit like Melville's Captain Vere. Like Vere, he has little appreciation of fiction. Most of his criticism had to do with Melville's fictional distortion of the actual state of affairs on the *United States.* Never, he declared, had he known a work professing to "give a true picture of men and things" in which there were "so many misnomers, misstatements and inconsistencies – so many improbabilities, false premises and false conclusions – so much of the marvellous and absurd." Putting "complaints into men's mouths that we never heard uttered," denouncing "ceremony and etiquette, and all discipline that does not square with his own peculiar notions," Melville would "make us believe there is nothing but wrong and injustice within the wooden walls of a ship of war." Worse, he "strives to convince his readers that all corporal punishment, for whatever offence, is no more nor less than tyranny; and that men would be justified in resisting this mode of correction even so far as to bring their conduct under the title of mutiny."[26]

Rear Admiral Selfridge's response to Melville's attack on undemocratic naval discipline reminds us how similar the military officer's code of honor and duty was to the code of honor and duty governing the behavior of the antebellum's upper class. Just as Commander Mackenzie cited duty and honor in defending his hanging of the three sailors on the *Somers,* so Rear Admiral Selfridge's father cited duty and honor in defending his killing of young Austin. In Melville's final work of prose fiction, the trial of Billy Budd interweaves considerations of class conflict emphasized by the *Selfridge* case and Thomas Fry's story of injustice in *The Confidence-Man* with considerations of a proper code of military discipline and duty raised by the *Somers* affair and *White-Jacket.* Considered by many readers a tragedy of innocence, the story of Billy Budd nonetheless reconfirms their sense of the system of things, since, like Thomas Fry's fabricated account of how he became a cripple while serving in the glorious Mexican War, it emphasizes the need of individual sacrifices to defend a country's honor and system of justice. Read another way, however, the tale is more like Fry's original story of injustice, since it raises important questions about the justice guaranteed by the honored tradition of Anglo-American law.

Part III

Billy Budd and Re-righting Legal History

9

Measured Forms

With *Billy Budd, Sailor* we return to a compelling but familiar story, the story told by James Fenimore Cooper in *The Pioneers* and repeated in America throughout the nineteenth century about the conflict between the demands of individual freedom and the need of society to be governed by rational, impartial laws. In Billy, Melville presents us with one of his most sympathetic individual characters, and in Captain Vere he presents us with his most eloquent spokesman for social order. Captain Vere is highly persuasive because he defends social order in the name of mankind, not a specific class interest. Describing Vere's response to the disruption of rule by law during the French Revolution, the narrator writes,

> His settled convictions were as a dike against those invading waters of novel opinion social, political, and otherwise, which carried away as in a torrent no few minds in those days, minds by nature not inferior to his own. While other members of that aristocracy to which by birth he belonged were incensed at the innovators mainly because their theories were inimical to the privileged classes, Captain Vere disinterestedly opposed them not alone because they seemed to him insusceptible of embodiment in lasting institutions, but at war with the peace of the world and the true welfare of mankind.[1]

In Lemuel Shaw, Melville had a convenient model for his fictional captain. According to Shaw's modern biographer, Shaw was as impartial as Captain Vere. "He made his name a synonym for integrity, impartiality, and independence. Towering above class and party, doing everything for justice and nothing for fear or favor, he was a model for the American judicial character." Like Vere, Shaw also believed strongly in the importance of preserving institutions and upholding rule by law, so strongly that he argued that even a bad law, "so long as it remains in force . . . is to be respected as law, and because it is the law, not grudgingly and reluctantly, but with honesty and sincerity, because any departure from this fundamental rule of conduct, would put in jeopardy every interest and every institution which is worth saving."[2]

As Robert Cover has demonstrated, Shaw's belief in the necessity to uphold established law forced him to face the conflict between head and heart confronted by Captain Vere. Against the dictates of his heart Captain Vere upholds the law demanding Billy's execution. Against the dictates of his heart Shaw upheld the law demanding the return of fugitive slaves.[3]

It might seem tenuous to think of Shaw, who died in 1861, in connection with *Billy Budd,* written a quarter of a century later. But we should remember that it was indirectly because of Shaw's generosity that Melville gained the economic freedom to write again. When Lemuel Shaw, Jr., died in 1884 he left a valuable estate inherited from his father. From this estate Elizabeth Shaw Melville was bequeathed a legacy that allowed Herman to quit his job at the Custom House and devote energy once again to writing. Furthermore, in 1885, the year in which Melville started thinking about *Billy Budd,* Samuel Shaw, another of Shaw's sons, contributed to a biography of Shaw for the New England Historic and Genealogical Society. Samuel's entry deals with his father's "Early and Domestic Life." The other entry, by P. Emory Aldrich, L.L.B., reviews Shaw's "Professional and Judicial Life."[4] Although there is no proof that Melville knew of this biography, it is hard to imagine that family members would not have told him about a work reporting his marriage to Elizabeth. Whether Melville knew about it or not, the Shaw biography lets us know what people in the late nineteenth century remembered about Melville's father-in-law. Of special interest for readers of *Billy Budd* is the mention in this biography of the Webster murder trial. Melville certainly knew about the trial and Shaw's role in it, because when it occurred in 1850 it was the most sensational murder trial in America. Having already looked at the controversy over Shaw's fugitive slave decisions in Chapter 4, we can turn to the *Webster* case to see what it might tell us about the critical controversy concerning Captain Vere's judgment of Billy Budd.

On trial was Dr. John W. Webster, a professor of chemistry at the Harvard Medical School, accused of murdering Dr. George Parkman, a wealthy Bostonian who had recently provided the money to finance the school. Trained at Harvard and at Guy's Hospital Medical School in London, where he had been a friend and classmate of John Keats, Webster had always lived beyond his means, never adjusting to his disappointment at finding that much of the money he had hoped to receive from his father's estate was tied up in almost worthless Charles River Bridge shares. In debt, he borrowed money from Parkman, the uncle of historian Francis Parkman. Webster acknowledged that on the day Parkman disappeared Parkman had visited him at the school to discuss the debt. But suspicion did not fall on Webster until a week later, when the school janitor found a butchered body in Webster's laboratory, some parts burned in a furnace, some hidden in a trunk, and some thrown down a privy.

The social prominence of all involved and the gruesome circumstances ensured the trial wide publicity. Dr. Webster tried to hire Rufus Choate for his defense, but Choate refused to serve unless Webster would admit he had killed Parkman. Choate was convinced that with Webster's confession he could gain a verdict of manslaughter.[5] Webster, however, refused to confess and ended up with defense attorneys who had no experience in criminal cases. At the same time, the most important voice for the prosecution was not a public official but George Bemis, Boston's foremost criminal lawyer, hired for the case by Parkman money, just as twenty years earlier Daniel Webster had been hired by White money.

To prove the body was Parkman's the prosecution relied heavily on the janitor's testimony, the identification of Parkman's false teeth by his dentist, and the majestic authority of Oliver Wendell Holmes, who claimed, "I am familiar with the appearance of Dr. Parkman's form, and I saw nothing dissimilar from it."[6] The defense countered by offering testimony of Webster's gentle nature from prominent Bostonians such as Jared Sparks, president of Harvard, and the expertise of Dr. William Morton, the celebrated discoverer of anesthesia, who claimed that fire damage made it impossible to identify Parkman's false teeth.

When Dr. Webster was found guilty, there was a general outcry, and many knowledgeable lawyers blamed his attorneys. During the trial, presided over by Shaw, Webster, like accused fugitive slaves, was not allowed to testify on his own behalf, because Massachusetts law feared that his self-interest would make him incompetent. When finally allowed to speak, although not under oath and consideration of the jury, he condemned his lawyers for refusing to consider his detailed notes constructed for his own defense. Basing their defense on the assumption that he had killed Parkman, his lawyers had maneuvered, as Choate would have done, for a verdict of manslaughter. But, as the testimony reveals, the court had never fully established whether the body was actually Parkman's. Furthermore, some, including Attorney General Clifford in his private notes, considered it a "rational hypothesis" that the janitor, who dealt in the underground market for cadavers, had killed Parkman and framed Webster.[7] Like Billy Budd, Webster had entrusted his defense to those who had already prejudged his guilt.

The loudest public outcry, however, was directed not against Webster's lawyers but against Shaw, because of his charge to the jury. Shaw saved many of the letters and newspaper articles protesting his behavior, and they remained within the family until they were finally donated with the Shaw papers to the Massachusetts Historical Society. Among these documents is an anonymous pamphlet by a "member of the legal profession," published in New York City, where Melville was then living. Commenting on Shaw's charge, the author writes, "From beginning to end it is but an argument against the prisoner. Proceeding from the Bench, it is an argument with all the moral force of a positive dictation to the jury; a dictation which made the pretended trial by *twelve* men a farce and a mockery." He continues, "What ulterior purpose was to be accomplished, or what feeling of interest or resentment was to be gratified by such an extraordinary judicial usurpation as this, we do not pretend even to conjecture; but we do not hesitate to declare, that to find a parallel for such an unscrupulous prostitution of dignity, such an unblushing betrayal of the sanctity of the judicial office, we must go back to the days of Jeffries."[8] George Jeffreys, lord chief justice of England, flagrantly violated the code of justice in his "Bloody Assizes" of 1685 when he condemned over three hundred people to death after Monmouth's Rebellion. In *The Confidence-Man* we hear of a "judicial murderer and a Jeffries, after a fierce farce trial condemning his victim to bloody death" (*CM* 207).

In addition to the anonymous pamphlet, there were unfavorable newspaper accounts of Shaw's conduct. A Philadelphia paper called Webster's conviction the "result of an inquisition, in which everything of law, nearly, was forgotten, except its forms, and a verdict was hurried into with a blind recklessness and infatuation heretofore unknown to Courts and jury-boxes."[9] The affair was compared to Puritan witch trials and the hanging of Quakers. An anonymous note to Shaw charged that "you have in this case performed the double duty of judge and juror; and it is owing to your outrageous conduct that [Webster] was convicted."[10] Professor Joel Parker of Harvard, former chief justice of New Hampshire, published a long critique of Shaw's rulings on homicide in the *North American Review* in 1851.[11]

Often the outcome was seen in terms of class bias. A letter to the *New York Globe,* signed "A Mechanic," stated, "The time has passed in this land when the few can govern the many. Our bodies may be chained, but our minds never! We begin to ascertain that the class claiming all the learning, honesty, and piety in our country, are not the Simon Pures they would have us believe. Do you, or does any one suppose, that if the positions of Webster and Parkman had been reversed, that Parkman would have been convicted on such testimony?" The *Globe* itself claimed that "pusillanimity or prejudice, or something worse had swerved [Shaw] from the path of judicial integrity." Another Philadelphia paper printed an editorial headed "Judicial Murder in Boston," claiming that "judges, jury, and even the prisoner's counsel, have been awed by the wealth of the [Parkman] family."[12]

Much of the outcry against Shaw was provoked by the criteria he used for establishing the fact of homicide. According to common-law tradition, in a murder trial the fact that a homicide was committed had to be proved by direct evidence, beyond the least doubt. Once the fact of homicide was established, the prosecution had to show beyond a reasonable doubt that the defendant had committed the crime. In his charge, however, Shaw required that the commission of homicide be proved "beyond a reasonable doubt" only. As our "Member of the Legal Profession" argued, "This again is law manufactured for the occasion. It is not the law of the land. It is not the common law of England. It is not the law of Massachusetts. It will be found nowhere but in the charge of Chief Justice Shaw. To verify his position he cites no authority, for the simple reason that none exists."[13]

Despite these criticisms, Shaw seemed to be exonerated when Dr. Webster's confession was printed in the *Boston Traveler*. But there were irregularities even about Webster's confession. It was not made in public but in private, through Rev. George Putnam, who during the trial had been in contact with the Parkmans and had written to the attorney general, making suggestions to help gain a conviction. The Boston press, except for the *Traveler,* considered Putnam's confession a hoax.

There are obvious similarities between the accusations made against Shaw and the ones critics have made against Vere. Vere has been accused, as Shaw was, of manufacturing law for the occasion and of swerving from the path of judicial integrity. To many observers, only some ulterior motive could account for Vere's and Shaw's vigorous argument for conviction, and especially for the death sentence, from reluctant juries. Having finally been convinced by Vere that Billy must be found guilty, a member of the drumhead court asks falteringly, "Can we not convict and yet mitigate the penalty?" (*BB* 108). In Webster's trial, when finally the jury had agreed that Webster had killed Parkman, it still hesitated on the question of willful murder. "Quite a pause ensued. One juror, in his sympathies of kindness for the prisoner (who was his personal acquaintance or friend) and his afflicted family, shrunk from the 'fiery ordeal.' 'Can't we stop here? – can't the law be vindicated and justice satisfied, if we pause here? Must we take the *life* of the unhappy prisoner?' "[14] That Webster's life was taken was due in part to Shaw's charge to the jury, just as Vere's rhetoric virtually commands the drumhead court to hang Billy.

But if Vere's and Shaw's critics interpret their vigorous pursuit of a conviction as evidence of bias, their supporters cite it as evidence of their judicial character. Any bias that might have existed was not evident in their outward manner. For both, execution of the law seemed a painful duty. Just as Vere feels drawn toward Billy, so Shaw felt sympathy for Webster, whom he had met socially while serving as a fellow and over-seer at Harvard. Similarly Vere, as he leaves a last, private interview with Billy, meets the senior lieutenant, who observes the captain. "The face he beheld, for the moment one expressive of the agony of the strong, was to that officer, though a man of fifty, a startling revelation. That the condemned one suffered less than he who mainly had effected the con-demnation was apparently indicated by the former's exclamation in the scene soon perforce to be touched upon" (*BB* 113). In his obituary notice of Shaw, Charles Loring remarks, "Indeed, in witnessing his discharge of his painful duty of his office upon the prisoner, it was often difficult to believe that he was not at the time the greater sufferer of the two."[15] Witnesses at the Webster trial reported that in his last address to Webster, Shaw was "at times quite interrupted by emotion."[16] Describing the difficulty of making his judgment, Shaw declared, "Nothing but a sense of imperative duty imposed on us by the law, whose officers and minis-ters we are, could sustain us in pronouncing such a judgment." The sentence was, after all, the "voice of the law, and not our own."[17] Similarly, Vere, soon after reminding his fellow officers that their uni-forms signal their duty to the king, not nature, remarks, "Our vowed responsibility is in this: That however pitilessly that law may operate in any instances, we nevertheless adhere to it and administer it" (*BB* 106). Shaw's sympathetic biographer summarizes Shaw's behavior with a de-scription that could just as easily have been written by a sympathetic literary critic describing Vere. "Had Shaw's sense of duty been less profound, or had he been a weaker man, he would have availed himself of his acquaintance with the prisoner as a reason for declining to sit in the case. He did not waver, however, in his determination to do whatever his obligation to the law demanded, and performed his office, with private feelings repressed, the embodiment of stern, impartial justice."[18]

The controversy over Shaw's determination to do whatever his position of authority demanded in the Webster murder trial recalls the controver-sy over the case most often cited as a source for *Billy Budd* – the *Somers* affair. I have already looked briefly at the *Somers* affair in Chapter 6. As I noted there, important pro-Union Whigs supported Mackenzie, who claimed that his duty as commander had forced him to hang three sailors at sea in order to save his ship from the threat of mutiny. Mackenzie himself, we saw, was an important figure. Like Vere, he was a man with literary tastes. In addition to his naval articles in Lieber's *Encyclopedia Americana* and his well-received *Year in Spain,* he had written biographies of commodores Perry and Decatur. (Hawthorne once tried to arrange for

Melville to write a biography of Perry's brother, Matthew, who "opened" Japan.) Mackenzie's family had connections with the Democratic party in New York and his personal connections were to prove valuable, because his opponents were also powerful. One of the three men hanged at sea by Mackenzie, and the alleged ringleader, was Philip Spencer, the son of Secretary of War John Spencer.

The secretary of war was an able lawyer with enough scholarly leanings to have edited an edition of Alexis de Tocqueville's *Democracy in America*. Appointed by President Tyler, he had drifted with Tyler away from the Whigs in the direction of the Democratic party. After the *Somers* affair he was made secretary of the treasury, and in 1844 he was nominated for a seat on the Supreme Court. Opposition from Whigs and from enemies made during the controversy over the *Somers* affair, however, ruled out his confirmation by the Senate.

Much of the controversy grew out of Spencer's attempt to have Mackenzie tried for murder. Outraged over his son's death and by Mackenzie's failure to wait four days until he could conduct the trial on the island of Saint Thomas, Spencer demanded civil prosecution. Mackenzie's supporters feared the outcome of a civil trial and arranged to have him tried in a naval court-martial. Although Mackenzie was acquitted, he did not escape criticism. Some of that criticism came from Melville in *White-Jacket,* in which Melville's first-person narrator asserts the right to mutiny and alludes to the *Somers* affair as an example of the injustice that can result from granting absolute power to a captain. Although Melville was far away in the South Pacific when the *Somers* affair occurred, he had good reason to pay attention to accounts of it. First, he had just participated in a mutiny himself. Second, as I mentioned earlier, his cousin, Lt. Guert Gansevoort, was second-in-command on the *Somers*. It was Gansevoort, in fact, who had relayed the threat of mutiny to Mackenzie, presided over the trial, and given the hanging order.

Melville's mention of the *Somers* affair in *Billy Budd* indicates that it influenced his depiction of Captain Vere's devotion to duty. Describing the decision of members of the drumhead court to hang Billy, the narrator writes,

> Not unlikely they were brought to something more or less akin to that harassed frame of mind which in the year 1842 actuated the commander of the U.S. brig-of-war *Somers* to resolve, under the so-called Articles of War, Articles modeled upon the English Mutiny Act, to resolve upon the execution at sea of a midshipman and two petty-officers as mutineers designing the seizure of the brig. Which resolution was carried out though in a time of peace and within not many days sail of home. An act vindicated by a naval court of inquiry subsequently convened ashore. History, and here cited without comment. True, the

circumstances on board the *Somers* were different from those on board
the *Bellipotent*. But the urgency felt, well-warranted or otherwise, was
much the same. (*BB* 109–10)

To reconstruct the legal reasoning that Melville would have heard in
defense of Mackenzie, we can turn to an article written by Charles
Sumner for the *North American Review*. Sumner's defense of Mackenzie's
actions has remarkable similarities with Captain Vere's justification of his
hanging Billy Budd.

Appearing after Mackenzie's acquittal of court-martial charges,
Sumner's essay had first been requested by Lt. Charles H. Davis (later a
rear admiral). Davis wrote to Sumner that he admired the "manner in
which you have treated public questions of legal interest," and he urged,
"I make bold to ask you to lend your influence, through the press, to keep
the public sentiment in Boston sound and right upon this subject."[19]

Sumner's defense begins with a brief history of the nature and danger
of mutinies. He concentrates on the events at Spithead and the Nore,
which provide the background for the setting of *Billy Budd*. His description of those mutinies shares remarkable similarities with the description
in *Billy Budd*. According to Sumner, "Perhaps no event during the reign
of George the Third seemed, for a while, more to endanger the empire,
or threw the people into a deeper consternation. The wooden walls of
England appeared to rock to their foundation, and the defenses against
the public enemy to be overturned." In *Billy Budd* we hear that the Nore
was a "demonstration more menacing to England than the contemporary manifestos and conquering and proselyting armies of the French
Director. To the British Empire the Nore Mutiny was what a strike in
the fire-brigade would be to London threatened by general arson" (*BB*
21–2). Nonetheless, as Sumner admits, "These mutinies had a not unnatural origin in the shameful nature of the provisions which were supplied to the navy, in the injustice of impressment, in the hardships of the
service, and the inadequate compensation which it received." Similarly,
Billy Budd's narrator records, "Reasonable discontent growing out of
practical grievances in the fleet had been ignited into irrational combus-
tion, as by live cinders blown across the Channel from France in flames"
(22). Sumner, like *Billy Budd*'s narrator, emphasizes the danger of mutinies by comparing them to an irrational, ungovernable fire. According to
him, "While the mutiny at Spithead was dying away, a flame broke out
in the fleet of the Nore, which was destined to rage with a wilder and
more ungovernable fury."[20]

Having used history to establish the danger of mutinies, Sumner goes
on to admit that in hanging three sailors Mackenzie had deviated from
accepted legal procedures. Nonetheless, in an argument that is important
for understanding the conception of the law in the nineteenth century, he

concludes that even so, Mackenzie's actions were legal. "We venture with diffidence upon the discussion of a question which has opened the field for such animated debate. It is acknowledged that Commander Mackenzie has taken the lives of three men without the customary forms of law. Does the law contain, within itself, any principle, which under the circumstances of the case, will justify this apparent violation of it? Our answer is, that it clearly does."[21]

Given the circumstances of the case, Sumner argues, Mackenzie had both judicial and executive duties. "The judicial authority does not depend on the ermine or the robe. It may be muffled even under a military cloak." As a judge Mackenzie was entitled to the full protection of the law as stated by James Kent. "Judicial exercise of power is imposed upon the courts. They *must decide and act according to their judgement;* and therefore, the law will protect them." It would not do to have a judge liable for his judgment, so long as it was, in the words of another authority, *"an honest and zealous intention."* "God forbid that a magistrate should suffer from an error in judgement, if his purpose was honestly to discharge his trust." The question the court had to answer, therefore, was simply "whether, under the circumstances of the case, [Mackenzie] acted honestly, to the best of his judgment, and without any corrupt motive, or wilful thought."[22]

Anticipating complaints that there was no real threat of mutiny or that the means used to prevent it were too extreme, Sumner argues that a real necessity "for a resort to extraordinary means to arrest the mutiny" did not need to be proved. What was important was whether Mackenzie felt an *"apparent necessity."*[23] According to legal precedent, the distinction between an apparent and real necessity lies at the foundation of the right of self-defense, and, Sumner argues, stopping a mutiny is clearly a form of self-defense.

The criterion of apparent necessity means that it was not incumbent on Mackenzie to "establish the *actual* guilt of each one of the three persons executed. . . . The utmost that can be required of him is to establish the *apparent* guilt of these persons. But even this is not imperative. And here we conclude, as we began, this portion of the argument, by saying that it is sufficient, if it be shown that the Commander, in taking the steps that he did towards the suppression of the mutiny, acted in good faith, even supposing subsequent knowledge may have made it evident that he erred in judgment." Therefore, even the question of whether Mackenzie should have conducted the trial aboard the ship or waited to take the prisoners to Saint Thomas or the United States is not to the point. The question is "whether, *at the time of the execution,* it did not *appear* impossible to do it, without imminent danger to the ship and all on board."[24]

According to Michael Rogin, the fact that Sumner's defense is based on Mackenzie's intent constitutes a major difference between the *Somers* affair and *Billy Budd*. Vere, after all, tells the drumhead court that "Budd's intent or non-intent is nothing to the purpose" (*BB* 108). This difference is more apparent than real. When Sumner argued for a consideration of intent, he argued for Mackenzie, not the executed crew members. When Vere declares that "intent or non-intent" is irrelevant, he refers to Billy's act of striking Claggart, not to his own hanging of Billy. As far as the guilt of the crew members is concerned, Sumner agrees with Vere. He explicitly argues that their actual intent, *even their guilt,* was not important. What mattered was the appearance of their actions and the appearance of their guilt. Similarly, Vere, immediately before commenting on intent, asserts, "War looks but to the frontage, the appearance. And the Mutiny Act, War's child, takes after the father" (108). For Vere, whether Billy's act was intended to be mutinous is not important – only that it appeared mutinous.[25]

Sumner places great emphasis on Mackenzie's intent and the crew members' appearance of guilt because he bases his defense on the established precedent for the natural right of self-defense. Clearly, if a ship is threatened by mutiny, a captain has a right to defend himself and his ship. The cases Sumner cites to establish what constitutes legitimate self-defense are revealing. One is the trial excusing British soldiers for firing on citizens in the Boston Massacre. The court ruled that to justify their actions the soldiers needed to prove only that their lives were apparently, not actually, threatened. As a result, the soldiers were acquitted.

The other case cited is the early nineteenth-century trial of Thomas O. Selfridge, in which both Lemuel Shaw and Maj. Thomas Melvill had served as witnesses. Sumner, writing to Lieutenant Davis, tells him that the *Selfridge* case had been drawn to his attention by Justice Joseph Story. "The Judge had not the least doubt that Mackenzie was justified in the alternative he took. He thought the circumstances would form a complete defense for a homicide on shore, in view of an enlightened civil tribunal; *a fortiori,* they would at sea, on shipboard, and under the stern laws of war. The question here was presented in the trial of Selfridge; and the court decided (your father was counsel) that it would be a sufficient defence for taking life, if the party had reasonable ground to fear for his own life."[26]

In 1843 Sumner appealed to the *Selfridge* decision to eliminate controversy over Mackenzie's acquittal by proving that it rested on the "immovable foundation of law."[27] As we saw in the last chapter, however, in 1806 the court's ruling on self-defense allowing for Selfridge's acquittal was as controversial as the ruling allowing for Mackenzie's acquittal. Indeed, although Lieutenant Davis's father had served as a counsel in the Selfridge trial, he was on the side of the prosecution. With many, he was appalled that Selfridge's killing of young and beloved Charles Austin was excused in part because Judge Parsons had altered the existing criteria for justifiable self-defense in his charge to the grand jury. It is even more appalling, then, that these new criteria could be invoked to justify Mackenzie's hanging of three sailors on the *Somers*.

Considered together, the *Webster, Somers,* and *Selfridge* cases might cause us to question Captain Vere's defense of the measured forms of the law. According to him, social order can be maintained only by submitting to the immutable principles embodied in law. But Parsons's alteration of the criteria for justifiable self-defense and Shaw's modification of the existing criteria for proof of homicide show that the forms of the law we submit to are not immutable. It comes as no surprise, then, that Captain Vere has also been accused of deviating from the legal forms and usages he claims to honor. For instance, as the surgeon implies, according to the Articles of War Vere should have rejoined the fleet before trying Billy. Similarly, the surgeon, the lieutenants, and the captain of marines are surprised when Vere does not "refer [the case] to the admiral" (*BB* 96), which is also required under the Articles.[28]

The most thorough criticism of Vere's deviation from established usages comes from Richard Weisberg. By looking at the existing law of the land, Weisberg has meticulously listed Vere's procedural errors, including ones not explicitly alluded to in the text. Weisberg's own procedure has caused some critics to object that he assumes too much.[29] First, he assumes that we should apply actual military regulations to judge Melville's fictional work. Second, he assumes that Melville knew the regulations accurately. Weisberg can respond that the surgeon's awareness of some of Vere's errors indicates that Melville wanted to direct us to actual regulations and that Melville's reference to the Articles of War in *White-Jacket* proves his knowledge of them. Moreover, additional textual evidence suggests that Melville wanted the reader to catch Vere deviating from the very forms and usages he cites as his authority. The narrator, who explicitly calls our attention to some of Vere's "variance from usage" (*BB* 130), is careful to point out that it is in "public" proceedings that "strict adherence to usage was observed" (115). This could indicate that Vere strictly observed established forms only when it was necessary to put on a show for the crew. Furthermore, there are occasional suggestions that Vere, the defender of rationality, is not as rational and impartial as he appears. His deviation from accepted procedures causes the surgeon to wonder if Vere is temporarily "unhinged" (96).

The problem with Weisberg's argument is not that he goes too far but that he does not go far enough. Although claiming to question Vere's legalistic mind, Weisberg retains the typical legalistic point of view that focuses on technicalities. I do not mean either to excuse Vere's technical errors or to argue that technicalities are unimportant. To be sure, the technicalities of legal procedure allow some of the most subtle ideological control. But the emphasis on procedural technicalities often diverts people from questioning the assumptions of the entire legal system. For instance, Weisberg is rightly concerned that Vere did not refer Billy's case to the admiral, but he does not go on to speculate whether, if Vere had done so, Billy's fate would have been any different. Billy, no longer "a 'King's Bargain'" (*BB* 88), becomes a political liability the moment he strikes Claggart, and the admiral's court would probably have disposed of him accordingly. To base criticism of the legal order on procedural errors is to risk explaining injustice as the acts of corrupt, or even just well-intentioned but confused individuals in positions of authority. It avoids questioning the order to which the legal system is intricately related. In fact, Weisberg's reading implicitly legitimizes the legal forms that Vere claims to uphold, since Vere's actions become illegitimate when they do not conform to them.

Billy Budd raises a more complicated issue than that of Captain Vere's procedural errors. It offers an account of how such behavior is accepted by a culture even when it would seem to contradict the culture's definition of legitimacy, just as Parsons's alteration of the criteria for self-defense became the established law of the land so that Sumner could cite it to defend Mackenzie for violating customary procedures, and just as parts of Shaw's controversial charge to the jury are cited today by students of criminal justice needing definitions of reasonable doubt, circumstantial evidence, alibi, murder, and manslaughter.[30]

One lesson that we might draw from our historical cases and from *Billy Budd* is that Vere, Shaw, and Parsons are corrupt and hypocritical men, employing a rhetoric of strict adherence to the law in order to disguise their conscious manipulation of the law. Or, more generously, we might conclude that they are sincere men who are so concerned with fulfilling their duty that they unconsciously violate the very principles they claim to uphold. A more fruitful line of inquiry is to try to understand what it is about the logic of the legal order they have sworn to defend that causes three well-intentioned men seemingly to contradict their own most sacred principles.

One reason judges claim strict adherence to established forms and usages in controversial cases is to reassure the public and themselves that a case is decided by the law, not by political and social pressure. In the *Selfridge* case, for instance, Judge Parker went out of his way to caution the jury to decide Selfridge's fate according to the law, not politics. In the *Webster* case Shaw worked hard to counter accusations that Parkman's high social position had influenced Dr. Webster's fate. And Shaw's strict adherence to the letter of the law in his fugitive slave law decisions was partially a response to the political pressures surrounding the cases.[31] Similarly, Captain Vere is extremely careful to respect established forms and usages. Given the recent events at the Nore and the Spithead, he knows that the law will maintain its authority only if the crew detects no deviance from accepted procedures.

But if, as these examples suggest, judges and those in positions of authority are especially prone to appeal to the established forms of the law in times of social unrest, it is possible to interpret that appeal as a response to political pressures, rather than a way to transcend them. For instance, although Captain Vere argues for the necessity of strict adherence to the letter of the law, he reminds the drumhead court of the ship's particular situation. He is very sensitive to the need to come up with an opinion that will elicit the proper response from the crew. Similarly, Shaw was aware of the national significance of his ruling in the *Sims* case. Furthermore, although Shaw does not mention outside pressures in the *Webster* case, there is evidence that the sternness of his charge to the jury might in part have been a response to social conditions in Boston.

In 1850 the established social structure of Boston was felt to be threatened as the result of mass immigration from Ireland. In his inaugural speech of January 7, 1850, the newly elected mayor of Boston decried the "large numbers of paupers from Ireland," who "became instantly and permanently a charge upon our public charities." He especially addressed the rise of crime. His solution was a call for law and order and an attack on the judiciary for excessive leniency to criminals. Whether in response to the mayor or not, Shaw was not in a mood lenient to criminals in early 1850. Two weeks before the Webster trial opened in March 1850, Shaw oversaw another murder case in which the jury declared the defendant guilty but unanimously recommended mercy because he was mentally retarded. Shaw reversed the jury and delivered the death sentence. In a case receiving the wide publicity that the *Webster* case did, there were political consequences if no criminal was convicted. As Attorney General Clifford wrote in his notes, "Somebody must answer!"[32] In making Webster answer, Clifford enhanced his own political reputation. Shortly after the trial he became the Whig candidate for governor and was elected to that post by the legislature, even though he lacked a majority of the popular vote.

Of course Shaw himself, although applauded by some, also suffered severe criticism from others. The controversy over his charge to the jury, as well as the controversy over the *Selfridge* case, the *Somers* affair, and the *Sims* case, indicates the difficulty that the legal order has in resolving conflicts in times of social unrest. Although defenders of the legal order may argue that a case has been decided by the logic of the law, not by the logic of politics, these cases demonstrate that the logic of the law is often political. We can see its logic most clearly in Sumner's account of the *Somers* affair.

Sumner's defense of Mackenzie illustrates the limitations of criticism like Weisberg's, which focuses on Vere's procedural errors, because it openly admits that the commander acted beyond "customary forms of law" and still claims that his actions are lawful. Sumner, in the course of his defense, even addresses some of the objections that Weisberg raises. He notes that Mackenzie played multiple roles, but argues that he should have. "The character cast upon him was at once *judicial* and *executive*." He raises the possibility that Mackenzie could have waited for the ship to dock in the Virgin Islands before calling the trial, but argues that the pressures of the situation demanded a trial at sea. In defending Mackenzie's actions as lawful, despite their violation of the letter of the law, Sumner carries formalist doctrine to a logical but contradictory conclusion. For someone who subscribes to the formalist belief that the function of law is to guarantee social order, it is all too easy to conclude that any action preserving the social order is legitimate. Although Sumner never explicitly makes this identification, by looking at one of his metaphorical descriptions of the law we can see how it forms the foundation of his entire argument. Having warned of the "suddenness with which the force of mutiny may subdue a ship," Sumner goes on to describe the "retribution which is sure to fall upon the miserable offenders from the unsleeping power of the law."[33] When Mackenzie contains the threat of a potential mutiny, he is merely acting in the service of the law's unsleeping power. Although he violates the letter of the law, he conforms to principles contained within the law itself.

Sumner's open admission that in order to serve the law Mackenzie had to violate its written manifestations can help us to see the mentality generating Vere's, Shaw's, and Parsons's contradictions of their stated fidelity to the letter of the law. There are, it seems, times when strict adherence to the established forms of the law might not be enough to preserve social order. At those times, the law of the land is likely to undergo a rapid metamorphosis as, protean, it takes on whatever forms are necessary to preserve order. Far from stable, the forms of the law are constantly shifting.

The frightening implication of Captain Vere's procedural errors is that even the "rational" forms from which he deviates are pervaded by the irrationality that they are supposed to guard against.[34] Convinced of the necessity to preserve formal order, Captain Vere feels that he must wage a war to silence the threat of the revolutionary spirit coming from

France. But perhaps the system Vere so eloquently defends is as much "at war with the peace of the world and the true welfare of mankind" (*BB* 37), if not more so, than the revolutionary spirit he condemns. Although Vere claims that his system of justice stands for liberty, it denies Billy Budd the rights of man. Although it stands for law and order, it allows prisons to be emptied of lawbreakers and defies the law of nations by impressing innocent sailors in order to man the ships that are supposed to protect its law and order. Although its institutions are supposed to represent rationality against a revolutionary power's irrationality, it is ruled by the Mutiny Act, which Captain Vere himself calls the "child of war," a most irrational force. Finally, although, as Vere claims, the officers who administer its laws owe allegiance to the king, not nature, that very king is reputed to be mad. It is a very distinct possibility that the entire system that rests on the king's paternal authority is also mad.

In *Moby-Dick* Melville constructs a frightening political allegory by portraying the consequences of one individual's madness. The allegory is especially frightening because Ahab's madness, which causes him to misuse his authority and lead the ship of state on a course to destruction, grows out of a humanistic desire to conquer a force of nature – the great whale – described as "indomitable" (*MD* 452). In *Billy Budd* Captain Vere serves on a ship that Melville first called the *Indomitable*. In this case what is indomitable is no longer a product of nature but a product of man, a ship whose purpose is to defend man-made institutions by serving the man-made institution of war. If *Moby-Dick* is about the madness of the romantic quest in which an individual tries to wrest a realm of freedom from indomitable nature, *Billy Budd* suggests the madness involved when man-made institutions themselves become indomitable and limit human possibility. Whereas the indomitable social forms ruling the *Bellipotent* are supposed to control cases of individual madness, like Ahab's, which grow out of the attempt to find alternatives to the existing order, the action of *Billy Budd* suggests the madness involved when society succumbs to the belief that all alternatives to the existing order are mad.

The difference between the madness on the *Pequod* and that on the *Bellipotent* marks the difference between the kinds of ideological control challenged by Melville's fiction. Ahab's madness was a type familiar to antebellum audiences. Rather than submitting himself to the rule of reason, Ahab is governed by an irrational force and uses his authority to further his own aims. Admitting that he is mad, even if his madness is special – "They think me mad – Starbuck does; but I'm demoniac. I am madness maddened! That wild madness that's only calm to comprehend itself" (*MD* 226) – Ahab cannot control himself. Nonetheless, this madman gains control of the *Pequod*.

For antebellum conservatives, Ahab's type of madness was personified by Andrew Jackson. Placing personal ambition above social duty, Jackson, they thought, had inaugurated a reign of passion that threatened the rational republican principles of the founding fathers. Conservatives emphasized Jackson's threat by comparing him to Cromwell and Napoleon, passionate rulers responsible for leading their revolutions astray. Since Jackson, according to John William Ward, represented "nature," "providence," and "will," his opponents countered by stressing civilization and law, history, and submission to duty.[35] Ahab is even more frightening than Jackson because he knows how to use rationality to further irrational ends. As Ahab says, "All my means are sane, my motive and my object mad" (*MD* 250). Most important, social forms are no defense against Ahab because, in control of them, he knows how to use them for his mad objectives. "Captain Ahab was by no means inobservant of the paramount forms and usages of the sea. Nor, perhaps, will it fail to be eventually perceived that behind those forms and usages, as it were, he sometimes masked himself; incidentally making use of them for more private ends than they were legitimately intended to subserve" (198). Rather than submit himself to civilization's measured forms, Ahab makes them submit to him.

The ease with which society's forms and usages lend themselves to Ahab's mad quest has caused a number of critics to read *Moby-Dick* as Melville's indictment of the social formations accompanying a capitalist economy.[36] There is no doubt that *Moby-Dick* records the irrational side of a whaling voyage that claims to be nothing more than a business enterprise, an attempt to turn whales into profit. In his detailed look at the whaling industry, Melville shows how the production of rationalized commodities for the civilized world both exploits workers and contributes to the bloody destruction of nature. Furthermore, in linking his description of the whaling industry with metaphysical speculation, Melville exposes the exploitative and destructive potential of the philosophical ideals of capitalist culture, anticipating Max Horkheimer's and Theodor Adorno's *Dialectic of Enlightenment,*[37] which shows the connection between Enlightenment thinking and a will to dominate nature. But in *Moby-Dick,* no matter how easily the forms and ideas of capitalist society lend themselves to irrational goals, they alone are not the cause of the *Pequod*'s tragic fate. Ahab's powerful personality remains the force steering the *Pequod* on a mad course of destruction.

In *Billy Budd* the situation is different. Captain Vere's submission to duty, his devotion to civilization, law, and history, would seem to make him the perfect answer to Ahab and his unchecked assertion of individual will. In performing his duty by taking on a judicial function, Vere would even seem to confirm the conservative belief that social order must be entrusted to the rational care of a disinterested judiciary. The suggestion in *Billy Budd* of Captain Vere's madness disrupts this reassuring vision by raising the possibility that the judiciary itself is pervaded by the irrational. As Ahab speculates, "Where do murderers go, man! Who's to doom, when the judge himself is dragged to the bar?" (*MD* 685) – a question that Melville most likely composed soon after his father-in-law was accused of misconduct in the Webster murder trial.

The question of insanity is raised a number of times in *Billy Budd*. The most extended description of madness is intended to describe Claggart.

> But the thing which in eminent instances signalizes so exceptional a nature is this: though the man's even temper and discreet bearing would seem to intimate a mind peculiarly subject to the law of reason, not the less in his heart he would seem to riot in complete exemption from that law, having apparently little to do with reason further than to employ it as an ambidexter implement for effecting the irrational. That is to say: Toward the accomplishment of an aim which in wantonness of atrocity would seem to partake of the insane, he will direct a cool judgement sagacious and sound.
>
> These men are true madmen, and of the most dangerous sort, for their lunacy is not continuous but occasional, evoked by some special object; it is protectively secretive, which is as much as to say it is self-contained, so that when moreover, most active, it is to the average mind not distinguishable from sanity, and for the reason above suggested, that whatever its aims may be – and the aim is never declared – the method and the outward proceeding are always perfectly rational. (*BB* 60–1)

Although it is disturbing enough that the man responsible for order on the ship is irrational, it is even more disturbing if we apply the technique of indirection suggested throughout the story and apply the narrator's definition of Claggart's madness to the ship's captain. If we do, we get an almost perfect fit. Vere's "cool judgement sagacious and sound" to condemn Billy, which would seem to be "peculiarly subject to the law of reason," may be the act of a true madman "of the most dangerous sort." Like Claggart, Vere may hide irrationality under a cloak of rationality.[38]

Because Captain Vere seems so fair and just, the possibility that even his measured judgments partake of the irrational suggests a more frightening political allegory than that of *Moby-Dick* and Melville's earlier works. In *White-Jacket* a cruel captain controls the crew by relying on a code of physical punishment, a code so harsh that its ideological bias in favor of those in authority is unmistakable. In *Moby-Dick,* the situation is somewhat different. A similar code of discipline operates on the *Pequod,* but Melville also emphasizes Ahab's ability to further his own irrational ends by using rhetoric to elicit the crew's consent. Effective in convincing the crew, Ahab's rhetoric has an ideological bias that remains clear to both Ahab and the reader. It is rhetoric calculated to manipulate and deceive. In *Billy Budd* ideological control is accomplished in a subtler manner.[39]

Like other naval officers, Captain Vere can rely on physical punishment to elicit consent. Certainly Billy's hanging is a symbolic act that reminds the crew of what is in store for mutineers. Nonetheless, Vere's most important power is his rhetoric, a rhetoric he uses to convince the officers and crew that Billy's hanging is both necessary and just, a rhetoric different from Ahab's. If Vere uses his rhetoric to manipulate opinion, he does not consciously use it to serve his own ends. Instead, he sincerely believes that it is based on an authority outside of himself, an authority that he submits to as much as the crew. Thus, although we can work to uncover the ways in which it legitimizes the present order, ideology in *Billy Budd* is no longer represented as a conscious weapon of the ruling class imposed on an innocent laboring class from without. Emanating from a set of impersonal laws outside the self, rather than from a single, powerful individual, ideology so pervades each person's consciousness that no one seems capable of escaping its constraints.

Peter Gabel, a recent legal critic, refers to the power of rule by law to exert the sort of ideological control we find on board the *Bellipotent* as the reification of the law. Gabel argues that rule by law has become an effective political weapon because it is able to offer reassurance while it contributes to repression. It reassures by appearing to demonstrate that seemingly unjust actions are actually just because human society follows a legal, rational system of laws. It is repressive because its demonstration depends on the assumption that the legal, rational system of laws governing society is just. This reification of the law keeps people from asking whether seemingly unjust actions may be caused by the very system that the logic of the law justifies. Ask, for instance, whether Billy's execution, which is judged necessary to preserve a rational system of law and order, may not also be caused by the system. As Gabel puts it, "Through the law we tell ourselves . . . that what is, ought to be – that the system follows a law."[40] The effect of this circular reasoning is to exclude the possibility for radical social transformation by defining alternatives to the present system as outside the law, and therefore illegitimate and irrational.

Appropriately, one of the clearest examples of how the rhetoric of legal formalism was used as a conservative political weapon occurs in late eighteenth-century Britain. Douglas Hay, in his study of late eighteenth-century penal codes, shows how the British ruling class responded to the threat of the French Revolution by glorifying the manner in which the established forms of common law seemed to guarantee individual rights and equality under the law. Convincing itself and the working classes of the justice of its laws, the propertied class was able to pass "one of the bloodiest penal codes in Europe" and still "congratulate itself on its humanity."[41] That sense of humanity was promoted by the standard rhetoric of judges pronouncing the death sentence. Evoking the culture's belief in the justness of a patriarchal system, the judge adopted both the stance of a stern, impartial agent through whom the law speaks and the role of a paternalistic, caring father. If people were hanged, they were at least hanged justly. We find a similarly effective use of rhetoric at work in *Billy Budd,* where the effectiveness of ideological control depends on its appearance of fairness.

Far from biased, Captain Vere seems the embodiment of impartial justice. Rather than silence voices of opposition aboard ship, he goes so far as to call a drumhead court, in which he lets members of the court, including a representative of the crew, speak, while he adopts the role of an impartial witness. But constrained within the formal control of the court system, these voices are heard without any chance of reversing the judgment that Captain Vere made at the moment of the homicide – "Struck dead by an angel of God! Yet the angel must hang!" (*BB* 95). The moment Vere drops the role of an impartial witness and adopts the role of the prosecutor, his "prejudgment" of Billy becomes clear (104). One by one he opposes the scruples of the members of the court and assigns them to a realm of silence. Captain Vere, a member of the class that wrote the laws of the land, takes on the role of witness, prosecutor, and judge. It is in the interests of that class that Billy Budd be hanged, yet Captain Vere projects such an image of fairness that not even Billy himself protests the call for his execution. Instead, like numerous condemned criminals in late eighteenth-century England, Billy ends up blessing the man who sentences him to hang.

Traditional readings see *Billy Budd* recording the ambiguous effects of the triumph of rule by law because it pits the demands of individual freedom against the social need for rational, impartial laws. Ironic readings claim that those laws are not always as rational and impartial as they appear, a possibility confirmed by our look at historical cases. Billy's blessing of Captain Vere suggests a situation even bleaker than that of our historical cases. In each of these cases, people actively protested judgments that deviated from the previously established law of the land. In *Billy Budd,* no one openly questions either the established forms of the law or Vere's deviation from them. Thus *Billy Budd* raises the possibility that the triumph of rule by law is an ambiguous achievement not because innocent individuals must be sacrificed to socially necessary laws but because, in appearing fair, rule by law can make people accept as lawful even judgments that violate established criteria of legitimacy. To understand how that acceptance occurs we have to turn from the logic behind

Vere's judgment to the object of his judgment – seemingly innocent Billy Budd. Captain Vere's measured forms are not the only ones questioned in the story. When the narrator tells us, "The form of Billy Budd was heroic" (63), it turns out that Billy's form is as flawed as the formal order Captain Vere defends. More than a tragedy of innocence or justice, *Billy Budd* suggests how the notion of presocial innocence can help perpetuate injustice. In the first chapter, my analysis of *The Pioneers* raised the same possibility, but I questioned Natty's innocence only by reading against the grain of Cooper's narrative. *Billy Budd,* by undercutting its own formal symmetries, invites us to read it against the grain and to question the very terms of the conflict between head and heart.[42]

From the start we are told that Billy has a flaw. Significantly, this flaw is a speech defect – an inability to speak out clearly in a time of excitement. Many commentators see his defect as a sign of his innocence. Illiterate Billy seems to have his origins in a world prior to signification, a world in which gesture has priority over language.[43] Such a reading is undercut, however, when we realize that it is precisely his inability to speak that causes Billy to produce a gesture that ends in violent death. Explaining why he hit Claggart, Billy maintains, "No, there was no malice between us. I never bore malice against the Master-at-arms. I am sorry that he is dead. I did not mean to kill him. Could I have used my tongue I would not have struck him. But he foully lied to my face and in presence of my Captain, and I had to say something, and I could only say it with a blow, God help me!" (102). Rather than offer a narrative that sentimentalizes Billy's innocence, Melville places Billy's innocence on trial. From that trial we learn not how innocence must be sacrificed in a world of civilization but how the desire of people like Billy to *appear* innocent allows them to be controlled.

The day following his impressment, Billy witnesses his first "formal gang-way-punishment." He does not protest the violence of the beating. Instead, he is so impressed by the scene that he resolves that "never through remissness would he make himself liable to such a visitation or do or omit aught that might merit even verbal reproof" (49). Billy's desire to avoid the judgment meted out to sailors who disobey the accepted forms and usages of the navy makes him easy to control because it renders him silent. Silence in *Billy Budd,* as it does in *Moby-Dick,* signals consent to the existing system of authority. In *Moby-Dick* it is when Starbuck can no longer speak that Ahab knows he has controlled him: "Speak, but speak! – Aye, aye! thy silence, then, *that* voices thee. . . . Starbuck now is mine; cannot oppose me now, without rebellion" (*MD* 222). Unable to speak against Ahab, Starbuck can only contemplate violent revenge. Unable to commit violence, Starbuck continues to acquiesce. Billy, of course, does commit a violent act, but, unconscious, it is easily contained by Captain Vere's system of rhetorical authority, since it is caused by Billy's fear that Captain Vere will not consider him innocent. Just as Starbuck's weakness is a conscience that would judge him for committing violence against his captain, so Billy's weakness is his juvenile "good nature" that wants to please.

"Now Billy, like sundry other essentially good-natured ones, had some of the weaknesses inseparable from essential good nature; and among these was a reluctance, almost an incapacity of plumply saying *no* to an abrupt proposition not obviously absurd, on the face of it, nor obviously unfriendly, nor iniquitous" (69). The inability to say no is Billy's biggest flaw, a flaw that becomes more significant when we compare Billy to Jack Chase, to whom the book is dedicated. Chase, unlike Billy, was a man who said no to an exploitative order and achieved reform. Chase, like the Hawthorne whom Melville so admired, knew how to say "No, in thunder."[44] Billy, in contrast, given the "order" that condemns him to death, "in silence, mechanically obeyed" (94).

Billy's failure to speak out denies him the role promised to him early in the book, the role of the Handsome Sailor. Although Billy has "as much of masculine beauty as one can expect anywhere to see," he fails to fit the role allotted to him, because of his vocal defect. We first see the Handsome Sailor in the "centre of a company of his shipmates. These were made up of such an assortment of tribes and complexions as could have well fitted them to be marched up by Anacharsis Cloots before the bar of the first French Assembly as Representatives of the Human Race" (4). The final allusion to Cloots in Melville's works, this description of the Handsome Sailor establishes his role as a leader. Cloots, known as the "Speaker of Mankind," had produced his mute representatives of the tongue-tied nations of the world as witnesses for the universal republic that he hoped the French Revolution would make possible. Similarly, from the Handsome Sailor's tales of prowess we learn that "ashore he was the champion; afloat the spokesman; on every suitable occasion always foremost" (4–5). Although Billy is a foretopman, he is by no means a spokesman.[45]

Instead of speaking out against Captain Vere, Billy lets the fatherlike captain speak for him. In doing so he entrusts his life to a man who sacrifices him in the name of the law. Remaining silent until singing out at his death, "in the clear melody of a singing-bird": "God Bless Captain Vere!" (124), Billy, like the composer Didbin, becomes "a song-writer" who is "no mean auxiliary to the English government at that European conjuncture" (22). Commenting in *White-Jacket* on how Didbin's songs "breathe the very poetry of the ocean," Melville goes on to expose their ideological value.

> But it is remarkable that those songs − which would lead one to think that man-of-war's-men are the most care-free, contented, virtuous, and patriotic of mankind − were composed at a time when the English Navy was principally manned by felons and paupers. . . . Still more, these songs are pervaded by a true Mohammedan sensualism; a reckless acquiescence in fate, and an implicit, unquestioning, dog-like devotion to whoever may be lord and master. Didbin was a man of genius; but no wonder Didbin was a government pensioner at £200 per annum. (*WJ* 383)

Although he does not earn two hundred pounds per annum, Billy serves the English government in more ways than Didbin. First, as portrayed by the narrator, Billy is the perfect subject for one of Didbin's songs. Impressed into the navy, he exhibits "uncomplaining acquiescence" to his new lord and master (6). "Like the animals, though no philosopher, he was, without knowing it, practically a fatalist. And, it may be, that he rather liked this adventurous turn in affairs, which promised an opening into novel scenes and martial excitements" (12). The "novel" scenes Billy enters make him pay with his life; nonetheless, he remains true to a narrative that Didbin might have composed. He goes so far as to take on Didbin's role at the end of his life by melodiously singing out a blessing for Captain Vere. We can only imagine what would have followed if Billy had condemned Vere rather than blessed him, but it is certainly possible that if Billy had not blessed the captain his sentence, which was calculated to discourage a mutiny, might well have provoked one. Instead, with Billy's consent, Vere is able to silence oppositional voices in the crew, a crew that expresses its sorrow in a Didbin-like poem rather than take political action.

In *The Confidence-Man* Melville had written, "Silence is at least not denial, and may be consent" (*CM* 116–17). *Billy Budd*'s comment on Billy's silence could well be Melville's indirect comment on his own silence of thirty years, his own refusal to speak out against a potentially repressive legal order in his chosen medium of prose fiction. If so, it would be no accident that in order to write fiction again Melville had to kill off in his imagination a figure who represents innocence prior to speech.[46] Writing again, Melville adopts, not the technique of innocent direction but the technique of subversive indirection that he employed in his short works of the 1850s. Once again he adroitly exposes the contradictions in orthodox ideology by undercutting the authoritarian narrative point of view but offers no direct alternative to the order he undercuts. Although Billy Budd is presented with more sympathy than Babo or Bartleby, he proves as unlikely an alternative as either. Yet, as in the earlier works, Melville's technique of indirection suggests the possibility of an alternative. In "Benito Cereno" and "Bartleby" this alternative world is represented by a character. Bartleby suggests a world of repressed workers who remain a repressed element of Melville's story, just as Babo suggests a world of repressed slaves. In *Billy Budd,* however, the alternative world is suggested by the setting, not a character.

By writing a story set in the wake of the French Revolution, Melville returns to a question that occupies the margins of many of his works: Is a violent revolution necessary to bring about lasting social change? As in those previous works, Melville's answer to that question is by no means clear. But if *Billy Budd* does not offer Melville's definitive statement on revolution, a look at the social conditions in late nineteenth-century America can help us see why Melville's imagination returned to the theme of revolution so widely debated a century earlier. In turn, the historical perspective we have gained from looking at *Billy Budd* in conjunction with antebellum cases can help us better understand the legal ideology that dominated at the time when Melville wrote his final story.

10

Ragged Edges

Billy Budd, Sailor presents a special problem for anyone interested in connections between nineteenth-century literary and legal history. Melville's only major work of prose fiction after the Civil War, it was written in a period dominated by a legal ideology different from that dominating antebellum America. Thus there is a strong temptation to see *Billy Budd* as recording transformations from antebellum to postbellum law. Specifically, the sacrifice of Billy to Captain Vere's need to maintain social order has been read as a comment on the postbellum triumph of secular authority over antebellum beliefs in a transcendental realm of natural law and an autonomous, presocial individual with self-evident, inalienable natural rights.[1] Such a reading adds a historical dimension to the traditional interpretation of *Billy Budd* as an example of the universal story of the inevitable sacrifice involved when an innocent individual abandons the state of nature to enter society. But essentially such an interpretation remains the same as more traditional ones. Perpetuating the myth repeated in American literature from Cooper on of the sacrifices incurred in America's fall from a more innocent, natural state into a world of civilization, it posits antebellum America, with its belief in an organic order and the natural rights of man, as the state of nature that must be abandoned to enter secular, postbellum America.

In the last chapter I complicated the traditional reading that sees *Billy Budd* as a classical narrative expressing the inevitable conflict between the individual and society, between the public and private spheres. To be sure, the work's formal structure seems to posit such a conflict, but its ragged edges destabilize the very symmetrical oppositions it establishes, oppositions central to the romance. *Billy Budd,* the narrator warns us, is no romance. Indeed, the legal cases that we looked at demonstrate the danger of opposing advocates of individual rights to defenders of social order. Often the loudest defenders of individual rights are also the loudest supporters of social order. For instance, Thomas O. Selfridge warned against Jacobin "fiends of anarchy" who perpetrated outrages against "liberty, security, and the legitimate rights of man."[2] Charles Sumner defended the actions that Commander Mackenzie took to preserve order on board the *Somers* at the same time that he powerfully defended the "natural rights" of blacks who had bloodily taken control of the *Amistad* and the *Creole* in order to gain their liberty. Sumner's continued defense of the rights of blacks soon brought him into conflict with Lemuel Shaw over the constitutionality of the Fugitive Slave Act. Yet Shaw, who was, like Captain Vere, a powerful defender of social institutions, was also one of the court's strongest advocates of the free-agent ideology.

In this chapter I will detail some historical circumstances in late nineteenth-century America that make it easier to see the inadequacies of a narrative based on the opposition between the individual and society. In doing so I will challenge the tendency to read *Billy Budd* as one more historical allegory of America's fall from a state of natural innocence. My reading does not deny that *Billy Budd* expresses historical transformations, but it does caution against claiming too much historical significance for Vere's sacrifice of Billy. Although I ultimately disagree with those critics who read *Billy Budd* ahistorically, they do have much evidence on their side, since the notion that the individual must be sacrificed to the larger interests of society is not one that Melville would have first encountered after the Civil War. The idea has, of course, an ancient tradition and was evoked in prewar as well as postwar decisions. To be sure, before the Civil War more appeals were made to a transcendental realm of natural law than after the war. Antebellum conservatives often relied on a rhetoric of natural law and organic cohesion. At one time even Rufus Choate cites the authority of Samuel Taylor Coleridge to define the "spirit of Law" as the "true necessity which compels man into the social state, now and always, by a still beginning never ceasing force of moral cohesion." But as Perry Miller points out, Choate's use of the "striking Platonisms" of England's foremost literary authority on the power of organic form had an important message to American proponents of natural law. Coleridge, after all, like Captain Vere, used his notion of the "spirit of Law" to oppose the disruption of forms by rebellious Frenchmen who were appealing to the authority of natural law. For Coleridge, the "spirit of the Law" is the "lute of Amphion – the harp of Orpheus."[3] For Captain Vere, "With mankind . . . forms, measured forms, are everything; and that is the import couched in the story of Orpheus with his lyre spellbinding the wild denizens of the wood."[4] As the *Selfridge, Webster, Somers,* and fugitive slave law cases demonstrate, neither a recognition of an appeal to the authority of natural law nor the use of organic rhetoric kept antebellum conservatives from choosing the authority of man-made over natural law. Any interpretation of *Billy Budd* as an expression of transformations from a prewar to a postwar legal mentality must come to terms with the similarity between such antebellum judgments and that made by Captain Vere.

In addition, such an interpretation must ask why Melville set his work in a period prior to, not after, the antebellum period. In other words, if we are to use *Billy Budd* to read the significance of changes from prewar to postwar attitudes toward the law at the same time that we read *Billy Budd* in light of those changes, we need to ask what conditions in late nineteenth-century America prompted Melville's imagination to turn to the late eighteenth century and the conflict between England and France. To ask that question implies a double focus that I will maintain throughout this chapter, a focus that frames the antebellum period. By showing where the assumptions underlying antebellum law came from and where they led, that focus should give us a better perspective on the significance of antebellum law. An important function of that perspective will be to help us detect continuities in the Anglo-American legal mentality. To admit the existence of continuities is not to deny the existence of changes, but it is to acknowledge that only by recognizing continuities can we distinguish real differences.

One of the best ways to understand how a recognition of continuities is necessary in order to understand change is to return to the comparison between Captain Vere and Chief Justice Lemuel Shaw. As I emphasized in the last chapter, in the fugitive slave law cases Shaw faced the same conflict between higher law and positive law as Vere does in *Billy Budd*. In addition, the wording that Shaw used in sentencing Dr. John Webster to hang is almost the same as that used by Melville's fictional captain to hang Billy. Furthermore, both Shaw and Vere rely on an appeal to the forms of the law as a way of ensuring the objectivity of their judgments, even though it can be demonstrated that such an appeal is not neutral but a highly charged political act. Thus the comparison between Shaw and Vere indicates that Shaw, like Vere, is a great defender of "forms, measured forms." And, in fact, Shaw did defend the authority vested in the forms of the law. For him, Anglo-American common law yielded a symmetrical, scientific set of principles generating its own rational authority.

But to stress only Shaw's belief in measured forms would be to misrepresent his attitude toward the law. Today he is widely recognized as an instrumentalist, the judge whom, as we saw, Justice Oliver Wendell Holmes commended for his "accurate appreciation of the requirements of the community" and "understanding of the ground of public policy to which all law must ultimately be referred."[5] In addition, Shaw frequently appealed to natural law to justify his opinions. Thus, three different types of legal thought coexisted in Shaw's decisions: formalism, instrumentalism, and natural-law doctrine. To compare Shaw to Vere is to emphasize Shaw's formalism at the expense of the other types of thought.

Indeed, through Captain Vere's belief in measured forms, *Billy Budd* highlights the formal strain that has long been a part of Anglo-American legal thought. It can be traced at least as far back as Coke, who derived the formal authority of the law from what he called the artificial reason of the law, a reason derived from a careful study of the common law by a specially trained elite of the legal profession. But if formalism has always already been present, it has not always dominated. In the early years of the American republic, for instance, natural-law doctrine was in the ascendancy, followed by an instrumentalism that helped to transform American law in the formative era. Not until after the Civil War did formalism emerge as the dominant legal ideology. The brand of formalism that developed was popularized by Christopher Columbus Langdell's introduction of the case method to the Harvard Law School. One of the most important effects of postbellum formalism was to "freeze" legal doctrine that had recently been established in the antebellum period to aid the growth of the market economy. Thus, the formalists' belief that the body of law could be reduced to a set of timeless formal principles through the study of selected common-law cases actually served the interests of laissez-faire economics.

Recent legal historians have referred to this period's particular formalism as a *boundary theory,* because it conceived of social action as the exercise of absolute rights and powers within bounded spheres. In every instance of dispute, the legal question was whether the relevant actors had stayed within their own protected sphere of activity or had crossed over the boundary and invaded the sphere of another.[6] The most important boundary defined was between the public and private sphere. The most immediately influential works were Thomas M. Cooley's *Treatise on the Constitutional Limitations which Rest Upon the Legislative Power of the States of the American Union* (1868) and Christopher Tiedeman's *Limitations of Police Power* (1886), both of which tried strictly to define the boundaries of government interference into the private realm, especially by limiting the government's power to interfere with the "liberty of contract," a term not to be found in legal treatises before the Civil War. The untrammeled right to make promises grew out of the economic theory of laissez-faire. Cooley and Tiedeman intended to prove that it was part of the U.S. Constitution.

The triumph of the North in the Civil War, leading to the ratification of the Fourteenth Amendment, greatly aided the cause of those intent on fully incorporating laissez-faire economics into constitutional law. Today we associate the due process clause of the Fourteenth Amendment with the protection of the civil rights of minorities, but in postbellum America the clause was used most often to protect the economic rights of a few from government interference. Legal historians generally agree that constitutional laissez-faire gained full ascendancy during 1885–6, just as Melville started thinking about *Billy Budd*.[7]

The ascendancy of formalism at this time gives Captain Vere's defense of measured forms an added significance. To be sure, Vere's intense belief in the necessity for maintaining formal order is not a belief confined to the postbellum era. Melville, for instance, would have heard people – including his father-in-law – espousing similar beliefs throughout the antebellum period. But in antebellum America, formalism was only part of the orthodox legal ideology. Writing in the 1880s, Melville was in a better position to see the consequences of the triumph of formalism in all areas of the law. For instance, a work like Tiedeman's made it clear that in the American context an appeal to the protection of individual rights helped to preserve the social order more often than it challenged it.

Tiedeman, like his conservative antebellum precedessors, was a great defender of individual liberty and social order. To define liberty, Tiedeman quotes Daniel Webster, who opposes it to that "authorized licentiousness that trespasses on right." "The creature of law," liberty is a "legal and refined idea, the offspring of high civilization, which the savage never understood, and never can understand." Arguing that liberty exists in proportion to "wholesome restraint," Webster claims that "it is an error to suppose that liberty consists of paucity of laws." Telling those who want few laws to go to Turkey, he concludes that only "our complex system" of "checks and restraints" is a safeguard to "individual rights and interests."[8]

A champion of individual rights, Tiedeman set out to prove that the "substantial rights of the minority" must be "free from all lawful control or interference by the majority, except so far as such control or interference may be necessary to prevent injury to others or the enjoyment of their rights." If this sounds like liberal doctrine, we must remember that the minority rights Tiedeman argued for were not those of ethnic groups. They were largely the economic privileges of a rich elite, privileges that had frequently been written into the law as rights during the antebellum period. In order to protect these economic "rights" of the rich, Tiedeman strictly defined the limits of government interference in the private sphere. These limits were necessary because in a democracy the government is ruled by the masses.

> Contemplating these extraordinary demands of the great army of discontents, and their apparent power, with the growth and development

of universal suffrage, to enforce their views of civil polity upon the civilized world, the conservative classes stand in constant fear of the advent of an absolutism more tyrannical and more unreasoning than any before experienced by man, the absolutism of a democratic majority.[9]

Condemning the present situation, Tiedeman constructed a history in which laissez-faire had dominated political rule for centuries in English-speaking countries.

Under the influence of [laissez-faire], the encroachments of government upon the rights and liberties of the individual have for the past century been comparatively few. But the political pendulum is again swinging in the opposite direction, and the doctrine of governmental inactivity in economical matters is attacked daily with increasing vehemence. Governmental interference is proclaimed and demanded everywhere as a sufficient panacea for every social evil which threatens the prosperity of society. Socialism, Communism, and Anarchism are rampant throughout the civilized world.

Fearful of those political agitators who would use the power of government to infringe on individual rights, Tiedeman hoped that his book would "awaken the public mind to a full appreciation of the power of constitutional limitations to protect private rights against the radical experimentations of social reformers." For Tiedeman, private rights could not exist in times of social disorder.[10]

Rhetoric like Tiedeman's that influenced legal thinking in the late nineteenth century makes clear how at that time an appeal to the protection of individual rights did not challenge the social order but helped to preserve it. If the rhetoric did not reveal this in and of itself, the growing tension between rich and poor did, for even though boundary theorists like Tiedeman argued, in the name of private rights, for strict limits to police power, his theory did not rule out armed action to protect social order such as was taken in 1886, when the poor demanded their rights in the Haymarket riot.[11]

In antebellum America James Fenimore Cooper had declared that laws were necessary to "protect the feeble against the violence of the strong."[12] Melville's father-in-law had claimed that all citizens of the Commonwealth, no matter how poor, were entitled to the paternal protection of its laws. To be sure, the weak and poor were not always protected, but for some thinkers in the late nineteenth century it was no longer necessary to offer even rhetoric promising to protect all of the country's citizens. For example, Tiedeman explicitly complained that "the State is called on to protect the weak against the shrewdness of the stronger, to determine what wages a workman shall receive for his labors, and how many hours he shall labor."[13]

It was in this context that Melville created his fictional Captain Vere, who abandons orphaned Billy to his execution. Like Tiedeman, Vere links the preservation of individual liberty with the preservation of social order. Like Tiedeman, Vere fights against the disorder caused by social reformers. And just as Tiedeman's allies suppressed the Haymarket riot in the name of social order, so Vere attempts to suppress the French Revolution by denying impressed sailors the rights of man. Finally, like Tiedeman's, Vere's view of justice is justified by constructing a history in which social welfare is served by minimizing irrational rule by the people. The people, according to Vere, "have not that kind of intelligent responsiveness that might qualify them to comprehend and discriminate" (*BB* 108).

To compare Vere to Tiedeman is not to imply that their thought is identical. To establish that *Billy Budd* responds to late nineteenth-century conditions, there is no need to turn Vere into a late nineteenth-century thinker. In Vere Melville has accurately captured the mentality of conservative British opposition to the French Revolution. For instance, when Vere evokes the story of Orpheus to counter the "disruption of forms going on across the channel" (*BB* 130), he recalls Carlyle's call for the "Lyre of some Orpheus, to constrain, with the touch of melodious strings, these mad masses into Order."[14] Further, Vere's sincere paternalism is in stark contrast to the late nineteenth-century social Darwinism of Tiedeman.

Nonetheless, the comparison between Vere and Tiedeman does show how well Vere represents a strain of Anglo-American formalism stretching from eighteenth-century Britain through antebellum America to late nineteenth-century America. The central doctrine of this formalism is that freedom can be guaranteed only by maintaining the institutions supporting the formal order of the law. This doctrine receives concise expression in different periods from three figures: Vere, Shaw, and Tiedeman. Vere, we are told, serves the "flag of founded law and freedom defined" (*BB* 22). Shaw claimed that he defended existing institutions precisely because they protected the "dearest rights of humanity."[15] Tiedeman argued that his book on police powers served the "cause of social order and personal liberty."[16] Proclaimed in the interest of the entire society, such statements were repeatedly used to counter threats to the social order by those seeking liberty, whether those threats were the French Revolution, Jacksonian mob rule, radical abolitionism, or labor agitation. Recording the triumph of such formalism, *Billy Budd* exposes whose interests that triumph served.

Of course, as my discussion of earlier works indicates, *Billy Budd* is not Melville's only story to question the assumptions of formalism. One of

Melville's most perceptive recent critics, Michael Rogin, has used Morton Horwitz's account of the rise of formalism in antebellum law to compare the effect of Melville's fiction from the 1850s with the effect of the legal decisions of Lemuel Shaw. Horwitz points to two competing ideological tendencies operating in antebellum law. In public law the major triumph of the Marshall court had been the triumph of a formalism that "depoliticized" the law. By creating formal doctrine such as that concerning "vested property rights," the Marshall Court was able to establish judicial control over legislative efforts to meddle with private economic rights. In private law, however, instrumentalism prevailed, as judges transformed common law to suit the needs of a market economy. By the late 1840s and early 1850s the market economy had essentially replaced the older agrarian order. About this time the formalist strain of public law was starting to enter the realm of private law. This increased formalism declared as fixed those rules of law that had been established in the previous half century to implement a market regime. Emphasizing the apolitical, scientific character of legal reasoning, this formalism completed its triumph after the Civil War as it helped to legitimize laissez-faire economics.[17]

Rogin detects a similar move to formalism in Melville's fiction of the 1850s. Increasingly Melville's fiction confined itself to a self-enclosed, formal world that cuts off ties to the transcendental world pointed to by his earlier romances. But the formalism of Melville's fiction had a different effect from the formalism of judges such as Melville's father-in-law. "Melville's literary and Shaw's legal formalism both worked within self-contained textual worlds. The two were, nonetheless, at odds. Legal formalism bolstered institutions. It protected corporations from economic challenge and defended a Union divided by slavery. Melville's formalism exposed institutional fragility; it was the shadow side of Shaw's."[18]

Rogin's analysis suggests a provocative way to read *Billy Budd*. But he prefers not to read it that way. According to Rogin, if the fiction of the 1850s challenged formalist doctrine, *Billy Budd* marks Melville's submission to it. "Like Melville's fiction of the 1850s, *Billy Budd* confines us to a denuded, mundane world, from which all possibility of transformation has fled. But unlike the earlier stories, *Billy Budd* gives that world its blessing."[19] Concerned with showing how *Billy Budd* closes the rift opened between external authority and claims of the heart, Rogin joins those critics who read the story as Melville's final testament of acceptance.

One reason that Rogin refuses to admit that *Billy Budd* exposes the institutional fragility of formalism as much as, or even more than, Melville's earlier works is the desire he shares with so many of us to offer his own narrative of dramatic change. I too am interested in understanding change, but I am convinced that we can do so only by admitting continuities, such as those between prewar and postwar law and those between Melville's fiction of the 1850s and *Billy Budd*. Not to recognize certain continuities is to periodize too rigidly. For example, take Rogin's description of the rise of formalism in antebellum law. "Judges like Shaw, who had once made the law serve human interests, now separated legalism from the living, contingent world. They shifted away from appeals to facts, lived experience, and the particularities of the case, and toward precedent and formal, legal logic. Judges had once acknowledged their own innovative role; now they insisted the system they helped to shape was fixed in timeless stone."[20] As Horwitz has shown, there was indeed a move toward formalism in the antebellum period, but judges did not change their attitudes as dramatically as Rogin claims. Throughout the antebellum period, judges, especially in public-law decisions, appealed to timeless legal principles. Furthermore, even when Shaw's formalist strain came to the forefront, it continued to coexist with instrumentalism and natural-law doctrine. In a case as late as 1854, Shaw justified an opinion by appealing to "reason, natural justice, and enlightened public policy."[21]

To recognize the persistence of formalist thought in the antebellum legal mentality, and its coexistence with other types of legal thought even when formalism begins to dominate, is to better appreciate the impact of postbellum formalism. After the Civil War, residual elements of natural law and instrumental doctrine played less and less a role. With fewer and fewer alternatives to formalism, a situation like that aboard the *Bellipotent,* in which measured forms have total control, takes on greater significance.

But even in postwar America, formalism did not exercise total hegemonic control. At the very time when formalism gained ascendancy, a challenge to it emerged. If, in antebellum America, the alternatives to formalism were residual elements of natural law and instrumental doctrine, the alternative in the 1880s was a new brand of thought. Its most powerful exponent was Oliver Wendell Holmes, Jr., who is often cited as a precursor to the legal realist movement that would dominate during the Progressive Era.

Not strictly a realist himself, Holmes was somewhat influenced by boundary ideology. In *The Common Law* he tried to define the boundary between contracts and torts. No radical, he was known to have made wisecracks about socialism and reformers.[22] Furthermore, like the formalists, he questioned the theory of natural rights. Certain statements of his – such as "Justice to the individual is rightly outweighed by the larger interests [of society]" – have caused a number of critics to compare him to

Captain Vere.[23] For instance, Rogin, in a provocative reading, uses Holmes's famous attempt to separate law from morality to establish the similarity between Vere's attitudes and accepted late nineteenth-century legal thought. Like Holmes, Vere "split apart the realms of law and morals, appearance and interior, which antebellum Americans had tried to connect. . . . The law, as Vere insisted, avoided intent; it remained in the realm of appearances. Morals addressed intentions, wrote [Justice] Holmes; the law had to do with external signs and deeds."[24] Rogin uses this similarity between Vere and Holmes to argue that *Billy Budd* records a change from antebellum to postbellum thought. According to him, Vere's denial of the relevance of intent is in direct contrast to Mackenzie's defense, based on intent, used in the *Somers* affair trial. But this argument neglects Charles Sumner's claim that Mackenzie was justified in hanging three sailors on the *Somers* because their acts merely appeared to be mutinous. Their actual intent, he concluded, citing the *Selfridge* case, was not important. Thus, as we saw in the last chapter, on the question of intent and appearances Vere's argument is almost identical to Sumner's antebellum one. Mackenzie's intent is given consideration, but the intent of the accused sailors who correspond to Billy is not.

On close scrutiny, other attempts to link Holmes with Vere turn out to be based on apparent rather than real similarities. For instance, John P. McWilliams, Jr., writes that "like Captain Vere, Holmes is prepared to argue that 'Public policy sacrifices the individual to the general good.'" To emphasize his point he compares Vere to "many thoughtful men of the 1870s and 1880s," including Holmes, who began to "suspect that natural rights, if they existed at all, must give way to the general welfare."[25] But, as McWilliams admits, Holmes's attack on rights was directed against economic "rights" such as the "liberty of contract" defended by people like Tiedeman. His most famous dissents argue against the assumption that laissez-faire philosophy is part of American law.[26] Thus, when McWilliams cites Holmes's famous statement "The life of the law has not been logic: it has been experience" as proof that Holmes, like Vere, reacted against a theory of natural law, we should remember that Holmes's main target was the formalists' claim that timeless legal principles could be deduced from a logical study of selected cases. As Holmes's next sentence makes clear, he gives no sanctity to the eternal, measured forms of the law. "The felt necessities of the time, the prevalent moral and political theories, intuitions of public policy, avowed or unconscious, even the prejudices which judges share with their fellowmen, have had a good deal more to do than the syllogism in determining the rules by which men should be governed."[27]

Furthermore, Holmes's thought helped lead to the overthrow of the paradigm of objective causation that was an important part of nine-

teenth-century legal orthodoxy. Courts used objective causation to justify rewarding damages in tort cases. Only if it could objectively be
proved that A caused an injury to B would courts take money from A to
give damages to B. The idea of objective causation was supported by
two metaphorical notions. The first distinguished between proximate
and remote causes. The law concerned itself only with proximate causes.
The second was the scientific metaphor of objective "chains of causation." The courts felt that it was possible to trace a single "scientific
cause," in order to identify a single responsible defendant. The metaphorical basis of this presumably scientific establishment of causation
was first pointed out by Nicholas St. John Green, who along with
Holmes, William James, and Charles Sanders Peirce was a member of the
informal Metaphysical Club in Cambridge in the 1870s. The club's discussions helped to shape pragmatism and Holmes's legal philosophy.
According to Green, "To every event there are certain antecedents. . . .
It is not any one of this set of antecedents taken by itself which is the
cause. No one by itself would produce the effect. The true cause is the
whole set of antecedents taken together." If this is true, the objective
establishment of a single agent responsible for an action is impossible.[28]

Green's thought influenced Holmes and anticipated his famous "prediction theory of the law." It also anticipated the argument used by the
legal realists a half century later against the doctrine of objective causation. According to the realists, courts claimed to base their awards of
damages on a scientific determination of cause. But since a single cause
could not be scientifically determined, what they actually were doing
was making policy decisions about the award of damages, policy decisions disguised under the cover of scientific objectivity.

The realists' argument can be applied to *Billy Budd*. Captain Vere
makes his case for Billy's execution by referring to the "facts. – In war-
time at sea a man–of–war's man strikes his superior in grade, and the
blow kills" (*BB* 107). Captain Vere establishes a clear chain of causality,
paying attention to proximate, not remote, causes. Yet the effect of
Melville's narration is to show that the cause of Claggart's death is much
more complicated. As Green argues, there is no one antecedent to the
event, taken by itself, that can be called the true cause. Instead, we have
an overdetermination of causes. One of these – Claggart's hatred of Billy
– is admittedly impossible to explain. Although Melville certainly did
not read Green's or Holmes's legal philosophy, he does create a fictional
narrative that questions the narrative model that the orthodox legal
thinkers used to assess blame. Furthermore, just as Green's ideas, ig-
nored in his day except by Holmes and his friends, did not replace
orthodox thought until years later, so it took many years for critics to
recognize that Melville's narrative might challenge that of his sym-

pathetic captain. Very likely, the triumph of the legal realists' paradigm indirectly helped the next generation of literary critics to see the subversive potential of Melville's narrative.

As this example shows, if the ideas in Melville's story have similarities with the thought of Holmes and his circle, they are reflected not so much in Captain Vere as in the way Melville questions Vere's orthodox thinking. Holmes's belief that law changes with changing social circumstances is not at all compatible with Captain Vere's philosophy of measured forms, nor was it compatible with late nineteenth-century orthodox legal thought. In such thought, truth "was an ascertainable entity."[29] For Holmes it was not. Nor was it for Melville, who recognized that truth always has its ragged edges. Those ragged edges, as we saw in the last chapter, subvert the balanced narrative based on an opposition between the individual and society. Similar to Melville's work of fiction, Holmes's legal philosophy questioned formalist assumptions while denying the alternative of appealing to a theory of natural law or the natural rights of man. And, just as Melville's narrative takes shape by looking back at historical events that led to the domination of formalism, so Holmes's legal theory grew out of his scrutiny of legal history.

Legal theorists who appeal to history are often considered to be conservative. Formalists, for instance, defended the status quo by turning to historical precedent and tradition. This aspect of their thought caused the legal realist Roscoe Pound to refer to them as the "historical school."[30] But the history the formalists appealed to was one that separated law from the specific historical conditions to which it responded. An analysis of the law that takes into account historical specificity can often undermine prevailing doctrine. Holmes is a case in point. Holmes wrote *The Common Law* only after his long and tireless editing of Kent's *Commentaries*. For him, legal history revealed that the law had no ahistorical logic. Its origin was not civilized reason, but primitive social need.

> The customs, beliefs, or needs of a primitive time establish a rule or a formula. In the course of centuries the custom, belief, or necessity disappears, but the rule remains. The reason which gave rise to the rule has been forgotten, and ingenious minds set themselves to inquire how it is to be accounted for. Some ground of policy is thought of, which seems to explain it and to reconcile it with the present state of things; and then the rule adapts itself to the new reasons which have been found for it, and enters on a new career. The old form receives a new content, and in time even the form modifies itself to fit the meaning which it has received.[31]

For Holmes, history is the "means by which we measure the power which the past has had to govern the present in spite of ourselves, so to speak, by imposing traditions which no longer meet the original end."[32]

Melville was not a legal scholar, but through his family's close contact
with the law he had personal knowledge of how old legal forms receive
new content and how forms themselves are modified to fit new meanings. In *Billy Budd* he, like Holmes, uses history to question the unexam-
ined assumptions of formalism.

Written by someone whose writing habits were formed in antebellum
America, *Billy Budd* clearly has the outward appearance of a romance.
Written in an age of literary realism, it also has aspects of realistic fiction.
Like a romance, it suggests the existence of alternative ways of interpreting the world. But that alternative is not to be found in a transcendental
realm, a realm that *Billy Budd,* like works of realism, denies. Instead, the
alternative that *Billy Budd* suggests is found in a realm of history. Offering us an inside view of the past, *Billy Budd* provides indirect evidence
that Captain Vere's is not the only interpretation of the past.

Throughout I have argued that the interpretation of laws is in part
conditioned by the historical presuppositions of those who interpret
them and the historical circumstances out of which those interpretations
arise. This view of the law, which undercuts formalist claims that legal
interpretations are based on a set of eternal logical principles, would seem
to have been apparent to anyone in Melville's lifetime making the most
elementary critical study of a history of American law, since the Constitution itself resulted from balancing the interests of thirteen separate
states and different economic forces at a unique time in history, and sixty
years later that same Constitution could be interpreted by either North
or South to support its position. But the historically conditioned bias of
an age's interpretation of its law is more difficult to detect than we might
suspect. What can make it so difficult to detect is the ability of people like
Vere to use historical presuppositions to demonstrate the historical inevitability of interpreting the law the way he does. This use of history to
deny alternative possibilities within history is one of the most subtle
ways in which formalist legal thought legitimizes the status quo. Thus,
Billy Budd's questioning of Captain Vere's version of history turns out to
be one of the most subtle ways in which the story exposes the fragility of
the captain's measured forms.

Captain Vere bases his legal philosophy on an understanding of the
nature of man that he has found confirmed in his reading of biographies
and histories. The narrator describes the captain's avid reading: "With
nothing of that literary taste which less heeds the things conveyed than
the vehicle, his bias was towards those books to which every serious
mind of superior order occupying any active post of authority in the
world naturally inclines: books treating of actual men and events no
matter what era – history, biography, and unconventional writers like

Montaigne, who, free from cant and convention, honestly and in the spirit of common sense philosophize upon realities. In this line of reading he found confirmation of his own more reserved thoughts – confirmation which he had vainly sought in social converse, so that as touching most fundamental topics, there had got to be established in him some positive convictions which he forefelt would abide in him essentially unmodified so long as his intelligent part remained unimpaired" (*BB* 36). Because his convictions are based on the actual facts of history, not the "*novel* opinions social, political, and otherwise" (36, my emphasis) coming from revolutionary France, Captain Vere can be relatively certain of them. It is on the basis of these convictions that he executes Billy Budd.

But Melville's novel casts doubt on the objectivity of Vere's interpretation of history. First, Vere does not read his texts free from presuppositions. In them he finds confirmation of thoughts he already has, confirmation that he cannot find through contact with people inhabiting the real world. Thus, he is either reading histories and biographies in a biased manner, selecting isolated passages to support his already existing prejudices, or selecting those texts that tend to confirm his prejudices.

That Vere interprets his authoritative texts selectively is suggested if we read what one of his favorite writers, Montaigne, has to say about the law in "Of Experience." Decrying the injustice of the law, Montaigne laments, "How many innocent people we have found to have been punished – I mean by no fault of their judges – and how many there have been that we have not found out about! . . . In short, these poor devils are sacrificed to the forms of justice." According to Vere's literary authority, "Now laws remain in credit not because they are just, but because they are laws. That is the mystic foundation of their authority; they have no other. And that is a good thing for them. They are often made by fools, more often by people who, in their hatred of equality, are wanting in equity; but always by men, vain and irresolute authors. There is nothing so grossly and widely and ordinarily faulty as the laws. Whoever obeys them because they are just, does not obey them for just the reason he should."[33]

Such passages from Montaigne do not confirm Vere's belief that the law serves rationality and order. Nonetheless, *Billy Budd* lets us see why so many histories and biographies confirm a conservative view of the past. Unlike works of fiction, which are the product of a suspect imagination, Captain Vere's objective histories and biographies are constructed from factual documents. The "authorized" account of Billy Budd, reported under the heading "News from the Mediterranean," in which Claggart becomes a patriotic hero and Billy a ruthless villain, is an example of how objective such "factual" documents are. The official version's total distortion of the events on the *Bellipotent* recalls the narrator's remark early in the story that historians often "naturally abridge" accounts unflattering to a country. Discussing accounts of the Nore mutiny, he admits,

> Nor are these readily to be found in the libraries. Like some other events in every age befalling states everywhere, including America, the Great Mutiny was of such character that national pride along with views of policy would fain shade it off into the historical background. Such events cannot be ignored, but there is a considerate way of historically treating them. (*BB* 23)

There are few better examples of such a "historical" treatment of an event than Charles Sumner's account of the *Somers* affair.

Responding to the request of Theodore Sedgwick, Jr., that he write an essay making certain that "all the Organs of 'Public Opinion' sound the right tune," Sumner starts with a history of past mutinies, including a description of the events at the Nore.[34] Sumner hopes that the "confusion and obscurity" that have surrounded discussions of the case will be cleared up so that we can see the decision to acquit Mackenzie "like the country's flag revealed in the smoke of battle." A historical account of the affair will offer such clarity because the history of past mutinies provides the clear lesson that the "outbreak of mutiny may be sudden, unexpected, and overwhelming, even among a crew that has given no previous sign of disaffection." Comparing the "spirit of mutiny" to the vapor in the box drawn up by the net of the fisherman in *The Arabian Nights Entertainments,* a vapor that grew until it assumed the "form of a Genie of gigantic proportions," Sumner concludes, "Woe to the unfortunate commander, who, in a moment of irresolution, or through fear of exercising a power corresponding to the stern necessities of the occasion, allows the small vapor to swell till it stalks like a giant over the ship."[35] Given such an unequivocal lesson from history, Captain Mackenzie had no alternative but to act as he did.

But a close look at Sumner's essay shows that it contains the seeds of its own subversion. In addition to taking as his historical source for his treatment of the Nore and Spithead mutinies an authorized naval history written by a British naval captain, Edward Pelham Brenton, Sumner occasionally refers to a book written by an unnamed person who is described as "the friend of the seaman," who "writes almost with the spirit of a mutineer." According to this person, Brenton's account of the mutinies is "inaccurate and of interest only because Brenton was held a prisoner in the fleet at the time."[36] He also offers terrible stories about the misuse of mutiny laws, such as when a commander (who later received a peerage) successfully appealed to the threat of mutiny to defend his having killed a sailor for complaining about the quality of wine used when rum was not available. Although such details crop up in Sumner's account, they are always consigned to footnotes. A reading of Sumner's footnotes provides a very different lesson about the history of mutinies from the one we get by reading the body of the text. The notes provide a model for the technique that Melville employs throughout his "inside story" of events aboard a potentially mutinous ship. Read against the grain, Sumner's article shows that one of the most effective ways to expose the contradictions in an argument is not to argue directly against it but to reproduce it along with a few well-placed details that do not fit into its formal logic.

The most explicit subversion of Captain Vere's formal logic occurs late in the story when the narrator remarks that "the symmetry of form attainable in pure fiction cannot so readily be achieved in a narration essentially having less to do with fable than with fact. Truth uncompromisingly told will always have its ragged edges" (*BB* 131). Coming shortly after Captain Vere supports his philosophy by referring to the myth of Orpheus, this passage suggests the extent to which his measured forms have more to do with fable than fact. The formally closed version of history imagined by Captain Vere and other minds of "superior order occupying any active post of authority" (36) cannot fully account for the events on board the *Bellipotent*. The ragged edges that remain suggest that an alternative to the authorized account exists. Even the myth that forms the basis of Vere's philosophy offers a lesson unnoticed by the captain. Orpheus, in addition to using the forms of art to tame the "wild denizens of the wood" (130), used his art to try to restore the dead to life. Too often the dead, in authorized versions of history, are those not reported in the history books and biographies read by Captain Vere. They are excluded because, as *Billy Budd* reminds us, events "affecting the least significant class of mankind have all but dropped into oblivion" (43).

One event affecting the least significant class of mankind that cannot drop into oblivion is the French Revolution. At the time when Melville conceived *Billy Budd,* national attention turned to that historical event as plans were made to celebrate its centenary, not long after the first centennial celebration of America's own revolution. Ties between the American and French quests for liberty were highlighted when the Statue of Liberty was constructed in New York Harbor, not far from where Melville lived. Nonetheless, many Americans found a way of treating the ties between France and America "historically," especially any connection between the countries' two revolutions. The Napoleonic aftermath of the French Revolution was one of their prime bits of evidence. As I noted in my discussion of the *Selfridge* case, in the days of Melville's grandfather Americans were engaged in a heated debate over whether the British or the French were the true representatives of republican princi- ples. According to *Billy Budd,*

> That era appears measurably clear to us who look back at it, and but read of it. But to the grandfathers of us graybeards, the more thoughtful of them, the genius of it presented an aspect like that of Camoen's Spirit of the Cape, an eclipsing menace mysterious and prodigious. Not America was exempt from apprehension. At the height of Napoleon's unexampled conquests, there were Americans who had fought at Bunker Hill who looked forward to the possibility that the Atlantic might prove no barrier against the ultimate schemes of this French portentous upstart from the revolutionary chaos who seemed in act of fulfilling judgement prefigured in the Apocalypse. (*BB* 44)

This passage takes on more significance when we remember the loy- alties of Melville's paternal grandfather, which can be gleaned from a toast that he made at a meeting of the Bunker Hill Association held on July 4, 1812. After speeches by William and Benjamin Austin, uncle and father, respectively, of the Billy Budd-like Charles Austin, Major Melvill con- demned the "Monarchist" Federalists as "The Traitors in the United States; may they follow the example of *Judas,* and save the necessity of Judge, Jury, and Executioner."[37]

Despite widespread American hostility toward Britain and sympathy for France at the time, the revolutionary judgment that Napoleon claim- ed to represent never established itself in America, checked as it was in part by the rhetoric typical of antebellum conservatives. According to this rhetoric, the fairness of constitutional order established in America after the Revolution of 1776 made further rebellion unnecessary and dangerous. Working hard to unmask the true nature of the "French portentous upstart," antebellum conservatives sounded very much like Captain Vere as they took for their authority Edmund Burke. Burke's respect for the tradition and organic form of the common law suited their reverent wish to preserve the established institutions that rebellious ap- peals to higher law threatened. Furthermore, Burke gave them a model for a conservative thinker who had supported the American Revo- lution.[38]

The enshrinement of Burke meant the desecration of his rival, Thomas Paine. Explaining how the ship *Rights-of-Man* received its name, the narrator of *Billy Budd* reports,

> The hard-headed Dundee owner was a staunch admirer of Thomas Paine, whose book in rejoinder to Burke's arraignment of the French Revolution had then been published for some time and had gone every- where. In christening his vessel after the title of Paine's volume, the man of Dundee was something like his contemporary shipowner, Ste-

phen Girard of Philadelphia, whose sympathies, alike with his native
land and its liberal philosophers, he evinced by naming his ships after
Voltaire, Diderot, and so forth. (9–10)

When Daniel Webster addressed the Supreme Court in the *Girard Will*
case, denouncing Girard's plan to leave his money to found a school for
orphans because it did not allow for proper Christian education, he cited
Paine as the source of Girard's dangerous scheme. "The idea was drawn
from Paine's *Age of Reason,* where it is said, 'let us propagate morality
unfettered by superstition.' "[39]

Webster's hatred of Paine was shared by other antebellum conservatives. In an essay that appeared in 1843 in the same issue of the *North
American Review* as Sumner's defense of Mackenzie, an author promising
"impartiality" proposes to "dig from an almost forgotten grave the
intellectual character of Thomas Paine," even though he assumes that
there is not a "human being in this wide world . . . who cares a jot for
him or his memory." The author's foremost purpose was to refute the
mistaken belief that "Paine really was one of the great men of the
[American] Revolution." In doing so, he makes the distinction between
the American Revolution and the French Revolution that was considered
essential by American conservatives. Paine, "the infidel, the scoffer, the
libertine, the drunkard, and, worse than all perhaps in anti-republican
judgment, the stay-maker," could not have been a true American because "he renounced [America's] moderate republicanism for the exag-
gerations of French democracy."[40]

Wondering why the American Revolution was "so little contaminated
by the cooperation of unworthy men, and especially unworthy for-
eigners," the author remarks that "the Revolution was no affair of the
barricades, of an infuriate, outraged populace rising suddenly to revenge.
It was (thank Heaven!) no brigand revolt, no revolution of squatters,
who, planting themselves on lands which belonged to others, raised the
standard of rebellion, and solicited the kindred aid of all fugitives from
justice throughout the world." The American Revolution was "very
gradual. From 1763 to 1774, it was a matter of grave, deliberate re-
monstrance and reasoning. . . . How dilatory would the process of revolt, as it was exhibited in this country, have seemed to the self-sufficient
reviler of all established institutions!" America's friends were not people
like Paine but those like Burke. "It was oppressed, not revolutionary,
America, which they defended."[41]

Burke's support of the American Revolution and his opposition to the
French Revolution allowed American conservatives to interpret the
founding fathers as true conservatives who had protected traditional
rights against violations from London. According to this view of history, Thomas Paine was turned into a foreign supporter of un-American

activities, whereas the Irishman Edmund Burke became a true American for embodying the "highest human qualities, the love of virtue and truth, with a meek and humble sense of the powers with which God has endowed us, and the love of freedom with a decent reverence for authority and example, which constitute the perfection of human character, that of the conservative and Christian patriot."[42]

The conservative interpretation of the French and American revolutions was an important part of Lemuel Shaw's political philosophy. In his Fourth of July Oration in 1815, delivered while the outcome of Waterloo was still unknown to his listeners, Shaw said that he feared that the American Revolution had "suffered an irreparable injury by being compared with that of France." For him the French Revolution had been deplorable, for "after a few feverish years of liberty, this horrible revolution terminated, as all reflecting men had foreseen that it must terminate, in a government of physical force, cruel, ferocious, military despotism. The rule of Bonaparte was little more than a continued scene of oppressive outrage and contempt of social rights."[43]

Shaw was so fascinated by Bonaparte that, as his son Samuel reports in the biography of his father that he published in 1885, Shaw was prompted by his French tutor in 1802 to translate *A Political and Historical View of the Civil and Military Transactions of Bonaparte, First Consul of France*, by J. Chas. Shaw never found a publisher, but his son reports speeches in which Shaw's views on Napoleon were published. Commenting on an address that his father gave to the Humane Society in 1811, Samuel Shaw notes that Shaw touched on the "growing philanthropy of the age, the partial abolition of the slave-trade, the prospect of a suitable asylum for lunatics." He then quotes the following passage from Shaw's speech.

> It is the misfortune of the present age to witness the most tremendous experiments upon the flexibility of human character that the world has ever exhibited. In alluding to the ferocious despotism that has desolated the fairest portions of Europe, let me earnestly hope that no party feeling will be imputed to me. God forbid that on this solemn occasion I should cherish or impart an ungenerous prejudice so inauspicious to its design. But as the humble advocate of the cause of humanity, whose interests are this day intrusted to my charge, it is impossible not to feel and it would be a dereliction of duty not to express the deepest abhorrence of a despotism equally at war with the dictates of justice, the precepts of religion, and the rights of humanity. Struggling for the preservation of life, shall we patiently see the lives of millions of innocents sacrificed without remorse to satiate the rapacity of individual ambition?[44]

Like Captain Vere, unprejudiced Lemuel Shaw felt it his duty to denounce Napoleon's despotism for being "at war" with the welfare of mankind.

When he wrote his biography, even Shaw's son could recognize that this "bit of Anti-Bonapartism," although sincere, was "good federal politics." As the narrator of *Billy Budd* remarks, "That era appears measurably clear to us who look back at it, and but read of it" (*BB* 44). But the clarity with which late nineteenth-century America saw the Napoleonic era was not merely the result of increased objectivity. If even conservatives could recognize that the French Revolution had led to important advances,[45] the debate over whether France or Britain was the truly republican power of the time had been unequivocally decided in favor of Britain. Essentially, the conservative interpretation of that era put forth by people like Shaw had triumphed. Authoritative histories unambiguously favored Britain, and rule by law, over France and its ambitious dictator. By now, even liberal reformers cited Burke as their authority, and Paine was described by Theodore Roosevelt as that "filthy little atheist."[46]

As a result, interpretations of American constitutional history were often informed by philosophies similar to those of antebellum conservatives and Captain Vere. There was of course the exceptional case of Holmes, who edited Kent's *Commentaries* and wrote *The Common Law*. The typical spokesman, however, was Cooley, whose constitutional theory was influenced by his editing of Story's *Commentaries on the Constitution*.[47] In turn, Cooley's copious annotations of the fourth edition meant that Story was now read through the lens of postbellum conditions and used to justify Cooley's laissez-faire economics. Furthermore, America's economic success was explained by the country's adoption of the time-tested British tradition of individual liberty and constitutional order. Writing of "The Embryo of a Commonwealth" for the *Atlantic Monthly*, Brook Adam argued that the political genius of the American people "did not lie in sudden inspiration, but in the conservative and at the same time flexible habit of mind which enabled them to adapt the institutions they had known and tested as colonists to their new position as an independent people."[48] James Bryce emphasized that the Constitution trained Americans to "habits of legality" and strengthened "their conservative instincts, their sense of the value of stability and permanence in political arrangements."[49]

At the same time many of the country's political leaders looked to Anglo-American political institutions as the hope of the world. Under Secretary of State Thomas F. Bayard, the United States increasingly pursued a foreign policy reflecting this Anglo-American bias. For Bayard, the United States and Great Britain were the twin conservators of world civilization.[50] Such an Anglo-centric view is confirmed by traditional, conservative readings of *Billy Budd*.

Although they call the story a tragedy of innocence, those who read it in the traditional way take comfort in a reassuring historical allegory. For them, when the *Bellipotent* defeats the *Athée,* orderly civilization triumphs, just as, for postbellum Americans, when the British defeated Napoleon, rule by law triumphed over militarism. Masquerading as the representative of liberty while spreading military rule, Napoleon had to be contained.

Yet, as I have already suggested, *Billy Budd* does not necessarily confirm such a reassuring view of history. Details in the margins of Melville's text confirm a reading of history closer to that offered by Paine in *The Rights-of-Man.* According to Paine, the British monarchy masqueraded as the defender of civilized rule by law, yet it had originated with a "banditti of ruffians" that had overrun the country and then allowed the "chief of the band" to "lose the name of robber in that of monarch." Conceived in violence, a monarchy led to a "continual system of war and exhortation."[51]

Read against the grain, the triumph of the· *Bellipotent* is not an unambiguous triumph for rational order over irrationality, or for Christianity over infidelity. Instead, it is a victory for the barbaric power of war and war's irrationality. When the narrator tells us that the *Athée* is the "aptest name, if one consider it, ever given to a war-ship" (*BB* 132), he seems to forget that the name of the British ship is even more apt. What defenders of British constitutional order fail to acknowledge is that in order to defeat Napoleon, Britain itself had to subordinate itself to the rule of war. "If our judgements approve the war, that is but coincidence," Vere claims (106), but shortly thereafter he admits that the Mutiny Act that he upholds is the "child of War." The outcome of the Napoleonic Wars may not have been the subordination of French militarism to Britain's legal, rational form of government but an alliance between the irrationality of militarism and forms of law serving an elite few. Events in postbellum America put Melville in a position to conceive of such an alternative interpretation of history. As a youth Melville could have heard antebellum conservatives denounce Andrew Jackson by comparing him to Napoleon and arguing that his militarism was incompatible with American constitutional principles. Later in his life he would have watched as the North waged a war to protect those principles and to expand them in order to ensure that black Americans were also protected by their provisions. In *Battle-Pieces* Melville wrote that the war had resulted because Southerners were "entrapped into the support of a war whose implied end was the erecting in our advanced century of an Anglo-American empire based on the systematic degradation of man."[52] After the war he lived in a country where the Fourteenth Amendment was used to protect the rights of rich capitalists as well as former slaves, a country that elected Gen. Ulysses S. Grant and three other Civil War generals president and used its military forces to occupy the South while many of its public officials in both North and South were shown to be corrupt. Meanwhile, in foreign affairs the country began to pursue a policy that linked hands across the sea to establish an Anglo-American alliance, as both the United States and Britain expanded their imperialistic control into territories Melville had visited and written about as a young man. Finally, in the years preceding his work on *Billy Budd,* Melville lived in a country that expanded its military power at home and abroad under the guise of protecting the Anglo-American tradition of constitutional order.[53]

In *The Rights-of-Man* Paine had favorably compared the American system of government to those in the Old World. In America, he writes, "The poor are not oppressed, the rich are not privileged. . . there is nothing to engender riots and tumults."[54] One hundred years after the American Revolution, he would not have made the same claim.

Prior to railroad labor disputes in 1877, the regular army had rarely been used in America in cases of civil disorder, but with increased labor unrest federal troops were marshaled on numerous occasions to aid state militias. In Congress, and in the *North American Review,* former general James A. Garfield, soon to meet a violent death after his election to the presidency in 1881, demanded an increase in the size of the army, citing its need in case of strikes.[55] In opposition, Congressman Abram S. Hewitt supported the reduction of the army on economic grounds and defended the right to strike as just. Rather than reduce social discontent, he argued, a larger army would increase it. "If you have a great standing Army in this country, you have got to pay for it; the working industry of the country has got to pay for it. Their sufferings will go on increasing from day to day until they break out into revolution."[56]

Instead of accepting Hewitt's advice, Congress began to expand the navy as well as the army. The expansion was considered .iecessary to protect American economic interests abroad. In 1877, Secretary of the Navy Richard W. Thompson wrote, "Without foreign commerce, we must sink into inferiority; and without a Navy amply sufficient for this purpose, all the profits of our surplus productions will be transferred from the coffers of our own to those of foreign capitalists."[57] The administration of Chester A. Arthur (1881–5) responded by constructing the first modern navy, armed with the ironclads that had so impressed Melville during the Civil War. On its way to ruling the waves that Captain Vere had fought so hard to protect for Britain at the end of the eighteenth century, the United States, like Vere, claimed to be protecting legal institutions that operated for the welfare of mankind.

Read in this context, *Billy Budd* does not offer an allegory about the transformation from antebellum rule by natural law to postbellum rule by secular law, but an alternative way of interpreting both the triumph of

British constitutional order at the end of the eighteenth century and the triumph of formalism in American law at the end of the nineteenth century.

In exposing the ragged edges of Captain Vere's philosophy of measured forms, *Billy Budd* might seem to advocate the revolutionary alternative embraced by radicals at the end of both centuries, yet this is not necessarily the case. *Billy Budd*'s setting in the wake of the French Revolution is itself enough to contest the conservative argument, in the late nineteenth century, that if America hoped to progress there was no alternative to current social relations of inequality. It also suggests that the revolutionary alternative is not always what it claims to be. The fear that antebellum conservatives had of the consequences of bloody revolution were to some extent justified by Napoleon's rise to power. Captain Vere's measured forms mask the very irrationality that he hopes to combat, but it does not necessarily follow that the Napoleonic forces he fights against become the representatives of rationality and the hope of humankind. For instance, Napoleon ordered the return of slavery to the island of Santo Domingo after the 1799 rebellion had brought about liberation. Potentially the supreme confidence man, Napoleon espoused the noble cause of the French Revolution while spreading the irrationality of war throughout Europe. No account of the rise of the modern military state would be complete without a section on Napoleon.

In addition, although Melville undercuts Captain Vere's philosophy he shared some of Vere's distrust of the masses' ability to reason. One of the ironies of the story's ironic subversion of Vere's logic is that it indirectly confirms his elitist pronouncements about the sailors. Unable to judge their own best interests, they willingly submit to Captain Vere's ordered world. Melville, rejected by the mass reading public, might have had good reason to agree with Vere that the people "have not that kind of intelligent responsiveness that might qualify them to comprehend and discriminate" (*BB* 108).

If Melville tempered his criticism of the status quo with a distrust of a revolutionary alternative, he was not alone. The period's most famous reformist writer, Edward Bellamy, offered criticism of both the present social structure and the revolutionary mentality. A brief look at Bellamy's fiction can help us define *Billy Budd*'s historical position and lead us to a final discussion of the historical conditions helping to shape the form of Melville's fiction.

In responding to conditions of late nineteenth-century America, Melville returns to the past, whereas Bellamy turns to a vision of the future. Nonetheless, there is a kinship between the tradition of utopian fiction and the tradition of the historical romance to which *Billy Budd* belongs. That kinship becomes clearer when we remember that before he wrote *Looking Backward,* Bellamy composed *The Duke of Stockbridge,* a historical romance. "The utopian novel is only the historical novel inverted," writes Harry B. Henderson.[58] Serialized in the *Berkshire Courier* in 1879, *The Duke of Stockbridge* responds to the bloody agitation of 1877 by returning to Shays' Rebellion, which had occurred almost one hundred years earlier in the Berkshire hills so familiar to Melville. Thus, like *Billy Budd,* Bellamy's romance responds to the present by looking backward at revolutionary class conflict at the end of the eighteenth century. Moreover, the American response to Shays' rebellion was similar to its response to the French Revolution. Supporters of Shays felt that the rebellion was necessary to complete the liberation of the people started by the American Revolution. Opponents dismissed the rebellion as an affair led by men of "one of three classes, viz: adventurers, demogogues, and desperados."[59] To them, once the colonies gained their freedom from Britain further rebellion was not justified. No longer a struggle for legitimate self-determination, it raised the threat of anarchy. As Josiah Gilbert Holland writes in his *History of Western Massachusetts: The Counties of Hamden, Hampshire, Franklin, and Berkshire* . . . (1855), Shays' Rebellion proved "that the rebellion of a people against a government *established by themselves* is not justifiable, even in an extreme case, and can only result in dishonor to the State, and calamity and disgrace to those who participate in it."[60]

Bellamy does not portray Shays' Rebellion as a "shame to the Commonwealth," one of those events from the past that the narrator of *Billy Budd* says every country tries to overlook in authorized histories. Nonetheless, Bellamy does not offer what Henderson describes as a "proletarian romance of Shays' Rebellion."[61] The lesson he draws from the revolt is to distrust working-class agitation. The leadership is depicted as dangerous and unstable. The "mobs which had done the business had been chiefly recruited from the idle and shiftless. Each village had furnished its contingent of tavern loafers, neerdowells, and returned soldiers with a distaste for industry."[62]

Having first looked to the past, Bellamy turns to the future and writes his utopian *Looking Backward.* In *Looking Backward* the conflicts associated with working-class agitation disappear. The problem of how to pay for the large standing army used to control striking workers is solved by creating an industrial army that maximizes production. In Bellamy's utopian vision, social transformation will occur through bloodless evolution. The perfect society will be shaped within American history, without class struggle and violence, a logical continuation of the American Revolution. For Bellamy, no second revolution was necessary to continue the reforms set in motion by the Revolutionary War.

If Melville had a distrust of revolutionary chaos, it did not lead him, like Bellamy, to imagine a utopian future achieved through evolution. In *Billy Budd* Melville once again exposes the injustice of the reigning order without being able to embrace an alternative to it. Melville's fiction is in part shaped by this inability to imagine the very alternatives to present forms of society that his texts suggest should exist.

In "The Encantadas," Melville describes the "crowning curse" of the Galapagos tortoises as "their drudging impulse to straight-forwardness in a belittered world" (*E* 105). Trying to avoid their fate, he adopted techniques of indirection, which he hoped would make possible the "grand Art of Telling the Truth" in "this world of lies."[63] *Billy Budd*'s capacity to undercut Captain Vere's authoritative version of history has led some critics to conclude that Melville's "inside narrative" offers a fictional account of the past that is true, whereas the account found in "objective" histories is false. But *Billy Budd*'s technique of indirection does not result in a vision of Truth. Instead, the story self-consciously undercuts any claim it makes fully to represent the past. A fiction, *Billy Budd* occupies the space of the *"might-have-been,"* which, we are told, is "but boggy ground to build on" (*BB* 27). Constructed on this boggy foundation, Melville's later works subvert any attempt to establish an authoritative position, including their own. Although his formally subversive fiction undercuts the narrative point of view he adopts, that undercutting does not let us extract the truth of a text independently from its point of view. To say this might seem merely to confirm the formalist doctrine that the point of view of fiction is part of its truth. But Melville's fiction lets us see the social and political consequences of such statements.

In 1889 *Cosmopolitan* printed a three-part account of the *Somers* affair entitled "The Murder of Philip Spencer." Admitting that Spencer was "by no means a blameless lad," the author argues that the closeness of death brought out the "true Philip Spencer, . . . the heroic soul he was born to be." In contrast, the *Somers* affair revealed the truly deceitful nature of Commander Mackenzie. As proof the author cites a "sinister fact" that came to light in the court-martial. According to the *Cosmopolitan* account, before his death Spencer had asked to write his parents. Handcuffed, he could not write himself and was forced to dictate a letter to Mackenzie. "Thus Spencer could not write to his own father and mother a dying message. Everything had to pass through the commander's hands. No one was permitted to be near enough to hear what Spencer said. No one will ever in this world know what Spencer said, for the commander wrote what he chose." Nonetheless, the author claims to be able to glean the truth from this distorted message. "Yet truth is so divine and eternal, so independent of effort to destroy or uphold it, that it can be *precipitated* from this hideous narrative, aided by the sinister and suppressed paper, almost as pure and clear as if truth had been the original intent."[64]

We could argue that Melville's situation is analogous to Spencer's. Forced by ideological constraints to speak through a censorious, authoritative point of view, Melville cannot speak the truth directly. But in Melville's world there is no divine and eternal truth that can be disentangled from the point of view he adopts, no innocent voice free of ideology. Instead, Melville's works remind us that all discourse is produced within a system of constraints. Or, to put it another way, the inevitability of ideological distortion is part of the truth Melville narrates.

The consequences of Melville's techniques of indirection do not stop with that insight. Postmodernist aesthetics have a tendency to privilege techniques leading to the kind of ambiguous, open-ended texts that Melville wrote. Showing the search for an innocent truth to be impossible, such texts are termed more "rigorous" than others. Embracing the free play of signification, they are said to expose the nostalgia involved in the old-fashioned search for truth.[65] But the ambiguities growing out of the silences in Melville's fiction are as much a sign of inadequacy as of lucidity, an indication that Melville could not offer an authoritative version of the truth in response to the ones he undercut. If Melville's texts expose the ragged edges that result from all attempts at formal closure, they also display sympathy for those figures like Vere who attempt to establish order or like Benito Cereno who regret the passing of an older order. If they demonstrate the impossibility of employing techniques of direction to tell the truth, through their negative portrayal of characters like Babo, Bartleby, and Claggart they also record suspicion at the endless subversion brought about by their techniques of indirection and masquerade.

Melville even hints at the similarities between his role as a writer and the satanic behavior of Claggart, a man who never means what he says. Billy's speech defect, we are told, is the work of the "envious marplot of Eden," the "arch interferer's" way of reminding us that "I too have a hand here" (*BB* 19). A "marplot" himself, Melville raises the possibility that the hand writing his fiction not only reports the conditions of the world but, in producing endless subversive texts, contributes to the world's "belittered" state.

As effectively as any other literary texts, Melville's dramatize how the belief that truth is to be found in formal wholeness contributes to both legal and literary philosophies of exclusion. But Melville's texts also offer a salutary caution to those on the scene of contemporary criticism who, under the banner of political radicalism, condemn as reactionary any desire for wholeness or identity. As much a result of our inequitable and divided world as an alternative to it, such theories too often lock themselves into a world view in which a belittered condition becomes inevitable. The ragged edges of *Billy Budd* subvert more than attempts at formal closure. Generated by the subversive negativity of Melville's vision, they turn us to a historical world beyond a closed textual universe in which all possibility for transformation has vanished and keep open a space in which an alternative to our present condition can be imagined.

A Closing Statement

To make a closing statement after discussing a text woven together with ragged edges is not easy, for our task is not to provide closure but to keep open the space needed to name and create an alternative world to our present one. Even so, at this present historical moment some tentative conclusions can be made as to how the study of law and literature can be used as a tool to accomplish that task. First of all, we need to avoid simplistic mergers of the two. Specifically, we need to guard against the tendency to construct symmetrical parallels between legal and literary history. For an example, we can take the attempt by John P. McWilliams, Jr., to link the rise of legal and literary realism after the Civil War.[1]

For McWilliams the chief casualties of the realist movement were the antebellum traditions of romance and legal theories of natural rights. Literature lost its transcendental, otherworldly quality, whereas law lost its appeal to a higher realm of self-evident, absolute standards.

The problem with McWilliams's formulation is that the symmetrical parallel that he creates – romance leads to realism as natural-law philosophy leads to realism – needs qualification. First of all, no literary or legal period is quite as pure as McWilliams's analysis would indicate. Not every work written before the Civil War was a romance; not every work after it was a work of realism. In antebellum law, instrumentalism, formalism, and natural-law doctrine coexisted. Second, even when we confine ourselves to dominant literary forms and the major trends in legal thought, parallels are not so neat. If the romance has affinities with a natural-law philosophy, it dominated at a time when legal thought was dominated by the instrumentalism that overshadowed the eighteenth-century concept of natural law. Similarly, although McWilliams rightly points to affinities between legal and literary realism, and although the legal-realism movement did have its beginnings during the time when realism predominated in literature, historically, boundary theory had prevailed in the law.[2] Legal realism did not gain ascendancy until literature moved toward modernism.

The asymmetries between the two histories suggest that a period's dominant literary form can just as likely contest a period's dominant legal ideology as resemble it. This is not to argue that literature takes its form by directly responding to legal ideology. Nor is it to argue that literature can transcend its historical conditions. But the disciplines of literature and law are relatively autonomous.[3] Although both are ultimately related to the period's modes of production and reproduction of social structures, each develops according to a logic of its own. This internal logic is most apparent in law. Legal history cannot be explained merely by reference to social history, because the legal profession's emphasis on precedent and tradition strongly influences how judges interpret laws. Throughout this book I have tried to point to some of the social effects of the profession's reliance on an intrinsic legal reasoning, as well as to suggest that it tends to rely on such reasoning more rigorously in certain social situations. Nonetheless, the logic is appealed to and does affect the shape of the law. Even changes in dominant legal thought from one period to the next can in part be explained by a logic intrinsic to the discipline. Realism can be seen as a reaction to formalism, just as formalism was a reaction to instrumentalism, and so on. The same sort of intrinsic logic can be seen at work in literature, where literary realism self-consciously responds to romanticism.

Having argued for a notion of the relative autonomy of the two disciplines, I think it is also important to emphasize that, of the two, literature is relatively more autonomous. Law is a vital part of the manner in which a society is governed; literature is not. Literature's distance from the direct mode of governance accounts for its capacity to contest a period's dominant legal ideology. Thus, even literature that does not directly engage legal issues can occupy a potential space in which it is informed by a different set of ideological assumptions from those that inform law. Those assumptions, I should emphasize, are by no means outside of history. As our look at antebellum legal philosophy makes clear, at no one time does one theory have total, hegemonic control. The period's dominant art form often shares affinities with oppositional ideologies that can be either progressive or nostalgic.

For instance, in challenging the instrumentalism that prevailed in antebellum America, transcendentalists and writers of romance often nostalgically relied on older, natural-law notions. To make this challenge they posited an autonomous individual whose rights are threatened by socially expedient law that conflicts with the higher laws to which the individual has private access. As a result, the nineteenth-century American romance was based on the same split between the public and private realms that was legitimized by the dominant legal order.

If the romance's criticism was limited by assuming separate public and private realms, the realism and naturalism that replaced it as a dominant literary mode had its own limitations. Like the legal realists, they questioned the well-defined split between public and private, but, like both legal realists and formalists, they denied a transcendental realm that could offer an alternative vision to the status quo. In basing their criticism on social "realities," not transcendental visions, they ran the risk of losing a ground for their critique, since their sense of the real was all too easily conditioned by already existing realities. To be sure, the romancers' transcendental visions were also influenced by already existing realities, but by positing them as otherworldly they at least suggested the possibility of a truly different alternative.

The dilemma for many today is how to restore a ground for criticizing the present system without lapsing into a nostalgic longing for a transcendental world. For me, this ground must be found in historical analysis. Unfortunately, some of the more popular trends in literary criticism dismiss a historical approach. Some contemporary critics, rediscovering with seeming amazement the connection between history and *histoire,* feel it their duty to remind historians that histories are, after all, stories told. Those influenced by structuralism add the insight that what seems to be a diachronic study of the past is actually a synchronic alignment written in the present. Having identified the historical approach with those who claim to tell us how the past really was, such critics go on to declare the impossibility of writing history and sometimes prematurely celebrate our liberation from the burden of the past.[4]

This attack on history assumes that all historians are narrow empiricists. To be sure, there are historians who fit the stereotype that these critics have constructed, but it is equally true that many of those who continue to take history seriously also criticize a naive view of how the past can be reconstructed. In his "Theses on the Philosophy of History" Walter Benjamin argues that "to articulate the past historically does not mean to recognize it 'the way it really was' (Ranke)." Rejecting the notion that historians "who wish to relive an era" should "blot out everything they know about the later course of history," Benjamin asserts,

> Historicism contents itself with establishing a causal connection between various moments in history. But no fact that is a cause is for that very reason historical. It became historical posthumously, as it were, through events that may be separated from it by thousands of years. A historian who takes this as his point of departure stops telling the se-

quence of events like the beads of a rosary. Instead, he grasps the constellation which his own era has formed with a definite earlier one.[5]

Melville achieves such a historical sense in *Billy Budd*. Fully aware of the problems involved in constructing histories, Melville writes a work set almost one hundred years in the past, a work in which he grasps the constellation that his own era has formed with an earlier one.[6]

In my own way, I too, writing one hundred years after Melville, have tried to use a method that will produce this historical sense. As Benjamin knows, histories are often constructed in the service of conservative interests. This was especially true of most legal histories written in the nineteenth century. But, as Robert Gordon has recently argued, the situation today is quite different.[7] The lack of a historical perspective in legal education clearly contributes to the maintenance of the status quo. Lawyers, receiving a technical training that suppresses any historical understanding, accept as legitimate the laws they are paid to administer. Thus, it is regrettable that some of the most popular recent attempts to link law and literature encourage an ahistorical perspective. Applying contemporary literary theory to legal interpretation, Sanford Levinson asks, "What does one do, then, when studying opinions, if one gives up the enterprise of determining whether or not they are 'correct'? Are cases simply historical fragments which should be studied for insight into the ideology of the time?"[8]

A major purpose of this study has been to counter this trend that dismisses a historical analysis of legal ideology so easily. By using literary texts to interpret a period's legal history and a period's legal history to interrogate literary texts, I have tried to combat the ahistorical sense of history that has resulted from an inadequate historical method. "Its method," Benjamin argues, "is additive; it masters a mass of data to fill the homogeneous empty time." But, Benjamin responds, "Thinking involves not only the flow of thoughts, but their arrest as well. Where thinking suddenly stops in a configuration pregnant with tensions, it gives that configuration a shock, by which it crystalizes into a monad." A literary text, though not revolutionary in and of itself, offers historians the opportunity to construct that monad, one whose structure allows them to "blast a specific era out of the homogeneous course of history."[9] An era blasted out of the homogeneous course of history reveals that although history happened one way, it could have happened another.

Literary texts become an aid to a historical investigation precisely because they expose the ragged edges of attempts to construct a continuum of history. In a consideration of legal history, those ragged edges help expose the contradictions involved in the law's attempt to close the case on events from the past. There is no inevitable law to history or history of the law. If the texts we have studied remind us of the difficulties involved in constructing histories, they also remind us that the struggle to understand the past should not lead us to forget the struggles in the past. Heirs of a legal tradition that has been both an arena of struggle and a means by which struggle has been suppressed, Americans can enrich their history through actions and understandings today that will construct a new constellation with the past, thus making it possible in the future to articulate the alternatives that American writers in the nineteenth century could express only as nostalgia, utopia, or silence.

Notes

AN OPENING STATEMENT

1 Joseph Story, "Value and Importance of Legal Studies," in *The Miscellaneous Writings of Joseph Story,* ed. William W. Story (Boston: Little, Brown, 1852), 548.

2 Abraham Lincoln, "Address before the Young Men's Lyceum of Springfield, Illinois, delivered Jan. 27, 1838," in *The Collected Works of Abraham Lincoln,* ed. Roy P. Basler, 8 vols. (New Brunswick, N.J.: Rutgers University Press, 1953), 1:112.

3 Rufus Choate, "The Importance of Illustrating New-England History by a Series of Romances Like the Waverly Novels," in *The Works of Rufus Choate with a Memoir of His Life,* ed. Samuel Gilman Brown, 2 vols. (Boston: Little, Brown, 1862), 1:320, 343–4.

4 Herman Melville, "The Marquis de Grandvin," in *Great Short Works of Herman Melville,* ed. Warner Berthoff (New York: Harper and Row, 1969), 400.

5 Robert A. Ferguson, *Law and Letters in American Culture* (Cambridge, Mass.: Harvard University Press, 1984), 26, 9, 243.

6 Choate, "Illustrating New-England History," 323, 334, 340.

7 Ferguson, *Law and Letters,* 249.

8 Choate, "Illustrating New-England History," 339.

9 William Charvat, Roy Harvey Pearce, and Claude M. Simpson, eds., *The Centenary Edition of the Works of Nathaniel Hawthorne* (Columbus: Ohio State University Press, 1972), 7:21–30.

10 Robert W. Gordon, "New Developments in Legal Theory," in *The Politics of Law,* ed. David Kairys (New York: Pantheon Books, 1982), 286. The essays collected in this volume offer a useful introduction to work done by members of the critical legal-studies movement.

11 G. Edward White, *The American Judicial Tradition* (New York: Oxford University Press, 1976), 33. See also Wallace Mendelson, *Capitalism, Democracy, and the Supreme Court* (New York: Appleton-Century-Crofts, 1960), 28. "Marshall's majestic prose, his premise-obscuring rhetoric and inspired generalizations tend to hide the shabby side of the claims which his great opinions protected. More important, Marshall served well the conservative interests of

his day – and for a long while it was conservatives who wrote history books."

12 Peter Gabel and Jay M. Feinman, "Contract Law and Ideology," in *Kairys, Politics of Law*, 172–84.

13 James Kent, *Commentaries on American Law*, 12th ed., ed. Oliver Wendell Holmes, Jr., 4 vols. (Boston: Little, Brown, 1873), pt. 2, lecture xvi, 343–4.

14 Robert M. Cover, "*Nomos* and Narrative," *Harvard Law Review* 97 (1983): 4–5.

15 See Winfried Fluck, "Literature as Symbolic Action," *Amerikastudien* 28 (1983): 361–71.

16 Claude Lévi-Strauss, "The Structural Study of Myth," in *Structural Anthropology*, trans. C. Jacobson and B. G. Schoepf (New York: Basic Books, 1963), 206–31.

17 Fredric Jameson, *The Political Unconscious* (Ithaca: Cornell University Press, 1981).

18 Theodor Adorno, *Prisms*, trans. Samuel Weber and Shierry Weber (London: New Left Books, 1967), 32.

19 Morton J. Horwitz, *The Transformation of American Law, 1780–1860* (Cambridge, Mass.: Harvard University Press, 1977).

20 Albert H. Marckwardt, "The Chronology and Personnel of the Bread and Cheese Club," *American Literature* 6 (1935):389–99.

21 Ferguson, *Law and Letters*, 271–2.

22 Maria Melvill to Mrs. Peter Gansevoort, New York City, December 28, 1826, in *Melville Society Extracts* 58 (1984):1.

23 See Stephen Nissenbaum, "The Firing of Nathaniel Hawthorne," *Essex Institute Historical Collections* 114 (1978):57–86. I will return to a discussion of Hawthorne's response to his firing in my chapters on *The House of the Seven Gables*.

24 Joseph Story, "Developments of Science and Mechanic Art," in *Miscellaneous Writings*, 477.

25 On the contrast between the useful olive and the barren laurel see Robert A. Ferguson, "The Emulation of Sir William Jones in the Early Republic," *New England Quarterly* 52 (1979):13–14.

26 Ferguson, *Law and Letters*, 200.

27 For an argument that the American romance reacts against the assumptions of the Scottish Common Sense School see Terence Martin, *The Instructed Vision* (Bloomington: Indiana University Press, 1961), 136–45.

28 For conflicting views on the sentimental aesthetic see Jane Tompkins, *Sensational Designs* (New York: Oxford University Press, 1985), and Ann Douglas, *The Feminization of American Culture* (New York: Avon Books, 1977).

29 For a concise statement of the position that literary history should be solely literary see Northrop Frye, "The Critical Path: An Essay on the Social Context of Literary Criticism" (1970), rpt. in *Issues in Contemporary Criticism*, ed. Gregory T. Polletta (Boston: Little, Brown, 1973), 50–7.

30 John Dewey, "The Historical Background of Corporate Personality," *Yale Law Review* 35 (1925–6):655.

31 William Peterfield Trent, John Erskine, Stuart P. Sherman et al., eds., *The Cambridge History of American Literature*, 4 vols. (New York: Putnam, 1918), vol. 2.

32 Harrison Hayford and Merton M. Sealts, Jr., introduction to *Billy Budd, Sailor* (Chicago: University of Chicago Press, 1962), 29–31.

33 The work of Michel Foucault is responsible for increasing our awareness of how specialized discourses administer silences.

34 E. P. Thompson, *Whigs and Hunters* (New York: Pantheon Books, 1975), pp. 263–5. See also Hans-Georg Gadamer's claim that "the ideal of law implies the idea of equality under the law," "Hermeneutics as Practical Philosophy," in *Reason in the Age of Science,* trans. Frederick G. Lawrence (Cambridge, Mass.: MIT Press, 1981), 96.

35 See especially Stanley Fish's "Working on the Chain Gang: Interpretation in the Law and in Literary Criticism," which is his response to Ronald Dworkin's "Law as Interpretation," in *The Politics of Interpretation,* ed. W. J. T. Mitchell (Chicago: University of Chicago Press, 1983), 271–86. This exchange also appeared in the *Texas Law Review* 60 (1982), an issue devoted to the topic of law and literature.

1. THE PIONEERS; *OR THE SOURCES OF AMERICAN LEGAL HISTORY: A CRITICAL TALE*

1 Henry Nash Smith, *Virgin Land* (Cambridge, Mass.: Harvard University Press, 1950), 66, 68.

2 George Dekker, *James Fenimore Cooper* (New York: Barnes and Noble, 1967), 59.

3 Perry Miller, *The Life of the Mind in America* (New York: Harcourt Brace and World, 1965), 100, 99.

4 James Fenimore Cooper, *The Pioneers; or the Sources of the Susquehanna: A Descriptive Tale,* ed. James Franklin Beard (Albany: State University of New York Press, 1980), 15, hereafter abbreviated *Pioneers* and cited parenthetically in the text. (A complete list of the abbreviations used for the works that I frequently cite appears in the front matter of this volume). For a comprehensive analysis of Cooper's fiction and the law see Charles Hansford Adams, " 'The Guardian of the Law': Authority and Identity in James Fenimore Cooper," Ph.D. thesis, University of Virginia, 1985.

5 See Robert A. Ferguson's brief discussion of this description in *Law and Letters in American Culture* (Cambridge, Mass.: Harvard University Press, 1984), 300, and William P. Kelly, *Plotting America's Past* (Carbondale: Southern Illinois University Press, 1983), 1–44.

6 Marvin Meyers, *The Jacksonian Persuasion* (Stanford: Stanford University Press, 1960), 237. Meyers's work remains one of the most important for those interested in the complexities of Jacksonian beliefs; I rely on it throughout. There are other accounts of the 1821 convention, in Dixon Ryan Fox, *The Decline of Aristocracy in the Politics of New York,* Columbia Studies in History, Economics and Public Law, vol. 86, no. 198 (New York: Columbia University, 1919); John Theodore Horton, *James Kent: A Study in Conservatism* (New York: Appleton-Century, 1939); Lee Benson, *The Concept of Jacksonian De-*

mocracy (New York: Atheneum, 1967), 7–11; and Shaw Livermore, Jr., *The Twilight of Federalism* (Princeton: Princeton University Press, 1962). On the original constitution, see Frederic G. Mathes, "First Constitution of the State of New York," *Magazine of American History* 17 (1887):310–13.

7 Fox, *Decline of Aristocracy*, 241.

8 Perry Miller speculates that Cooper's conservative lawyer, Thomas Dunscomb, in *The Ways of the Hour*, is modeled on Kent. See Miller's *Life of the Mind in America*, 180, 249. David Hackett Fischer offers a valuable interpretation of William Cooper's politics. Although Cooper, like Judge Temple, mingled with the people, his belief in his paternal authority distinguished him as a true Federalist. "Implicit even in his most intimate gestures was an elitist spirit, an expectation of deference." See Fischer's *Revolution of American Conservatism* (New York: Harper and Row, 1965), 16.

9 Kent, quoted in Fox, *Decline of Aristocracy*, 254.

10 See Cooper to John Jay, September 6, 1821, in *Letters and Journals of James Fenimore Cooper*, ed. James F. Beard, Jr. (Cambridge, Mass.: Harvard University Press, 1960–3), 1:70–1.

11 John P. McWilliams, Jr., *Political Justice in a Republic* (Berkeley: University of California Press, 1972), 21–2; James Fenimore Cooper, *The American Democrat*, ed. George Dekker and Larry Johnston (Baltimore: Penguin Books, 1969), 75. See McWilliams's recent discussion of *The Pioneers* in "Innocent Criminal or Criminal Innocence: The Trial in American Fiction," in Carl S. Smith, John P. McWilliams, Jr., and Maxwell Bloomfield, *Law and American Literature* (New York: Knopf, 1983), 56–71.

12 The quotation is from the section of Kent's speeches reprinted in *Documents of American History*, ed. Henry Steele Commager (New York: Appleton-Century-Crofts, 1963), 233. Kent's acceptance of Jeffersonian agrarianism has two motivations. First, the most important Federalists in upstate New York were large landowners, fearful of losing power to New York City. Second, as David Hackett Fischer has shown, after 1800 the Federalists in general "came to terms with every major argument of the Jeffersonians' majoritarianism, individuality, the ever-broadening concept of equality, states' rights, even agrarianism and Anglophobia." In Fischer's terms, Kent remained a "Federalist of the old school," but even he had to come to terms with increasing Jeffersonian control. See *Revolution of American Conservatism*, 153.

13 James Fenimore Cooper, *The Monikins* (New York: Darley-Townsend, 1859), 408.

14 In *The Pioneers*, Cooper indulges in one of the favorite attacks on lawyers by satirizing their legalistic jargon. One lawyer's use of Latin causes a woman to exclaim, "Spake it out in king's English; what for should ye be talking Indian, in a room full of Christian folks?" (150). The lawyer, Mr. Van der School, speaks with a "parenthetical style, that frequently left to his auditors a long search after his meaning" (281).

15 James Kent, *Commentaries on American Law*, 12th ed., ed. Oliver Wendell Holmes, Jr., 4 vols. (Boston: Little, Brown, 1873), pt. 2, lecture xi, 227; pt. 3, lecture xx, 450. I follow conventional practice by citing Kent according to part and lecture.

16 Kent, quoted in Horton, *James Kent,* 251–2.

17 Fox, *Decline of Aristocracy,* 136, 140–1.

18 McWilliams, *Political Justice,* 120. McWilliams argues that "Cooper does not admire Judge Temple because he was modeled upon William Cooper, nor because the judge speaks for James's Federalist heritage, nor because the judge has mastered the realities of frontier life. Temple exemplifies Cooper's definition of a just judge" (116–17). McWilliams forgets how much Cooper's definition of a just judge grew out of his Federalist heritage.

19 On antilawyer sentiment, see Gerard W. Gawalt, *The Promise of Power* (Westport, Conn.: Greenwood Press, 1979); Perry Miller's chapter "The Rise of a Profession," in *Life of the Mind in America,* 99–116, and Maxwell Bloomfield's chapter "Antilawyer Sentiment in the Early Republic," in *American Lawyers in a Changing Society, 1776–1876* (Cambridge, Mass.: Harvard University Press, 1976), 32–58. For an excellent account of the attempt of the legal profession to upgrade its image, especially in popular literature, see Bloomfield, *American Lawyers,* 136–90. See also n. 14, above.

20 Morton J. Horwitz, *The Transformation of American Law, 1780–1860* (Cambridge, Mass.: Harvard University Press, 1977). For the notion of a "release" of energy, see J. Willard Hurst, *Law and the Conditions of Freedom in the Nineteenth Century United States* (Madison: University of Wisconsin Press, 1964).

21 Joseph Dorfman, "Chancellor Kent and the Developing American Economy," *Columbia Law Review* 61 (1961):1292, 1315.

22 Kent, quoted in Dorfman, "Chancellor Kent," 1297.

23 Ibid., 1306.

24 Ibid., and Hurst, *Law and the Conditions of Freedom,* 15–18.

25 For a discussion of *The Pioneers* and conservation laws, see E. Arthur Robinson, "Conservation in Cooper's *The Pioneers,*" *PMLA* 82 (1967):564–78. For a much more thorough discussion see Charles Swann, "Guns Mean Democracy: *The Pioneers* and the Game Laws," in *New Essays on Cooper,* ed. Robert Clark (New York: Barnes and Noble, [Vision Press] 1985), 96–120. This stimulating essay appeared after I had completed my book.

26 Kent, *Commentaries,* part 5, lecture xxxiv, 328–9.

27 Kent, quoted in Horton, *James Kent,* 283.

28 Dorfman, "Chancellor Kent," 1292.

29 Kent, quoted in Dorfman, 1292. For Kent's record of changes from British to American property law, see Horton, *James Kent,* 278–83.

30 Alexis de Tocqueville, *Democracy in America,* ed. Phillips Bradley (New York: Knopf, 1945), 2:166.

31 Quoted in Michael P. Rogin, *Fathers and Children* (New York: Knopf, 1975), 103.

32 William Priest, *Travels in the United States of America* (London, 1802), 132.

33 James Fenimore Cooper, *The Chainbearer; or, The Littlepage Manuscripts,* 2 vols. (New York: Burgess, Stringer, 1845), 1:171–2.

34 See *Fairfax Devisee v. Hunter's Lessee* (1813). Another important Supreme Court case involving a title dispute was *Fletcher v. Peck* (1810), which grew out of the Yazoo land scandal. It is worth noting that Kent's friend Joseph

Story gained national prominence by lobbying for New England Yazooists before he was named to the Supreme Court. His first important opinion of court came in the *Fairfax* case. Story's friend Chief Justice John Marshall, the embodiment of the Federalist ideal for a judge, was also a speculator in western lands. See *The Papers of John Marshall,* ed. Herbert A. Johnson (Chapel Hill: University of North Carolina Press, 1974–), 1:100–4, 2:140–9. For more on the Yazoo affair, see my next chapter.

35 On the controversy between common law and codification, see Miller, *Life of the Mind in America,* 105–16, 239–54, and Horwitz, *Transformation of American Law,* 1–30, 256–9.

36 Brackenridge, quoted in Horwitz, *Transformation of American Law,* 24.

37 See Joel R. Kehler, "Architectural Dialecticism in Cooper's *The Pioneers,*" *Texas Studies in Language and Literature* 18 (1975):124–34.

38 See Thomas Philbrick, "Cooper's *The Pioneers:* Origins and Structure," *PMLA* 79 (1964):592.

39 James Fenimore Cooper (grandson), ed., *Correspondence of James Fenimore Cooper,* (New Haven: Yale University Press, 1922), 1:77. See also Stephen Railton, *Fenimore Cooper* (Princeton: Princeton University Press, 1978), 131.

40 Daniel Peck, *A World by Itself* (New Haven: Yale University Press, 1977). Peck tries to concentrate on Cooper's aesthetic effects as opposed to his political effects. I am trying to suggest the politics of Cooper's aesthetics.

41 On Doolittle's role, see Robert Barton, "Natty's Trial, or the Triumph of Hiram Doolittle," *Cimarron Review* 36 (1976):29–37.

42 James Fenimore Cooper, *The Prairie* (New York: Appleton, 1892), 31. In *The Chainbearer* Cooper relies on his faith that laws are necessary to protect the poor in arguing that the poor, even more than the rich, have a stake in preserving rule by law. When a woman hopes that the "laws should be considerate of the poor," Littlepage responds: "Not more so than of the rich. The laws should be equal and just; and the poor are the last people who ought to wish them otherwise, since they are certain to be the losers when any other principle governs. . . . No class suffers so much by a departure from the rule, as the rich have a thousand other means of attaining their ends, when the way is left clear to them, by setting up any other master than the right" (1:92).

43 My entire discussion of the foundations of Cooper's political system depends on C. B. Macpherson, *The Political Theory of Possessive Individualism* (New York: Oxford University Press, 1962), 263–4.

44 David Noble, "Cooper and the Death of the American Adam," *American Quarterly* 16 (1964):426.

45 See also David Levin's argument, in *History as Romantic Art* (Stanford: Stanford University Press, 1959), that romantic historians of the period, as well as Cooper, construct narratives that locate the irresolvable conflict between "artificial" and "natural" conflicts in the past as a way of implying its irrevocability and thus reinforcing mid-nineteenth-century conceptions of destiny and progress.

46 Rogin, *Fathers and Children,* 254.

47 France, quoted in Isaac D. Balbus, *The Dialectics of Legal Repression* (New York: Russell Sage Foundation, 1975), 5.

48 For a discussion of how *The Ways of the Hour* reacts against the 1848 New York State property laws granting more rights to women, see Barbara Ann Bardes and Suzanne Gossett, "Cooper and the 'Cup and Saucer' Law: A New Reading of *The Ways of the Hour*," *American Quarterly* 32 (1980):499–518. The change in inheritance laws in New York would have forced Cooper to change his standard plot in which a lone daughter becomes a vehicle for transferring property. See Nina Baym, "The Women in Cooper's Leather-stocking Tales," *American Quarterly* 23 (1971):698.

49 Kent, quoted in Thomas R. Lounsbury, *James Fenimore Cooper* (Boston: Houghton Mifflin, 1882), 128.

2. THE HOUSE OF THE SEVEN GABLES: *HAWTHORNE'S LEGAL STORY*

1 Nathaniel Hawthorne, "The Ambitious Guest," in *Twice-Told Tales,* vol. 9 in *The Centenary Edition of the Works of Nathaniel Hawthorne,* ed. William Charvat, Roy Harvey Pearce, and Claude M. Simpson (Columbus: Ohio State University Press, 1965), 329, hereafter abbreviated *TT.* Further page references to this and other works from this edition will be given parenthetically in the text. The other works cited are *The House of the Seven Gables* (vol. 2), *HSG,* and *The Scarlet Letter,* (vol. 1), *SL.*

2 Quoted in Charles M. Haar, *The Golden Age of American Law* (New York: Braziller, 1965), 206.

3 Morton J. Horwitz, *The Transformation of American Law, 1780–1860* (Cambridge, Mass.: Harvard University Press, 1977), 33.

4 Edward S. Corwin, "The Basic Doctrine of American Constitutional Law," *Michigan Law Review* 12 (1914):255.

5 Leonard W. Levy, *The Law of the Commonwealth and Chief Justice Shaw* (Cambridge, Mass.: Harvard University Press, 1957), 280.

6 For a discussion of the case, see Stanley Kutler, *Privilege and Creative Destruction: The Charles River Bridge Case* (Philadelphia: Lippincott, 1971).

7 Charles River Bridge v. Warren Bridge, 11 Peters 608 (1837).

8 The essays are "The Supreme Court of the United States – Its Judges and Jurisdiction," *United States Magazine and Democratic Review* 1 (1838):143–71; Charles J. Ingersoll, "Speech . . . in the Convention of Pennsylvania, on Legislative and Judicial Control over Charters of Incorporation," *United States Magazine and Democratic Review* 5 (1839):97–144; and "The Supreme Court of the United States," *United States Magazine and Democratic Review* 6 (1840):497–515. "Foot Prints on the Sea Shore" by "the author of 'Twice Told Tales'" appears in the January 1838 issue (vol. 2, no. 2); "Tales of the Province-House. No. IV – Old Esther Dudley," by Nathaniel Hawthorne, Esq., appears in the January 1839 issue (vol. 5, no. 13).

9 "Judges and Jurisdiction," 143; "Supreme Court of the United States," 515; "Judges and Jurisdiction," 144; ibid.

10 "Judges and Jurisdiction," 143.

11 Ibid., 163.

12 William Austin, "Martha Gardner; or Moral Re-action," *American Monthly*

Magazine, n.s. 4 (1837):564–74. I want to thank Hans-Joachim Lang for drawing my attention to this story, in "Classic American Writers and Jacksonian Democracy: Some Preliminary Remarks and Case Studies," *Amerikastudien* 28 (1983):97–8. Choate's and Higginson's remarks can be found in *William Austin: The Creator of Peter Rugg,* ed. Walter Austin (Boston: Marshall Jones, 1925), 38, 121–6.

13 Austin, "Martha Gardner," 572. This is standard rhetoric against corporations. In an essay entitled "Corporations," *American Jurist* 4 (1830):300–1, the anonymous author laments that the doctrine "describing corporations as having no souls or consciences" has led managers of corporations to sometimes "forget that *they* had souls and moral responsibility."

14 John Locke, *The Second Treatise of Government* (1690), sec. 85; quoted in Douglas Hay, "Property, Authority and the Criminal Law," in *Albion's Fatal Tree,* ed. Douglas Hay, Peter Linebaugh, and John G. Rule (London: Allen Lane, 1975), 18.

15 Johnson, quoted in C. Peter Magrath, *Yazoo* (Providence: Brown University Press, 1966), 103.

16 Edward Christian, ed., *Commentaries on the Laws of England, by William Blackstone,* 12th ed. (1793–5), 2:2; quoted in Hay, "Property," 19.

17 Quoted in Vernon Parrington, *Main Currents in American Thought* (New York: Harcourt Brace and World, 1927), 2:276–7.

18 Joseph Story, "History and Influence of the Puritans," in *The Miscellaneous Writings of Joseph Story,* ed. William Wetmore Story (Boston: Little, Brown, 1852), 468. In his talk Story lists the Pynchons with the Hathornes as important Pilgrim ancestors. "Where are Winthrop, and Endicott, and Higginson, and Dudley, and Saltonstall, and Bradstreet, and Pickering, and Sprague, and Pynchon, and Hathorne, . . . and the other worthies? . . . They are here. This is their home. These are their children" (415).

19 John Theodore Horton, *James Kent: A Study in Conservatism, 1763–1847* (New York: Appleton Century, 1939), 266.

20 Wilkinson v. Leland, 2 Peters 657 (1829).

21 Story, quoted in Gerald T. Dunne, *Justice Story and the Rise of the Supreme Court* (New York: Simon and Schuster, 1970), 181.

22 Story to Kent, Salem, Mass., August 21, 1819, in William Wetmore Story, ed., *Life and Letters of Joseph Story* (Boston: Little and Brown, 1851), 1:331.

23 George Parsons Lathrop, ed., *Complete Works of Nathaniel Hawthorne* (Boston: Houghton Mifflin, 1883), 3:9.

24 Story to Webster, Cambridge, Mass., April 17, 1830, in *Life and Letters,* 1:331.

25 Parker, quoted in James McClellan, *Joseph Story and the American Constitution* (Norman: University of Oklahoma Press, 1971), 283.

26 Howard A. Bradley and James A. Winans, *Daniel Webster and the Salem Murder* (Columbia, Mo.: Artcraft Press, 1956), 219. F. O. Matthiessen suggests comparing the rhetoric of Webster's speech with Hawthorne's set-piece description of the death of Judge Pyncheon. See *American Renaissance* (New York: Oxford University Press, 1941), 214. Constraints of space have kept

me from making such a comparison, but I believe that there are more possible connections than even Matthiessen suggests. See Chapter 6, n. 30, for more on this speech.

27 Rufus Choate, "Eulogy on Daniel Webster," in *Addresses and Orations of Rufus Choate,* ed. Samuel Gilman Brown (Boston: Little, Brown, 1878), 267. Choate devotes a good deal of space to Webster's role in the White murder affair. Other accounts include that of Walker Lewis, in *Speak for Yourself Daniel* (Boston: Houghton Mifflin, 1969), and Rita Pollard, "Against the Law and beyond the Evidence," *American Bar Association Journal* 63 (1977):204-10. A letter from Webster to Story (Salem, Mass., August 6, 1830) indicates Webster's reliance on Story for legal advice. Webster writes, "I pray you collect your thoughts on this point [the problem of proving Knapp a principal], look to the cases, if convenient, and I will send to you, or more probably see you, on Sunday." Cited in Lewis, *Speak for Yourself,* 233.

28 Bradley and Winans, *Webster,* 10.

29 On the Crowninshields see William T. Whitney, Jr., "The Crowninshields of Salem, 1800-1808," *Essex Institute Historical Collections* 94 (1958):1-36, 79-118. Richard Crowninshield was also linked to Zachary Taylor, whose election led to Hawthorne's removal from the Custom House, see Henry C. Wright, *Dick Crowingshield [sic], the Assassin, and Zachary Taylor, the Soldier: The Difference Between Them* (Hopedale, Mass.: Non-resident and Christian Office, 1848). Perhaps Hawthorne connected the Pyncheons' acquisition of land with Taylor's grabbing of land from Mexico.

30 Magrath, *Yazoo,* 50-4.

31 Mrs. Benjamin Crowninshield to her husband, Salem, Mass., March 21, 1815, in Dunne, *Justice Story,* 158.

32 Hawthorne to John Dike, Salem, Mass., September 1, 1830, in E. B. Hungerford, "Hawthorne Gossips about Salem," *New England Quarterly* 6 (1933): 455.

33 In "Mr. Higginbotham's Catastrophe" three men – a white, a black, and an Irish servant – plot the murder of a rich merchant. The first two lose courage, leaving the Irishman alone to commit the deed. The hero of the story interrupts him, saves the merchant, and marries the rich and beautiful niece. Recalling the original suspicion directed against a black or a servant as White's murderer, Hawthorne's tale, despite its wittiness, did nothing to combat the racial and class prejudices of well-to-do Salem, which saw the poor and blacks as a threat to social stability. His use of the White murder in *The House of the Seven Gables* is more extensive and more radical.

34 Rufus Wilmot Griswold, ed., *The Prose Writers of America* (Philadelphia: Carey and Hart, 1847), 139. The portrait of Story is by J. E. Johnson. Hawthorne mentions Griswold in *The Blithedale Romance* for placing Coverdale "at a fair elevation among our minor minstrelsy, on the strength of my pretty little volume, published ten years ago" (226).

35 Cited in Norman Holmes Pearson, "The Pynchons and Judge Pyncheon," *Essex Institute Historical Collections* 100 (1964):240.

36 Hawthorne to Bridge, Salem, April 13, 1850, quoted in Pearson, "The Pynchons and Judge Pyncheon," 237. Griswold, *Prose Writers,* 471.

37 Elizabeth Hawthorne to Nathaniel Hawthorne, Montserrat, May 3, 1851, in Julian Hawthorne, *Hawthorne and His Wife* (Boston: Ticknor, Reed, and Fields, 1884) 1:438–9.

38 Henry Nash Smith, "The Morals of Power," in *Essays on American Literature,* ed. Clarence Gohdes (Durham: Duke University Press, 1967), detects similarities with Story's friend Daniel Webster (96). Sarah I. Davis, "The Bank and the Old Pyncheon Family," *Studies in the Novel* 16 (1984):150–65, uses Judge Pyncheon's Whig politics to associate him with Nicholas Biddle, president of the Second United States Bank. Judge Pyncheon's interest in horticulture and agriculture also suggests Rev. Henry Colman, who was deeply involved in the White murder case. A year after the event, Colman left the ministry and devoted himself to the study of agriculture. In 1845 he went to England, with letters of introduction that gave him entree to the homes of the rich. Carlyle wrote to Emerson that Colman was much in vogue in England as a "kind of Agricultural Missionary." Colman's two-volume book on European agriculture eventually went through six editions, and on his return to America in 1848, he wrote a gossipy book on people he had met in Europe. Gloria C. Erlich shows that Hawthorne drew on his uncle Robert Manning for his portrait of Judge Pyncheon. Manning was also a horticulturist. See *Family Themes and Hawthorne's Fiction: The Tenacious Web* (New Brunswick, N.J.: Rutgers University Press, 1984).

39 Bentley, quoted in Dunne, *Justice Story,* 142.

40 Lathrop, *Works of Hawthorne,* 9.

41 Kent to Story, New York City, June 19, 1833, and New York City, October 10, 1836, in Story, *Life and Letters,* 2:135, 218.

42 Charles Sumner, "The Scholar, the Jurist, the Artist, the Philanthropist. An Oration before the Phi Beta Kappa Society of Harvard University, at Their Anniversary, August 27, 1846," in *Orations and Speeches* (Boston: Ticknor, Reed, and Fields, 1850), 1:131–98.

43 Henry James, *William Wetmore Story and His Friends* (Boston: Houghton, Mifflin, 1904), 1:21.

44 James, *Story,* 1:23–4. James started the biography in 1897 and completed it in 1903. See Joseph Hynes, "The Transparent Shroud: Henry James and William Story," *American Literature* 46 (1975):506–27.

45 Griswold, *Prose Writers,* 21.

46 Story, *Life and Letters,* 2:552.

47 Ingersoll, "Speech," 126–7.

48 Thomas Pynchon, *Gravity's Rainbow* (New York: Viking, 1973), 265.

3. THE HOUSE OF THE SEVEN GABLES: *HAWTHORNE'S ROMANCE OF ART*

1 Joseph Story, "History and Influence of the Puritans," in *The Miscellaneous Writings of Joseph Story,* ed. William Wetmore Story (Boston: Little and Brown, 1852), 460. The section of Story's talk dealing with the Indians was reprinted in two collections that also had selections by Hawthorne. See *The Prose Writers of America,* ed. Rufus Wilmot Griswold (Philadelphia: Carey and

Hart, 1847), 140, and *The Boston Book* (Boston: George W. Light, 1841), 95–7.

2 Story, "History and Influence of the Puritans," 465, 462, 453, 462, 464–5. Also, see Philip Fisher's discussion of narratives about the Indians, in *Hard Facts* (New York: Oxford University Press, 1985), 22–86.

3 Nathaniel Hawthorne, *The House of the Seven Gables,* vol. 2 in *The Centenary Edition of the Works of Nathaniel Hawthorne,* ed. William Charvat, Roy Harvey Pearce, and Claude M. Simpson (Columbus: Ohio State University Press, 1965), 19. Further page references to this and other works from this edition will be given parenthetically in the text. The other works cited are *The Scarlet Letter* (vol. 1), *SL; The Blithedale Romance* (vol. 3), *BR; The Marble Faun* (vol. 4), *MF;* and *Mosses from an Old Manse* (vol. 10), *MM.*

4 Rudolph Von Abele, *The Death of the Artist: A Study of Hawthorne's Disintegration* (The Hague: Martinus Nijhoff, 1955), 66.

5 Marvin Meyers, *The Jacksonian Persuasion* (Stanford: Stanford University Press, 1960), 115.

6 Sumner, quoted in William Wetmore Story, ed., *Life and Letters of Joseph Story* (Boston: Little, Brown, 1851), 2:616. On the attempt to grant legal reasoning the status of science see Perry Miller, *The Life of the Mind in America* (New York: Harcourt Brace and World, 1965).

7 Ralph Waldo Emerson, "The Transcendentalists," in *The Complete Works of Ralph Waldo Emerson,* Centenary Edition, ed. Edward Waldo Emerson, (Boston: Houghton Mifflin, 1903–4), 1:331–2.

8 Story, "Characteristics of the Age," in *Miscellaneous Writings,* 367.

9 Emerson, "The Fugitive Slave Law," in *Complete Works,* 11:217.

10 Morton J. Horwitz, *The Transformation of American Law, 1780–1860* (Cambridge, Mass.: Harvard University Press, 1977), 255.

11 Ibid., 254.

12 Jonathan Arac, "The Politics of the *Scarlet Letter,*" in *Ideology and Classic American Literature,* ed. Sacvan Bercovitch and Myra Jehlen (Cambridge: Cambridge University Press, 1985), 247–66.

13 Stephen Nissenbaum, "The Firing of Nathaniel Hawthorne," *Essex Institute Historical Collections* 114 (1978): 57–86.

14 See Michael T. Gilmore, "The Artist and the Marketplace in *The House of the Seven Gables,*" *ELH* 48 (1981):172–89.

15 Story, "Characteristics of the Age," 350, 353.

16 Ibid., 341, 344, 346, 346, 347, 346.

17 Story to McLean, Cambridge, Mass., August 16, 1844, cited in Maxwell Bloomfield, *American Lawyers in a Changing Society* (Cambridge, Mass.: Harvard University Press, 1976), 235.

18 Daniel Webster, "Summation in the Trial of John Francis Knapp for the Murder of Joseph White," in *The Law as Literature,* ed. Ephraim London (New York: Simon and Schuster, 1960), 408.

19 Less than a year before starting *The House of the Seven Gables* Hawthorne checked out from the Salem Athenaeum Charles J. Ingersoll's *Historical Sketch of the Second War Between the United States and Great Britain* (Philadelphia: Lea

and Blanchard, 1849). In his account of the National Bank controversy, Ingersoll argues that the Bank was supported by an aristocracy, that the Bank's defeat was a "plebian" victory, and that the "discernment and attachment of the illiterate are less selfish and more reliable than those of the aristocratic" (2:285). Hawthorne would have had reason to disagree, which is not to say that he would have favored the Whig "aristocracy." Quoted in Sarah I. Davis, "The Bank and the Old Pyncheon Family," *Studies in the Novel* 16 (1984):160.

20 Fredric Jameson's discussion of the romance as a genre, in *The Political Unconscious* (Ithaca: Cornell University Press, 1981), is useful here. According to Jameson, the preconditions of the romance are "to be found in a transitional moment in which two distinct modes of production, or moments of socioeconomic development coexist. Their antagonism is not yet articulated in terms of the struggle of social classes, so that its resolution can be projected in the form of a nostalgic (or less often, a Utopian) harmony" (148). Written as the country was changing from an agrarian to a commercial society, *The House of the Seven Gables* fits the precondition that Jameson describes. It also, as Jameson argues about the romance, defuses the class conflict it portrays by turning that conflict into a battle between good and evil, felt as magical forces.

21 Henry James, *Hawthorne* (New York: 1887; rpt. AMS Press, 1968), 124.

22 Gerald T. Dunne, *Justice Story and the Rise of the Supreme Court* (New York: Simon and Schuster, 1970), 142–3.

23 See Nissenbaum, "Firing of Hawthorne."

24 See, for example, F. O. Matthiessen, *The American Renaissance* (New York: Oxford University Press, 1941), 332, and Edgar F. Dryden, "Hawthorne's Castle in the Air: Form and Theme in *The House of the Seven Gables*," *ELH* 38 (1971):294–317.

25 John Gatta, Jr., "Progress and Providence in *The House of the Seven Gables*," *American Literature* 50 (1978):47–8. On the romantic historians see the second chapter of David Levin's *History as Romantic Art* (Stanford: Stanford University Press, 1959).

26 Hawthorne, *Life of Pierce*, in *Complete Works of Nathaniel Hawthorne* (Boston: Houghton Mifflin, 1883), 12:417. See the discussion in Arac, "Politics of the *Scarlet Letter*."

27 For a discussion of the *Webster* case, see Chapter 9, this volume.

28 This coincidence and numerous others are pointed out by Thomas J. Allen, *The Accomplice: The Truth of Vigilante Salem: Hawthorne, Melville, Robert Rantoul, Jr., and the Captain White Murder Trial* (Salem, Mass.: Common School Press, 1965).

4. "BENITO CERENO": MELVILLE'S NARRATIVE OF REPRESSION

1 Chafee, quoted in Leonard W. Levy, *The Law of the Commonwealth and Chief Justice Shaw* (Cambridge, Mass.: Harvard University Press, 1957), 336.

2 Oliver Wendell Holmes, Jr., *The Common Law*, ed. Mark DeWolfe Howe

(Cambridge, Mass.: Harvard University Press [Belknap Press], 1963), 85. Holmes first used this praise of Shaw in "Trespass and Negligence," *American Law Review* 14 (1880):20.

3 For discussions of Melville and Shaw see the following: Charles R. Anderson, *Melville in the South Seas* (New York: Dover, 1966), 432–3; Robert M. Cover, *Justice Accused* (New Haven: Yale University Press, 1975), 1–7, 250–2; James Duban, *Melville's Major Fiction* (DeKalb: Northern Illinois University Press, 1983), 82, 104, 110–11, 246; Charles H. Foster, "Something in Emblems: A Reinterpretation of *Moby-Dick,*" *New England Quarterly* 34 (1961):3–35; Robert C. Gale, "Bartleby – Melville's Father-in-Law," *Annali Instituto Universitario Orientale, Napoli, Sezioni Germanica,* 5 (1962):57–72; Keith Huntress, "'Guinea' of *White Jacket* and Chief Justice Shaw," *American Literature* 43 (1972):639–41; Carolyn L. Karcher, *Shadow over the Promised Land* (Baton Rouge: Louisiana State University Press, 1980), 9–11, 40; Herschel Parker, "Melville and Politics: A Scrutiny of the Political Milieux of Herman Melville's Life and Works," Ph.D. thesis, Northwestern University, 1963; Michael Paul Rogin, *Subversive Genealogy* (New York: Knopf, 1983); John Stark, "Melville, Lemuel Shaw, and 'Bartleby,'" in M. Thomas Inge, *Bartleby, the Inscrutable* (Hamden, Conn.: Archon Books, 1979), 166–73.

4 Jean-Paul Sartre, *Search for a Method,* trans. Hazel E. Barnes (New York: Random House [Vintage Books], 1968), 124.

5 Story to Loring, Cambridge, Mass., November 5, 1836, in William W. Story, ed., *Life and Letters of Joseph Story* (Boston: Little and Brown, 1851), 2:235.

6 Huntress, "'Guinea,'" 639–41.

7 Shaw, quoted in Levy, *Law of the Commonwealth,* 70.

8 Ibid., 59, 81.

9 Nevius, quoted in Cover, *Justice Accused,* 58. Clearly, Judge Nevius forgot Shaw's *Latimer* ruling, as does Rogin, who claims that prior to 1850 Shaw always ruled in favor of fugitive blacks (142). Nonetheless, Shaw opposed slavery more vigorously than James Kent, who admitted that slavery was an evil but believed that the South "ought to be left alone, and [that] time will gradually undermine domestic slavery in those states, as it has done in New York." Kent also felt that "the African race even when free are essentially a degraded race." See John Theodore Horton, *James Kent: A Study in Conservatism, 1763–1847* (New York: Appleton-Century, 1939), 274–5.

10 *Prigg v. Pennsylvania,* 16 Peters 611 (1842).

11 Joseph Story, quoted in William Story, *Life and Letters,* 2:392–3.

12 Ibid., 431.

13 Levy, *Law of the Commonwealth,* 89–90.

14 Herman Melville, in "Benito Cereno," *Great Short Works of Herman Melville,* ed. Warner Berthoff (New York: Harper and Row, 1969), 279, hereafter abbreviated *BC.* Future page references will be included parenthetically in the text.

15 See Allen Guttmann, "The Enduring Innocence of Captain Delano," *Boston University Studies in English* 5 (1961):42. "The official and attested view of the matter, the view put forth by Don Benito and ingenuously accepted by

Captain Delano, is *the very thing which Melville is subverting*. With its legalistic pretensions of objectivity, the deposition misses the truth as widely as did Delano in his complete innocence." See also Edgar Dryden, *Melville's Thematics of Form* (Baltimore: Johns Hopkins University Press, 1968), 199–216, and Karcher, *Shadow over the Promised Land*, 134–5.

16 Carl B. Swisher, *The Taney Period, 1836–64*, vol. 5 of *The Oliver Wendell Holmes Devise History of the Supreme Court of the United States*, ed. Paul A. Freund (New York: Macmillan, 1974), 693–5.

17 Adams, quoted in Swisher, *Taney Period*, 193. For discussions of "Benito Cereno" and the *Amistad* case, see Sidney Kaplan, "Herman Melville and the American National Sin: The Meaning of 'Benito Cereno,'" *Journal of Negro History* 41 (1956):311–38, and 42 (1957):11–37, and Rogin, *Subversive Genealogy*, 212–13. Rogin seems confused when he writes, "Melville did not fictionalize the *Amistad* or *Creole* uprisings, where slaves threw off illegitimate authority and then appealed to the American government for help." The blacks on the *Amistad*, like the blacks on the *San Dominick*, demanded to be taken back to Africa but were outwitted by the Spanish crew, and the ship was taken into custody by the United States. The blacks on the *Creole*, as Rogin notes earlier, sought British protection.

18 Story, quoted in Cover, *Justice Accused*, 112.

19 Webster to Story, Washington, D.C., March 17, 1842, and Story to Webster, Cambridge, Mass., March 26, 1842, in *Writings and Speeches of Daniel Webster*, ed. J. W. McIntyre (Boston: Little, Brown, 1903), 16: 364–5.

20 Story, *Life and Letters*, 2: 348.

21 Cover, *Justice Accused*, 116. This understanding of the *Amistad* decision qualifies Marvin Fisher's claim that the *Sims* and *Burns* cases reversed the *Amistad* decision. (Fisher does not note that Shaw decided the first two cases.) See Fisher's *Going Under: Melville's Short Fiction and the American 1850s* (Baton Rouge: Louisiana State University Press, 1977), 109.

22 William Jay(?), quoted in Cover, *Justice Accused*, 114.

23 H. Bruce Franklin. "'Apparent Symbol of Despotic Command': Melville's 'Benito Cereno,'" *New England Quarterly* 34 (1961):462–77.

24 William Johnson, quoted in John Quincy Adams, "The Argument of John Quincy Adams before the Supreme Court of the United States" in *The Amistad Case* (New York: Johnson Reprint, 1968), 109.

25 Story, quoted in Cover, *Justice Accused*, 101.

26 Franklin, "'Apparent Symbol of Despotic Command,'" 462–77.

27 Gloria Horsley-Meacham, "The Monastic Slaver: Images and Meaning in 'Benito Cereno,'" *New England Quarterly* 61 (1983):261–6. Karcher, in *Shadow over the Promised Land*, notes echoes of the Spanish inquisition. See also Charles Swann, "The *San Dominick*, Black Friars, and Jacobins," *Journal of American Studies* 19 (1985):112–14. Swann reminds us that from reading Carlyle's *French Revolution* Melville would have known that in France the Dominicans were once called Jacobins. Thus, we have the irony that Dominicans/Jacobins/Black Friars enslaved blacks who, when they rebelled on Santo Domingo, were considered by conservatives to be black Jacobins unleashed by the French Revolution.

28 Shakespeare, *Othello* 1.1. 42–4. On Babo as Iago see Kaplan, "Herman Melville," 20; Charles Nicol, "The Iconography of Evil and Ideal in 'Benito Cereno,'" in *Studies in the Minor and Later Work of Melville*, ed. Raymona E. Hull (Hartford: Transcendental Books, 1970), 29; and Michael T. Gilmore, *The Middle Way* (New Brunswick, N.J.: Rutgers University Press, 1977), 167.

29 Adams compares America's support of slavery and Britain's abolition of it. "The reasons of the British Judge glow with the flame of human liberty; those of the American Judges are wedged in thrilling regions of thick ribbed ice. Vituperation of the slave trade in words, with a broad shield of protection carefully extended over it in deeds. Slavery acknowledged an evil, and the inveteracy of its abuse urged as an unanswerable argument for its perpetuity. . . . The British Court has at least the consistency of harmonizing practice and profession. The American Courts profess humanity and practice oppression," *Amistad Case*, 110.

30 An illuminating discussion of "Benito Cereno" and American expansionism is in Allan Moore Emery, "'Benito Cereno' and Manifest Destiny," *Nineteenth-Century Fiction* 39 (1984):48–68. Emery emphasizes Melville's response to Manifest Destiny over his response to slavery. I find it hard to separate these two issues.

31 Sandra A. Zagarell notices that the crew's actions are piratelike. "Reenvisioning America: Melville's 'Benito Cereno,'" *ESQ* 30 (1984):256. Rogin offers a valuable comparison of Melville and Cooper in terms of slavers and pirates in *Subversive Genealogy*, 3–11, 211–13.

32 *Amistad Case*, 109.

33 Sumner, quoted in Levy, *Law of the Commonwealth*, 86.

34 Ibid., 82, 91.

35 Thomas, quoted in ibid., 102. Edwin Haviland Miller notes in passing a similarity between Captain Delano and Shaw, in *Melville* (New York: Braziller, 1975), 299.

36 See Joyce Sparer Adler, *War in Melville's Imagination* (New York: New York University Press, 1981), 104–5. The vision of injustice that Melville presents in "Benito Cereno" is similar to that described by Michel Foucault: "Following traditional beliefs, it would be false to think that total war exhausts itself in its own contradictions and ends by renouncing violence and submitting to civil laws. On the contrary, the law is a calculated and relentless pleasure, delight in the promised blood, which permits the perpetual instigation of new dominations and the staging of meticulously repeated scenes of violence." "Nietzsche, Genealogy, History," in *Language, Counter-Memory, Practice*, ed. Donald R. Bouchard, trans. Sherry Simon (Ithaca: Cornell University Press, 1977), 150–1.

37 Kaplan, for instance, argues that Melville's story reinforces all of the antiblack prejudices of his 1855 audience. For an argument against Kaplan that does not deny the story's complexity see Charles Swann, "Who Dunn It? Or, Who Did What? *Benito Cereno* and the Politics of Narrative Structure," *American Studies in Transition*, ed. David Nye (London: Odense University Press, 1985), 199–234. For Swann, "The ending of *Benito Cereno* is open, problematic – not out of a liberal pluralism but because the history that Melville was living through is alive to just this set of [complex] issues" (223).

38 Karcher writes, in *Shadow over the Promised Land*, "I find Babo on the whole a favorable portrayal of a black rebel, despite the fearsomeness with which he is tinged in his role as white America's nemesis" (140). Later, however, she admits, "moving as I find this glimpse, I do not believe one can honestly deduce from it an unequivocal endorsement of revolutionary violence as a means of ending slavery" (142).

39 Allan Moore Emery, "The Topicality of Depravity in 'Benito Cereno.'" *American Literature* 55 (1983):330–1. Edward S. Grejda, *The Common Continent of Man* (Port Washington, N.Y.: Kennikat Press, 1974), also eloquently argues for a color-blind Melville.

40 Jean Fagan Yellin, "Black Masks: Melville's 'Benito Cereno,'" *American Quarterly* 22 (1970):687–8. As Karcher points out, in *Shadow over the Promised Land*, Babo's silence recalls Frederick Douglass's characterization of the plight of the slave: "Ask the slave what is his condition – what is his state of mind – what he thinks of enslavement? and you had as well address your inquiries to the *silent dead*. There comes no *voice* from the enslaved" (141).

41 Marianne DeKoven, "History as Suppressed Referent in Modernist Fiction," *ELH* 51 (1984):137–52, argues that slavery is a suppressed referent in "Benito Cereno," but her discussion of slavery so lacks historical specificity that her interpretation does little to recreate a historical context for the story.

5. A SENTIMENTAL JOURNEY: ESCAPE FROM BONDAGE IN UNCLE TOM'S CABIN

1 Harriet Beecher Stowe, *Uncle Tom's Cabin*, ed. Alfred Kazin (New York: Bantam Books, 1981), xviii, hereafter abbreviated *UTC*. Further page references to this edition will be given parenthetically in the text, as will references to Harriet Beecher Stowe, *A Key to Uncle Tom's Cabin* (Boston: John P. Jewett, 1853), hereafter abbreviated *Key*, and Harriet Beecher Stowe, *Dred; A Tale of the Great Dismal Swamp*, 2 vols. (Boston: Phillips, Sampson, 1856), hereafter abbreviated *Dred*.

2 James Baldwin, "Everybody's Protest Novel," *Partisan Review* 16 (1949): 578–85.

3 Kermit Vanderbilt, "'Benito Cereno': Melville's Fable of Black Complicity," *Southern Review* 12 (1976):317–18. Vanderbilt argues that Melville's work is concerned with the effect that slavery had on the masters, whereas Stowe's is concerned with its effect on slaves, but Stowe often refers to the negative effects of slavery on masters as well as slaves.

4 For examples see David Levin, "American Fiction as Historical Evidence: Reflections on *Uncle Tom's Cabin*," *Negro American Literature Forum* 5 (1971):132–6, 154; John E. Martin, "Approaches to the Reality of the Slave Family in *Uncle Tom's Cabin* and the Work of Eugene Genovese," in Hans-Heinrich Freitag and Peter Huhn, eds., *Literarische Ansichten der Wirklichkeit: Studien zur Wirklichkeitskonstitution in englischsprächiger Literatur: To Honour Johannes Kleinstuck* (Frankfurt: Lang, 1980); and Moody E. Prior, "Mrs. Stowe's Uncle Tom," *Critical Inquiry* 5 (1979):635–50.

5 Mark Tushnett, *The American Law of Slavery* (Princeton: Princeton University Press, 1981), and Stanley M. Elkins, *Slavery* (Chicago: University of Chicago Press, 1959).

6 Tushnett, *American Law of Slavery*, 44, 58.

7 George Fitzhugh, *Sociology for the South, or the Failure of Free Society* (1854; rpt. New York: Burt Franklin, 1965), 167. My discussion of Fitzhugh is indebted to Peter Wenzel, "Pre-Modern Concepts of Society and Economy in American Pro-Slavery Thought: On the Intellectual Foundations of the Social Philosophy of George Fitzhugh," *Amerikastudien* 27 (1982):157–75.

8 George Fitzhugh, "Popular Institutions," *DeBow's Review* 28 (1860):523; *Cannibals All! or Slaves without Masters,* ed. C. Vann Woodward (1857; rpt. Cambridge, Mass.: Harvard University Press, 1960), 248, 69.

9 Fitzhugh, *Sociology,* 7.

10 Stowe's detailed discussion of *State v. Mann* in *Key* (77–9) does not necessarily mean that she used this case as a source for *Uncle Tom's Cabin.* Much of the material in *Key* was collected after *Uncle Tom's Cabin* was published. But even if *State v. Mann* was not a source for Stowe in writing *Uncle Tom's Cabin,* her later insistence that the case perfectly illustrates what she tried to dramatize in her book means that it can help us to define her attitude toward slave law. In her preface to *Key* she gives special thanks to "those legal gentlemen who have given her their assistance and support in the legal part of the discussion" (iii). According to E. Bruce Kirkham, *The Building of Uncle Tom's Cabin* (Knoxville: University of Tennessee Press, 1977), her brother-in-law John Hooker was probably one of the most important of these advisers (80).

11 See Tushnett's discussion of *State v. Mann,* in *American Law of Slavery* (34–65; quotation on 58).

12 Ruffin, quoted in Tushnett, *American Law of Slavery,* 62.

13 George F. Holmes, "Review of *Uncle Tom's Cabin,*" *Southern Literary Messenger* 18 (1852):630–8, rpt. in *Critical Essays on Harriet Beecher Stowe,* ed. Elizabeth Ammons (Boston: Hall, 1980).

14 Isabella Beecher, quoted in Kirkham, *Building of Uncle Tom's Cabin,* 64.

15 In *Uncle Tom's Cabin* the role of lawyers is usually, as in this case, mechanically to carry out the law. Lawyers do the dirty work, allowing Brother B. to avoid facing the human consequences of his action.

16 Hans-Joachim Lang, "Classic American Writers and Jacksonian Democracy: Some Preliminary Remarks and Case Studies," *Amerikastudien* 28 (1983):103. See also Philip Fisher, *Hard Facts* (New York: Oxford University Press, 1985), 87–127.

17 Quoted in Michael Paul Rogin, *Subversive Genealogy* (New York: Knopf, 1983), 27.

18 Warner's book appeared in December 1850. Since she had been forced to write for money because of her family's economic losses after the panic of 1837, she knew the uncertain power of the market firsthand.

19 Elizabeth Ammons, "Heroines in *Uncle Tom's Cabin,*" *American Literature* 49 (1977):161–79.

20 Ibid., 163. Levin too, in "American Fiction as Historical Evidence," notes the intelligence of the women's responses. Jane P. Tompkins, "*Sentimental Power:*

Uncle Tom's Cabin and the Politics of Literary History," *Glyph* 8 (1981), boldly argues that women's sentimental fiction in the nineteenth century, especially *Uncle Tom's Cabin*, represents a "monumental effort to reorganize culture from the woman's point of view"; that "this body of work is remarkable for its intellectual complexity, ambition, and resourcefulness"; and that "in certain cases, it offers a critique of American society far more devastating than any delivered by . . . Hawthorne and Melville" (81). After making such a revolutionary pronouncement, she later concludes that the "argument over whether the sentimental novelists were radical or conservative is a false issue" (102). As will become clear, I do not think it is a false issue, nor, at times, does Tompkins. My own position on Stowe and the "sentimentalists" is that we cannot ignore the conservative aspects of their thought pointed out by Ann Douglas in *The Feminization of American Culture* (New York: Knopf, 1977), attacked by Tompkins; see also three studies by Mary Kelley: "At Home with Herself: Harriet Beecher Stowe as Woman in Conflict within the Home," *American Studies* 19 (1978):23–40, "The Sentimentalists: Promise and Betrayal in the Home," *Signs* 4 (1979):434–46, and *Private Woman, Public Stage* (New York: Oxford University Press, 1984); Myra Jehlen, "Archimedes and the Paradox of Feminist Citicism," in *Feminist Theory: A Critique of Ideology*, ed. Nannerl O. Keohane, Michelle Z. Rosaldo, and Barbara C. Gelpi (Chicago: University of Chicago Press, 1982), 189–215, and Stephen Railton, "Mothers, Husbands, and *Uncle Tom*," *Georgia Review* 38 (1984):129–44.

Part of the blindness of Tompkins's position grows out of the idealist ideology that she shares with the sentimentalists. She writes, "Rhetoric *makes* history by shaping reality to the dictates of its political design; it makes history by convincing the people of the world that its description of the world is the true one. . . . If history did not take the course these writers recommended, it is not that they were not political, but because they were insufficiently persuasive" (94). I am not one to deny the power of rhetoric, but to make it the motor of history is naive – and reactionary. More recently Gillian Brown, "Getting in the Kitchen with Dinah: Domestic Politics in *Uncle Tom's Cabin*," *American Quarterly* 36 (1984):501–23, asserts that Stowe's message is that "domesticity itself requires reformation" (511). "Housekeeping in *Uncle Tom's Cabin*," Brown argues, "becomes not merely politically significant, but a political mode" (512). What she fails to see is that Stowe's belief that political change can start in the kitchen reveals Stowe's acceptance of the public and private spheres.

21 Harriet Beecher Stowe, *My Wife and I* (New York: J. B. Ford, 1871), 257.

22 Dorothy Berkson, "Millennial Politics and the Feminine Fiction of Harriet Beecher Stowe," in *Critical Essays on Harriet Beecher Stowe*, ed. Elizabeth Ammons (Boston: Hall, 1980), 252.

23 Another member of the Semi-Colon Club was Judge James Hall, whose *Wilderness and the Warpath* served as Herman Melville's source for the Indian hater episode in *The Confidence-Man*.

24 Review of Timothy Walker's "Reform Spirit of the Day," *North American Review* 71 (1850):515–16.

25 Diane Polan, "Toward a Theory of Law and Patriarchy," in *The Politics of*

Law, ed. David Kairys (New York: Pantheon Books, 1982), 298. See also Jean Bethke Elshtain, *Public Man, Private Woman* (Princeton: Princeton University Press, 1981), 298–353, and Julie A. Matthaei, *An Economic History of Woman in America* (New York: Schocken Books, 1982), especially the chapter "Women's Work and the Sexual Division of Labor under Slavery," 74–100, and pt. 2, "Women's Work and the Sexual Division of Labor under the Cult of Domesticity," 101–234.

26 "The Death of Chief Justice Shaw," *Monthly Law Reporter* 24 (1861):10.

27 Here I take issue with those who try to turn Stowe into a radical, such as James M. Cox, who writes that "*Uncle Tom's Cabin* is revolutionary in that it is written directly *against the law.*" See his "Harriet Beecher Stowe: From Sectionalism to Regionalism," *Nineteenth-Century Fiction* 38 (1984):455. Stowe opposed the law of slavery, but she was not, as Cox argues, "deeply against the social order" (456). Indeed, her opposition to slavery laws was closer to the position of antislavery constitutionalists than that of radical abolitionists. On this distinction see William M. Wiecek, *The Sources of Antislavery Constitutionalism in America, 1760–1848* (Ithaca: Cornell University Press, 1977), and Robert M. Cover, "*Nomos* and Narrative," *Harvard Law Review* 97 (1983):35–40.

28 The connection between Stowe's antislavery sentiments and her belief in free labor is typical. See Eric Foner, *Free Soil, Free Labor, Free Men* (New York: Oxford University Press, 1970). Charles Foster, in *The Rungless Ladder* (Durham: Duke University Press, 1954), 56, overlooks Stowe's compromise with capitalist ideology in arguing that Stowe's attack on laissez-faire capitalism provides the "masculine edge, the intellectual bite of *Uncle Tom's Cabin.*"

29 See James Fenimore Cooper's judgment that the "American slave is better off, so far as mere animal wants are concerned, than the lower order of the European peasants," quoted in Robert E. Spiller, "Fenimore Cooper's Defence of Slave-owning America," *American Historical Review* 35 (1930):580. In contrast, Harold T. MacCarthy, in *The Expatriate Perspective: American Novelists and the Idea of America* (Rutherford, N.J.: Fairleigh Dickinson University Press, 1974), claims that Cooper expresses a covert antislavery message in *The Headsman* consistent with his belief, stated in *Notions of the Americans,* that slavery is a "prodigious evil" (25–46).

30 See Maxwell Bloomfield, "Law and Lawyers in American Popular Culture," in Carl S. Smith, John P. McWilliams, Jr.. and Maxwell Bloomfield, *Law and American Literature* (New York: Knopf, 1983), 145–7.

31 Here I take issue with Walter Benn Michaels's claim, in his "Romance and Real Estate," *Raritan* 2 (1983):84, that "Stowe, fearing slavery . . . as an emblem of the market economy, nevertheless thought for many years that the solution to the slave problem could be repatriation to Africa, as if exorcising the slaves would rid the South of feudalism and the North of capitalism." Michaels admits that Stowe "spoke for free labor and against slave labor" but adds that "insofar as her critique of slavery came to be a critique of the 'Southern market,' it had inevitably to constitute a repudiation of free labor as well" (86). As Stowe's praise of free labor shows, it was not inevitable that she had to repudiate free labor. In fact, she did not. What is inevitable logic for Michaels was not for Stowe. Michaels fails to see how residual "feudal-

ism" in the North, embodied in the domestic economy, gave Stowe a sphere of influence from which she could effect a compromise with the market. She could not, however, compromise with the combination of slavery *and* the market. Michaels needs to pay more attention to gender roles within the market economy than he does. This is especially true of his attempt to link capitalism and masochism in "The Phenomenology of Contract," *Raritan* 4 (1984):47–66. Brown, "Getting in the Kitchen with Dinah," agrees with Michaels that Stowe's attack on slavery is really an attack on the market economy. "As long as the marketplace, of which the slave trade is the worst version, exists, the domestic sphere remains vulnerable" (510). One wonders why, then, Stowe's solution for slavery is to teach freed slaves the work habits she associates with the northern market economy. The ideal kitchen that Stowe describes is a testimony to the habits of discipline and order fostered by her ideal image of the northern system of free labor in harmonious marriage with the private sphere.

32 Herman Melville, *Moby-Dick; or, The Whale,* ed. Charles Feidelson, Jr. (Indianapolis: Bobbs-Merrill, 1964), 28. Michael Paul Rogin writes, "Melville's fiction after *Moby-Dick* found slavery everywhere in the democratic future," *Subversive Genealogy,* 151.

6. EXPLOITATION AT HOME AND AT SEA

1 Herman Melville, *Moby-Dick; or The Whale,* ed. Charles Feidelson, Jr. (Indianapolis: Bobbs-Merrill, 1964), 683, hereafter abbreviated *MD.* Further page references to this edition will be given parenthetically in the text, as will references to Harrison Hayford, Hershel Parker, and G. Thomas Tanselle, eds., *The Writings of Herman Melville,* The Northwestern-Newberry Edition (Evanston and Chicago: Northwestern University Press and Newberry Library), vol. 5, *White-Jacket: or The World in a Man-of-War* (1970), abbreviated *WJ,* and vol. 7, *Pierre; or, The Ambiguities* (1971), abbreviated *Pierre;* Herman Melville, *The Confidence Man: His Masquerade,* ed. H. Bruce Franklin (Indianapolis: Bobbs-Merrill, 1967), abbreviated *CM;* and Herman Melville, "Benito Cereno," in *Great Short Works of Herman Melville,* ed. Warner Berthoff (New York: Harper and Row, 1969), abbreviated *BC.*

2 Michael Paul Rogin, *Subversive Genealogy* (New York: Knopf, 1983), 100. Marvin Fisher titles his last chapter "A House Divided" and uses the phrase to discuss "I and My Chimney," in *Going Under: Melville's Short Fiction and the American 1850s* (Baton Rouge: Louisiana State University Press, 1977), 202–3.

3 Lemuel Shaw, Jr., quoted in Amy Puett Emmers, "New Crosslights on the Illegitimate Daughter in *Pierre,*" in *Critical Essays on Herman Melville's "Pierre; or, The Ambiguities,*" ed. Brian Higgins and Hershel Parker (Boston: Hall, 1983), 239.

4 Review of "An Oration delivered at the Celebration in Philadelphia of the 106th Anniversary of the Birthday of Thomas Paine, by John Alberger, Philadelphia, 1843," *North American Review* 107 (1843):5–6.

5 Sacvan Bercovitch, *The American Jeremiad* (Madison: University of Wisconsin Press, 1978).

6 Story, quoted in Carl B. Swisher, *The Taney Period, 1836–64,* vol. 5 of *The*

Oliver Wendell Holmes Devise History of the Supreme Court of the United States, ed. Paul A. Freund (New York: MacMillan, 1974), 544.

7 Story, quoted in Morton J. Horwitz, *The Transformation of American Law, 1780–1860* (Cambridge, Mass.: Harvard University Press, 1977), 247.

8 James Fenimore Cooper, *The Chainbearer,* 2 vols. (New York: Burgess, Stringer, 1845), 1:iii–iv.

9 Leon Howard, "Historical Note" to *Pierre,* 365.

10 *Pierre* also challenges the ideological assumptions that underlay the transcendentalists' attack on slavery. Like Stowe, Emerson and Thoreau saw the answer to slavery in private reform of public institutions and opinions. But for Stowe the private is the realm of the family bound together by sentiment; for Emerson and Thoreau it is the realm of individual genius. Celebrants of the individual, Emerson and Thoreau distrust the imprisoning capacity of the family, for its sentimental bonds threaten to stifle individual genius. Emerson counsels, "The doctrine of hatred must be preached, as the counteraction of the doctrine of love, when that pules and whines. I shun father and mother and wife and brother when my genius calls me." See "Self-Reliance," in *The Collected Works of Ralph Waldo Emerson,* ed. Joseph Slater, Alfred R. Ferguson. and Jean Ferguson Carr (Cambridge, Mass.: Harvard University Press, [Belknap Press], 1979), 2:30. Thoreau, more prudent than Emerson, never took a wife, who might have muffled the call of his genius.

Emerson and Thoreau's doctrine of self-reliance seems to align them with the "masculine," public values of individualism that Stowe fears, but for them there is an important distinction between private and public individualism. The individualism of the public realm is conditioned by the market economy, whose calculating values fragment the world, just as industrialization mechanizes the world. Like Stowe, Emerson and Thoreau oppose the logic of the public realm with the resources of the private heart, but the heart has a different function for them. For Stowe the heart is the source of sentiment; for Emerson and Thoreau it is the source of imagination. In either case, the heart is associated with the organicism of a residual mode of production, in opposition to the effects of the mechanized market economy and its business rationality. Alone in nature, private man synthesizes. In the marketplace, man fragments. Private man is in touch with higher, moral laws. Public man is ruled by the expediency of man-made laws. For Emerson and Thoreau, northern support of the Fugitive Slave Act can be understood according to these oppositions. Daniel Webster, a public individual lacking in private genius, was responsible for the law, and acts of private individuals must resist the law. See Stanley M. Elkins, "The Abolitionists as Transcendentalists," in *Slavery* (Chicago: University of Chicago Press, 1959), and a response by Aileen S. Kraditor, "A Note on Elkins and the Abolitionist," in *The Debate over Slavery,* ed. Ann J. Lane (Urbana: University of Illinois Press, 1971), 87–101.

11 Myra C. Glenn, "The Naval Reform Campaign against Flogging: A Case Study in Changing Attitudes toward Corporal Punishment, 1830–1850," *American Quarterly* 35 (1983):408–25; Hale quotation, 419–20. For a recent discussion of *White-Jacket* and flogging see H. Edward Stessel, "Melville's *White-Jacket:* A Case against the 'Cat,'" *Clio* 13 (1983):37–55.

12 Eric Foner, "The Causes of the American Civil War: Recent Interpretation and New Directions," in *Politics and Ideology in the Age of the Civil War* (New York: Oxford University Press, 1980), 25.

13 George F. Holmes, "Review of *Uncle Tom's Cabin*," *Southern Literary Messenger* 18 (1852):630–8, rpt. in *Critical Essays on Harriet Beecher Stowe*, ed. Elizabeth Ammons (Boston: Hall, 1980); quotation, 19.

14 William Gilmore Simms, "*White-Jacket; or the World in a Man-of-War*," *Southern Quarterly Review* 17 (1850):515. Simms does support Melville's indictment of naval discipline. Carolyn Karcher, assuming that Melville's indictment of naval discipline is Melville's indirect way of indicting the slave system, in turn indicts Simms for failing to perceive the connection. See *Shadow over the Promised Land* (Baton Rouge: Louisiana State University Press, 1980), 45. But, as I argue, it is not so clear that Melville's covert argument is directed only against proslavery factions.

15 In *Battle-Pieces* Melville writes, "Those of us who always abhorred slavery as an atheistical inequity, gladly we join in the exulting chorus of humanity over its downfall," but he quickly makes an appeal for understanding of the Southerners' position. "In imagination let us place ourselves in the unprecedented position of the Southerners – their position as regards the millions of ignorant manumitted slaves in their midst." See *Battle-Pieces*, ed. Sidney Kaplan (Amherst: University of Massachusetts Press, 1972), 268. Marvin Fisher recognizes that Melville adopts his own version of the hireling and slave argument in his fiction of the 1850s and adds, "But despite his use of an argument which was itself a rationalization favoring slavery, Melville never seems the least sympathetic to slavery"; *Going Under*, 104. Nonetheless, as the case of Lemuel Shaw indicates, a lack of sympathy for slavery does not make someone a militant abolitionist. Melville's position on slavery is more complicated than the one Fisher sketches in his interpretation of "Benito Cereno."

16 Hans-Joachim Lang and Fritz Fleischmann, " 'All This Beauty, All This Grace': Longfellow's 'The Building of the Ship' and Alexander Slidell MacKenzie's 'Ship,' " *New England Quarterly* 54 (1981):104–18. I draw on this essay throughout my discussion of "The Ship."

17 Henry Wordsworth Longfellow, *Works*, ed. Samuel Longfellow (Boston: Houghton Mifflin, 1886). 1:225.

18 For accounts of the *Somers* affair see Harrison Hayford, ed., *The Somers Mutiny Affair* (Englewood Cliffs, N.J.: Prentice-Hall, 1959); Rogin, *Subversive Genealogy*, 80–6, 295–315; and Hans-Joachim Lang, "Melville's 'Billy Budd' und seine Quellen: Eine Nachlese," *Festschrift für Walther Fischer* (Heidelberg: Carl Winter Verlag, 1955).

19 Alexander Slidell Mackenzie, *Case of the Somers' Mutiny: Defense of Alexander Slidell Mackenzie, Commander of the U.S. Brig Somers, Before the Court Martial Held at the Navy Yard, Brooklyn* (New York: Tribune Office, 1843), 30.

20 Longfellow, quoted in Lang and Fleischman, " 'All This Beauty,' " 113.

21 Mackenzie, quoted in Lang and Fleischman, " 'All This Beauty,' " 115.

22 Ibid., n. 29.

23 Dana, quoted in Robert Cover, *Justice Accused* (New Haven: Yale University Press, 1975), 106, note.

24 William M. Wiecek, *The Sources of Antislavery Constitutionalism in America*,

1760–1848 (Ithaca: Cornell University Press, 1977). Antislavery constitutionalists such as Dana and Sumner need to be distinguished from radical abolitionists who completely disregarded the law.

25 Shaw, quoted in Leonard W. Levy and Douglas L. Jones, eds., *Jim Crow in Boston* (New York: DaCapo Press, 1974), 227.

26 Sumner, quoted in Levy and Jones, *Jim Crow,* 216.

27 On the composition of *Moby-Dick* see Robert Milder, "The Composition of *Moby-Dick:* A Review and a Prospect," *Emerson Society Quarterly* 23 (1977):203–16.

28 See Robert S. Ward, "Longfellow and Melville: The Ship and the Whale," *Emerson Society Quarterly,* 22 (1961):57–63.

29 Charles H. Foster, "Something in Emblems: A Reinterpretation of *Moby-Dick,*" *New England Quarterly* 34 (1961):3–35.

30 Daniel Webster, "Summation in the Trial of John Francis Knapp for the Murder of Joseph White," in *The Law as Literature,* ed. Ephraim London (New York: Simon and Schuster, 1960), 439. Most contemporary accounts of Webster's career refer to this passage. It is quoted in Charles W. Marsh, *Reminiscences of Congress* (New York: Baker and Schribner, 1850), 180. Rufus Choate also quotes part of it in his "Discourse Commemorative of Daniel Webster," reprinted in *Addresses and Orations of Rufus Choate* (Boston: Little, Brown, 1878), 266. See Chapter 2, n. 26, on the possibility of a relationship between this speech and *The House of the Seven Gables.*

31 Henry D. Thoreau, "Herald of Freedom," in *Reform Papers,* ed. Wendell Glick (Princeton: Princeton University Press, 1973), 56, 49–50, 50. One more example of how politicized the question of duty had become occurs in the review of *Pierre* in the *Southern Literary Messenger.* The reviewer writes that the purpose of the book is to illustrate the fact that it is possible for a young soul, "acting strictly from a sense of duty, and being therefore in the right, to erect itself in direct hostility to all the universally-received rules of moral and social order." See Higgins and Parker, *Critical Essays on Pierre,* 46.

32 Allan Moore Emery makes the same argument as I do but then tries to minimize the role of slavery too much. See "'Benito Cereno' and Manifest Destiny," *Nineteenth-Century Fiction* 39 (1984):48–68, and "The Topicality of Depravity in 'Benito Cereno,'" *American Literature* 55 (1983):316–31.

7. "BARTLEBY, THE SCRIVENER": FELLOW
SERVANTS AND FREE AGENTS ON WALL STREET

1 Harold H. Scudder, "Melville's *Benito Cereno* and Captain Delano's Voyages," *PMLA* 43 (1928):502–32. For background materials on "Bartleby" intended for a discussion of its legal aspects see Merton M. Sealts, Jr., *Resources for Discussing Melville's Tale, "Bartleby, the Scrivener"* (Madison: Wisconsin Humanities Committee, 1983).

2 Johannes Dietrich Bergmann, "'Bartleby' and *The Lawyer's Story,*" *American Literature* 47 (1975):432–6.

3 George Greenville, "Death of a Poor Debtor in Boston Jail," printed in Charles M. Haar, ed., *The Golden Age of American Law* (New York: Braziller, 1965), 381.

4 Readings that turn Bartleby into an alienated worker are H. Bruce Franklin, *The Victim as Criminal and Artist* (New York: Oxford University Press, 1978), and Michael T. Gilmore, "'Bartleby, the Scrivener' and the Transformation of the Economy," in *American Romanticism and the Marketplace* (Chicago: University of Chicago Press, 1985).

5 Leonard W. Levy, *The Law of the Commonwealth and Chief Justice Shaw* (Cambridge, Mass.: Harvard University Press, 1957), 305–6.

6 Ibid., 305, 326.

7 Morton J. Horwitz, *The Transformation of American Law, 1780–1860* (Cambridge. Mass.: Harvard University Press, 1977), xiv, and Michael Paul Rogin, *Subversive Genealogy* (New York: Knopf, 1983), 248.

8 For a discussion of the social consequences of Shaw's decisions see Lawrence M. Friedman and Jack Ladinski, "Social Change and the Law of Industrial Accidents," in *American Law and the Constitutional Order*, ed. Lawrence M. Friedman and Harry N. Scheiber (Cambridge, Mass.: Harvard University Press. 1978), 269–82.

9 Roscoe Pound, *The Spirit of the Common Law* (Boston: Marshall Jones, 1921), 49.

10 Quoted in Horwitz, *Transformation*, 210.

11 Horwitz, *Transformation*, 209, cited by Rogin, *Subversive Genealogy*, 248.

12 Quoted in William L. Prosser, *Handbook of the Law of Torts* (St. Paul: University of Minnesota Press, 1941), 514. See Shakespeare, *Romeo and Juliet*, 5.1.75.

13 Brown v. Kendall, 60 Mass. 292 (1850). See John Stark, "Melville, Lemuel Shaw, and 'Bartleby,'" in M. Thomas Inge, ed., *Bartleby, the Inscrutable* (Hamden, Conn.: Archon Books, 1979), 169–70.

14 Herman Melville, "Bartleby, the Scrivener: A Story of Wall-Street," in *Great Short Works of Herman Melville*, ed. Warner Berthoff (New York: Harper and Row, 1969), 40, hereafter abbreviated *B*. Further page references will be given parenthetically in the text, as will references to Herman Melville, "The Paradise of Bachelors and the Tartarus of Maids," in *Great Short Works*, abbreviated *PB/TM*, and Herman Melville, *Pierre; or, The Ambiguities*, vol. 7 in *The Writings of Herman Melville*, The Northwestern-Newberry Edition, ed. Harrison Hayford, Hershel Parker, and G. Thomas Tanselle (Evanston and Chicago: Northwestern University Press and Newberry Library, 1971), abbreviated *Pierre*.

15 Hershel Parker, "The 'Sequel' in 'Bartleby,'" in Inge, *Bartleby the Inscrutable*, 159–65.

16 Girard's will, quoted in Maurice Baxter, *Daniel Webster and the Supreme Court* (Amherst: University of Massachusetts Press, 1966), 157–8.

17 Webster, quoted in James McClellan, *Joseph Story and the American Constitution* (Norman: University of Oklahoma Press, 1971), 131; churchmen quoted in Baxter, *Webster*, 164–5.

18 Story, quoted in Perry Miller, *The Life of the Mind in America* (New York: Harcourt Brace and World, 1965), 200.

19 Adams, quoted in Baxter, *Webster*, 166.

20 Baxter, *Webster*, 167–8.

21 Kent, quoted in Lawrence M. Friedman, *A History of American Law* (New York: Simon and Schuster, 1973), 211.

22 Michael Grossberg, "Who Gets the Child? Custody, Guardianship, and the Rise of a Judicial Patriarchy in Nineteenth-century America," *Feminist Studies* 9 (1983):236.

23 Scott Donaldson, "The Dark Truth of *The Piazza Tales*," *PMLA* 85 (1970):1086.

24 See Herbert F. Smith, "Melville's Master in Chancery and His Recalcitrant Clerk," *American Quarterly* 17 (1965):736. John Carlos Rowe's attempt to use the narrator's position as a master of chancery to support his deconstructive reading causes him to make misleading statements about a master's duties. According to Rowe, a "Master is concerned primarily with 'original sources.'" The master's duties were much more complex. See John Carlos Rowe, *Through the Custom-House* (Baltimore: Johns Hopkins University Press, 1982), 121.

25 Horwitz, *Transformation,* 265.

26 See, for instance, Mordecai Marcus, "Melville's Bartleby as a Psychological Double," *College English* 23 (1962):365–8.

27 Leo Marx, "Melville's Parable of the Walls," *Sewanee Review* 61 (1953):619. The first to argue that Bartleby was modeled on Thoreau was Egbert S. Oliver, *College English* 6 (1945):431–9.

28 Thoreau, *Reform Papers.* ed. Wendell Glick (Princeton: Princeton University Press, 1973), 86–7. See Walter Benn Michaels, "*Walden*'s False Bottoms," in *Glyph* 1 (1977):132–50, for a discussion of this passage.

29 Thoreau, *Reform Papers,* 104, 75.

30 Donald H. Craver and Patricia R. Plante, "Bartleby Or, The Ambiguities," *Studies in Short Fiction* 20 (1983):132–6. Parker, "Sequel," makes a similar association.

31 Leo Marx, *The Machine in the Garden* (New York: Oxford University Press, 1964), 174–91.

32 Joseph Story, "Developments of Science and Mechanic Art," in *The Miscellaneous Writings of Joseph Story,* ed. William Wetmore Story (Boston: Little, Brown, 1852), 475–502.

33 John Theodore Horton, *James Kent: A Study in Conservatism, 1763–1847* (New York: Appleton-Century, 1939), 276–7.

34 Shaw, quoted in Levy, *Law of the Commonwealth,* 176.

35 Marx, "Melville's Parable of the Walls."

36 Hershel Parker, "Why *Pierre* Went Wrong," *Studies in the Novel* 8 (1976):7–23.

37 Richard Chase, *Herman Melville* (New York: MacMillan, 1949), 16.

8. CONTRACTS AND CONFIDENCE MEN

1 Herman Melville, *The Confidence-Man,* ed. H. Bruce Franklin (Indianapolis: Bobbs-Merrill, 1967), 323, hereafter abbreviated *CM.* Further references to this edition will be included parenthetically in the text, as will references to Herman Melville, *Redburn, His First Voyage, Being the Sailor-boy Confessions and Reminiscences of the Son-of-a-Gentleman, in the Merchant Service,* vol. 4 in *The Writings of Herman Melville,* The Northwestern-Newberry Edition, ed. Harrison Hayford, Hershel Parker, and G. Thomas Tanselle (Evanston and

Chicago: Northwestern University Press and Newberry Library, 1969), abbreviated *R;* Herman Melville, *Moby-Dick; or, The Whale,* ed. Charles Feidelson, Jr. (Indianapolis: Bobbs-Merrill, 1964), abbreviated *MD;* and Herman Melville, "Bartleby, the Scrivener: A Story of Wall-Street," in *Great Short Works of Herman Melville,* ed. Warner Berthoff (New York: Harper and Row, 1969), abbreviated *B.*

2 This assumption is a starting point for "deconstructive" criticism. As Barbara Johnson writes, "[Jacques] Derrida's critique of Western metaphysics focuses on its privileging of the spoken word over the written word." Translator's introduction to Derrida, *Dissemination* (Chicago: University of Chicago Press, 1981), viii.

3 Michael Paul Rogin, *Subversive Genealogy* (New York: Knopf), 239.

4 Peter Coleman, *Debtors and Creditors in America* (Madison: State Historical Society of Wisconsin, 1974), 283–5.

5 See Morton J. Horwitz, *The Transformation of American Law, 1780–1860* (Cambridge, Mass.: Harvard University Press, 1977), 160–210, for a discussion of the changing hermeneutical principles applied to the interpretation of contracts during the antebellum period. (Horwitz's discussion is sometimes confusing because of his imprecise use of the terms *subjective* and *objective.*)

6 Hugh Kenner, *The Counterfeiters* (Bloomington: Indiana University Press, 1968).

7 The prejudice that Irish emigrants faced from some important legal thinkers is shown by James Kent's attitude toward them. When more than five hundred New York City residents died in plagues caused by poor sanitary conditions, Kent consoled himself that most were Irish immigrants. See John Theodore Horton, *James Kent: A Study in Conservatism, 1763–1847* (New York: Appleton-Century, 1939), 117.

8 An excellent discussion of Pitch's attitude toward labor and of the period's faith in machine labor is in Carolyn Karcher, *Shadow over the Promised Land* (Baton Rouge: Louisiana State University Press, 1980), 237–57.

9 Rogin, *Subversive Genealogy,* 27.

10 Some of Walter Benn Michaels's ingenious attempts to study economic representation in nineteenth-century American fiction overemphasizes the role that confidence plays in the generation of a capitalist economy. See, for instance, his "*Sister Carrie's* Popular Economy," *Critical Inquiry* 7 (1980):373–90.

11 Rogin, *Subversive Genealogy,* 238.

12 In her desire to show the role that chattel slavery played in Melville's works, Karcher, in *Shadow over the Promised Land,* too often neglects the metaphysical aspect of his treatment of slavery. For her, chattel slavery is central. For instance, Thomas Fry's story is important to her because it implies "that a person need not be black to fall victim to a society that enslaves blacks" (206).

13 Rogin, *Subversive Genealogy,* 249.

14 Rufus Choate, "The Importance of Illustrating New-England History by a Series of Romances Like the Waverly Novels," in Samuel Gilman Brown, *The Works of Rufus Choate with a Memoir of his Life* (Boston: Little, Brown, 1862), 1:338.

15 "Bartleby" includes its own reflection on a homicide similar to the one

reported by Fry. Even the prudent lawyer of "Bartleby" admits the capacity to kill in anger. Agitated and alone with Bartleby, he thinks of the Colt murder case, in which Colt "imprudently" worked himself into a rage and murdered Adams in the solitary confines of his office. Pondering the subject, the lawyer concludes that "had that altercation taken place in the public street, or at a private residence, it would not have terminated as it did." It was the setting of a "solitary office, up stairs, of a building entirely unhallowed by humanizing domestic associations" that "greatly helped to enhance the irritable desperation of the hapless Colt" (B 63–4). Fry's story does not confirm the lawyer's speculation. The gentleman kills the pavior in public, apparently unafraid of the legal consequences. For an attempt to link the form of modern fiction with the legal mentality, see Richard Weisberg, *The Failure of the Word* (New Haven: Yale University Press, 1984).

16 Quotation from Charles Warren, *Jacobin and Junto* (Cambridge, Mass.: Harvard University Press, 1931), 188–9.

17 Ibid., 189.

18 Thomas Oliver Selfridge, *A Correct Statement of the Whole Preliminary Controversy between Tho. O. Selfridge and Benj. Austin* (Charlestown, Mass.: Samuel Etheridge, 1807), 39.

19 Quotations from Warren, *Jacobin and Junto,* 191, 197.

20 Thomas C. Amory, *Life of James Sullivan with Selections from His Writings* (Boston: Phillips, Sampson, 1859), 167–8.

21 Sullivan, quoted in ibid., 180.

22 Warren, *Jacobin and Junto,* 205.

23 Parker, quoted in Warren, *Jacobin and Junto,* 203, and Selfridge, *Correct Statement,* 6.

24 Warren, *Jacobin and Junto,* 211.

25 Amory, *Life of Sullivan,* 169.

26 Charles R. Anderson, "A Reply to Herman Melville's *White Jacket* by Rear-Admiral Thomas O. Selfridge, Sr.," *American Literature* 7 (1933):126.

9. MEASURED FORMS

1 Herman Melville, *Billy Budd, Sailor (An Inside Narrative),* ed. Milton R. Stern (Indianapolis: Bobbs-Merrill, 1975), 36–7, hereafter abbreviated *BB.* I use Stern's edition rather than that of Harrison Hayford and Merton M. Sealts, Jr., because I agree with Stern's more inclusive editorial decisions. Future page references to this edition will be included parenthetically in the text, as will references to Herman Melville, *Moby-Dick; or, the Whale,* ed. Charles Feidelson, Jr. (Indianapolis: Bobbs-Merrill, 1964), abbreviated *MD;* Herman Melville, *White-Jacket: or The World in a Man-of-War,* vol. 5 in *The Writings of Herman Melville,* The Northwestern-Newberry Edition, ed. Harrison Hayford, Hershel Parker, and G. Thomas Tanselle (Evanston and Chicago: Northwestern University Press and Newberry Library, 1970), abbreviated *WJ;* and Herman Melville, *The Confidence-Man: His Masquerade,* ed. H. Bruce Franklin (Indianapolis: Bobbs-Merrill, 1967), abbreviated *CM.* A resource for studying *Billy Budd* in the context of the law is Merton M. Sealts, Jr., *Innocence*

and Infamy: Resources for Discussing Herman Melville's "Billy Budd, Sailor"
(Madison: Wisconsin Humanities Committee, 1983).

2 Shaw, quoted in Leonard Levy, *The Law of the Commonwealth and Chief Justice Shaw* (Cambridge, Mass.: Harvard University Press, 1957), 336, 329.

3 Robert M. Cover, *Justice Accused* (New Haven: Yale University Press, 1975), 1–7, 250–2.

4 Samuel S. Shaw, "Lemuel Shaw, Early and Domestic Life," in *Memorial Biographies of the New England Historic and Genealogical Society,* no. 4 (Boston: New England Historic and Genealogical Society, 1885), 200–29.

5 Frederic Hathaway Chase, *Lemuel Shaw* (Boston: Houghton Mifflin, 1918).

6 Holmes, quoted in Robert Sullivan, *The Disappearance of Dr. Parkman* (Boston: Little, Brown, 1971), 89. Sullivan's account of the murder is the most thorough.

7 Ibid., 164.

8 A Member of the Legal Profession, *Statement of Reasons Showing the Illegality of that Verdict Upon Which Sentence Has Been Pronounced Against John W. Webster for the Alleged Murder of George Parkman* (New York: Stringer and Townsend, 1850), 23–4.

9 *Philadelphia North American,* April 3, 1850.

10 Shaw Papers, the Massachusetts Historical Society, Boston, Mass.

11 Joel Parker, "The Law of Homicide," *North American Review* 72 (1851):178–204.

12 *New York Daily Globe,* April 8, 1850; *Philadelphia Daily Sun,* April 3, 1850.

13 Member of the Legal Profession, *Statement of Reasons,* 32.

14 Chase, *Shaw,* 205.

15 Charles G. Loring, "Obituary Notices of the Late Chief Justice Shaw and Judge White," *Proceedings of the American Academy* 5 (1861):7.

16 Chase, *Shaw,* 210.

17 Shaw, quoted in Sullivan, *Disappearance,* 150.

18 Chase, *Shaw,* 210.

19 Davis to Sumner, New York City, December 28, 1842. On March 26, 1843, Theodore Sedgwick, Jr., wrote to Sumner asking. "Can you not review [George] Griffin's Argument in the McKenzie [sic] case for the North American [Review] – It is desirable to have all the Organs of 'Public Opinion' sound the right tune – & you can do it better than any one I know of – " Both letters are reprinted in *The Somers Mutiny Affair,* ed. Harrison Hayford (Englewood Cliffs, N.J.: Prentice-Hall, 1959), 27, 153. Another event in 1842 that caused concern for those intent on maintaining rule by law was the Dorr Rebellion in Rhode Island. Discontent with an outdated state constitution limiting suffrage to freeholders, Thomas W. Dorr organized an alternative government. Dorr was defeated and the petitions of his supporters were denied in the courts, most notably by Justice Story.

20 Charles Sumner, "The Mutiny on the Somers," *North American Review* 107 (1843):200–1. James Duban, in *Melville's Major Fiction* (DeKalb: Northern Illinois University Press, 1983), 238–40, notes the similarity between Sumner's review of the mutinies at Spithead and the Nore and the opening of

Billy Budd. Duban argues that Melville, because of his interest in the case and his personal acquaintance with Sumner, probably read Sumner's defense. If so, it is also interesting to speculate that he read the essay in the same issue of the *North American Review* that attacks Thomas Paine (see this volume, chap. 10). See also William J. Kimball's "Charles Sumner's Contribution to Chapter XVIII of *Billy Budd*," *South Atlantic Bulletin* 23 (1967):13–14.

21 Sumner, "Mutiny," 228.

22 Ibid., 229–31 (quotation from Kent on 230).

23 Ibid., 231.

24 Ibid., 236, emphasis added.

25 Rogin argues that Captain Vere's refusal to take Billy's intent into account is similar to postbellum theories of the law, like that of Justice Oliver Wendell Holmes, Jr., which minimized intent. In contrast, Rogin argues, antebellum law stressed intent. "Mackenzie's trial turned on Spencer's intent and on his own" (298). But Rogin is misleading. For his argument about Mackenzie's intent to have force, he would have to compare Mackenzie's defense with a defense that Vere would have made if he had been tried, a defense that does not exist. As far as Spencer's intent is concerned, Sumner's antebellum legal philosophy coincides exactly with Vere's. Spencer's intent is no more important than Billy's. See Michael Paul Rogin, *Subversive Genealogy* (New York: 1983), 298–300. One of the problems is that Rogin relies on the excerpts from Sumner's essay reprinted in Hayford, *Somers Mutiny Affair*. A reading of the entire essay provides a different perspective. See my discussion in Chapter 10.

26 Sumner to Davis, Boston, January 3, 1843. Rpt. in Edward L. Pierce, *Memoir and Letters of Charles Sumner* (Boston: Roberts Brothers, 1878), 2:255.

27 Sumner, "Mutiny," 238. Robert Lucid, in his introduction to *The Journal of Richard Henry Dana* (Cambridge, Mass.: Harvard University Press [Belknap Press], 1968), uses Dana's different responses to the *Somers* case and the *Webster* case to illustrate the ideological bias of upper-class Boston. Dana immediately decided that Webster was guilty of murder in the first degree and reported in his journal that he had met no one in Boston who disagreed – something highly unlikely, given the controversy about the case. In contrast, he assumed Mackenzie's innocence from the start. According to Lucid, Dana's responses show that "position and authority in [his] world were inseparable partners. To a member of that fraternity who erred while attempting to protect his station, all the support of a powerful class was to be rallied; but for one who sinned on the side of undisciplined passion, at the expense of duty, no punishment was too severe. The granite foundation of conservatism, asserting the transcendence of institution over individual, could hardly be more overwhelmingly apparent" (1.xx).

28 As Edgar Dryden points out, the text also suggests that ambition for promotion may have secretly motivated Captain Vere. In this case, Billy would have been sacrificed on the altar of his captain's ambition. See *Melville's Thematics of Form* (Baltimore: Johns Hopkins University Press, 1968), 212–13. A recent essay stressing Captain Vere's class bias is Christopher S. Durer's "Captain Vere and Upper-class Mores in *Billy Budd*," *Studies in Short Fiction* 19 (1982):9–18.

29 Richard Weisberg, "How Judges Speak: Some Lessons on Adjudication in *Billy Budd, Sailor* with an application to Justice Rehnquist," *New York University Law Review* 57 (1982):1–69. A different version appears in his *Failure of the Word: The Protagonist as Lawyer in Modern Fiction* (New Haven: Yale University Press, 1984). As Weisberg points out, Captain Vere's deviation from accepted procedures may be suggested in his name. Critics have noted that Vere implies "truth," as in *veritas,* but it may also imply "to veer," which was a naval term meaning "to wear a ship." See also William Domnarski, "Law and Literature Criticism: Charting a Desirable Course with *Billy Budd,*" *Journal of Legal Education* 34 (1984):702–13.

30 Sullivan, *Disappearance,* vii.

31 Cover, *Justice Accused,* 249–52, 265–7.

32 Sullivan, *Disappearance,* 22, 165. The controversy over Shaw's conduct in the Webster trial could well have influenced Hawthorne's imagination as he composed *The House of the Seven Gables.*

33 Sumner, "Mutiny," 230, 205.

34 See Dryden, *Melville's Thematics,* 215–16.

35 John William Ward, *Andrew Jackson, Symbol for an Age* (New York: Oxford University Press, 1962); Daniel Walker Howe, *The Political Culture of the American Whigs* (Chicago: University of Chicago Press, 1979), 211.

36 Leo Marx, *The Machine in the Garden* (New York: Oxford University Press, 1964), 277–319; Rogin, *Subversive Genealogy,* 102–51.

37 Max Horkheimer and Theodor W. Adorno, *Dialectic of Enlightenment* (New York: Seabury Press, 1972).

38 Others who have drawn attention to the possibility of matching this description of insanity with Captain Vere are Phil Withim, *"Billy Budd:* Testament of Resistance," *Modern Language Quarterly* 20 (1959):122; Merlin Bowen, *The Long Encounter* (Chicago: University of Chicago Press, 1960), 218–21; H. Bruce Franklin, *The Victim as Criminal and Artist* (New York: Oxford University Press, 1978), 68–9; and Carolyn L. Karcher, *Shadow over the Promised Land* (Baton Rouge: Louisiana State University Press, 1980), 301–2. Henry Nash Smith, "The Madness of Ahab," in *Democracy and the Novel* (New York: Oxford University Press, 1978), 39–55, compares Ahab's madness to Lemuel Shaw's definition of insanity in *Commonwealth v. Rogers* (1844). Space does not permit an application of Shaw's definition to *Billy Budd,* but I should note that Shaw family members feared Melville was insane. Melville, in indirectly suggesting that a figure whose most admirable characteristic is his judicial rationality is actually insane, could be achieving a subtle revenge. For a discussion of insanity in Melville's earlier works see Paul McCarthy, "Facts, Opinions, and Possibilities: Melville's Treatment of Insanity through *White-Jacket,*" *Studies in the Novel* 16 (1984):167–81.

39 Rogin remarks on the "shift Melville's fiction enacts, from patriarchal oppression in *White-Jacket* to mother-love in *Pierre*" as a "shift in discipline from the whip to the wall" (190). Melville's short works of the 1850s, he argues, reflect a psychological rather than a physical discipline. But he eventually sees. *Billy Budd* as Melville's submission to this form of ideological control, not his unmasking of it. On his reading of *Billy Budd,* see my Chapter 10.

40 Peter Gabel, "Reification in Legal Reasoning," *Research in Law and Sociology* 3 (1980):29.

41 Douglas Hay, "Property, Authority, and the Criminal Law," in *Albion's Fatal Tree,* ed. Douglas Hay, Peter Linebaugh, John G. Rule et al., (London: Allen Lane, 1975), 48.

42 My questioning of Billy's innocence distinguishes my reading from other "ironic" readings, which usually turn Billy into a tragic hero. The first of these ironic readings to appear was Joseph Schiffman's "Melville's Final Stage, Irony: A Reexamination of *Billy Budd* Criticism," *American Literature* 22 (1950):128–36. Withim, "Testament of Resistance," comes closest to my judgment of Billy's silence.

43 See, e.g., Charles A. Reich, "The Tragedy of Justice in *Billy Budd,*" *Yale Review* 56 (1967):368–89, and Walter L. Reed, "The Measured Forms of Captain Vere," *Modern Fiction Studies* 23 (1977):227–35.

44 Melville to Hawthorne, Pittsfield, Mass., April 16, 1851, rpt. in Herman Melville, *Moby-Dick; or, the Whale,* ed. Harrison Hayford and Hershel Parker (New York: Norton, 1967), 555.

45 Schiffman, "Melville's Final Stage," points out that Billy is no spokesman. Others who have questioned his innocence are James E. Miller, Jr., "*Billy Budd:* The Catastrophe of Innocence," *Modern Language Notes* 73 (1958):168–76; Barbara Johnson, "Melville's Fist: The Execution of *Billy Budd,*" in *The Critical Difference* (Baltimore: Johns Hopkins University Press, 1980), 79–109; and Lyon Evans, Jr., "'Too Good to Be True': Subverting Christian Hope in *Billy Budd,*" *New England Quarterly* 55 (1982):323–53.

46 See my "*Billy Budd* and the Judgment of Silence," in *Literature and Ideology,* ed. Harry R. Garvin (Lewisburg, Pa.: Bucknell University Press, 1982), 51–78. This is a response to Johnson's "Execution of *Billy Budd.*"

10. RAGGED EDGES

 1 See John P. McWilliams, Jr., "Innocent Criminal or Criminal Innocence: The Trial in American Fiction," in Carl S. Smith, John P. McWilliams, Jr., and Maxwell Bloomfield, *Law and American Literature,* (New York: Knopf, 1983), 45–124, and Michael Paul Rogin, *Subversive Genealogy* (New York: Knopf, 1983), 288–316. The original version of Rogin's essay appeared as "The *Somers* Mutiny and *Billy Budd:* Melville in the Penal Colony," in *Criminal Justice History: An International Annual,* no. 1 (1980), 186–224.

 2 Thomas Oliver Selfridge, *A Correct Statement of the Whole Preliminary Controversy between Tho. O. Selfridge and Benj. Austin* (Charlestown, Mass.: Samuel Etheridge, 1807), 35.

 3 Coleridge, quoted in Rufus Choate, "The Position and Functions of the American Bar, as an Element of Conservatism in the State: An Address Delivered before the Law School in Cambridge, July 3, 1845," in *Addresses and Orations of Rufus Choate,* ed. Samuel Gilman Brown (Boston: Little, Brown, 1878), 165. Miller's comments are in his notes to Choate's essay, reprinted in *The Legal Mind in America,* ed. Perry Miller (Ithaca: Cornell University Press, 1962), 272–3.

 4 Herman Melville, *Billy Budd, Sailor (An Inside Narrative),* ed. Milton R. Stern

(Indianapolis: Bobbs-Merrill, 1975), 130, hereafter abbreviated *BB*. Future page references will be included parenthetically in the text, as will references to Herman Melville, "The Encantadas or Enchanted Isles," in *Great Short Works of Herman Melville,* ed. Warner Berthoff (New York: Harper and Row, 1969), abbreviated *E*.

5 Oliver Wendell Holmes, Jr., *The Common Law,* ed. Mark DeWolfe Howe (Cambridge, Mass.: Harvard University Press [Belknap Press], 1963), 85. *The Common Law* first appeared in 1881. Holmes first used this praise of Shaw in "Trespass and Negligence," *American Law Review* 14 (1880):20.

6 See Elizabeth Mensch, "The History of Mainstream Legal Thought," in *The Politics of Law,* ed. David Kairys (New York: Pantheon Books, 1982), 18–39.

7 Clyde E. Jacobs, *The Influence of Thomas M. Cooley, Christopher G. Tiedeman, and John F. Dillon upon American Constitutional Law* (Berkeley: University of California Press, 1954), 50–8.

8 Webster, quoted in Christopher G. Tiedeman, *A Treatise on the Limitations of Police Power in the United States* (St. Louis: Thomas Law Book, 1886), 67.

9 Tiedeman, *Treatise,* vii. If William E. Nelson's thesis is correct, Tiedeman's concern with the threat that government posed to minority rights leads to a paradox. According to Nelson, the rise of government bureaucracy in the late nineteenth century was due to the desire to institutionalize pluralism and thus to protect minority rights against the tyranny of the majority. See William E. Nelson, *The Roots of American Bureaucracy* (Cambridge, Mass.: Harvard University Press, 1982).

10 Tiedeman, *Treatise,* vi–viii.

11 Brief mentions of *Billy Budd* in connection with the Haymarket riot occur in Alan Trachtenberg, *The Incorporation of America* (New York: Hill and Wang, 1982), 203, and Robert K. Wallace, "*Billy Budd* and the Haymarket Hangings," *American Literature* 47 (1975):108–13.

12 James Fenimore Cooper, *The American Democrat,* ed. George Dekker and Larry Johnston (Baltimore: Penguin Books, 1969), 75.

13 Tiedeman, *Treatise,* vi.

14 Carlyle, cited in James Duban, *Melville's Major Fiction* (De Kalb: Northern Illinois University Press, 1983), 229.

15 Shaw, quoted in Leonard W. Levy, *The Law of the Commonwealth and Chief Justice Shaw* (Cambridge, Mass.: Harvard University Press, 1957), 329.

16 Tiedeman, *Treatise,* viii.

17 Morton J. Horwitz, *The Transformation of American Law, 1780–1860* (Cambridge, Mass.: Harvard University Press, 1977), 253–66.

18 Rogin, *Subversive Genealogy,* 158.

19 Ibid., 302.

20 Ibid., 158.

21 Norway Plains Co. v. Boston & Me. R.R., 1 Gray 267 (1854).

22 On Holmes's attempt to define the boundary between contracts and torts see Frederic Rogers Kellogg, *The Formative Essays of Justice Holmes* (Westport, Conn.: Greenwood Press, 1984), 3–74. On his wisecracks see Morton White, *Social Thought in America: The Revolt against Formalism* (Boston: Beacon Press, 1947), 237. Holmes has been accused of being an authoritarian; see Ben W.

Palmer, "Hobbes, Holmes, and Hitler," *American Bar Association Journal* 31 (1945):569.

23 See both McWilliams, "Innocent Criminal," and Rogin, *Subversive Genealogy*. Robert A. Ferguson also argues that Vere's thought is similar to Holmes's. For Ferguson, "The modernity of *Billy Budd* consists in its portrayal of a legal system that explicitly denies all natural and spiritual connections." See his *Law and Letters in American Culture* (Cambridge, Mass.: Harvard University Press, 1984), 289. The Holmes quotation is from *Common Law*, 41. McWilliams writes, "The similarity of Vere's and Holmes's arguments also suggests that Melville's perception of the problem of criminal justice has diverged from the ideas of his eminent father-in-law, Chief Justice Lemuel Shaw," (76). On the contrary, as I have argued throughout, there are numerous similarities between Shaw and Vere. See n. 34 in this chapter for more on Shaw and Vere. Holmes mentions reading *Moby-Dick* in a letter to Sir Frederick Pollock, Beverly Farms, Mass., August 30, 1928, in *The Holmes-Pollock Letters*, ed. Mark DeWolfe Howe (Cambridge, Mass.: Harvard University Press, 1941), 2:227.

24 Rogin, *Subversive Genealogy*, 299. Holmes's theory of the relationship between law and morals remains a subject of debate. See Kellogg, *Formative Essays*, 58–74.

25 McWilliams, "Innocent Criminal," 74, 79–80.

26 See especially Lochner v. New York, 198 U.S. 45 (1904).

27 Holmes, *Common Law*, 5. Specifically, Holmes was responding to the thought of John Austin; see Kellogg, *Formative Essays*, 3–22.

28 Nicholas St. John Green, "Proximate and Remote Cause," *American Law Review* 4 (1870):201. See Morton J. Horwitz, "The Doctrine of Objective Causation," in *The Politics of Law*, ed. David Kairys (New York: Pantheon Books, 1982), 201–13, and Kellogg, *Formative Essays*, 14–18. For Holmes's connection to pragmatism see Kellogg, 3–74, and Max H. Fisch, "Justice Holmes, the Prediction Theory of Law, and Pragmatism," *Journal of Philosophy* 39 (1942):85.

29 G. Edward White, *Patterns of American Legal Thought* (Indianapolis: Bobbs-Merrill, 1978), 66.

30 Pound, quoted in Jacobs, *Influence of Cooley*, 10.

31 Holmes, *Common Law*, 8.

32 Holmes, "Law in Science and Science in Law," *Harvard Law Review* 12 (1899):452.

33 Montaigne, "Of Experience," in *The Law as Literature*, ed. Ephraim London (New York: Simon and Schuster, 1960), 760–2. W. G. Kilbourne, Jr., "Montaigne and Captain Vere," *American Literature* 33 (1962):514–17, argues that Montaigne's ideas on the law support Vere's position, interpreting the comments in "Of Experience" quite differently from the way I understand them. That Montaigne does not unequivocally support Vere's position undercuts Vere's appeal to the authority of Montaigne's commonsensical philosophizing upon realities.

34 Sedgwick to Sumner, New York, March 26, 1843, rpt. in *The Somers Mutiny Affair*, ed. Harrison Hayford (Englewood Cliffs, NJ: Prentice-Hall, 1959),

153. See Duban, *Melville's Major Fiction,* 236–42, for a discussion of Vere's conservative sense of history and its connection to Sumner's defense of Mackenzie.

The Webster murder trial is another example of the "historical" treatment of an event. Most accounts of the trial assume Webster's guilt, because they rely on documents as questionable as the account in "News from the Mediterranean." They include Putnam's version of Webster's "confession"; Bemis's *Report of the Case of John Webster,* told from the prosecutor's perspective, and the published account of Shaw's charge to the jury, which, because of the criticism that his oral charge received, was revised for the offical record. In uncritically accepting the perspective in these documents, people such as Leonard Levy, Shaw's biographer, justify the court's ruling (see Levy, *Law of the Commonwealth,* 218–28). Relying on Levy, McWilliams refers to Shaw's ruling in the *Webster* case as showing that Shaw was a "vigorous defender of due process for the accused – as Vere clearly is not" (McWilliams, "Innocent Criminal," 76).

35 Charles Sumner, "The Mutiny on the Somers," *North American Review* 107 (1843):238, 213–14.

36 Ibid., 202.

37 Melvill, quoted in *William Austin: The Creator of Peter Rugg,* ed. Walter Austin (Boston: Marshall Jones, 1925), 82. This radical streak in the Melville family history complicates Rogin's reading of *Billy Budd,* which sees Melville as ultimately submitting to the family order that he once rebelled against.

38 See Daniel Walker Howe, *The Political Culture of the American Whigs* (Chicago: University of Chicago Press, 1979), 227–37.

39 Vidal v. Girard's Executors, 2 Howard 174–5 (1844).

40 Review of "An Oration delivered at the Celebration in Philadelphia of the 106th Anniversary of the Birthday of Thomas Paine; by John Alberger. Philadelphia. 1843," *North American Review* 107 (1843):1, 3, 3–4, 2.

41 Ibid., 4–5.

42 Ibid., 58. In *Billy Budd* the authorized version turns possibly foreign Claggart into a true patriot and Anglo-Saxon Billy into a foreign alien. The neglect of Paine is mirrored in Captain Vere's thought. Searching for support of his conservative, Burkean political opinions, Vere looks to philosophers with "common sense." He ignores the most obvious appeal made to common sense, Paine's pamphlet justifying the American Revolution, and instead turns to Montaigne. Ironically, then, he relies on the thought of a Frenchman to justify opposition to the French Revolution, while neglecting the thought of his countryman Paine, who went on to support the French.

43 Shaw, quoted in Frederic Hathaway Chase, *Lemuel Shaw* (Boston: Houghton Mifflin, 1918), 308–9.

44 Samuel S. Shaw, "Lemuel Shaw, Early and Domestic Life," *Memorial Biographies of the New-England Historic and Genealogical Society,* no. 4 (Boston: New-England Historic and Genealogical Society, 1885), 215.

45 See, for instance, Emilio Castelar, "The Progress of Democracy in Europe," *North American Review* 141 (1885):416. Castelar lists the great modern revolutions as, first, the Dutch against the Burgundian dynasty; second, the British against the Stuarts; third, the American Revolution; and finally the French Revolution, "which may be called the motor of universal democracy in Europe."

46 See Robert Kelley, *The Transatlantic Persuasion: The Liberal-Democratic Mind in the Age of Gladstone* (New York: Knopf, 1969), 80–100. The Roosevelt remark is quoted in Eric Foner, *Tom Paine and Revolutionary America* (New York: Oxford University Press, 1976), 270.

47 Joseph Story, *Commentaries on the Constitution of the United States,* 4th ed. with notes and additions by Thomas M. Cooley (Boston: Little, Brown, 1873).

48 Brook Adam, "The Embryo of a Commonwealth," *Atlantic Monthly* 54 (1884):619.

49 Bryce, quoted in Herman Belz, "The Constitution in the Gilded Age: The Beginnings of Constitutional Realism in American Scholarship," *American Journal of Legal History* 13 (1969):117.

50 Charles Callan Tansill, *The Foreign Policy of Thomas F. Bayard, 1885–1897* (New York: Fordham University Press, 1940).

51 Paine, *The Rights-of-Man,* in *The Complete Writings of Thomas Paine,* ed. Philip S. Foner, 2 vols. (New York: Citadel Press, 1945), 1:361–2.

52 Herman Melville, *Battle-Pieces,* ed. Sidney Kaplan (Amherst: University of Massachusetts Press, 1972), 261.

53 H. Bruce Franklin correctly notes that during the time when Melville was writing *Billy Budd,* Great Britain and the United States frequently came into conflict in their desire to conquer foreign territory. These conflicts led to a desire to create an alliance of Anglo-American interests. On the American side this policy was forged by Secretary of State Bayard, although at first he had to disguise it because of political pressure to retain the Irish-American vote. Thus, I stress the unity of Anglo-American efforts, whereas Franklin stresses the discord, but our points are essentially the same: America joins Britain as an imperial power. See Franklin's "From Empire to Empire: *Billy Budd, Sailor,*" in *Herman Melville: Reassessments,* ed. A. Robert Lee (New York: Barnes and Noble, 1984), 199–216.

54 Paine, *Rights-of-Man,* 360. Clearly Paine indulges in his own bit of distortion. At the time when he wrote *Rights-of-Man,* there was class tension in America. Shays' rebellion is a perfect example.

55 James A. Garfield, "The Army of the United States," *North American Review* 126 (1878): 193–216, 442–65.

56 Hewitt, quoted in Arthur A. Ekirch, Jr., *The Civilian and the Military* (New York: Oxford University Press, 1956), 117–18.

57 Thompson, quoted in Ekirch, *Civilian and Military,* 126.

58 Harry B. Henderson, *Versions of the Past: The Historical Imagination in American Fiction* (New York: Oxford University Press, 1974), 199.

59 Quoted in Hans-Joachim Lang, "Looking Backward at the Second Revolution in Massachusetts: Edward Bellamy's *The Duke of Stockbridge* as Historical Romance," *Amerikastudien* 28 (1983):319. I am indebted to Lang's discussion.

60 Holland, quoted in ibid., 321.

61 Henderson, *Versions of the Past,* 199.

62 Edward Bellamy, *The Duke of Stockbridge: A Romance of Shays' Rebellion,* ed. Joseph Schiffman (Cambridge, Mass.: Harvard University Press, 1962), 263.

63 Melville, "Hawthorne and His Mosses," rpt. in *Moby-Dick,* ed. Harrison Hayford and Hershel Parker (New York: Norton, 1967), 542.

64 Gail Hamilton, "The Murder of Philip Spencer," pt. 3, *Cosmopolitan* (1889):347.

65 The notion of the rigorous text is Paul de Man's. See Barbara Johnson's "Rigorous Unreliability," *Critical Inquiry* 11 (1984):278–85. De Man is fully aware of the link between a text's "rigor" and its author's experience of inadequacy. My argument is with the implication in de Man's work that such a link is inevitable. I also argue with those who distort de Man by trying to use his position in a politically radical manner.

A CLOSING STATEMENT

1 John P. McWilliams, Jr., "Innocent Criminal or Criminal Innocence: The Trial in American Fiction," in Carl S. Smith, John P. McWilliams, Jr., and Maxwell Bloomfield, *Law and American Literature* (New York: Knopf, 1983), 45–124.

2 This entire discussion becomes complicated by the question of the difference between literary realism and naturalism. Certainly, one of the most explicit literary challenges to the orthodoxy of objective causation occurs in Stephen Crane's conclusion to "The Blue Hotel," a work usually described as naturalistic. In contrast, Mark Twain's "realistic" *Pudd'nhead Wilson* subscribes to the notion of objective causation, since Pudd'nhead uses fingerprints to establish a scientific "chain" of events leading to a murder. A full discussion of this problem is beyond the scope of my study of antebellum law and literature.

3 The concept of "relative autonomy" is usually attributed to Louis Althusser, but I find an earlier use in John-Paul Sartre, *Search for a Method,* trans. Hazel E. Barnes (New York: Random House [Vintage Books], 1968), 48, 66, 111.

4 For a survey of the debate over a poststructuralist history, see Andrew Parker, "'Taking Sides' (On History): Derrida: Re-Marx," *Diacritics* 11 (1981):57–73.

5 Walter Benjamin, "Theses on the Philosophy of History," in *Illuminations,* trans. Harry Zohn (New York: Schocken Books, 1969), 255–6, 263.

6 James Duban, in *Melville's Major Fiction* (DeKalb: Northern Illinois University Press, 1983), argues that Melville is "not as concerned with history as he is with something like a Nietzschean 'historical sense'" (xvii). Duban, however, gives Melville more of a liberal than a Nietzschean historical sense.

7 Robert W. Gordon, "Historicism in Legal Scholarship," *Yale Law Journal* 90 (1981):1017–56. See also Morton J. Horwitz, "The Historical Contingency of the Role of History," *Yale Law Journal* 90 (1981):1057–9.

8 Sanford Levinson, "Law as Literature," *Texas Law Review* 60 (1982):386.

9 Benjamin, "Theses," 262.

Index